Shakespeare's Symmetries

Shakespeare's Symmetries

The Mirrored Structure of Action in the Plays

James E. Ryan

McFarland & Company, Inc., Publishers

Jefferson, North Carolina

ISBN 978-1-4766-6370-8 (softcover : acid free paper) ∞
ISBN 978-1-4766-2416-7 (ebook)

LIBRARY OF CONGRESS CATALOGUING DATA ARE AVAILABLE

BRITISH LIBRARY CATALOGUING DATA ARE AVAILABLE

Front cover image of William Shakespeare and *The Winter's Tale*
© 2016 duncan1890/iStock

Printed in the United States of America

*McFarland & Company, Inc., Publishers
Box 611, Jefferson, North Carolina 28640
www.mcfarlandpub.com*

To Christine

Table of Contents

Preface

My original title for this book was "Shakespeare's Action: The Chiastic Design of the Plays." "Chiastic" was judged too unfamiliar to appear in the title, though it is retained in the text and thus requires some clarification. According to the Oxford English Dictionary, "chiasmus" is derived from a Greek word meaning "crossing, a diagonal arrangement, esp. of clauses of a sentence." Hence, the definition: "a grammatical arrangement by which the order of words in one of two parallel clauses is inverted in the other": "Fair is foul, and foul is fair" (*Macbeth*); "I wasted time and now doth time waste me" (*Richard III*). In recent criticism, particularly of the Bible, the term "chiasmus" is not limited to the grammatical arrangement of words but is applied to larger structures of inverse parallelism as well, such as the narrative design of Exodus ("ABCDXDCBA"). It is in this larger sense that I deploy the term throughout this book, more or less interchangeably with terms like "symmetrical structure" or "mirroring actions." I do not, however, extend the term so far as to leave behind specific repeated elements, such as individual actions or characters, that confirm the pattern. We might say of *King John*, for example, that it has an "X-shaped, or chiastic, pattern similar to that in *Richard II*: like Richard, King John declines; like Bolingbroke, the Bastard rises" (Braunmuller, 72). But this use of the term, untethered as it is from details of the play, provides only an impression of the overall action and serves little analytical purpose.

My original title was intended to emphasize what I take to be a neglected aspect of Shakespeare's art, his action. Though drama is, in substance and etymology, action, Shakespeare's language receives far more attention than his equally brilliant and subtle plot and character actions. Surely, our greatest dramatist must be a connoisseur of action, and his resonant language must be in the service of that essential element, the very stuff of any play. Shakespeare's "perfect hold on the Aristotelian action," in Una Fermor-Ellis's phrase, allows a more nuanced presentation of action than is usually appreciated. The final transformation of, say, Antonio—the action of his reform—in *The Merchant of Venice* is completed in a single line; and Gobbo's service to Bassanio in the same play is echoed, amplified and judged by Portia's analogous disguised service at the trial. Furthermore, some actions crucial to the meaning of a play as so finely threaded through the narrative as to be nearly invisible; the six analogous meals in *Othello*, traced in a later chapter, are an especially elusive instance. Shakespeare's actions warrant closer attention than they have so far received.

My original main title was also intended to hint at the action of Shakespeare himself in constructing the plays. Our ignorance of the playwright's constructive practice is implicitly lamented by John Jones: "*Antony and Cleopatra* and *The Tempest* [are 'masterpieces'] about

1

the making of which almost nothing can be inferred. If some purchase could be gained from the inside upon just these two very disparate works, our impression of the creative process in Shakespeare might be significantly different, and it would certainly be richer" (38). It is exactly "some purchase ... from the inside," not just of these two plays but of the entire mature canon, that the analysis of Shakespeare's symmetrical structures provides.

This book, then, isolates and interprets the chiastic designs structuring Shakespeare's mature, non-collaborative plays. It demonstrates that essential thematic elements, usually actions, are disposed in a reflecting pattern, ABCBA, in all the mature plays, and that this pattern is foundational for the narrative, the imagery and other dramatic elements. It is this pattern, for example, not the usual considerations of cleared stage or "continuous action," that explains the scene designations in Folio *Measure for Measure* and other Folio plays whose scene breaks are routinely changed by modern editors; the chiastic design determines Shakespeare's scene divisions. Furthermore, once shown to be invariable, Shakespeare's structural chiasmus becomes a predictive tool, as any departure from it must be, to whatever extent, non-Shakespearean. As every play has an unrepeated central element and thus an odd number of scenes, the 24-scene Quarto *Lear*, for example, could never have been intended to be a "final form" of the play, as some critics and editors have maintained. Nor could the central, keystone scene of *2 Henry IV*, missing from the earliest Quarto, have been part of an extensive revision to the play; it must have been an overlooked sheet of the original composition. In some cases the chiastic design also illuminates plays whose structures have long been disparaged. The "badly proportioned" *King John*, the "peculiarly uncertain" structure of *The Merry Wives of Windsor*, and the *Antony and Cleopatra* that "bewilders the mind" are seen to be thematically organized, rigorously crafted and surprisingly unified.[1] Finally, by heightening unnoticed reflections and structural rhythms, the chiastic design often reveals subtleties otherwise invisible.

I have most often referred to the chiastic design as an arch, the most convenient (and historically appropriate) rendering of the symmetry of Shakespeare's thematic patterns. They can be likened to, say, Gothic portals with keystones and historiated columns, the sculptures on each side reflecting Old and New Testament figures as Shakespeare mirrors essential actions in the first and second halves of his plays. This thematic arch is not to be confused with the well-known Freytag triangle, which is a largely metaphorical tool of narrative analysis. Even the terms used to describe parts of a play—exposition, rising action, climax, denouement—are inextricably sequential, their meanings determined by what precedes or follows in the play. That is, a play is treated as a dramatized narrative only, with no other unifying structure, no other possible patterning of its plot. Of course, Shakespeare's myriad other "patterns"—of imagery, character, dramatic situation, stage action, etc.—are the very stuff engaging most criticism. But these "patterns" are confluences of meaning rather than structural configurations with a definite periodicity. To posit a "pattern" of food imagery in *Much Ado About Nothing*, say, is not to claim a spatial relationship between the individual images. Nor does the Freytag triangle claim anything more than a rough figurative approximation of the "movement" of a play's conflicts, whereas the chiastic thematic arch is a precisely mirroring structure of identical and contrasting actions.

In at least one respect my procedure differs from what might be expected in literary analysis. My spatial approach continually refers the reader back to the thematic arch, somewhat as though it were a painting under the eye of an art critic, both the source and the end of analysis. That Cassius and Caesar both consider omens of their deaths does not occasion a detailed comparison of their characters or speculation on the place of superstition and the supernatural in *Julius Caesar*, as it might in traditional criticism. Rather, the repeated action is fitted into the larger gestalt of the symmetrical structure for no other purpose than to demonstrate that the reflected action constitutes one element in a meaningful spatial and thematic pattern. Therefore, I hope the reader will avoid the understandable temptation to merely glance at the outlines I provide or to skip them altogether, thinking that the commentary will sufficiently compensate. I allude to but do not repeat quotes from the thematic outlines, for example, and trust that each thematic arch, sufficiently considered, will ultimately be perceived as a significant whole in itself.

In more or less detail, I have analyzed all of Shakespeare's mature, non-collaborative plays. The six chapters of Part One explain Shakespeare's chiasmus, the nature of the actions isolated by the chiastic design, their symmetrical disposition in an arch-like structure, my methodology, and the implications of the thematic arch for scene division. Part One also includes three chapters of illustrative analysis. Part Two consists of interpretive readings of the remaining plays in light of the thematic arch. Though some plays receive only brief treatment, I thought it better to include the thematic arches of all the plays rather than risk the inference that absent plays might not conform to Shakespeare's chiastic pattern, particularly since many of my inferences and extrapolations depend on the fact that the thematic arch always structures Shakespeare's mature plays.

1

The Chiastic Design

Shakespeare's mature, non-collaborative plays have an intertwined and variously overlapping double structure of narrative actions and thematic actions. The narrative movement, the linear unfolding of the story, has been studied by Gustave Freytag, A. C. Bradley, Bernard Beckerman, Emrys Jones and others.[1] It is usually described in the familiar terms of exposition, conflict, climax and central turn, of sequential movements ("rising and falling action") and denouement. This structure is loose-jointed and variable. Episodes and even whole scenes can be cut from a play without narrative coherence or continuity appearing to suffer. The "third-act climax" might occur anywhere in the third or fourth act, and the two movements universally discerned in the plays might similarly turn from one to the other in the second, third or fourth act.[2]

In contrast to the shifting design of the narrative action, the second, interpenetrating structure of thematic actions is invariant. It is a chiastic design in which each scene of the first half of the play reflects an essential thematic action in the corresponding scene of the second half. The same action or contrasting actions occur in paired scenes, as described below. Isolating and distinguishing the narrative and thematic structures reveals that, in one aspect at least, Shakespeare's plots are not *sui generis*, as critical commentary on their narrative shapes has concluded. Rather, there is a recurring pattern in his carpet, a kind of Platonic form created by the chiastically patterned actions underlying the design of all the plays.

The exact relationship between the narrative and the thematic structures varies from play to play, with most individual actions of necessity functioning in both structures. The assassination of Caesar is not only a narrative incident but a thematic one as well, one of many perversions of "sacrifice" in the play. But other actions, which seem to have little or no place in the storyline and are often cut by directors, function almost exclusively as thematic actions. The Poet who interrupts the quarrel between Brutus and Cassius is often cut from productions of *Julius Caesar*, but he is crucial to the thematic design in mirroring Artimedorus in the chiastically paired scene, another advocate of love, who is dismissed by Caesar as the Poet is dismissed— for significantly different reasons—by Brutus. Individual actions may have a place in one or in both interpenetrating structures; the thematic design includes actions from every scene.

Shakespeare's Chiasmus

Chiasmus—a mirror pattern in which key elements are repeated in reverse order, either with or without an unrepeated central element (ABCBA or ABBA)—is a common organizing principle, employed both rhetorically and structurally. It is used to pattern sentences, speeches, narrative incidents and whole works of literary art, including ancient Greek texts, books of the Old Testament and French epics.[3] There are simple and complex forms of chiasmus, and the pattern is so prevalent it is known by a variety of names. The simplest rhetorical form, "basic" chiasmus, ABBA, corresponds to the figure of antimetabole ("O brawling love! O loving hate!" [*Romeo and Juliet* 1.1.176]). The form with an unrepeated central element, ABCBA, variously known as "chiastic inclusion" or "symmetric" chiasmus, might also be designated an "envelope" or "framing" pattern in which the flanking reflections heighten the importance of the central element; many of the best known episodes in Shakespeare's plays, such as Malvolio's tortured reading of Maria's letter in *Twelfth Night*, are structurally emphasized in this way (see below). Chiasmus, or "inverse parallelism," as it is also known, is common in Shakespeare, both as a rhetorical device organizing sentences and speeches[4] and as a structural device organizing individual scenes and—as I will illustrate—entire plays.

The basic chiasmus is illustrated in the quotes from *Macbeth* and *Richard II* above. A short speech from *Richard III*, analyzed by William Davis, will serve as an example of a slightly more complex rhetorical chiasmus and will suggest the kinds of variations possible within the pattern. The speech is by Brackenbury (*RIII* 1.4.76–83) and is introduced by a standard parallelism and a basic chiasmus; then follows the symmetrical chiasmus or ABA pattern, as indicated:

> Sorrow breaks seasons and reposing hours,
> Makes the night morning and the noontide night: [basic chiasm]
> A: Princes have but their titles for their glories,
>   An outward honor for an inward toil,
>   B: And for unfelt imaginations
>   They often feel a world of restless cares
> A: So that between their titles and low name
>   There's nothing differs but the outward fame.

Though the same words are not both repeated in the basic chiasmus of line two, the idea of broken hours is closely repeated and—as with the slight change of wording in the symmetrical chiasmus from "outward honor" to "outward fame"—the repetition of the idea is enough to create chiasmus. The mirroring may be verbal or conceptual. Instances of Shakespeare's rhetorical chiasmus, whether simple or much more complicated than this example, are easily found throughout his work.

Chiasmi structuring scenes have been frequently noted. Marjorie Garber remarks the ABBA pattern in scene 4.3 of *Love's Labor's Lost* when the King of Navarre and his lords are exposed as having fallen in love:

One by one the shamefaced courtiers come forward, announce the dilemma of being in love against the vows they have sworn, and declaim sonnets they have written to their ladies. The scene unfolds brilliantly, almost itself like a sophisticated verse form, *abcd dcba*. First Berowne appears, soliloquizes about his plight, notes that he has written a sonnet to Rosaline and sent it to her, wishes the others were similarly affected, and then moves aside, out of sight, to be followed immediately by the King, Longueville and Dumaine, each of them with a sonnet in hand. They read their sonnets, then hide, but overhear the next-comer. Once the last sonnet has been read, the accusations begin in reverse order, Dumaine accused by Longueville, Longueville's love unmasked by the king, and finally Berowne.[5]

The obvious key elements repeated in reverse order are the characters, each performing the same action. In the letter scene of *Twelfth Night*, as described by Emrys Jones, the characters are again the most obvious elements of the chiasmus:

> The scene itself is severely economical and purposefully shaped; as soon as it gets going the nature of the "device" [the letter] becomes obvious. Sir Toby, Sir Andrew, and Fabian appear first. Then Maria runs in to announce the approach of Malvolio, and runs out again. And Malvolio appears. The main business of the scene follows. Malvolio ... reads ... the letter ... and hurries away crying, "I will smile: I will do everything thou wilt have me." The three dupers emerge from their hiding place, and are joined by Maria before they leave the stage.

Jones comments that the scene can be visualized in "almost symmetrical terms. First, the three dupers enter; then, briefly, Maria; lastly Malvolio. The main business of the scene follows. Malvolio leaves the stage to the dupers again, who are again joined by Maria, before they too leave."[6] Again, the order in which characters enter and leave the stage forms a chiasmus: ABCBA—dupers: Maria: Malvolio: Maria: dupers.

In his indispensable *Shakespearean Design* Mark Rose analyses any number of scenes organized by a "frame principle," that is, as symmetrical chiasmi. The opening scene of *King Lear* is an instance; however, rather than the same characters as repeated key elements, as in the examples of *Love's Labor's Lost* and *Twelfth Night*, the repeated elements are the topics of conversations by different characters. Rose first outlines the largest pattern, the "frame and centerpiece." The scene opens with a prologue between Kent and Gloucester about Lear's judgment and the subplot villain, Edmund. After the public court centerpiece, the scene ends with Cordelia denouncing her sisters, who then discuss among themselves Lear's judgment. Lear's judgment: subplot villain: court centerpiece: main plot villains: Lear's judgment. Rose further finds the court centerpiece to be "symmetrically patterned," and the overall scene thus to be "a triad within a triad," that is, an extended symmetrical chiasmus. "The centerpiece opens with the formal love-tests of the daughters.... The closing episode ... brings on Burgundy and France to judge dowerless Cordelia's worth.... The two analogous episodes, each a love test ... frame the central episode in which Kent dares come between the dragon and his wrath."[7] The conversational topics of the scene in order then are: Lear's judgment, subplot villain, love test, Kent's "treason," love test, main plot villains, Lear's judgment.

Crediting the observation to Michael Holahan, Rose also points out a larger chiastic structure in Shakespeare, the "triple frame of distinct character groups" around the central scene of *The Tempest*, i.e., a symmetrical chiasmus in which the repeated units are the character groupings of entire scenes or parts of scenes.

3.1 Miranda and Ferdinand.	
2.2 Caliban's party.	3.2 Caliban's party.
2.1 King's men.	3.3 King's men.
1.2 (last segment) Prospero, Ferdinand and Miranda.	4.1 (first segment) Prospero, Ferdinand and Miranda.

While Rose dismisses the pattern as having "little dramatic function," "merely a display of virtuosity," it is, in fact, the invariant organization of all Shakespeare's mature plays. Most often with actions as key elements rather than character groups, symmetrical chiasmus is Shakespeare's fundamental dramatic structure.[8]

Following is a summary of Folio *Measure for Measure* illustrating the chiastic pattern. The thematic reference in the central scene and the paired reflecting actions are in bold type.

2.4 Angelo tells Isabella, **"You must lay down the treasures of your body ... or else let [Claudio] suffer"** and die. Isabella, certain Claudio would not want her to sin, goes to prepare him for death.	

2.3 **The duke as friar visits the prison** and meets with Juliet, who expresses both her love for Claudio and her repentance for the sinful act that made her pregnant. As he exits, "Friar" tells Juliet that Claudio is to die.	3.1 **"Friar" visits prison**, persuades Claudio death is preferable to life. When Isabella tells Claudio that he can be freed if she yields to Angelo, Claudio wants to live even on those terms. Isabella is horrified. *** "Friar," who has eavesdropped, tells Isabella of a way to save Claudio and her own honor: Angelo's abandoned fiancé will sleep with Angelo in Isabella's place. Pompey is brought to prison. Lucio refuses to bail him out and slanders the absent duke to the "Friar," who warns him he will pay for the slander when the duke returns. The "Friar" tells Escalus that Claudio is ready to die.
2.2 **Isabella pleads with Angelo for Claudio's life.** Angelo refuses but, desiring Isabella, tells her to return the next morning for his answer.	4.1 **Isabella** reports to "Friar" on arrangements with Angelo for that night's assignation and **pleads with Mariana to save Claudio** by sleeping with Angelo.
2.1 Escalus suggests leniency but **Angelo orders Claudio to be executed** the next morning. Escalus tells Froth to stay out of alehouses and Pompey that he will be whipped if he offends again.	4.2 Pompey becomes assistant to Abhorson, the executioner. "Friar" awaits Angelo's pardon of Claudio but **Angelo orders Claudio's immediate death** and that his head be brought to Angelo. "Friar" plans to bring head of another prisoner, Bernardine.

1.5 **Lucio tells Isabella that Claudio is to be executed** and persuades her to intercede with Angelo.	4.3 Bernardine says he is not ready to die. "Friar" and Provost send head of a dead prisoner. When Isabella asks, **"Friar" tells her that Claudio has been executed.**
1.4 **To avoid slander, the duke** explains while **disguising himself** as a friar, he appointed Angelo and plans to secretly observe him.	4.4 **Angelo** confident **no scandal** can touch the **"credent bulk" of his "authority,"** when he learns of the duke's return.
1.3 **Claudio**, sentenced to be executed, **sends Lucio to summon** Isabella to intercede with Angelo on Claudio's behalf.	4.5 **Duke sends Peter to summon** duke's friends in preparation for his return.

1.2 **Mistress Overdone brings news** that Angelo has had Claudio arrested as **a fornicator** because his fiancé is pregnant.	4.6 **Isabella** to take Mariana's "part" and **speak indirectly** against Angelo as **a fornicator.**
1.1 **The Duke of Vienna confers authority** on Angelo: "Be thou at full ourself."	5.1 The duke is met by Isabella, who accuses Angelo of violating her chastity. She is arrested for slander. Mariana claims Angelo as her

husband. Angelo protests his innocence until **the duke**, who re-enters disguised as the friar, is stripped of his hood by Lucio and **retrieves his authority**. Angelo confesses. He is sentenced to marry Mariana and then to be executed for Claudio's death. Mariana begs for Angelo's life and Isabella joins her plea. The duke refuses and has a prisoner brought in who, unmuffled, is revealed to be Claudio. Angelo's death sentence is revoked, Lucio must marry Kate Keepdown, Claudio must marry Juliet. The duke proposes marriage to Isabella.

The key element in the chiastic design is action. The halves of the play reflect the same action in each pair of scenes. It may be performed by the same character or by different characters, or it may begin in one scene and end in the paired scene. The central segment of three scene pairs reflects in each pairing the same character performing essentially the same action. The Duke in 2.3–3.1 visits a prisoner, first Juliet and then Claudio; Isabella pleads for Claudio's life, in 2.2 with Angelo and again in 4.1 with Mariana; and Angelo twice orders the execution of Claudio, in 2.1 and 4.2. In the other three-pair segment the Duke's actions are reflected in the actions of other characters. In sending Peter to summon Flavius and other friends, the Duke mirrors Claudio's earlier action of sending Lucio to summon Isabella (1.3 and 4.5). In telling Isabella that Claudio is dead, the Duke falsely completes the news Lucius brought to Isabella earlier (1.5 and 4.3). The central pair of this three-pair segment (1.4 and 4.4) compares the Duke and Angelo in what might be called their "substitute selves," the Duke as Friar and Angelo as a figure of authority, both anxious to avoid being slandered. Finally, the two-pair segment contains both types of pairing—the same action by the same character, here initiated and ended, when the Duke confers and retrieves his authority in the center of the first and last scenes; and the same action performed by different characters when in the second and penultimate scenes a fornicator is publicly proclaimed, by Mistress Overdone and by Isabella. Like the Duke in the middle segment, Isabella is also shown to have moved closer to the street life of Vienna, in her case by performing the same action as Mistress Overdone performs in the corresponding scene (and in publicly proclaiming herself a sinner). Essential actions are chiastically related in what can be conveniently rendered as a symmetrical arch of mirroring halves with a keystone scene, in this case scene 2.4, in which Angelo articulates the play's basic thematic opposition between procreation and death.

The scene groupings are essentially thematic. Briefly, the central segment in which the reclusive characters' actions are exactly reflected in the second half of the play implies their self-involvement and enacts their attitudes toward sex and death. The second three-pair segment reveals the old duke, mirrored in Angelo, and the new duke breaking out of his sterile reclusiveness in reflecting the actions of Claudio and Lucio. Besides interweaving the two worlds of anarchic fecundity and sterile legalisms by means of this reflective structure, Shakespeare also emphasizes the importance of key actions. The duke's two visits to prison in the central flanking scenes, for example, illustrate that, like Angelo, the duke is an advocate for death until he overhears the conversation between Claudio and Isabella. Furthermore, the reflective structure bears on questions of scene division and revision, topics treated in subsequent chapters.

A word on my terminology. I have designated the arch as "thematic," though distinctions between narrative and theme or character and theme are impossible to draw exactly. Nevertheless, the distinction is structurally enforced in Shakespeare and warrants my use of the term. The final battle sequence in *Macbeth*, for example, is variously divided by editors who impose scene breaks at every cleared stage in the Folio's long last scene (5.7), as though the narrative should determine the breaks.[9] But Shakespeare has designed the Folio scene to emphasize the psychological change in Macbeth, the moment of his final break from the influence of the Weird Sisters; at the center of the Folio scene (49 of 104), at the news that MacDuff was untimely born, Macbeth says, "And be these juggling fiends no more believ'd." The disordered imaginings that have transported Macbeth through the whole play are at an end. Here as elsewhere in the canon, the narrative sequence needs no pointing to be apprehended; the thematic units, however, are often less evident. Shakespeare has usually arranged the thematic elements to be the structural focus of individual scenes.[10] Furthermore, mirror scenes in Shakespeare have long been recognized as thematic rather than narrative, and the thematic arch is essentially a description of the basic mirror design upon which the whole play is organized. Finally, studies of chiastic structure in other literary works have found the central element to be a "crux," and my contention that the central scene focuses the theme accords with these structural analyses.

Shakespeare's Action

As a first approach to Shakespeare's action and its chiastic disposition, consider the beginnings and endings of his plots, subplots and nested actions. In the clearest instances, the protagonist's action initiates the main plot in the first scene and ends it in the last scene with another action, as Duke Vincentio in *Measure for Measure* confers his authority on Angelo in the first scene and retrieves it in the last scene (1.1 and 5.1), initiating and ending the most encompassing of the play's many substitutions. In the tragedy *Coriolanus*, the eponymous hero initiates the action that ends with his death, the conflict with Tullus Aufidius; in the first scene Coriolanus promises he will "once more strike at Tullus' face" (240), and in the last scene, manipulated by Aufidius, defies the Corioles and suffers his fate when Tullus Aufidius stands on his body (5.6). In the same way, the beginning and ending actions of subplots and of significant nested actions are also disposed in paired scenes. In *Troilus and Cressida* the Achilles-Hector conflict begins in the third scene with Hector's challenge and ends with Hector's death in the third-last scene (1.3 and 5.8). Antonio's bond with Shylock begins in the third scene of *The Merchant of Venice* and ends in the third-last scene, the trial scene (1.2 and 4.1). The window trick, an action nested in the larger plot action of the Claudio-Hero courtship, also begins and ends in corresponding scenes of *Much Ado About Nothing* (2.2 and 4.2).

This is an invariant structural principle in Shakespeare: the main plot and the subplot begin and end with character actions in corresponding scenes of the first and second half of the play. These demarcations are not always as evident as in the examples above, for Shakespeare's plots are not always straightforwardly Aristotelian. They are not actions in which an agent has a clear goal to be pursued through the play, as in *Oedipus Rex*, the citizens of Thebes want to cure the city of the plague and this goal in turn entails Oedipus's search for the killer of Laius, or in *Philoctetes* Odysseus wants to possess Heracles' unerring bow and enlists Neoptolemus to con Philoctetes. Often Shakespeare's action is initiated to no clear purpose; the plot direction, the goal of the action, is not explicitly purposeful but unfolds (or not) as the play progresses. Even in as early a play as *Richard II*, the first scene provides no certain goal for the action, or, rather, it provides a misleading goal, since Bolingbroke intends to avenge Gloucester's death by challenging Mowbray. In the second scene, Gloucester's widow wants her husband's death avenged not on Mowbray but on Richard, and Gaunt refuses to harm "God's substitute." After Richard banishes both Bolingbroke and Mowbray in the third scene, the apparent revenge plot, which has had two suggested agents and two possible targets, has dissipated. The true "action" of the play turns out to be something more like a propositional transformation than an Aristotelian action, a change from "not-killing the king" (Gaunt in second scene) to "killing the king" (Eton in second-last scene), that is, a thematic action testing the divine right of monarchy. The chronicle narrative addresses, as the history plays so often do, the issue of succession in the deposition of Richard by Bolingbroke; but the action of the play, considered as Aristotelian, as an agent pursuing a goal, remains nebulous to the end, since Bolingbroke's articulated purposes are suspect and his most important actions, his revolt and his military campaign, are dramatized at their start and end only in the queen's reaction to them. It is almost as though Bolingbroke drifted into treason with no more intent than the clouds rolling overhead.

Or again consider the plot of *Macbeth*. No Aristotelian action is initiated by the witches' intention to meet Macbeth. What is the witches' purpose? But, as Kenneth Burke puts it, we immediately sense a curse on Macbeth, a chthonic charm of a sort.[11] Though the weird sisters later disappear from the play, their charm continues to transport Macbeth until the last scene, when he finally says, "And be these juggling fiends no more believed." The play seems rather to describe the beginning, middle and end of a charm as it varyingly affects the protagonist than to dramatize the course of a single purposeful action. The narrative of, say, Macbeth's ambitious climb (as the play is often described) is subsumed in the thematic action of Macbeth's transport, which begins in the first scene.[12]

Because Shakespeare's plot actions shift agents and their goals and are intricately woven together, his practice of beginning and ending actions in paired scenes provides a useful analytical tool. In *Troilus and Cressida*, for example, the actual affair of the lovers (as distinct from its preliminaries and consequences) clearly ends when Troilus tears up Cressida's letter to him, but it begins less obviously in the paired scene with Paris's promise to make Troilus's excuses at dinner (3.1 and 5.3). The romance plot of *The Merchant of Venice*, entails of necessity the transformation of the Antonio-Bassanio relationship, which, beginning with Antonio's promise of money in the first scene, ends quietly enough in the last scene with Antonio's promise to stake his soul (rather than his money/flesh) on the security of Bassanio's marriage bond (1.1 and 5.1). By symmetrically embedding the beginnings and endings of his plots in paired scenes, Shakespeare assures his perfect hold on the plot action, however muted its dramaturgy, and provides a convenient means of explicitly demarcating the various movements of the temporal narrative action and the segmentations of the thematic structure even in complex plays like *Cymbeline* and *Antony and Cleopatra*.

In addition to the character actions beginning and ending plots, other character actions are also disposed in corresponding scenes of the arch. Identical or contrasting actions by the same character may mark changes or fossilizations that have occurred between the first and second halves of the play. In corresponding scenes of *Much Ado* Claudio twice agrees to marry Hero, in the second instance as the "niece" he has never seen, a woman who, unlike Hero, has not been vetted by his friends (2.1 and 5.1). In *Measure for Measure* Isabella twice pleads for her brother's life, once with Angelo and again, after wishing Claudio dead, with Marianna (2.2 and 4.1). Identical or contrasting actions of different characters are also common in paired scenes—Iachimo voyeuristically violating Imogen and Cloten planning her physical violation in *Cymbeline* (2.2 and 4.1); Caesar and Cassius both considering omens of their deaths in *Julius Caesar* (2.2 and 5.1); Goneril casting out her father in Folio *King Lear* and Cordelia embracing him (1.4 and 4.6). Such character actions are carefully located on the thematic arch to mirror each other in paired scenes.

The actions in the two scenes flanking the numerically central scene are more prominently mirrored than actions in other paired scenes. The central flanking scenes, we might say, are a privileged position in the plays. Their mirroring actions are equivalently staged, making the repeated or completed action immediately evident to the audience. Coriolanus twice denounces the tribunes; Pisanio twice gives Imogen a letter; two suitors of Portia choose the wrong casket; Caesar and Cinna the poet are both murdered, etc. These identical actions all occur in the central flanking scenes. This is the case in all but three mature plays. The central flanking scenes reflect a clearly identical action. Either the same character performs the same action in both scenes, different characters perform the same action, or the same action is begun in one scene and ended in the other. Because most of Shakespeare's mirroring scene pairs are variations of this practice, I list here the actions reflected in the keystone flanking scenes of each of the mature, non-collaborative plays.

Same character performs the same action in both central flanking scenes:

A Midsummer Night's Dream: Oberon applies magic juice (2.2 and 3.2)
Henry IV Part Two: Falstaff recruits soldiers (2.4 and 3.2)
Henry V: French boast of their prowess (3.5 and 3.7)
Hamlet (variation): King Hamlet (as Player King and as Ghost) exhorts to memory and purpose (3.2 and [3.4 & 4.1])
Measure for Measure: Duke visits a prisoner (2.3 and 3.1)
King Lear: Lear identifies himself with "Poor Tom" (3.4 and 3.6)
Macbeth: Macbeth imagines a frightening Banquo (in dream and in hallucination) (3.2 and 3.4)
Coriolanus: Coriolanus denounces the tribunes (3.1 and 3.3)
Cymbeline: Pisanio gives a letter to Imogen (3.2 and 3.4)

Same action repeated by different characters:

Richard II: Bolingbroke's grievances expressed (by Bolingbroke and by Northumberland) (3.1 and 3.3)
Merchant of Venice: wrong casket chosen (by Moor and by Aragon) (2.7 and 2.9)
Henry IV Part One: squabbling (between Hotspur and wife and between Falstaff and Hostess) (3.1 and 3.3)
Julius Caesar: murder (of Caesar by assassins and of Cinna by the mob) (3.1 and 3.3)
Much Ado About Nothing (variation: "passion" rather than action): lovesickness (of Benedick and of Beatrice) (3.2 and 3.4)

Merry Wives of Windsor: quizzing (of Slender by Anne and of William by Hugh Evans) (3.4 and 4.1)

Twelfth Night: love expressed (by Viola and Olivia) (2.4 and 3.1)

A single action begun and ended:

Love's Labor's Lost: Berowne's letter sent and (mis)delivered (3.1 and 4.2)

Troilus and Cressida: exchange of Cressida revealed (to Troilus and Cressida) and accomplished (4.2 and 4.4)

All's Well That Ends Well: Bertram receives military orders and celebrates military victory (3.3 and 3.5)

Othello: Cassio enters and leaves Desdemona's residence (3.1 and 3.3)

Antony and Cleopatra: Antony previews and reflects on Actium (3.9 and 3.11)

The Tempest: Caliban drinks and is drunk (2.2 and 3.2)

King John (variation: a failed action, that of killing Arthur): Hubert is dissuaded from murder and protests his innocence in Arthur's death (4.1 and 4.3)

The three plays that do not contain the same action in the central flanking scenes contain contrasting actions.

Romeo and Juliet: marriage and (supposed) death of Romeo (2.6 and 3.2)

As You Like It: lands expropriated and appropriated (3.1 and 3.2.11–420)

The Winter's Tale (variation): the prologues of the parallel (and contrasting) plays, the tragedy of Mamillius and the comedy of Perdita (1.1 and 4.1)

As Francis Fergusson observes, "[W]e depend on the dramatists both to discover the infinitely various modes of human action, and to devise the cognate forms whereby they show them to us on stage."[13] By placing these reflecting actions in paired scenes before and after the central scene, Shakespeare has shown us the form action takes at the core of each play. These are Shakespeare's actions, whether or not we might have isolated them as significant. Their placement in paired mirroring scenes defines them for us as Shakespeare's examples of some of the "infinitely various modes of human action." Furthermore, as I show in essays on individual plays, these central flanking actions are elaborately complicated and ramified by their close connection to the keystone articulation of the play's theme, as, for example, the anointing of Demetrius and Lysander in *Midsummer Night's Dream* is connected to the analogous "translation" of Bottom in the keystone scene, or Lear's empathetic identification with Poor Tom is contrasted with Edmund's isolation, his "self-fathering" as the Duke of Gloucester, in the keystone scene of *Lear*.

These central flanking actions can help to define Shakespeare's "basic unit of action," to use a phrase of Charles Hallett's, and especially to distinguish Aristotelian or "sequential" actions from the simple deeds of Shakespeare's thematic structure. Fergusson explains Aristotle's action as follows:

> One must be clear, first of all, that *action* (*praxis*) does not mean deeds, events or physical activity: it means, rather, the motivation from which deeds spring. Butcher puts it this way: "The *praxis* that art seeks to reproduce is mainly a psychic energy working outwards" [*Aristotle's Theory of Poetry and Fine Art*, S. H. Butcher, 4th ed., London, 1932]. It may be described metaphorically as the focus or movement of the psyche toward what seems good to it at the moment—a "movement-of-spirit," Dante calls it.[14]

This is the action Hallett describes as the "sequence," composed of "beats," which are "essentially unit[s] of motivation." It is in sequences that "Shakespeare creates the fundamental 'rising action' of the drama—introduction, complication, climax, denouement." This is, as Hallett says, an application of Freytag to smaller units than the plot. In this view, scenes such as *Macbeth* 5.6 or *As You Like It* 2.6 are not themselves actions, nor do they contain actions. Hallett locates the short *Macbeth* 5.6 in the larger action expressed in the question "Will Macbeth fall?" then quotes the scene in full:

> Malcolm. Now near enough; your leafy screens throw down
>   And show like those you are. You, worthy uncle,
>   Shall with my cousin, your right noble son,
>   Lead our first battle. Worthy Macduff and we
>   Shall take upon's what else remains to do,
>   According to our order.
> Siward.   Fare you well.
>   Do we but find the tyrant's power tonight,
>   Let us be beaten, if we cannot fight.
> Macduff. Make all our trumpets speak, give them all breath,
>   Those clamorous harbingers of blood and death. *Exeunt*

Hallett comments: "Does this scene contain an action? Or is it *itself* an action? [Italics in original.] No. The scene tells us where we are. Its clamorous trumpets summon Macbeth to battle. But that in itself is not an action. The unit merely introduces an action."[15]

Hallett has isolated the narrative action, the fight against Macbeth, as the purposeful action this scene merely serves to introduce. We can see from the central flanking actions of Shakespeare's plays, however, particularly in a play like *Cymbeline*, that his basic actions, isolated by repetition, are not in themselves purposeful or sequential. They can be the mere physical deeds that Fergusson warns against confusing with Aristotelian action. *Macbeth* 5.6 therefore contains two actions in the monadic sense in which Shakespeare fundamentally presents action. The camouflaging boughs of Burnam Wood are cast down, and the trumpets are sounded. While the second of these is too common to battle scenes to have a special significance here, the initial action of throwing down the leafy screens certainly figures importantly in Macbeth's growing disenchantment with the witches' prophecies, that is, in the thematic action of the play, and is significantly reflected in the paired scene in which Duncan confers on Macbeth the title of the deceitful Thane of Cawdor. Similarly with the other scene Hallett mentions, *AYL* 2.6, in which Orlando carries off Adam. This is an iconic action, both as telling of Orlando's character and in recalling the classical action of Aeneus carrying his father from Troy. Furthermore, the action is reflected in Rosalind's contrasting evasion of her father in the paired scene (3.4), so that Orlando's action is thematically crucial. Any definition of Shakespearean action must encompass such significant moments. They are more fundamental, more foundational, than the sequential "basic unit of action" Hallett analyzes.

It is worth noting that recent work on mirror neurons confirms both Aristotle's view and Shakespeare's dramaturgical acuity. Even young children, neuroscientists have found, are "highly attuned to picking up the *goal* of other people's behavior" (italics in original).[16] However, the physical action itself causes a response in the brain; mirror neurons "fire when an individual kicks a soccer ball, sees a ball being kicked, hears a ball being kicked, and even just says or hears the word 'kick.'"[17] Shakespeare has structured his plays on this more fundamental perception of action than the Aristotelian, a more instinctive, basic grasp of human action. Indeed,

Shakespeare's basic unit of action is what neuroscientists in their experiments label simply "Action," which, if it is to be understood as purposeful, must be placed in "Context." The deed itself is perceived with or without the context necessary to attribute a goal or motive. Without our realizing, we respond neurologically to the recurring monadic actions in the plays.

The actions of the central flanking scenes confirm not only that Shakespeare's basic unit of action is monadic not sequential, but also that these monadic actions may be physical, verbal or mental. In the central flanking scenes of *Cymbeline* Pisanio hands a letter to Imogen, a simple physical action; in *Coriolanus* the eponymous hero twice denounces the tribunes, an act of performative speech that is the verbal equivalent of Pisanio's physical gesture. Both are accomplishing activities in themselves and need no motive or consequence to be apprehended as actions on the stage. Shakespeare repeats the actions precisely to highlight their different possible motives. In giving Imogen Posthumus's letter to *her*, Pisanio intends to conceal Posthumus's plan to have her murdered; in giving her Posthumus's letter to *him*, Pisanio intends to expose Posthumus's plan. The same deed of handing over a letter has different motives, the combination of act and motive each creating a different character action. Coriolanus denounces the tribunes spontaneously at first, but is goaded to it in the second instance, his "eloquence" defeated by the tribunes' "eloquence"; the successful warrior is a failed orator. Furthermore, in Shakespeare, mental actions can have the same monadic status as physical or verbal actions. In *King Lear*, for example, the titular hero twice identifies himself with Poor Tom, in one instance as a bare forked animal and in the other as a man driven mad. "Identifying with" is a monadic action directed toward different "objects," Poor Tom as beggar and Poor Tom as madman, in each case differently motivated. Of course we only know of Lear's mental action because he expresses it in words, but words here are used as though he is describing a physical action; Lear's expression in words of his "identifying with" is not itself a performative deed like Coriolanus's denunciation of the tribunes. Whether physical, verbal or mental, the monadic action is the basic building block of Shakespeare's drama. It is only because Shakespeare's fundamental apprehension of action is not sequential or purposeful that he can structure it chiastically, that a non-temporal order, a spatial syntax, an "arch," can pattern the basic actions of his plays. We grasp the basic action of, say, giving a letter, instinctively, and as that action is repeated we register the difference in motive, consequence, meaning, both sequentially and analogously, that is, narratively and thematically.

The monadic Shakespearean actions reflected in other paired scenes are not usually as evident as in the central flanking scenes. The same types of identical or contrasting mirrorings occur in all scenes, but their staging is not equivalently emphatic. Shakespeare seems to be proceeding on an assumption that neuroscientists have empirically confirmed, that even hearing a word denoting an action is sufficient for the audience's response. Consequently, the same action may be enacted in one scene and merely referenced or narrated in the other. In *Coriolanus*, for example, the titular hero embraces Cominius on stage in one scene and in the paired scene the contrasting action is narrated: Cominius tells how he was rebuffed by Coriolanus (1.6 and 5.1). And Shakespeare further attenuates our sensitivity to action. Analogous rather than identical actions may link paired scenes, as "service" links two scenes in *The Merchant of Venice*. In the fifth scene Lancelot enters Bassanio's service and is given a new livery; in the fifth-last scene Portia dons a new "habit" to serve Bassanio as the lawyer at Antonio's trial (2.2 and 3.4). Any number of variations and degrees of emphasis might be worked on these kinds of reflections. Occasionally, as thematically relevant, scenes may be paired by mirroring speeches rather than of actions. Not surprisingly, *Hamlet* and *1 Henry IV*, plays whose major characters displace much of their energy into language, often mirror speeches rather than actions; the rhetorical set pieces on honor by Hotspur and Falstaff, for instance, occur in paired scenes (1.3 and 5.1).

The focal point and keystone of this symmetrically mirroring structure, the central scene, is always thematically but seldom "dramatically" central. That is to say, the narrative climax and the keystone scene are rarely one and the same. True, a relatively early play like *Romeo and Juliet* has its thematic focus on Romeo as "Fortune's fool" in a big central scene: Romeo kills Tybalt, and Prince Escalus makes his fateful pronouncement amid a civic crowd (3.1). But most similarly extravagant scenes, though often thought to be central, are seldom so. In *Julius Caesar*, for example, the assassination scene (3.1), the narrative climax, occurs in the scene before Antony's keystone invocation of Caesar as a martyred saint (3.2), which makes blasphemous "sacrifice" a theme common to conspirators and revengers alike. In *The Merchant of Venice* the narrative climax is Bassanio's choice of the lead casket (3.2), but the central scene, 2.8, contains the thematically crucial conversation between Solanio and Salerio focusing the nexus of money and flesh in the losses of Shylock's money and Antonio's friend. The thematic center might also be coincident with an important character's transformation. Urging the essential action of substitution, Angelo propositions Isabel in the central scene of *Measure for Measure*, 2.4, asking her to exchange her chastity for her brother's life. In the central lines of the central scene of *1 Henry IV* Hal tells his father, "Henceforth I shall be more myself," addressing Henry's (and the play's) thematic concern with succession (3.2).

Because narrative and thematic designs have not been carefully distinguished, the precisely central focus and underlying symmetry of the plays has not been previously noticed. For example, Bernard Beckerman, in his useful discussion of Shakespeare's dramaturgy, argues against the idea of a keystone scene. He finds a "central plateau" rather than distinguishable keystone and central flanking scenes because the climax, the "emotional intensification at the center of a Shakespearean play," is diffuse. "For example," he asks, "is the play-within-the-play scene, the prayer scene, or the closet scene the climax in *Hamlet*?" The point is well taken that "none of these scenes alone reveal a point of climax." But Beckerman concludes that there is therefore no distinguishable single keystone scene and recommends "abandoning the conception of a climactic moment." The thematic action, however, does not depend on emotional intensity. Reversals, recognitions and "dramatic explosions" are indications of narrative climaxes only; the "unseen referent at the play's center" that Beckerman refers to is thematic.[18]

Hamlet is too complex to use as an example, but consider another play that Beckerman mentions, *Coriolanus*. The critic finds the banishment of Coriolanus to be the point of reversal but states that it is "blunted" because the scene of banishment duplicates the earlier struggle with the Tribunes; therefore, the apparently classical "climax" is really a central plateau extending over the three central scenes, the first struggle with the Tribunes (3.1), the discussion with Volumnia (3.2) and the second struggle with the Tribunes, which results in banishment (3.3).[19] In fact, the scene containing the discussion with Volumnia is numerically central and is the thematic heart of the play, the keystone of the arch, expressed in Volumnia's statement that "action is eloquence" (76). She introduces an idea of action as acting, as pretense, which Coriolanus attempts but fails to pull off. The two struggles with the Tribunes are therefore profoundly different in that Coriolanus uses a different idea of action in each, the warrior's angry spontaneity and the orator's practiced gestures and words. Failing in his second strategy where the Tribunes succeed, Coriolanus meets the first of his three defeats by "actors"—the Tribunes, Aufidius and Volumnia. While the action is the same in both flanking scenes, Coriolanus's intention is significantly different. This is a common pattern for the central three scenes. The strongly similar scenes of the flanking pair have a significant point of difference, often resulting from an expression in the central scene of a transforming idea, the theme of the play.

Scene Groupings

The remaining, paired scenes of each play are organized into groups consisting of from one to five scene pairs. The thematic actions of each group address an essential topic of the play. For example, as we have already seen, a group of three scene pairs in *Measure for Measure* addresses the character of the duke by mirroring his actions with precisely the same actions by Angelo and by characters of the demimonde.

1.5 Lucio tells Isabella that Claudio is to be executed.	4.3 "Friar" tells Isabella that Claudio has been executed.
1.4 To avoid slander, the duke explains, he disguised himself as a friar.	4.4 Angelo confident no scandal can touch the "credent bulk" of his "authority."
1.3 Claudio sends Lucio to summon Isabella.	4.5 Duke sends Peter to summon duke's friends.

This group is clearly distinct from the play's other three-pair group in which the main characters each perform an identical action in both scenes of each pair.

2.3 The duke as friar visits the prison and condemns Juliet's "sin."	3.1 "Friar" visits prison to persuade Claudio that death is superior to life.
2.2 Isabella pleads with Angelo for Claudio's life.	4.1 Isabella pleads with Mariana to save Claudio.
2.1 Angelo orders Claudio to be executed.	4.2 Angelo orders Claudio's immediate death.

This group reveals the settled attitudes of the three main characters, a sort of standard by which to measure their changes or fossilizations elsewhere in the play. Once the reflecting actions of paired scenes are isolated, the scene groupings are easily apprehended and distinguished.

Julius Caesar, to take one more example, consists of four groups of two scene pairs each (plus the keystone, not included in the outline below). The thematic actions of one group are (both directly and indirectly) devoted to Caesar; another to the main conspirators, Cassius and Brutus; a third to a comparison of Caesar with the conspirators; and a fourth to the public and private disorder caused by Caesar's assassination.

Disorder	
3.1 Caesar killed.	3.3 Cinna the poet killed.
2.4 Portia sends Lucius on errand.	4.1 Antony sends Lepidus on errand.

Caesar and conspirators

2.3 "Lover" Artemidorus reads warning he plans to present to Caesar.	4.2 [& 4.3] Poet advises Cassius and Brutus to "love, and be friends."
2.2 Caesar weighs dreams and auguries presaging his death.	5.1 Cassius now "partly" believes auguries; omens of his death.

Conspirators

2.1 Brutus: "Let us be sacrificers."	5.2 Brutus orders attack.
1.3 Cassius: "Cassius from bondage will deliver Cassius."	5.3 Cassius kills himself; "I am free," says Pindarus.

Caesar

1.2 Cassius, Brutus's "glass," reflects Brutus to himself: "A Brutus once..." Caesar offers his throat.	5.4 Lucilius, claiming to be Brutus, is captured and asks to be killed.
1.1 Flavius & Marcellus disperse workmen celebrating Caesar's triumph.	5.5 Brutus kills himself, confirming Caesar's triumph.

The reflecting actions are discussed in detail in a later chapter. The point to be made by this outline is that the organization by scene groups is both logical and comprehensive, collectively encompassing the main characters and essential actions of the play.

All the plays are similarly rigorous in their grouped arrangement of thematic actions and their careful inclusion of major characters, even plays like *Cymbeline* and *Antony and Cleopatra*, whose constructions are most lamented. With the significant exception of the two parts of *Henry IV*, however, no two mature plays have the same overall division into scene groups, though Shakespeare frequently uses the same total number of scenes.[20] The grouping of scenes is as various as their pairings. It is impossible to generalize, for each play has its own logic in sectioning off parts of the play into scene groups of varying numbers of scene pairs.

The overall symmetrical structure and the grouping of scenes may also pattern the imagery. Arranged on an invariant structure, images more readily reveal their changing significance over the course of the action. In earlier plays like *Richard II* and *King John*, imagery traces changes in the action and characters strictly in accordance with the overall symmetry of the play. That is to say, Shakespeare not only disposed the actions in a symmetrical pattern but also arranged the imagery to make use of the same pattern. Meaning is not only semantic but is positional as well. What is unspoken but "built in," implied only by position and structural location, is often what gives Shakespeare his resonance and elusiveness. In *King John*, for example, the few sun images seem to contribute little to the play, but once seen disposed in the symmetrical pattern the imagery becomes literally pivotal, central to our understanding of kingship in the play. In later plays the imagery is more complexly nuanced, but an awareness of the underlying symmetrical scaffolding is nonetheless often useful in tracing the interplay of imagery and action.

I want to emphasize that these generalizations are subject to an interesting range of variations on the basic chiastic pattern. Shakespeare may not perfectly mirror the halves of the play. After the spell-stopped tableaux signaling the end of Prospero's charm, *The Tempest* has a series of codas outside the symmetrical pattern to indicate the characters' return to reality. Or the playwright might alter the "rising" and "falling" action. *The Winter's Tale* begins a new play in the middle, the comedy of Bohemia matching the tragedy of Sicilia scene for scene. One of the pleasures of tracking Shakespeare's architectural symmetry is a renewed appreciation of the virtuosity he brings to every aspect of his art.

It is an understatement to say that an awareness of the thematic structure is useful. Scene designations become determinable by something more than the vague notion of "continuous action" or the often dizzyingly cleared stage in a battle sequence. Critical studies are significantly assisted by isolating the thematic designs of individual plays, which often qualify or even undercut the narrative. Almost without critical analysis a thematic arch suggests much about a play, often crystallizing common intuitive notions; for example, the tragic first half of *The Winter's Tale* and the comic second half are, it turns out, two exactly parallel plays, mirroring each other's thematic actions scene for scene. In fact, after some familiarity with the symmetrical design, the elusive unity of a Shakespeare play begins to reveal itself, and it is possible to apprehend each play whole, even a complex play like *Cymbeline*. Most consequentially for recent notions of Shakespeare's revision, the chiastic design establishes parameters for the number and placement of scenes in a play and calls into question the current orthodoxy about the revisions of *King Lear* and *2 Henry IV*. Modest as it is, even the present initial examination of the thematic structure and its architectural symmetry suggests much about larger questions of Shakespeare's writing methods, treatment of sources and aesthetic.

2

Isolating the Chiastic Design

In the summary of *Measure for Measure* in the previous chapter, one character action in each Folio scene was clearly mirrored in the corresponding scene of the other half of the play. This degree of clarity is rather the exception than the rule, and it would be misleading to leave the methodology described in the previous chapter unqualified. Ordinarily, a play contains both obviously reflecting actions in paired scenes, as in *Measure for Measure*, and more subtly mirroring actions. *Much Ado About Nothing* illustrates this combination.

Certain actions in *Much Ado*, like those in *Measure for Measure*, are identical or nearly identical. Claudio twice agrees to marry Hero, once as Leonato's "niece"; Benedick and Beatrice both exhibit symptoms of lovesickness; Claudio's slander of Hero is a specific instance of Benedick's more general slander of women. We can also mark the progress of the narrative, the beginning and end of its various sequences, such as the initiation and exposure of the window trick, or the beginning and end of Claudio's courting of Hero. It is hardly more than pattern recognition, a description of parts of the play, to arrange these inversely parallel incidents as they occur in the corresponding scenes of the first and second halves of the drama.

3.2 Benedick is lovesick.	3.4 Beatrice is lovesick.
2.3 Benedick said to "torment" Beatrice (with his "impossible slanders").	4.1 Claudio slanders Hero at church.
2.2 Borachio introduces window trick to Don John.	4.2 Watch questioned: window trick exposed.
2.1 Claudio agrees to wed Hero.	5.1 Claudio agrees to wed "niece."
1.1 Claudio's first interest in Hero.	5.4 Claudio marries Hero.

In the first and last scenes it is not simply that Claudio falls in love and marries Hero. These incidents are more specifically rendered by Shakespeare to have a thematic resonance. Claudio questions Benedick about Hero in the center of the opening scene (1.1.161 ff. of 328), and she unveils at the center of the last scene (5.4.60 of 129). Claudio's mediated approach to Hero begins even before the proxy courtship is arranged with Don Pedro, so the unveiling, which might seem to be only a conventional plot device, is enhanced as a moment of independent action by Claudio and of intimacy with Hero by virtue of its pairing with scene 1.1. The pairing should therefore read to reflect these specific actions.

1.1 Claudio questions Benedick about Hero.	5.4 Claudio offers himself to "niece," who unveils herself.

Expressed in this way, the basis of the pairing is not immediately clear, though its expression and inclusion in the outline are no more "interpretive" than the original pairing in the partial outline above. These are the monadic actions at the center of the first and last scenes that initiate and conclude the main plot. In the same way, other pairings may not immediately yield up the basis of scene reflections, but I hope the commentary clarifies what are basically descriptions.

The 2.3–4.1 pair also deserves some comment. Benedick is reported to "torment" Beatrice in 2.3 (160) as, in the pairing, Claudio torments Hero. In typically Shakespearean fashion, a referenced action is reflected in an identical staged action in the paired scene. But Benedick is also being "slandered" by his friends. He is not only like Claudio but also like Hero. And as she "dies" on Claudio's words, Benedick sickens on the words of his friends. As we would expect of Shakespeare, there is more than one analogy built into the pairing of the two scenes, but the basis of the pairing is the identical action of slander.

How much further can we pursue the pattern that seems to be emerging in *Much Ado*? There are certainly other suggestive pairs. In 1.3 Don John expresses his intention to poison Claudio's happiness, and in 5.2 Benedick informs Beatrice that he has challenged Claudio to a duel. Both men intend harm to Claudio. Thus, their contrasting motives for the same intended action are highlighted (and supplemented by the explicit self-characterizations of Don John and Benedick in these scenes). This mirroring of apparently opposing characters in paired scenes is typical of Shakespeare's practice in suggesting shadings of similarity and difference. Finally, the second and penultimate scenes also demarcate a thematic action. They initiate and terminate the mistakings of the main plot. As in *Romeo and Juliet* the couple's wedding is paired with Juliet's mistaken notion of Romeo's death, love and death, now both misconstrued, are similarly paired in scenes 1.2 and 5.3 of *Much Ado*:

1.2 Antonio wrongly reports that Don Pedro loves Hero.	5.3 Epitaph at tomb of Hero, wrongly thought dead.

If we outline the pairs discussed so far and add the central scene, the thematic reflections look like this:

	3.3 Dogberry instructs Watch. Borachio and Conrade arrested. ("I know that Deformed...")

3.2 Benedick is lovesick.	3.4 Beatrice is lovesick.
3.1	3.5
2.3 Benedick said to "torment" Beatrice (with his "impossible slanders").	4.1 Claudio slanders Hero at church.
2.2 Borachio introduces window trick to Don John.	4.2 Watch questioned: window trick exposed.
2.1 Claudio agrees to wed Hero.	5.1 Claudio agrees to wed "niece."
1.3 Don John intends to poison Claudio's happiness. (Don John's self-characterization.)	5.2 Benedick informs Beatrice he has challenged Claudio. (Benedick's self-characterization.)

1.2 Antonio wrongly reports that Don Pedro loves Hero.	5.3 Epitaph at tomb of Hero, wrongly thought dead.
1.1 Claudio questions Benedick about Hero.	5.4 Claudio offers himself to "niece," who removes her veil.

Since Dogberry and the Watch are the instruments of the plot resolution, they are fittingly central to the narrative of the play; their place in the thematic structure is suggested by the crucial distortion of language in the personification of Deformed. There is then only one remaining pair to complete the arch. In one scene of the pair, a reprise of the Benedick scene, Beatrice is manipulated into eavesdropping on her friends. As Benedick was accused of tormenting Beatrice, she is analogously charged at the center of 3.1. "I never yet saw man," Hero says, "But she would spell him backwards.... [T]urns she every man the wrong side out" (59–61, 68). Also like Benedick, Beatrice is herself "slandered," spoken of harshly—"Her wit Values itself so highly that to her All matter else seems weak. She cannot love.... She is so self-endeared" (52–6)—and, again like Benedick, she sickens at these words. Similar as this is to the treatment of Benedick, at first glance it does not seem to mirror the paired scene (3.5), in which the busy Leonato simply dismisses the information brought by Verges and Dogberry that a couple of "arrant knaves" have been taken into custody. But, in fact, the scene is not only analogous to the Beatrice scene (3.1) but is also structured like the slander of Hero (4.1). In the central speech, Dogberry, miffed that Verges has beaten him in blurting out the news of the capture, says to Leonato (in the Folio punctuation),

> A good old man, sir, he will be talking as they say, when the age is
> in the wit is out, God help us, it is a world to see: well said i'faith
> neighbor Verges, well, God's a good man, and two men ride of
> a horse, one must ride behind, an honest soul i'faith, sir, by my
> troth, he is, as ever broke bread, but God is to be worshipped,
> all men are not alike, alas good neighbor [3.5.33–40 of 64].

Dogberry's treatment of his friend is analogous to the treatment of Beatrice by her friends. Dogberry disparages Verges to Leonato and even indulges a feeble sarcasm to Verges himself: "well said, i'faith." And as the mirroring of Claudio's and Benedick's slanders is the basis of further analogies between the paired scenes, the mirrored slanders of Beatrice and Verges immediately suggest other similarities and pointed contrasts between the wits of the slandered and slanderer and their degree of self-endearment. It is the reflected slanders, however, that are the basis of the pairing.

3.1 Beatrice's "wit Values itself" too highly, Hero says.	3.5 Dogberry's denigration of Verges: "the wit is out."

Reduced to its essential mirroring pairs, then (and substituting the more general "speaks against" for "slander"), the structure of patterned actions in *Much Ado* is as follows. (The breaks indicate the segmentation of scene pairs, discussed below.)

	3.3 Dogberry instructs Watch. Borachio & Conrade arrested. ("I know that Deformed...")

3.2 Benedick is lovesick.	3.4 Beatrice is lovesick. [Hero dresses for wedding.]

3.1 Hero speaks against Beatrice.	3.5 Dogberry speaks against Verges.
2.3 His friends speak against Benedick.	4.1 Claudio speaks against Hero at church.
2.2 Borachio introduces window trick to Don John.	4.2 Watch questioned: window trick exposed.

2.1 Claudio agrees to wed Hero.	5.1 Claudio agrees to wed "niece."
1.3 Don John intends to poison Claudio's happiness. (Don John's self-characterization)	5.2 Benedick informs Beatrice he has challenged Claudio. (Benedick's self-characterization)
1.2 Antonio wrongly reports that Don Pedro loves Hero.	5.3 Epitaph at tomb of Hero, wrongly thought dead.
1.1 Claudio questions Benedick about Hero.	5.4 Claudio offers himself to "niece," who removes her veil.

Such then is the thematic arch of *Much Ado*. It requires a few further comments. The bracketed addition to the outline—"Hero dresses for wedding"—initiates the new phase of the action, the courtship now having progressed to preparations for the wedding, which will require the entire second half of the play to be performed (i.e., for Hero to unveil). Thus the new phase of the action starts, as in *Measure for the Measure* and in almost all of Shakespeare's mature plays, in the scene immediately after the keystone scene. Worth noting, too, is the focus on language, the play's thematic preoccupation, in the central scenes: the group of four scenes focused on slanders (2.3, 3.1, 3.5, 4.1); the physical effects of language on Benedick and Beatrice in the central flanking scenes; and the comic misuse of language in the keystone scene in which "the word becomes flesh" in the imagined person of Deformed. Finally, as to the paired scenes themselves. While not all the reflecting actions of the arch are immediately apparent, a careful comparison of corresponding scenes reveals the mirrored actions. It must be repeated that it is *actions* that are the basis of the pairing. The enrichments of language and spectacle—images, dramatic situations, stage actions or other possible analogies—follow from the foundation of identical actions upon which the thematic spatial pattern is based, dramaturgically understated though the actions may be. Emotional intensity marks narrative crises and climaxes; thematic actions are often muted. Indeed, they may be completely overlooked unless the spatial pattern guides our description of the play.

Shakespeare's plays, of course, have overlapping patterns. I do not always pursue multiple structural designs in analyzing the plays, so it might be well here to give some idea of Shakespeare's virtuosity. In addition to the scene pairings already outlined, there is a five-part structure organizing *Much Ado*, evident if we substitute other incidents from scenes 1.3, 5.2 and 5.3.

3.3 Dogberry instructs the Watch.
Borachio and Conrade arrested.

3.2 Window trick.	3.4 Hero dresses for wedding.
3.1 Gulling of Beatrice.	3.5 Dogberry disparages Verges to Leonato.
2.3 Gulling of Benedick.	4.1 Claudio slanders Hero at church.
2.2 Don John & Borachio plan to dupe Claudio with window trick.	4.2 Watch questioned: window trick exposed.

2.1 Claudio agrees to wed Hero.	5.1 Claudio agrees to wed "niece."
1.3 Borachio reports to John an overheard conversation between Claudio and Pedro.	5.2 Benedick repents his slanders of women: his "wit will not hurt a woman."
1.2 Antonio reports to Leonato an overheard conversation between Claudio and Pedro.	5.3 Claudio repents at supposed tomb of Hero.
1.1 Claudio expresses a liking for Hero to Benedick. Don Pedro offers proxy wooing.	5.4 Claudio offers himself to veiled, unknown bride.

Shakespeare may or may not have thought of these five segments as acts, but the play clearly has this intrinsic structure; to avoid confusion I will refer to these segments as Parts. The Part divisions are based on segments of the play's actions, not on time intervals. The initial segment of the courting action, from first liking to marriage agreement, determines Part One (1.1 through 2.1), and the first stage of the window trick, from Borachio's initiation of the plan to Don John (2.2) to its execution (3.2), demarcates Part Two. The window trick sequence resumes for the main plot lovers with Hero dressing for the wedding in 3.4 and ends with its effective exposure to the Sexton in 4.2. Part Five, which accords with the traditional act division, completes the last stage of the courtship, from Claudio's second marriage agreement (5.1) to the wedding dance (5.4). With the obvious exception of Part Three, each Part begins and ends with a scene devoted primarily to furthering (or obstructing) the action of the Hero-Claudio plot.

Again excepting Part Three, each Part is identically structured, with the two central scenes containing the same stage action. Scenes 1.2 and 1.3 both contain a report of a conversation between Claudio and Don Pedro about courting Hero. Scenes 2.3 and 3.1 contain the gullings of Benedick and of Beatrice. Scenes 3.5 and 4.1 both enact a "slander" before Leonato, the disparagement of Verges by Dogberry and the slander of Hero by Claudio. Scenes 5.2 and 5.3 enact the repentance of the courting males in the two love plots. Claudio places an epitaph on the supposed tomb of Hero and confesses to her murder in 5.3, and Benedick, mindful of his conscience, "Don Worm," submits to the women's wits in 5.2 (77). Both Margaret and Beatrice score on Benedick, and he good-naturedly accepts the insults and lays down his arms, so to speak, in saying that his wit will not hurt a woman. Both men have repented their earlier slanders of women and reformed. In each Part then the beginning and end of a Hero-Claudio segment frame a pair of identical actions in what is essentially a chiastic design—ABBA.

In addition to the chiastic design of reflecting actions and the five-part structure, I would like to point out one more pattern, one that would likely be overlooked without a perception of the overall structure of *Much Ado*. In what can only be called a structural metaphor, Shakespeare equates the final revelation of the truth about the window trick—the "news"—with food. In other plays "news" is often figured as food more explicitly. In *King John*, for example, the Bastard reports that he "saw a smith.... With open mouth swallowing a tailor's news" (4.2.193–95). In *Coriolanus* the long exchange between Aufidius's servants describing the off-stage meal of the titular hero and his enemy begins when a servingman enters with "news— news, you rascals!" and his companion's reply, "What, what, what? Let's partake" (4.5.172–203). In *Much Ado* the equation of news with food is entirely positional. Central to each Part— that is, between the second and third scenes—is a time interval that, while not material to the act breaks, is nevertheless significant in the overall food narrative. Between the end of 1.2 and 1.3 Leonato's supper, or part of it at least, takes place; at the end of 2.3 Benedick declines Beatrice's grudging invitation to dinner, the midday meal; at the end of 3.5 Dogberry and Verges are invited to "drink some wine" (49); and at the end of 5.2 Benedick accepts Beatrice's invitation to hear Margaret's "news" of Hero's innocence and Don John's villainy (92). Each Part has two scenes, a food interval and two further scenes, structurally corresponding to two acts interrupted by the Dogberry-Borachio scene (3.3) and followed by two acts. (Because the Dogberry-Borachio scene is a perfect diptych, the whole play divides exactly in half.) These intervals trace the play's slow progress toward the revelation of the truth about the window trick. There are—to varying extents depending on the degree of truth attained— "shared meals" within the intervals of each of the four parts. In Part One the central scenes contain a false report that Don Pedro loves Hero, and Don John is conspicuously absent from supper; in Part Two the scenes contain half-truths about Benedick and Beatrice, and Benedick declines to share in the meal; in Part Four the truth of the window trick is revealed by Verges but dismissed by Leonato, and Dogberry's and Verges' drinking is indulged alone; and in Part Five, finally, the literal truth is revealed, and Benedick accepts this invitation by Beatrice to hear the news of Hero's innocence and Don John's plot. In the final interval language—"news," the truth—is yet another meal in the sequence, the (increasingly incorporeal) sustenance the plot has been moving toward. Structurally embedded in this play about scandal and language generally is the strong imagistic suggestion that the truth is shared food, communal sustenance. Such subtle touches to the plays might not be perceived at all without an awareness of their larger structures, the chiastic design and the grouping of scenes.

3

Shakespeare's Scene Division

When Bottom and his fellow mechanicals are called upon to perform their "tedious and brief" version of Pyramus and Thisbe in *A Midsummer Night's Dream*, Quince as Prologue delivers the following speech:

> If we offend, it is with our good will.
> That you should think, we come not to offend,
> But with good will. To show our simple skill,
> That is the true beginning of our end.
> Consider then, we come but in despite.
> We do not come, as minding to content you,
> Our true intent is. All for your delight
> We are not here. That you should here repent you,
> The actors are at hand; and, by their show,
> You shall know all, that you are like to know [5.1.108–17].

His aristocratic audience is quick to comment on Quince's fractured delivery, remarking that he "doth not stand upon points" and "knows not the stop." His misplaced punctuation, I would suggest, resembles the misplaced structural punctuation in the plays—the much disputed act and scene divisions. As Quince's meaning is undermined and mangled by inappropriate stops, the action of the plays, particularly the thematic action, is too often compromised by inept divisions. Scene breaks, like Quince's stops, are arbitrarily inserted into the texts, or scenes are run together on the erroneous basis of "continuous action." In extreme cases, scenes are cut altogether in performance. Indeed, many critics frankly admit that they know not the stop and conclude that scene divisions are functionally meaningless. The editor of the New Cambridge *Antony and Cleopatra*, for example, considers both act and scene designations to be merely a "matter of editorial convenience," mere "benchmarks for reference."[1] Those critics who find scenes to be essential to Shakespeare's art cannot agree on exactly where the scene divisions should occur. *Antony and Cleopatra*, the most vexed instance, may have anywhere from 37 to 47 scenes, depending on the editor or commentator consulted. Does *Hamlet* have 19, 20 or 21 scenes? *Measure for Measure* 16, 17, or 18 scenes? And so on through dozens of disputed scenes in the canon. After illustrating the uncertainties directors and editors face, I will analyze *Romeo and Juliet* and *Twelfth Night* to demonstrate the value of the thematic arch in determining scene divisions.

What demarcates a Shakespearean scene? Since Capell, editors, critics and directors make do with the notion that, in the words of W.W. Greg, "a new scene begins whenever the stage is clear and the action is not continuous; whenever, that is, a change of locality is possible."[2]

Serviceable as this idea of a break at each cleared stage may appear, it hardly covers every case and must be hedged with caveats, as Greg immediately does in a footnote:

> There is, however, an element of uncertainty here. When one set of characters goes out on the approach of another set a new scene is marked [in the First Folio] on the ground that the stage is clear, whereas modern editors continue the scene on the ground that the action is continuous. On the other hand, in battle scenes, where combatants are constantly in and out, old texts seldom trouble to break up the scene: it is modern editors who are constantly imagining "another part of the field."[3]

Hence the first scene of the Folio *Cymbeline*, which I address later, is run into the second scene by modern editors because the two gentlemen exit as the Queen, Imogen and Posthumus enter. The battle that occupies one scene of the Folio *2 Henry IV* is usually granted three scenes in later editions. Any variorum text records centuries of disagreement among editors as to exactly what is and is not a separate scene. Scene designations depend, finally, on the individual editor's judgment. Without a fuller knowledge of Elizabethan stage conventions and with varyingly imperfect texts, editors construe scene divisions as best they can from the dialogue and stage directions around a cleared stage and from a sense of the immediate action. Beyond that, there is no compelling rationale for marking scene divisions. Since it is manifestly apparent that Shakespeare composed in scenes, our ignorance of his constructive principles is a serious gap.

As an example of the disagreements, consider the end of the Folio's first scene in *Cymbeline*, which I mentioned earlier. One Gentleman says to another, "Here comes the gentleman [Posthumus], the Queen, and Princess" (1.1.68–9), and both men exit. A new scene begins with the entrance of the characters referred to in the dialogue. Here is Roger Warren's rationale for ignoring the Folio division: "Although the Folio text marks a new scene after the Gentlemen's departure, the action is clearly continuous, so much so that Oxford brings Posthumus, the Queen and Imogen on stage before l.69."[4] To declare the action continuous begs the question. And to adduce as evidence another editor's complete disregard even of the cleared stage only emphasizes the highhandedness with which the Folio is often changed. But it must also be said that editors who retain the Folio designation do so tentatively, for they too depend on the immediate narrative action as a basis for their decision, rather than the overall thematic structure. After noting that most editors ignore the division, J.M. Nosworthy continues, "There is, however, a cleared stage together with a momentary pause in the action, and this justifies the division, which may relate to some original subtlety in production that is lost beyond recovery."[5] As I've said, whatever the editorial decision, it lacks any compelling rationale.

Troilus and Cressida illustrates differences in designating battle sequences. The Folio marks only the first scene of the play. The Riverside divides the play into 24 scenes, the Arden into 25, the Oxford into 27. The divisions in Act Five are one source of disagreement. Most of the act is taken up with the fighting between the Greeks and Trojans. The Riverside, inclined toward the Folio practice, ignores the cleared stage after Achilles leads the Myrmidons off to kill Hector and before Menelaus and Paris enter fighting under the caustic eye of Thersites. Pope, Capell and David Bevington, the Arden editor, prefer consistency and mark the break at the cleared stage, though Bevington comments that "the matter is arbitrary since the action is virtually continuous in the battle sequence."[6] The Oxford editors also mark this break (as well as two additional breaks in Act Four marked by no previous editors). If scene breaks are based on the local action, there is no definite way to determine the break. Neither convention, logical consistency nor "continuous action" leads editors to unanimity.

Romeo and Juliet is typical of the uncertainties of scene division generally. I hope to show that the local action, the individual scene structures and the thematic arch all confirm the play's division into 23 scenes. With respect to scene designations *Romeo and Juliet* is a problematic textual case. The early texts are of almost no help in determining scene divisions. The Second Quarto (Q2), the usual copy text, marks none, and the Folio, derived ultimately from Q2, marks only 1.1. The First Quarto (Q1), a corrupt perhaps memorial reconstruction, is nonetheless of some small help in that it has printer's ornaments between scenes beginning at 3.5. Early editors established what have come to be accepted as the traditional 24 scenes, which most modern editors follow for convenience of reference. But in their commentaries modern editors disagree with the traditional scene designations in four instances: at 1.5, in which the masquers enter Capulet's ball; at 2.2, in which Romeo comments on Mercutio's conjuring and sees Juliet on the balcony; at 4.4, after Juliet drinks the potion; and at 4.5, in which the Nurse discovers Juliet's "body."

Two of these editorial disagreements are easily resolved. All modern editors who comment agree that the scene break at 4.5 is incorrect. The Nurse is continually on stage and continually the focus while she goes from, presumably, Capulet's hall to Juliet's chamber. The change in location does not itself warrant a new scene, as the lack of a printer's ornament here in Q1 tends to confirm.

No such unanimous agreement obtains regarding the break at 4.4, but there seems to be little reason to question it. At the end of 4.3, according to the stage directions usually adopted from Q1, Juliet *falls upon her bed, within the curtain.* Lady Capulet and the Nurse then enter to some unspecified new location to discuss preparations for the wedding until the Nurse is sent to Juliet's chamber. While Juliet's collapse could be staged to signal her continuing though unseen presence on stage, the definite new location of Lady Capulet and the Nurse confirms that *within the curtain* is meant to indicate a cleared stage, a conclusion reinforced, if weakly, by the fact that Q1 also marks a break here.

Some editors argue that "no real scene division is implied" at 1.5[7] because the masquers, according to the Folio and Q2 stage directions, do not leave the stage: *They march about the stage and Servingmen come forth with napkins.* But the change of locale from the street to the hall, here (unlike 4.5) combined with the introduction of new speaking characters, the Servingmen, clearly indicates a new scene. And the structures of the two scenes, 1.4 and 1.5, also argue for the break. Scene 1.4 is a simple two-part scene in which Mercutio's Queen Mab speech and the reactions to it constitute the second half. Scene 1.5 is a triptych: the first part culminates in Romeo's infatuated sight of Juliet, the central panel is the argument between Tybalt and Capulet and the third part the conversation between Romeo and Juliet. The center of the scene is Capulet's assertion of his authority over Tybalt and his insistence on hospitality toward Romeo. As independent scenes, each has a firm structure, whereas the single scene created by combining 1.4 and 1.5 is disjointed and unfocused. Indeed, both the Oxford and Pelican editors are so convinced of the need for a break that they simply add a stage direction for the masquers to exit at the end of 1.4: *They march about the stage and [exeunt].* The new scene, 1.5, then begins with the rest of the original stage direction: *Servingmen come forth with napkins.* However the "break" is staged, there is little doubt either in the reading or in performance that a structural scene division occurs here.

The most consequential disagreement regards the break at 2.2. In spite of its hold on the popular imagination as "the balcony scene," 2.2 is generally accepted by modern editors to be part of 2.1. Beyond commenting to this effect, the Oxford editors go so far as to print the two scenes as one: the "conjuring" of Romeo by Mercutio and the professions of love by Romeo and Juliet thus become a single scene. In the received texts the only stage direction at the traditional break here is the exit of Mercutio and Benvolio; Romeo then makes a one-line comment on Mercutio's conjuration before exclaiming at the sight of Juliet. The question is then, where has Romeo been during Mercutio's speech, on stage or off? Editors must provide some additional stage direction for Romeo. Should it be *coming forward* or *enter*? The Oxford chooses the former, simply commenting that "the location is unchanged and the action continues."[8] Whether or not a new scene is marked here, the Oxford's stage direction is the generally accepted editorial view and the usual directorial choice in performance, with Romeo "hiding" somewhere on stage while Mercutio calls.

This staging derives in part from the difficulties in the opening of 2.1. The second quarto includes the solo entrance of Romeo and two lines later the entrance of Mercutio and Benvolio, calling out for Romeo. There are no further stage directions. The dialogue establishes that Romeo has leapt over the orchard wall. An actual wall is, of course, out of the question. After dismissing a number of other implausible alternatives for realizing onstage Romeo's leap, Gibbons suggests the usual solution: that Romeo conceal himself "behind a stage post when Mercutio and Benvolio enter seeking him." This simple expedient is reinforced for Gibbons by the rhyme between Benvolio's last line in 2.1 and Romeo's opening line in 2.2:

> Benvolio.   Go then, for 'tis in vain,
>   To seek him here that means not to be found.
> [Scene II]
>   [*Romeo comes forward.*]
> Romeo. He jests at scars that never felt a wound.

Gibbons notes that "Romeo has not left the stage; he emerges from behind whatever concealment he has found.... It is traditional, and hence convenient for reference, to mark a new scene here, but the opening line rhymes with Benvolio's last line, revealing the actual continuity."[9]

But it is precisely because Romeo has been out of the audience's sight that the rhyme is necessary. We need to be told that he has been within hearing and that no time has elapsed, though (*contra* the Oxford editors) the location has changed from outside the wall to inside, from the street to the orchard, a leap into "another world."[10] The sense of Mercutio's conjuring, as well, argues that Romeo should be off stage. The "Madman" (7) Mercutio calls no longer exists; Romeo has been transformed from his affected love of Rosaline, as the audience already knows. It is not his reaction that is paramount here but the doomed Mercutio's lively presence. Furthermore, the traditional balcony scene is brilliantly structured to carry almost the whole weight of the lovers' beleaguered commitment. Romeo's and Juliet's uninterrupted conversation of only 86 lines is the centerpiece of the three-part scene. The central conversation is set within two approximately equal parts, the first consisting of Romeo's soliloquies and Juliet's presumed soliloquies and the second enacting via the Nurse the intrusiveness of Juliet's own household. It is not until line 49 that Romeo makes his presence known to Juliet, and the Nurse first calls at 136 (of 193). At the center of the scene is Juliet's profession of love, her longest speech to Romeo in the entire play, in which she admits, "In truth, fair Montague, I am too fond" (97). Between dreamy solitudes and busy society, the love of Romeo and Juliet has its brief illumination. The structural integrity of the traditional balcony scene contributes significantly to that memorable poignance.

The traditional break at 2.2, then, like those at 1.5 and 4.4, should be retained. Except for 4.5, the traditional scene breaks are effective punctuations of the immediate action. More importantly, they also fit the overall thematic structure.

3.1 Tybalt kills Mercutio; Romeo kills Tybalt.	
2.6 Juliet joins Romeo and Friar for the wedding.	3.2 Juliet learns from Nurse of Romeo's "death" and Tybalt's death.
2.5 Impatient Juliet gets news of marriage from Nurse.	3.3 Distraught Romeo gets Juliet's ring from Nurse.
2.4 Nurse comes to learn marriage date from Romeo.	3.4 Capulet sets date for Juliet's wedding to Paris.
2.3 Romeo plans with Friar the marriage ceremony.	3.5 Romeo departs; Juliet told of plans for her to marry Paris.
2.2 Romeo and Juliet exchange vows of love ("balcony scene").	4.1 Paris arranges wedding and professes love to Juliet.
2.1 Mercutio conjures Romeo.	4.2 Capulet "calls" Paris to tell him of wedding.
1.5 Ball; Romeo and Juliet meet.	4.3 Juliet drinks potion.
1.4 Maskers on way to ball; Queen Mab speech.	[4.4 & 4.5] Preparation for wedding; "dead" Juliet discovered; Friar's consoling speech.
1.3 Mother and Nurse tell of Juliet's birth and Paris's intent to marry.	5.1 Romeo learns of Juliet's "death" and buys poison intending to die.
1.2 Romeo and Ben. with guest list (S.D.: "letter").	5.2 Friar John returns letter to Friar Lawrence.
1.1 Brawl; Romeo's lovesickness.	5.3 Romeo kills Paris and himself; Juliet kills herself.

The central scene, which contains (unusually) the narrative turn and the generic turn from comedy to tragedy, is reinforced by the love-death contrast of the immediately flanking scenes, 2.6 and 3.2, the offstage wedding and Romeo's "death," as Juliet first misunderstands the Nurse's hysterics. Both scenes of the next pair, 2.5 and 3.3, confirm the marriage, first to Juliet and then to the despairing Romeo. In the various divisions of his plays Shakespeare habitually distinguishes the agreement to marry from the marriage ceremony or its consummation; the grouping of the central five scenes in *Romeo and Juliet* suggests the same distinction. The next grouping of four scenes parallels Paris's courtship of Juliet with Romeo's. Setting the date, planning the wedding, professing love—each of these moments in the two courtships is symmetrically paired (2.4 & 3.4, 2.3 & 3.5, 2.2 & 4.1). The pairing of 2.1 and 4.2 continues the pattern. Told of Juliet's supposed change of heart, Capulet says, "Send for the County [Paris], go tell him of this" (4.2.23) and ends the scene by saying, "I will walk myself to County Paris, to prepare up him against tomorrow" (44–46). In the same minor key that parallels and contrasts Romeo and Paris so often in the play, each of these paired scenes summons an offstage suitor of Juliet's, in one case conjured by Mercutio and in the other called by Capulet. The next four-pair grouping sets the movement toward the first meeting of the lovers against that of their final separation, which begins with Juliet's drinking the potion in 4.3. The anticipated ball is darkly mirrored in the anticipated funeral (1.4-[4.4 & 4.5]); and the two suitors are once again contrasted in the 1.3–5.1 pair, in which the play's pervasive mingling of love and death is again explicit in Paris's intent to marry Juliet and Romeo's intent to lie beside her in the tomb. The guest list for Capulet's ball that initiated the meeting of Romeo and Juliet is contrasted with the letter returned to Friar Lawrence that means their irrevocable separation (1.2–5.2).

The structural parallels between the suitors confirm and particularize the conclusion of source studies, demonstrating just how carefully Shakespeare developed Paris into a rival to Romeo.[11] They also contribute to the stature of Romeo in the last scene. The mere fact of his duel with Paris contrasts with Romeo's absence from the brawl of the opening scene, marking the distance between his initial self-conceit and his final tragic perception. Romeo has become a fighter rather than a dreamer; his love has taken on commitment, finality. More particularly, Romeo is, in effect, killing his conventional self of the opening scene in killing Paris, whose flaccid rhetoric at Juliet's tomb strongly recalls Romeo's conventional rhyming couplets of the first scene. Harry Levin notes the way in which Paris continues Romeo's earlier affectations: "Long after Romeo has abandoned his sonneteering, Paris … pronounce[s] a sestet at Juliet's tomb."[12]

In large and small ways the other symmetrical pairings extend the analogies worked around the love-death contrast. The pair 1.4 & [4.4 & 4.5], for example, contrasts not only the preparations for the ball and for the wedding-turned-funeral. It also invites a comparison of Mercutio's fantasy of Queen Mab and Friar Lawrence's pretense of consolation over the drugged Juliet. Again, love and death are paired, here as the subjects of the respective speeches, and the quick, playful and genuinely moral imagination of Mercutio is set against the plodding and earnest but ultimately deadly imagination of Friar Lawrence. The pairing of 1.5 & 4.3 heightens the poignance of Juliet's isolation when taking the potion, her tragic moment of individuation, of "death," in separating herself from parents, nurse and confessor; her solitary toast to Romeo is contrasted with their meeting among a "feasting presence" at the ball.

Details in paired scenes are also highlighted by an awareness of the overall structure. Juliet is encouraged to "read" Paris's face, a "precious book of love" (1.3.81, 87); in the paired scene Romeo reads the Apothecary's face and finds "Famine … in thy cheeks, Need and oppression starveth in thine eyes" (5.1.69–70). Even the smallest touches take on added resonance in the context of the symmetrical structure. After Romeo and Benvolio read the guest list for Capulet's ball, Benvolio says,

> At this same ancient feast of Capulet's
> Sups the fair Rosaline, whom thou so loves,
> With all the admired beauties of Verona.
> Go thither and with unattainted eye
> Compare her face with some that I shall show
> And I will make thee think thy swan a crow [1.2.84–9].

The rest of the 103-line scene is given up to what will be seen in the faces of Rosaline and the other young women at the ball, Romeo expecting "splendour" (103) and Benvolio insisting "she shall scant show well" (101). The paired scene, in which Friar John returns with the unde-livered letter to Romeo, contains the grim but wholly Shakespearean confirmation of Benvolio's deflating view in the "searchers of the town" (5.2.8), "appointed to view dead bodies and report on the cause of death" (Arden n. citing OED). In a phrase Levin uses of the Apothecary scene, the grotesque detail of the searchers is rendered with "Flemish precision" (287), not only locally but across the symmetry of the play, threading the read list and unseen faces of 1.2 and the unread letter and seen faces of 5.2 into the play's fabric of love and death.

While the pairing of scenes is thus reinforced in large and small ways, it bears repeating that the structure depends on mirroring thematic actions not imagery, stage actions or other echoing elements. Indeed, the scenes that most obviously echo one another—the two balcony scenes, the scenes of Juliet with each of her suitors in Friar Lawrence's cell, Juliet's pleas for information from the teasing and the hysterical Nurse—are not chiastically paired. The mir-roring thematic actions occur in stage situations that are not reflections of each other, though the distinction—and therefore the scene designations—can sometimes be made only in the context of the overall gestalt of the thematic arch.

Like *Romeo and Juliet*, *Twelfth Night* is a useful illustration of the marked effect scene divisions can have in performance and of the contribution an awareness of the thematic struc-ture can make both to the determination of correct breaks and to an understanding of Shake-speare's scene structure. Editors of the play accept the First Folio's act-scene divisions, merely noting one anomaly: a cleared stage at 3.4.263[13] that is nevertheless not marked as a scene break. Without a marked scene, directors usually ignore the cleared stage altogether, producing a faltering, overlong 3.4. Marking the new scene indicated by the thematic symmetry divides the present shapeless 3.4 into two thematically unified scenes.

In a thorough analysis of the F1 text to determine the printer's copy, R.K. Turner observes that "the division of the text into acts and scenes is perfectly satisfactory."[14] Given the generally high quality of the text, editors have agreed with Turner, even as regards the anomaly at 3.4.263. The Riverside edition, for example, says, "the cleared stage at III.iv. 272 [TLN 1790] suggests the possibility that a new scene should have been marked at that point. The present text, however, adheres to the F1 division."[15] Even editors who recognize the break do not mark it; Herschel Baker notes in the Signet edition that the exit of Fabian and Viola "properly marks the ending of the scene, but the new scene that opens with the entrance of Sir Toby and Sir Andrew is not marked as such in the Folio."[16]

As generally printed then, the scene contains, in the words of the Oxford edition, the following incidents: "Malvolio's appearance in yellow stockings (ll. 1–136), Sir Andrew's chal-lenge (137–93), the third and final interview between Viola and Olivia (194–210), the mock duel (211–300), and Antonio's intervention and arrest (301–86)."[17] The cleared stage occurs during the mock duel. There are stage directions for the exit of Fabian and Viola, for the immediate entry of Sir Toby and Sir Andrew, and, 18 lines later, for the re-entry of Fabian and Viola. But no scene break. The sheer number of incidents, entrances and exits suggests the problem: the episodes are too disparate to stage coherently; the scene falls apart.

Attempts to find some common thread among the episodes vaporize into generality. Evans, for example, sees four sections unified by a lack of awareness: "first, that in which Malvolio's delusion is central; second, that in which Olivia's unawareness of 'Cesario's' identity is central; third, that in which Viola and Sir Andrew's unawareness of Toby's practice is central; fourth, that in which Antonio's mistaking of 'Cesario' for Sebastian is central."[18] Since the same lack of awareness is true of almost any scene in the play, this observation is not of much help in producing a unified scene on stage. Consequently, "it is a common theatrical experience that around the middle of the play the rhythm seems to falter, especially in the very long 3.4.... Performances that have moved well often seem to lose their way here, and the scene to fall into its discrete parts; it proves hard to discover the rhythm of individual sections or the overall shape of the scene."[19]

This faltering rhythm occurs because the sequence before and after the cleared stage is usually treated as the Oxford edition, in justifying the lack of a scene break, suggests it should be: as a "continuous action." But it begs the question to pronounce the dueling sequence a continuous action and thereby dismiss the possibility of a scene break. And it invites interpolated, farcical business: "directors often make comic capital by keeping both reluctant duelists on stage."[20] The Arden edition goes even further, concluding flatly that the text's two stage directions for the exit and re-entry of Viola and Fabian, though admittedly "derived from copy and not ... additions by the scribe," should be ignored, apparently because of recent directorial practice: "The directions of F are ... all retained in this ed., even though it is unlikely that Viola and Fabian are to leave the stage; in modern productions they seldom, if ever, do so" (107). The textual justification for keeping Viola and Fabian on stage is Sir Toby's "Fabian can scarce hold him yonder,"[21] interpreted as meaning that Viola and Fabian are on stage and visible to the audience as to Toby and Andrew. Obviously an offstage struggle is just as likely if one is not looking to add irrelevant slapstick.

And marking the scene break? It might encourage directors to respect the exquisite buildup to the duel. The sequence maintains and alternates Andrew's and Viola's two points of view, intentionally keeping the duelists apart for comic (as opposed to farcical) effect. Heavyhanded business would overwhelm what is after all not much in the way of excitement, the duel itself being, in effect, a non-duel that is aborted before it gets well under way. In fact, the duel's most important function is a further neat turn. With Antonio's entrance, the potential unmasking of Viola is deferred and the possible survival of Sebastian is suggested to Viola. By respecting the Folio's cleared stage and limiting Viola's "presence" to Toby's glancing offstage, a director ensures that the fears of Andrew and Viola do not detract from the more important moment of the duel itself.

The thematic structure of *Twelfth Night* confirms a break here. With five scenes in Act Three, *Twelfth Night* has a total of 19 scenes, with the keystone the scene in which Malvolio reads the forged love letter. The overall disposition of scenes can be represented as follows:

2.5 Malvolio reads forged love letter.	
2.4 Viola indirectly tells her love to Orsino.	3.1 Olivia tells her love to Viola.
2.3 Plan to gull Malvolio.	3.2 Plan to gull Andrew.
2.2 Viola given ring.	3.3 Sebastian given purse.
2.1 Sebastian discloses his identity.	[3.4.1–263] (Analogous self-disclosures): Malvolio in garters / Andrew's letter / Olivia's picture
1.5 Olivia mistakes Viola for a man.	[3.4.264–386] Antonio mistakes Viola for Sebastian.

1.4 Viola first seen with Orsino; in soliloquy tells her love.	4.1 Sebastian meets Olivia; agrees to be "ruled."
1.3 The gull Andrew mocked.	4.2 The gull Malvolio mocked.
1.2 Viola determines to serve Orsino.	4.3 Sebastian and Olivia agree to marry.
1.1 Orsino's melancholy; Olivia's grief.	5.1 The marriages.

Merely listing the essential action of each scene in this way is enough to demonstrate the symmetry of the scenic design. And this symmetry is reinforced by the fact that the secondary actions of paired scenes are also often parallel. In 2.4 and 3.1, for example, Orsino and Viola each have a prefatory encounter with Feste in which he mocks them and suggests that each of them is "nothing" (2.4.77 and 3.1.29). Feste's gibes point up that the professions of love in 2.4 and 3.1 are each made to a character wrapped in some folly of the imagination—Orsino as in "changeable taffeta" (74) and Viola in disguise. Thus these framing scenes set up further interesting parallels with the central scene—the forged letter's profession of love to the imagination-besotted Malvolio. To the extent that the object of each of their affections is womanish, Viola and Olivia are also victims of delusory self-love.

With the overall symmetry of the play in mind, we can see the advantages of marking the scene break at 3.4.263. The correspondence between the essential actions of 1.5 and 3.4.264–386 is clear: Olivia and Antonio both mistake Viola for, we might say, her brother. And both scenes have a prefatory "duel," the verbal fencing of Feste in one case and a physical duel in the other. Considered in this way, as a distinct unit in which hostilities are brought to a focus in the mistaken identity of Viola for Sebastian, the new scene is easily and effectively playable. The other new scene, 3.4.1–263, is more subtly analogous to its paired scene, 2.1. Malvolio's cross-gartering, Sir Andrew's letter and Olivia's portrait can be described as versions of an ultimate self-disclosure parallel to Sebastian's disclosure of his real name and condition. In each disclosure the character is truly revealed. The "rhythm" of the scene is thus constituted by a sequence of analogous actions linking Sebastian and Olivia by virtue of their true self-representations and contrasting them with the foolish self-expressions of Malvolio and Sir Andrew. The two separate scenes are each perfectly coherent and gain substantially from an awareness of their parallel scenes.

The proportioning of the scenes themselves is a further indication of their integrity as dramatic units. The precise midpoint of 3.4.264–386 (62nd of 123 lines) is the moment when Antonio, arrested, turns to address Viola: "This comes with seeking you." The escalating foolishness has come to the brink of violence, and the disguised Viola is its focal point. With Antonio's angry accusations of her, the confusion begins to clear. Scene 3.4.1–263 also divides neatly. Essentially, the episode of the cross-gartered Malvolio occupies the first half of the scene, and the delivery of Sir Andrew's challenge the second half. The challenge is itself enacted in two segments, Sir Andrew's letter and Sir Toby's spoken variant. Between these latter two segments is the brief interruption of Olivia's contrasting self-representation, the "jewel" (201), her picture.

The notion of "continuous action," so often invoked to justify eliminating a scene break, is obviously not the basis of Shakespeare's scene divisions. It is not the physical action occurring onstage that determines an integrated scene, but rather the thematic action, as in the incidents of self-disclosure revealed by the symmetrical structure of *Twelfth Night*.

From the symmetrical thematic structures of all the mature plays it is clear that there is no universally applicable definition of a scene break, no unalterable mathematical axiom. There is only the generally recognized dramatic convention, more or less conformable to Greg's definition—a convention subject in every instance to expressive variation. Shakespeare may or may not begin a new scene if there is a change in location. Brutus and Cassius go from outside to inside Brutus's tent without a new scene, and the Nurse is dispatched from another part of the house to Juliet's room without entering a new scene. *A Midsummer Night's Dream* is usually divided into nine scenes though Titania remains onstage sleeping during one scene break and the lovers remain onstage sleeping during an act break. Those editors who mark only seven scenes because of the sleeping characters miss the thematic and atmospheric relevance of such "softened" breaks by insisting on the inflexible application of an imperfectly deduced definition. It is telling that many of the plays whose Folio divisions are routinely changed—*Macbeth, Lear, Measure for Measure*, the two parts of *Henry IV*—are significantly distorted by the changes. So, while the conventional definition is generally accurate, scene breaks are thematic and ultimately serve the whole play as patterned in the chiastic arch, not merely the immediate action.

4

Shakespeare in Nine Scenes

The three plays that Shakespeare constructed in nine scenes—*Love's Labor's Lost, A Midsummer Night's Dream* and *The Tempest*—provide a convenient sketch of the thematic arch. They are firmly anchored in Aristotelian actions beginning and ending in paired scenes of the symmetrical arch, and they illustrate Shakespeare's habitual thematic emphasis at the center of the play and at the center of individual scenes. Grouping these plays also provides a glimpse into Shakespeare's development as a playwright, for they are sufficiently similar to make comparison meaningful. As printed in the *First Folio*, they are all comedies, dramatizing the rocky course of at least one pair of lovers. Each play also contains a prominent play-within-a-play, a feature that indicates their further likenesses as self-conscious artworks, pre-occupied with their own artifice—language and sonneteering in *Love's Labor's Lost*, play production and imagination in *A Midsummer Night's Dream,* and art and imagination generally in *The Tempest.* Not unrelated to this heightened consciousness of art and reality is the plays' similar use of a "place apart" that Stanley Wells has pointed out and the self-discovery made possible by the characters' sojourns in some less-than-fully-civilized locale, a park or wood or island.[1] The plays are all designed to engage us in a full, various and rich world of art and then to return us, more or less gently, to reality. Furthermore, and most significantly for my purposes, they are unique among Shakespeare's dramatic works in that they have no known plot sources. In an apparent departure from his usual practice of borrowing stories from other works, Shakespeare appears to have plotted these three plays himself. These are his most original plots, all constructed, again uniquely, in nine scenes. Thus they illuminate Shakespeare's constructive practice when unconstrained by an existing plot. Because they span almost his whole career, they also suggest, as I have said, something of the increasing complexity and sophistication Shakespeare brings to the thematic arch of each later play.

Love's Labor's Lost is a relatively simple example of the thematic arch:

4.1 Princess hunts deer. Armado's misdelivered letter read: "lion & lamb." Boyet and Rosaline "both did hit it."	
3.1 Armado gives letter to Costard to deliver to Jacquenetta. Berowne gives Costard letter for Rosaline.	4.2 Costard delivers Berowne's letter to Jacquenetta; read by Nathaniel.
2.1 Princess & ladies attract secret interest of Navarre & lords.	4.3 Navarre & lords exposed as lovers.

1.2 Armado confesses his love for Jacquenetta (famous lovers).	5.1 Armado consults Holofernes & others about pageant (of Worthies).
1.1 Navarre, Berowne & lords swear oath.	5.2 Navarre, Berowne & lords forswear oath.

The play symmetrically reflects the beginnings and ends of its actions. The framing action is the lords' vow of seclusion, sworn in the first scene and forsworn in the last scene. The structurally "inner" action, the subterfuge of the lords (set off by the break in the outline), begins in the third scene (2.1), with their first surreptitious interest in the ladies, and ends in the paired seventh scene (4.3), with the lords' exposures. The inner action is separated from the framing action by the paired scenes (1.2 and 5.1) devoted exclusively to the comic characters and their heroic models. The one other scene pair, 3.1 and 4.2, also contains an action begun and ended: Berowne's letter is sent (3.1) and (mis)delivered (4.2), to Jacquenetta instead of to Rosaline, the confusion allowing the exposure of the lords in the following scene. The main plot of the play thus consists of three nested (and, as the title promises, failed) actions: the vow sworn and forsworn, the subterfuge and its exposure, and the sonnet-letter sent and misdelivered. Though *Love's Labor's Lost* is usually thought to be without plot or action in the Aristotelian sense, it is more accurate to say that its actions are unemphatic, comparatively trivial. For all the verbal elaboration that Shakespeare lavishes on each incident, the play is structured firmly around the beginnings and ends of its essential actions.

The symmetry of these scene pairs focuses the play on the keystone scene. Collectively, its three incidents articulate the play's gender-equal view of courtship as hunting. In killing the deer, the Princess is explicitly compared to a lady subduing a lord (4.1.35–40); Armado likens his courtship of Jacquenetta to a lion preying on a lamb (88–93); and in the bawdy sparring of Boyet and Rosaline, punning on suitor/shooter, "they both did hit it" (129–30). At this point in the play, the violence implicit in the hunt and related images is deflected from our awareness by the light tone. The froth of language obscures the reality of death from the audience as from the lords. But intimations of mortality, first introduced in the King's opening speech, are certainly not absent from the keystone presentation of courtship as hunting, and as sudden as the appearance of Marcade seems in the last scene it is certainly not unprepared for.

The structural emphasis on the center of the play as a whole is repeated in individual scenes. The preoccupation with language in *Love's Labor's Lost* is structurally embedded at the center of each scene of the inner action. The following outline includes the (italicized) centers of each scene except the pair of exclusively comic scenes.

	4.1 Princess hunts deer. *Armado's letter read: lion & lamb (66–86 of 149).* Boyet & Rosaline "both did hit it."
3.1 Armado gives letter to Costard to deliver to Jacquenetta. *l'envoi & goose(the letters of) (99–104 of 205).* Berowne gives Costard letter for Rosaline.	4.2 Costard (mis)delivers Berowne's letter. *Jacq & Costard bring Berowne's letter to be read by Holofernes (82 of 166).*
2.1 Princess & Ladies attract secret interest of Navarre & lords. *Navarre on King of France's letter (127–41 of 260).*	4.3 Navarre & Lords exposed as lovers. *Jacq & Costard enter with Berowne's letter (186 of 383).*

1.2 Armado confesses his love for Jacquenetta (famous lovers).	5.1 Armado consults Holofernes & others about pageant (of Worthies).
1.1 Navarre, Berowne & Lords swear oath. *Berowne signs oath* (155 of 315).	5.2 Navarre, Berowne & Lords forsworn. Berowne: "*We are again forsworn, in will and error*" (471 of 931).

The scenes of the inner action have "letters" at their midpoints, either correspondence or the letters of the alphabet: the King of France's letter (2.1); the comic punning on *l'envoi* and "goose," repeatedly calling attention to the difference of a letter between them (3.1); and Berowne's sonnet-letter, brought in at the centers of 4.2 and 4.3. These central "letters" structurally anchor the proliferation of puns, malapropisms, errant billets-doux and other linguistic pyrotechnics in the play. The framing action is similarly emphasized at the centers of the first and last scenes, when Berowne signs the oath of seclusion and, in the final speech before the pageant is announced, articulates the breaking of the oath "in will and error" (471). This central emphasis in the play and in individual scenes is, we will see, a common feature of all three comedies.

The symmetrical structure of *A Midsummer Night's Dream* is identical to that of *Love's Labor's Lost*. The later play too has a framing action beginning and ending in the first and last scenes, an inner action beginning and ending in the third and seventh scenes, with the two actions separated by a pair of comic scenes; and it too contains a thematic keystone scene of lovers. *A Midsummer Night's Dream* also structurally anchors its theme by repetitions at the scene centers of the inner action. Following is an outline of the play's main actions.

3.1 Bottom "translated" during rehearsal. Titania falls in love with him.	

2.2 Puck anoints eyes of Lysander. Oberon anoints Titania.	3.2 Oberon anoints Demetrius. Lovers' confusion.
2.1 Oberon and Titania quarrel. Oberon recalls magic flower to Puck.	4.1 Oberon undoes anointing of Titania. Theseus, Hippolyta awaken lovers.

1.2 Bottom & others receive parts in play.	4.2 Bottom returns. Play to go on.
1.1 Theseus anticipates wedding, hears Egeus's complaint against Lysander. Lovers plan to elope.	5.1 Marriage celebration. Pyramus and Thisbe performed.

The framing action begins and ends in the first and last scenes with the planned wedding and the final celebration (counterpointed by a second, less harmonious courtship, similar to Costard's in the earlier play). The five central scenes contain the inner action, the transformations of the lovers, Bottom, and Titania; this action begins with Oberon's recollection of the flower love-in-idleness, the means of enchantment (2.1), and ends with the hunting horn waking the lovers from their "dream" (4.1). The inner action of *A Midsummer Night's Dream* is much more clearly demarcated from the framing action than that of *Love's Labor's Lost*. Not only are there paired scenes of comic characters in the second and penultimate scenes and the introduction of new characters in the third scene, as in *Love's Labor's Lost*, but there is also a different setting and time of day for the inner action, the forest at night. Furthermore, the characters introduced in the third scene, the fairies, are prominent throughout the inner action, whereas after their introduction the ladies of *Love's Labor's Lost* appear only in the keystone scene. As in *Love's Labor's Lost*, the central scene of *A Midsummer Night's Dream* (3.1) epitomizes the play's view of courtship and love, though with much more focus, economy and dramatic effect. The deer hunt of the earlier play is the only stage action in the keystone; otherwise the theme is fittingly but diffusely articulated in language, in a comic letter and dueling double entendres. In these ways Shakespeare succeeds in demonstrating his essential hunting image at work in both the serious and comic characters, but at the expense of concision and force. In *A Midsummer Night's Dream*, by contrast, the theme is fully dramatized in the misalliance of the literal-minded Bottom and the infatuated fairy queen by virtue of its analogies with the other lovers in the play.

The following outline, summarizing all the episodes of *A Midsummer Night's Dream*, will help isolate and explain the scene centers. The play is more complexly layered than *Love's Labor's Lost* and embeds the centers of some scenes as "third-act climaxes" in five-part sequences.

3.1 Mechanicals plan play (1–76). Bottom "translated" during rehearsal (77–119). Titania falls in love with him (120–201).	

2.2 **Oberon anoints sleeping Titania** (1–34). Hermia & Lysander sleep; Puck anoints him (35–83). Lysander falls in love with Helena (84–156).	3.2 Puck tells Oberon Titania is in love (1–40). Demetrius & Hermia enter; **Oberon anoints Demetrius.** Lovers' confusion (102–342). Oberon plans to restore Lysander & Titania (343–99). Lovers sleep; Puck restores Lysander (400–63).
2.1 Puck & Fairy in woods (1–59). Contention of Oberon & Titania (60–145). **Oberon commands Puck to fetch flower** (146–87). Demetrius & Helena squabble (188–246). Oberon & Puck take potion (247–68).	4.1 Bottom & Titania fall asleep (1–45). Oberon restores Titania (46–103). **Theseus & Hippolyta wake lovers (104–86).** Lovers puzzle over their "dream" (187–99). Bottom puzzles over his dream (200–19).

1.2 Mechanicals.	4.2 Mechanicals.
1.1 Theseus & Hippolyta on wedding (1–19). Theseus hears Egeus on Lysander (20–127).	5.1 Theseus & Hippolyta on lovers' story (1–27). Theseus & Hippoltya talk with lovers (28–107). Play: Prologue (108–26). Dumbshow (127–53).
Lysander & Hermia plan to leave Athens (128–79). They tell Helena of their plan (180–225). Helena determines to follow (226–51).	**Conversation** (154–218). Lion & Moon (219–62). Deaths (263–370). Fairies sing & dance (371–422). Puck delivers epilogue (423–38).

Within the symmetrical structure are five-part sequences keyed by the performance of Pyramus and Thisbe in the last scene. The performance is presented in a classical five-act structure: the Prologue, the dumb show, the conversation through the wall, the Lion and Moon, and the deaths of Pyramus and Thisbe. There are five structurally analogous sequences in the play: scenes 1.1, 2.1, 4.1 and 5.1, and the entirety of the forest action. In 5.1 the mechanicals' performance is also a single "act" in the overall scene; the final scene is thus a structural miniature of the entire play, with the five forest scenes, the inner action, analogous to the five acts of Pyramus and Thisbe.

The centers of four scenes in *A Midsummer Night's Dream* are paired "third-act climaxes." The conversation between Lysander and Hermia in 1.1, in which they plan to leave Athens at night, matches the conversation between Pyramus and Thisbe at the center of 5.1, in which they too plan to meet at night. In the central episode of 2.1 Oberon recalls to Puck the flower whose juice induces madness, initiating the hallucinatory forest action; in the central episode of 4.1 Theseus commands the hunting horn to wake the lovers, restoring them to the daylight world. Although not so clearly divided as to have a third-act climax, scene 3.2 has as its midpoint the lovers' confusion in the forest and thus fits the "narrative" sequence of scene centers in the inner action, that is to say, its initiation in 2.1, its implementation in 2.2, its consequences in 3.1 and 3.2, and its conclusion in 4.1. Where *Love's Labor's Lost* punningly repeats "letters" at the centers of the scenes of inner action, *A Midsummer Night's Dream* records the stages of a single action: Oberon recalls the flower (2.1), which is then applied to Lysander (2.2); Bottom is (analogously) translated (3.1) and the lovers suffer their confusions (3.2) before the dream is dispelled by Theseus' hunting horn in the morning (4.1). Analogous actions rather than puns and simple repetitions unify the inner action.

In its symmetry and in the broad disposition of its scenes, *The Tempest* is similar to *Love's Labor's Lost* and *A Midsummer Night's Dream*, though compared to the romance even the virtuoso structure of *A Midsummer Night's Dream* looks merely competent. It is clearer at first to include only the main characters in the scene outline of *The Tempest*, with actions indicated only in the keystone and first and last scenes:

3.1 The marriage agreement between Miranda and Ferdinand.	
2.2 Caliban's party.	3.2 Caliban's party.
2.1 King's men.	3.3 King's men.
1.2 Prospero, his people & spirits.	4.1 Prospero, his people & spirits.
1.1 The storm.	5.1 Spell-stopped tableaux.

Like the earlier plays, *The Tempest* has an enveloping action, the storm, that begins in the turbulent first scene, rages metaphorically through the subsequent scenes and ends in the spell-stopped tableaux of the last scene. As the lovers and Bottom are analogously transformed in the inner action of *A Midsummer Night's Dream*, the various characters of *The Tempest* are analogously affected by spirits, though the inner action of the romance, like its spirits, cannot be so easily confined to the five central scenes but also occupies the second and penultimate scenes, as I discuss below. The second obvious similarity between the romance and the earlier plays is the presence of lovers in the central scene. Miranda and Ferdinand occupy the same central position as do Titania and Bottom in *A Midsummer Night's Dream* and Boyet and Rosaline and the other "suitors" in *Love's Labor's Lost*, and like the earlier couples Miranda and Ferdinand epitomize the play's view of courtship, in this case as a realistic commitment, free of the illusions of spirits. In the central dialogue of the play (3.1.33–67) Ferdinand sees

Miranda not as a goddess, as he had earlier, but as "created of every creature's best" (3.1.47–48); and Miranda sees Ferdinand not as a "thing divine" (1.2.419) but as a "companion in the world" (55). ("Nor can imagination" she continues, implicitly rejecting the illusions her father has created, "form a shape, beside yourself, to like of" [56–57].) The framing action and the keystone scene of *The Tempest* are perfectly homologous with the earlier plays; in other respects the romance works variations on the earlier structure.

If we parse the structure more finely, the sophistication of *The Tempest* is clearer. Following is an outline of the character groupings within scenes. The *x*'s indicate that the pairings of the adjacent scenes are cross-related rather than direct.[2]

3.1 Ferdinand and Miranda agree to marry.	
2.2 Caliban's party.	3.2 Caliban's party.
2.1 King's men.	3.3 King's men.
1.2.378–506 Prospero and meeting of Miranda & Ferdinand.	4.1.1–163 Prospero and masque for Miranda & Ferdinand.
1.2.308–377 Prospero & Caliban.	4.1.164–264 Prospero and Caliban.
1.2.190–307 Prospero & Ariel.	5.1.1–57 Prospero & Ariel.
1.2.1–189 Prospero tells Miranda of Milanese. XXX	5.1.58–100 Spell-stopped tableaux. X X X
1.1 The storm.	5.1.100–171 Recognition of Prospero & Milanese.
	(Coda: return to reality.) Discovery of Miranda & Ferdinand. Enter ship's crew. Enter Caliban's party. Epilogue.

The character groupings form a second structure within and overlapping the scene divisions, though it is worth noting that, discounting the coda, both are effectively nine "scenes": the character groupings consisting of the five central scenes and the four additional "scenes" of the remaining segments. This structure of character groupings demonstrates a significant difference in the inner action as compared to the earlier plays. Though the King's party and Caliban's crew are vexed by spirits in a manner similar to the confusions of the inner action in *Love's Labor's Lost*—the misdelivered letters—and *A Midsummer Night's Dream*—the various "translations"—the confusions the spirits effect in *The Tempest* are not ended until the play returns to reality in the coda, when the king is reunited with his son and Caliban realizes how fine his master is. The inner action does not end in the seventh "scene" of either the scene structure or the character groupings. Instead it begins and ends in the second and penultimate "scenes" of the character groupings, in the positions earlier devoted to the comic characters. It is initiated by Prospero's rage against Ariel in 1.2.190–307 and resolved by the "rarer action" of forgiveness Prospero attains in 5.1.1–57. That is to say, the structurally inner action is a psychological action; the disturbing illusions of the inner action are framed by and issue largely from Prospero's mind, from his own struggle with spirits. Only after his inner turmoil is resolved are all storms quelled in the spell-stopped tableaux, and (as the scene centers below demonstrate) only then does Prospero recover his identity, return to himself, among the Milanese. The magus and his spirits, the baseless fabric of the play, dissolve, and, in a manner reminiscent of the entrance of Marcade in *Love's Labor's Lost*, the last segment of the play returns to reality, in the discovery of Miranda and Ferdinand and the subsequent appearance of the ship's crew and Caliban's party. (For a detailed analysis of Prospero's transformation, see my last chapter.)

As "letters" and the magic juice and its effects were centrally located in the scenes of the earlier plays, so the center of each scene of *The Tempest*, excepting the keystone and last scenes, is a version of tempest, a perturbation of spirits, a blowing, beating or angry "storm." The "spirits" in the first half of the play—Prospero's anger, Gonzalo's and the courtiers' "spirit[s] of persuasion" (2.1.235) and the spirits of alcohol—are "natural spirits"; those in the second half are artful, the creations of Ariel and Prospero. The productions of natural spirits in the first half are paired with corresponding art productions in the second half. For example, Gonzalo's vision of a Golden Age, in which no labor is required to produce food, is reflected and implicitly commented upon in the disappearing banquet of the paired scene. The following outline includes the "stormy" centers of each scene (italicized) and the "productions" of storms, if they occur.

Caliban mistaken for a monster.	Mimicked voice.
2.2. *Caliban drinks spirits of alcohol (86 & 93 of 188)*.	3.2. *Beating of Trinculo (76 of 152)*.
Stephano mistaken for a god.	Mimicked song.
Golden Age.	Banquet.
2.1 *"It is foul weather in us all" (142–84 of 327)*.	3.3 *Thunder and storm sounds (53 of 110)*.
Descending crown.	Harpy.
	Masque.
1.2. *Prospero berates Ariel (245–96 of 502)*.	4.1. *Storm and strange noises (137 of 266)*.
	Hound hunt.
1.1. *The storm on empty deck (33 of 68)*.	5.1. *"I am Prospero" (159 of 320)*.

All but the keystone scene and the last scene contain a central disorder, a storm, a turbulence of natural or artful spirits. The spirits of alcohol in 2.2 cause the mistaken identities of Caliban as a monster and Stephano as a god; in the paired 3.2 the artful mimicry of the spirit Ariel causes the mistaken identity and central beating of Trinculo and the "sweet airs" encouraging the drunkards' comic conspiracy, the new action of the second half of the play initiated, characteristically, in the scene immediately following the keystone scene. The "foul weather" of the King's men prompts the "spirit of persuasion" (2.1.235) to be loosed in 2.1: in Gonzalo as he attempts to comfort the king with a vision of the Golden Age; and in Antonio as he conjures a vision of a descending crown to convince Sebastian to kill the king. The mirroring, artful illusions in the paired scene, 3.3, are the disappearing banquet and accusatory harpy, performed before and after the central storm sounds. In the final pair of the inner action, Prospero's ambivalent anger toward Ariel at the center of 1.2 is reflected in the stormy confusion at the center of 4.1. Caught up in the same distraction that cost him his dukedom, Prospero, transported by the spirits' revels, forgets the conspiracy against him. However, he now recovers himself sufficiently to unleash all his pent-up anger against Caliban, and in the cathartic process of the hunt attain the calm of reason and forgiveness that immediately follows. Finally, precisely in the center of the last scene, Prospero recovers himself in his full identity, as friend, as brother, as subject, as duke. And in the paired first scene, in the storm raging on an empty stage, we glimpse not only the ultimate referent for all the scene centers of the play's inner action but also Prospero's inner life while on the island: barren, unpeopled, elementally disordered.

In plotting these three comedies, Shakespeare's craftsmanship is as meticulous as that of a goldsmith. He disposes the beginnings and ends of the action in a carefully symmetrical arrangement and constructs his scenes and plots with a rigorously central thematic emphasis. It is a solid and forthright dramatic structure, Aristotelian in being anchored by the logical arrangement of the play's actions. In *A Midsummer Night's Dream*, he elaborates the basic structure with an additional pattern of "five-act sequences," alluding to the design of classical Roman comedies, and in *The Tempest* he fashions a double structure that has something of the same metamorphic shimmer as the spirits and poetry of the play. The basic symmetrical ordering of the action, the thematic structure, evolved into a design of extraordinary subtlety and refinement.

5

Richard II
Thematic Arch and Imagery

Richard II illustrates both the difference between narrative and thematic structures and the disposition of the imagery on the thematic arch. Broadly speaking, the chronicle narrative is a vehicle for the psychological "inner plot," to use Una Ellis-Fermor's phrase, the psychological change in Richard, which constitutes the thematic action. One way in which this change is expressed is in the imagery of the contested sun, emblem of kingship, which changes as Richard's fortunes change. The narrative and the imagery are both disposed expressively on the thematic arch.

In the usual view the plot has its pivotal turn from Bolingbroke's rise to Richard's fall at Flint Castle, when the antagonists meet for the first time after Richard returns from Ireland. Mark Rose succinctly describes this view:

> There is no ambiguity about the basic structure, which rests upon the opposition of two anti-thetical characters, Richard and Bolingbroke. Indeed, it is a commonplace to point out the play's symmetrical pattern, and to cite Richard's image of two buckets, one rising, one falling, as an emblem for the overall design. Nor is there much ambiguity about the turning point. The play pivots in the Flint Castle scene (III. iii) in which Richard ... turns his descent to the main platform into a symbolic act: "Down, down, I come, like glist'ring Phaeton."[1]

Not only the symbolic stage action but the confrontation itself is taken as evidence of the narrative turn here. Brents Stirling, for example, points to the final lines of the scene as initiating the pivotal change: "the aptly timed climax of the episode, and of the play" is Bolingbroke's affirmative reply to Richard's question about going to London.[2] These opposing views are, of course, not incompatible. The conflict between Richard and Bolingbroke and the complex fall of Richard cannot be separated. They constitute the narrative and the thematic designs, what might be thought of as the temporal and the spatial structures. The narrative action, the temporal movement, develops as Rose suggests, with the turn occurring, as is characteristic of Shakespeare, in the scene following the keystone scene; but the play focuses on the psychological change Ure finds in the central scene, the keystone of the thematic arch. The change in Richard is expressed in the sun imagery (discussed below) that ties it to the play's thematic concern with succession and the divine right of kings. The fact that Richard's descent is expressed in the same solar imagery, as quoted by Rose ("glist'ring Phaeton"), suggests the way in which Shakespeare intertwines narrative, theme and imagery.

The thematic core of the play's nineteen scenes, then, is the numerically central tenth scene, 3.2, in which Richard collapses psychologically at the news of Bolingbroke's success.[4] Early in the scene Richard reiterates the security of the anointed king: "Not all the water in the rough, rude sea Can wash the balm off from an anointed king" (54–5); within a hundred lines he is lamenting his mortality, inviting "talk of graves, and worms, and epitaphs" (145), and, after rallying briefly, psychically surrenders altogether in the last lines of the scene: "Discharge my followers, let them hence away, From Richard's night to Bolingbroke's fair day" (217–18). Richard's volte-face, his turn from the sun of kingship, epitomizes the thematic action.

Richard's psychological collapse, his loss of faith in the efficacy of his anointing, is flanked by two scenes of a more pragmatic nature, asserting Bolingbroke's moral claim and achieved power.

	3.2 Richard gets "tidings of calamity," Bolingbroke's success.	
3.1 Bolingbroke lists his grievances in condemning Bushy and Green.		3.3 Northumberland petitions for redress of Bolingbroke's grievances. (Richard descends.)

Both 3.1 and 3.3, the scenes flanking the keystone, are centrally concerned with the grievances stemming from Richard's seizure of Bolingbroke's hereditary rights. Bolingbroke expresses these grievances himself in the earlier scene, when justifying his condemnation of Bushy and Greene. Bolingbroke tells them he has been "eating the bitter bread of banishment Whil'st you have fed upon my signories" (3.1.21–22 of 44). In the central speech of the paired scene Northumberland voices the same complaint to Richard. Diplomatically understating the extent both of Bolingbroke's grievances and his power, Northumberland says that Bolingbroke's "coming hither has no further scope Than for his lineal royalties" (3.3.112–13 of 209). Besides demonstrating Bolingbroke's power, both scenes of the central flanking pair insist on the illegality of Richard's actions, particularly as they violate "fair sequence and succession" (2.1.199). This reiterated thematic emphasis is immediately followed by the decisive narrative action, Richard's descent.

The comparison between Richard and Bolingbroke implicit in the central scene and the flanking pair is further developed in the chiastically mirroring pairs of the rest of the play. One two-pair section is devoted to the rise of Bolingbroke and the fall of Richard.

2.3 York accedes to Bolingbroke's cause.	4.1 Deposition. Richard accedes to Bolingbroke.
2.2 Sorrowing Queen receives news of revolt against Richard.	5.1 Richard and Queen parted by Northumberland.

The opposite fortunes of Richard and Bolingbroke are most obviously enacted in the deposition scene and the paired scene of York's entrance to Bolingbroke (4.1–2.3). In each scene there is what might be called a treasonous shift in allegiance: York proclaims himself "as neuter" (98), and Richard, in an act that he himself will call treasonous, gives up his kingship to Bolingbroke. In the 2.2–5.1 pair the pathos of Richard's fall is expressed by the Queen's suffering: her sorrow at Richard's departure for Ireland and the revolt against him is magnified in the paired scene of grief over his deposition and her final parting from her husband. The beginning and end of Bolingbroke's revolt is thus presented only in the reactions of the Queen, and Bolingbroke's agency is muted.

Another two pair section compares the kingship of Richard with that of Bolingbroke. In this early play the mirroring is less precise than in, say, *Measure for Measure*; it is rather of a thematic topic than of specific actions.

2.1 Gaunt dies. Richard seizes his lands.	5.2 York discovers his son's plan to kill Bolingbroke.
1.4 Richard on Bolingbroke's popularity: "as were our England in reversion his."	5.3 Duchess enters to plead for her son before Bolingbroke.

The York-Aumerle incident in scenes 5.2 and 5.3 contrasts with the implicit father-son incident of the paired scenes, 1.4 and 2.1, in which Richard violates the laws of succession after having separated Gaunt and Bolingbroke. Under Richard, Gaunt finds it necessary to vote for his son's banishment and, partly from his subsequent grief, dies. York turns even more decisively against his son, seeking his death for treason, but Bolingbroke forgives him. This "king and the beggar" scene has a conclusive thematic significance. In preserving Aumerle, Bolingbroke implicitly restores respect for the larger legal rights of succession; and in acceding to the Duchess's request to spare her son, Bolingbroke establishes an integral relationship to the larger associations clustering around women in the play: birth, nursing, land, etc., the balancing female side of the concern with succession. Overall, the "farcical" scene is an attempt to humanize Bolingbroke. He is concerned about his son but hopeful, grateful for York's loyalty, responsive to the Duchess, forgiving, humorous. And this scene is paired with an account of his popularity with the commoners (1.4), the very cynicism with which this account is delivered by Richard and seconded by Aumerle, the man Bolingbroke forgives, reinforcing rather than detracting from the humanity and breath of capacity in Bolingbroke.

This complimentary end to the sequence enacting Bolingbroke's kingship is quickly qualified by the final sequence, on the defining murders for which Richard and Bolingbroke are (to disputed extents) responsible. Richard's murder retrospectively casts an ironic light on Bolingbroke's actions in the opening scenes in response to the murder of Gloucester.

1.3 Banished Bolingbroke to Richard: "Your will be done."	5.4 As friend to Bolingbroke, Exton says, he will kill Richard.
1.2 Gaunt, insisting that Richard is "God's substitute," will not avenge Gloucester's death.	5.5 Richard is murdered.
1.1 Bolingbroke accuses Mowbray of treason and of killing Gloucester.	5.6 Richard's body is brought before Bolingbroke.

The loyalty Bolingbroke proclaims to Richard in 1.3 has the same ultimate outcome as the loyalty Exton expresses to Bolingbroke in the paired 5.4. Even when submitting to Richard's command of banishment, Bolingbroke fairly usurps the imagery of kingship: "Your will be done: this must my comfort be: That sun that warms you here shall shine on me" (144–45 of 308). If this is meant literally, it is vapid. Bolingbroke (or Shakespeare) seems to be suggesting equality with Richard by a proleptic use of the sun image, which in the central scenes will be invoked explicitly in its traditional kingly associations. Bolingbroke's submission then is highly qualified. Such loyalty as this and such equivocation find an apt echo in the paired scene, when Exton takes Bolingbroke at his word and plans to rid the new king of an old nemesis.

The murder of Richard (5.5) is ironically paired with Gaunt's earlier refusal to avenge the death of Gloucester (1.2) because "God's is the quarrel; for God's substitute ... has caused his [Gloucester's] death" (37–9 of 74). This is the first explicit statement in the play that Richard is responsible for Gloucester's death, information withheld in order to structurally mirror the two murders. The wisdom of Gaunt's deference to God's substitute is confirmed by the paired scene. In both the source and the play, Exton is immediately conscience-stricken at having killed Richard, suddenly aware that "this deed is chronicled in hell" (5.5.116). This pair of scenes demonstrates how complex, even this early, is the single action unifying a Shakespearean play. In delimiting the sprawling action of the historical record with the two murders—of Gloucester by Richard and of Richard by Bolingbroke—Shakespeare has brilliantly suggested that the action of the play, with its ceremonial, even ritualistic unfolding, is retributive, larger than the mere political machinations of either Richard or Bolingbroke.

The accusations of murder and treason Bolingbroke makes in 1.1 can be turned against him in the paired 5.6, when he views the body of the murdered Richard. In the central lines of 1.1 Bolingbroke accuses Mowbray of murdering the Duke of Gloucester, of having "Sluiced out his soul through streams of blood; Which blood, like sacrificing Abel's, cries ... to me for justice" (103–106 of 205). When Richard's body is brought before Bolingbroke in the last scene, he banishes the murderer Exton with a final reference to the Genesis story: "With Cain go wander thorough shades of night" (5.6.43). The prominent mention of Abel and Cain, the hinted shift in Bolingbroke's moral position from victim to victimizer, suggest his culpability for the "crimson tempest" of civil war begun by Richard's murder.

The one other pair of scenes in the play, 2.4–3.4, needs to be considered in the context of the entire outline:

3.2 Richard gets "tidings of calamity," Bolingbroke's success.	
3.1 Bolingbroke lists his grievances in condemning Bushy and Green (16–20 of 44).	3.3 Northumberland petitions for redress of Bolingbroke's grievances (101–120 of 209).
2.4 Omens of "fearful change" as Richard's troops disperse (24).	3.4 Gardeners on seizure of Richard.
2.3 York accedes to Bolingbroke's cause. (York enters at 81 of 171.)	4.1 Deposition. Richard accedes to Bolingbroke. (King enters at 162 of 334.)
2.2 Queen receives news of revolt against Richard (73–81 of 148).	5.1 Richard and Queen parted by Northumberland (who enters at 162 0f 334).
2.1 Gaunt dies. Richard seizes his lands (155–62 of 299).	5.2 York discovers his son's plan to kill Bolingbroke (56–72 of 117).
1.4 Richard on Bolingbroke's popularity: "as were our England in reversion his" (24–36 of 65).	5.3 Duchess first heard before entering to plead for her son before Bolingbroke (72 of 117).

1.3 Banished Bolingbroke to Richard: "Your will be done." (144–47 of 309).	5.4 As friend to Bolingbroke, Exton says, he will kill Richard (11).
1.2 Gaunt, insisting that Richard is "God's substitute," will not avenge Gloucester's death (37 of 74).	5.5 Richard is murdered (soliloquy 1–66 of 118).
1.1 Bolingbroke accuses Mowbray of treason and of killing Gloucester (100–106 of 205).	5.6 Richard's body is brought before Bolingbroke (29 of 52).

Scenes 2.4 and 3.4 comment emblematically on the action and set off the tympanum of the arch. The fearful omens in 2.4 and the Gardener's allegory in 3.4 widen the perspective while separating the central action from the rest of the narrative. Shakespeare frequently uses a pair of scenes of this kind to create a choric break of sorts punctuating the main action, sometimes, as here, to separate the central pinnacle, in other cases positioned elsewhere in the arch. (See, for other examples, *Macbeth* and *Lear*.) As we will see, this pair of scenes also initiates and concludes the storm-related imagery that is used to express the conflict between Richard and Bolingbroke.

The whole play then is symmetrically balanced around the central scene in which Richard's spirit breaks and he surrenders in imagination to Bolingbroke. The psychological change in Richard is the thematic focus. The central flanking scenes express Bolingbroke's grievances and superior power. Collectively, these three scenes present the essential conflict between Richard and Bolingbroke and are structurally highlighted by the two choric scenes of emblematic comment (2.4 and 3.4). The rest of the play is in three sections mirroring the rise of Bolingbroke and the fall of Richard (2.2–2.3 and 4.1–5.1), their kingships (1.4–2.1 and 5.2–5.3) and the murders each is involved in (1.1–1.3 and 5.4–5.6). It is worth noting that the essential entrance, action or speech of each scene is usually central and thus reproduces in miniature the central structural emphasis of the play's overall action. (There are two expressive variations from this pattern. In 3.1 the central speech is not Richard's upon descending but the conclusive assertion of Bolingboke's power; in 5.5 it is not the death of Richard but his transformation that is emphasized.)

Given this structural emphasis, it is not surprising to find that the central speech of the central scene uses the most significant image motif of the play: kingship as symbolized by the sun. It has been widely remarked that Shakespeare uses meteorological, diurnal and seasonal imagery to represent the struggle between Richard and Bolingbroke, the ways in which the sun can be darkened by clouds, by night, or by winter, depending on the stage of the underlying political struggle.[5] All of this imagery is orchestrated in a unified and coherent pattern determined by the symmetrical thematic structure already outlined. The following outline merely positions the relevant imagery, which is fully quoted in the commentary following. (The bracketed quotes in 1.1 and 5.6 are not directly part of the pattern. A solid horizontal line indicates that there are no sun or sun-related images in that scene)

3.2 Richard as the sun (37–53).	
"unseasonable stormy day" (106–120).	
Richard benighted (217–8).	

| 3.1 Bolingbroke: "sighed my English breath | 3.3 Richard as the sun (61–6). |

in foreign clouds" (20).	various storms (53, 61, 84). Richard: "down, down, like.... Phaeton" (177).
2.4 predicted storm: "The sun sets weeping, Witnessing storms to come" (21–2).	3.4 emblematic storm: Queen weeping in garden.
2.3 _____	4.1 Bolingbroke as sun (261).
2.2 _____	5.1 Richard into winter (40).
2.1 Storm and "rash ... blaze" of Richard's reign (263–69, 33). Gaunt as "setting sun" (12).	5.2 Bolingbroke's spring (47, 50).
1.4 "North-east wind" awakes "rheum" in ironic Aumerle (6).	5.3 emblematic magnanimity: "The King and the Beggar."
1.3 [basic images.]	5.4 _____
1.2 "heaven ... will rain hot vengeance on offenders' heads" (8).	5.5 _____
1.1 [Gloucester's "blood, like sacrificing Abel's, cries ... to me for justice."] [basic imagery introduced.]	5.6 ["with Cain thorough night."] "that blood should sprinkle me to make me grow" (46).

The first and third scenes introduce sun-related images in more or less neutral contexts. There are three storm images in these scenes, all referring to combat and hatred (1.1.41–2, 1.3.79 ff., and 1.3.187), a single reference to seasons (1.1.64), two references to the sun (1.3.145, 1.3.274, as "the eye of heaven") and one to night (1.3.176). Underlying the storm imagery are the elements of fire and water also introduced in the first scene (19). Richard is early associated with fire (e.g., 2.1.34–5, 2.4.19–20) and Bolingbroke with water (ambiguously at 1.1.19; in 2.2 derivatively as causing tears). The strife between them is fire and water on the land, lightning and rain on the garden of England. The storm imagery is particularly dominant in the central part of the play, from 2.4 to 3.3. In 2.4, the first of the choric, transitional scenes, Salisbury says of Richard, "Thy sun sets weeping in the lowly west, Witnessing storms to come, woe and unrest" (2.4.21–22); in the paired transitional scene, 3.3, the storm is concluded by the Queen's emblematic weeping in the garden. In the repeated storms of political strife between these two scenes Bolingbroke succeeds in taking power from Richard, so that by the deposition scene (4.1) it is Bolingbroke and not Richard who is associated with the sun, and the elements are reversed, Richard dissolving in tears and Bolingbroke associated with fire. Following is a more detailed analysis tracing this shift in power.

The elemental struggle between Bolingbroke and Richard is most explicitly and elaborately expressed by Bolingbroke before Flint Castle.

> Methinks King Richard and myself should meet
> With no less terror than the elements
> Of fire and water, when their thund'ring shock
> At meeting tears the cloudy cheeks of heaven.
> Be he the fire, I'll be the yielding water;

> The rage be his, whilst on the earth I rain
> My waters—on the earth, and not on him [3.3.53–59].

In his first speech responding to Bolingbroke's presence outside the castle, Richard also uses storm imagery, though naturally with a different import:

> Yet know, my master, God omnipotent
> Is mustering in his clouds on our behalf
> Armies of pestilence, and they shall strike
> Your children yet unborn and unbegot [84–7].

This political storm threatens the sun of kingship: Bolingbroke before Flint Castle:

> See, see, King Richard doth himself appear,
> As doth the blushing discontented sun
> From out the fiery portal of the East,
> When he perceives the envious clouds are bent
> To dim his glory, and to stain the track
> Of his bright passage to the Occident [3.3.61–66].

Consequently, in the central scene, Richard's psychic abdication, it is fitting that the central image should render Bolingbroke's success apocalyptically in a storm image of watery inundation. Scroop reports Bolingbroke's advance

> Like a unseasonable stormy day
> Which makes the silver rivers drown their shores
> As if the world were all dissolved to tears,
> So high above his limits swells the rage
> Of Bolingbroke, covering your fearful land
> With hard bright steel and hearts harder than steel [3.2.106–111 of 218].

When this flood of support for Bolingbroke is detailed for Richard, he immediately laments his own mortality, for it is as if the image is a direct rebuttal of Richard's earlier confident assertion that "not all the water in the rough rude sea Can wash the balm off from an anointed king" (54–5). After some vacillation, Richard imagines going down to darkness: "Discharge my followers, let them hence away, From Richard's night to Bolingbroke's fair day" (217–18).

This diurnal imagery has been elaborately explained in Richard's earlier speech (3.2.36–53), comparing himself to the sun. With the darkening of the sun at the end of 3.2 a pattern is established. After each variant of abdication—the psychological at Barkeley Castle, the political at Flint Castle and the ceremonial in London—Richard again imagines himself as descending into darkness, as having lost the sun of his kingship. In 3.3 the image takes on a mythological twist: "Down, down I come, like glist'ring Phaethon" (177); in 4.1 it is a symbol of his own identity as he smashes the mirror: "Was this the face That, like the sun, did make beholders wink?" (282–83).

Before this final destruction of himself as the sun, Richard transfers the image to Bolingbroke, re-introducing the seasonal imagery that disappeared after scene 1.3, shifting into a new temporal register. Richard wishes himself

> a mockery king of snow
> Standing before the sun of Bolingbroke
> To melt myself away in water drops [259–61].

Richard here anticipates his descent into winter in the next scene, when he parts from his

Queen (40, 76–7), and the spring of the new king's court in 5.2 (46–7, 50), the return of the monarchical ideals embodied in Gaunt as the setting sun of the paired scene (2.1). There is no further sun-related imagery, though it is importantly recalled by Bolingbroke's allusion to a storm variation in the last lines of the play: the shower of blood.

The motif of raining blood is first briefly and elliptically suggested by Gloucester in 1.2: "heaven … will rain hot vengeance on offenders' heads" (8). There is no further image until 3.3, when Bolingboke threatens to "lay the summers' dust with showers of blood Rained from the wounds of slaughtered Englishmen" (42–3). The image is immediately repeated by Richard (97–9) and again when the Bishop of Carlisle prophesies that "the blood of English shall manure the ground" (4.1.136–38). It is then not only the natural storm that is conjured in the play's last lines but this "crimson tempest" (3.3.45) as well: "Lords, I protest my soul is full of woe That blood should sprinkle me to make me grow" (5.6.45–6).

Like the plot incidents the sun imagery has also been arranged expressively on the symmetrical structure. The storm imagery—that is, the contested sun—is concentrated in the five central scenes, most emphatically in 3.3. Where the imagery exists in paired scenes, it forms a mirroring comment. For example, the storm of Richard's reign in 2.1 is contrasted with the spring of Bolingbroke's court, with "violets" in its "green lap," in 5.2 (46–7). Less obvious is the 1.4–5.3 pair. If 5.3 is intended, as I think, to be an emblem of Bolingbroke's sun-like magnanimity, his embodiment of the best qualities of kingship, the pairing with Aumerle's mention of the powerful wind in 1.4 provides another storm-sun contrast like that of 2.1 and 5.2. And Aumerle's sardonic account of the wind that may have caused his eyes to water when leaving Bolingbroke contrasts with the mother's tears that save Aumerle's life. The bracketed quotes in the first and last scenes take the final stitch connecting the leitmotifs of blood as familial bond (the imagery of succession which I have not considered here) and as a storm of violence.

In selecting and arranging source incidents to form mirroring halves of the play, Shakespeare has deepened and complicated the chronicle narrative in a reflexive thematic symmetry balancing Richard and Bolingbroke. Similarly, the imagery of the *roi du soleil* is carefully subordinated to the structural development of the drama. *Richard II* demonstrates nothing so much as the hand of a master playwright constructing an elaborate artifact with a symmetrical thematic structure.

6

The Merchant of Venice
Thematic Arch,
Scene Division and Imagery

The structural simplicity and elegance of *The Merchant of Venice* are particularly striking. It is organized in three segments, each with three scene pairs, plus the keystone scene. In one segment, the thematic arch pairs the beginnings and ends of the two main actions, Antonio's "courting" of Bassanio (mediated finally by Portia) and Antonio's bond with Shylock. The other two segments reflect the various marriage-related choices and bonds, respectively, of all the main characters. Additionally, the thematic arch structures the food imagery. It is arranged in two movements, rising and falling roughly along the two columns of the arch. The first movement extends from the opening scene to the scene of Jessica's elopement, i.e., to the scene of Bassanio's cancelled feast for Jew and Christian alike (2.6), and the second movement alternates scene by scene through the play's last half the vying substitutes for Bassanio's cancelled feast: the revenge feeding Shylock desires and the celebratory marriage feast of the Christians.

This structure obviously depends on the number of scenes in the play. Neither the two early Quartos nor the Folio text of *The Merchant of Venice* divide the play. Scene designations have evolved from the work of early editors to the present general agreement on a total of 20 scenes. Something of the difficulty and uncertainty of the process, however, can be inferred from Harley Granville-Barker's comment that "the confusion of scene-divisions in most modern editions (a very riot of it when Jessica is eloping) is not Shakespeare's."[1] In fact, it is exactly at Jessica's elopement that the usual logic of scene division weakens the performance of the play and distorts the overall symmetry of the design. The break at 2.6, though correct by conventional measures of scene designation, subtly diminishes the integrity of the single scene it interrupts and skews the structural mirroring of the two halves of the play.

The traditional 2.5 is a 57-line scene in which Shylock, leaving for the feast, warns his daughter to keep the house locked. After his departure Jessica ends the scene with a rhyming couplet: "Farewell—and if my fortune be not cross'd, I have a father, you a daughter lost" (56–7).[2] She exits, clearing the stage. Gratiano and Salerio then enter in their masquers' costumes, also on their way to the feast, at which point the traditional 2.6 begins. The cleared stage and rhyming couplet certainly seem to invite a new scene, but these indications of a scene break are not conclusive. Rhyming couplets are so common in the play, both within and at the end of scenes, that their mere presence cannot be taken as an infallible indication of a break.

52

Furthermore, in every other instance the cleared stage in *Merchant* is combined with a change in location, mostly between Venice and Belmont, reinforcing the fact that place is a structural and thematic device in the play. Of successive scenes only the traditional 2.5 and 2.6 are set in the same location. Consistency suggests that they should be combined, that the parallel actions of departing for the feast unify what has traditionally been divided. The play's overall symmetry and the disposition of the food imagery, both discussed below, also indicate there should be no break. The play then, at least provisionally, has nineteen scenes.

The keystone scene, the tenth scene, contains a conversation between Salerio and Solanio. They discuss two topics: Shylock's reaction to his daughter's elopement and the parting of Bassanio and Antonio (2.8). Solanio says that mocking boys follow Shylock through the streets crying, "his stones, his daughter, and his ducats" (24); Salerio quotes Antonio's telling Bassanio to take his time in courting Portia: "for the Jew's bond which he hath of me, Let it not enter in your mind of love" (41–2). The two archenemies embody the play's ultimate polarity and are at the center of the play each separated from what they most value—Shylock his money and Antonio his friend. For each man this entails the figurative loss of his very flesh. Shylock and his money are one flesh: his ducats are his "stones," ("testicles" in Elizabethan slang) more valuable to him than his "flesh and blood" in the person of his daughter (3.1.33). In giving his money, Antonio is giving his flesh, as Bassanio's reciprocal offer at the trial explicitly expresses: "The Jew shall have my flesh, blood, bones, and all, Ere thou shalt lose for me one drop of blood" (4.1.112). In Antonio's attenuated desire, anyway, he and Bassanio are one flesh. Essentially, the keystone scene focuses the fundamental terms of all four plots: the intricate nexus of money and flesh. As man and woman become one flesh in marriage and as a dowry is an inescapable part of this bond, Shylock's and Antonio's equation of money with flesh corrupts, to varying degrees, the marriage exchange. Portia's suitors in the central flanking scenes (2.7 & 2.9) confuse precious metals with a prospective wife and cannot get by the glitter of her wealth; Jessica elopes "gilded" with her father's stolen money. At the other extreme, also undermining the bond of marriage, is Bassanio's offer of his flesh for Antonio and his gift of the ring to the disguised Portia, both of which indulge the lack of self-possession underlying Bassanio's generosity and risk-taking. In her extraordinary self-possession Portia moderates the identification of valuables and flesh; the ring is "riveted" to Bassanio's "flesh" by "faith" (5.1.169). The play's reductive terms of money and flesh are transformed in Portia's person and Belmont home into a harmonious, spiritual world. The thematic extremes that she reconciles are focused in the play's keystone articulation of the fundamental commonality between Shylock and Antonio: in responding to the loss of what he most values, each reveals his confusion of his wealth with his self: "my purse, my person" (1.1.138).

The remainder of the play is divided into three sections, each composed of three pairs of mirroring scenes. In structure the groupings are like a tercet, a stanza rhyming A-B-A, in that the flanking pairs have a similar subject that is different from the subject of the central pair. Following is an outline of the central tercet:

2.7 The Moor chooses casket of gold.	2.9 Prince of Aragon chooses casket of silver. (Bassanio arrives.)
[2.5 + 2.6] Shylock leaves for banquet with Christians; Jessica elopes.	3.1 Shylock receives news of his daughter's spending & Antonio's losses.
2.4 Lorenzo reveals his choice of Jessica.	3.2 Bassanio chooses lead casket.

The tercet "rhymes" on the subject of choice, common to the pairs 2.7–2.9, the wrong choices of the Moor and the Prince of Aragon, and 2.4–3.2, Lorenzo's choice of the "gilded" Jessica and Bassanio's choice of the lead casket. The middle pair, [2.5 + 2.6]-3.1, bookends Shylock's fall from human relationships. He goes from being a father and member, however disliked, of the Venetian community in the early scene, [2.5 + 2.6], to suspecting a larger conspiracy in his daughter's flight and wishing revenge on her and on Antonio (3.1). Scene 2.9 is characteristic of Shakespeare's narrative structure as well in that the new action (or new phase of the main action) of the second half of the play is initiated in the scene immediately after the keystone scene. With Bassanio's arrival at Belmont the courtship proper begins. Similarly, the new action of the second plot is initiated in scene 3.1, with Shylock's revenge.

As the central tercet rhymed on the various choices made by the suitors, the middle tercet rhymes on the nature of the play's various bonds:

2.3 Launcelot takes Jessica's letter, an offer "to become a Christian and [Lorenzo's] wife."	3.3 Shylock: "I'll have my bond" of Antonio.
2.2 Launcelot taken into Bassanio's service.	3.4 Portia prepares for disguised service.
2.1 Portia barred by her father from "voluntary choosing" of husband.	3.5 Jessica, defying her Jewish father, will be saved by Christian marriage.

Jessica's offer of herself as wife to the Christian Lorenzo in the marriage bond (2.3) is paired with her father's insistence on the bond he has made with Antonio: "I'll have my bond… . I'll not yield … to Christian intercessors" (3.3.112, 115–6). Bonds and Christian intercession are also the topic of scene 3.5, in which Jessica and Lorenzo banter with Launcelot, who jokes that Jessica is damned because of the sins of her Jewish father and she retorts that she has been saved by her Christian husband. In the paired scene, 2.1, Portia explains that, far from betraying her father, she will follow even his puzzling casket test, though it bars her from any voluntary choice. Before Bassanio faces his test, she explains that she stands "for sacrifice" of her own will (3.2.57). The "B" pair, 2.2 and 3.4, central to this tercet and to both halves of the play, treats of willing service—Launcelot's to Bassanio and Portia's to Bassanio. Both Launcelot and Portia change clothes as a sign of their new allegiance, though servant and wife are far differently motivated, of course. Lancelot has been "famished in [Shylock's] service" and merely seeks a master with a "fairer table" (2.2.101,158). By contrast, Portia, in "godlike amity" and under cover of going "To live in prayer and contemplation," expends her wealth and herself to save her husband's friend (3.4.3, 28). These scenes of service are each the mid-point of its half of the play and derive an increased thematic emphasis from that position.

The final tercet:

1.3 Antonio agrees to bond for pound of flesh.	4.1 The trial: "The bond is forfeit."
1.2 Portia & Nerissa on departed suitors.	4.2 Portia given ring.
1.1 Antonio agrees to borrow money for Bassanio to woo Portia.	5.1 Portia arranges that Antonio become surety for Bassanio's fidelity.

In its rhyming pairs the final tercet resolves the polar views focused in the keystone scene. Shylock's bond is made and forfeit in the 1.3–4.1 pair, and Antonio's opening-scene melancholy, due to his affection for Bassanio, is, if not resolved, at least mitigated in the friendship Portia re-prioritizes in the final scene. As Shylock's identification of himself with his wealth requires that all his assets be taken if he is to reconstitute his identity, so Antonio, all his wealth, his flesh, lost, as he thinks, accepts a new bond, his *"soul* upon the forfeit," that Bassanio will be true to Portia (5.1.252, italics added), implicitly sacrificing the desired homosexual relationship implied in his original loan to his friend. In the "B" pair, Bassanio, in giving up the ring that should be "riveted with faith unto [his] flesh" (5.1.169) is implicitly compared to the earlier, mocked suitors in the paired scene (1.2), who abandoned the love trial completely. Though like the suitors Bassanio has been faithless, it is not from a lack of courage; he simply has to learn that the pledge the ring symbolizes has an even higher claim on his own flesh than did, in his earlier estimation, Antonio's loan. Hearing Portia's rebuke of Gratiano for giving his ring to the clerk, Bassanio says, "Why, I were best to cut my left hand off, And swear I lost the ring defending it" (5.1.177–78). It is not wealth that weds the marriage partners in one flesh. As Portia says to Bassanio after the casket test, succinctly expressing their new reciprocity of identity: "I am half yourself" (3.2.248).

In the rigorous patterning of its four plots *Merchant* is almost Euclidean in its precision. The complete outline:

2.8 Salerio & Solanio on Shylock's hysteria at loss of money/daughter and on parting of Bassanio & Antonio.	

2.7 The Moor chooses casket of gold.	2.9 Prince of Aragon chooses casket of silver. (Bassanio arrives.)
[2.5 + 2.6] Shylock leaves for banquet with Christians; Jessica elopes.	3.1 Shylock receives news of his daughter's spending & Antonio's losses.
2.4 Lorenzo reveals his choice of Jessica.	3.2 Bassanio chooses lead casket.

2.3 Launcelot takes Jessica's letter, an offer "to become a Christian and [Lorenzo's] wife."	3.3 Shylock: "I'll have my bond" of Antonio.
2.2 Launcelot taken into Bassanio's service.	3.4 Portia prepares for disguised service.
2.1 Portia barred by her father from "voluntary choosing" of husband.	3.5 Jessica, though a Jew's daughter, will be saved by Christian marriage.

1.3 Antonio agrees to bond for pound of flesh.	4.1 The trial: "The bond is forfeit."
1.2 Portia & Nerissa on departed suitors.	4.2 Portia given ring.
1.1 Antonio agrees to borrow money for Bassanio to woo Portia.	5.1 Portia arranges that Antonio become surety for Bassanio's fidelity.

Not only theme and narrative, but the imagery of food and feeding is disposed on this symmetrical structure in a meaningful pattern as well. The first half of the play builds to the threshold of an uneasy harmony between Jew and Christian in Bassanio's feast. With the cancellation of the feast, coincident with Jessica's elopement, the strained relationship between Jew and Christian collapses altogether, and the food imagery reappears as the alternating possibilities of Shylock's revenge feast and the Christian marriage feast. In the following outline the quotes are abbreviated or paraphrased, and the parsing of food imagery and related images—animals and animal meat, for example—is admittedly imprecise, as it must be, but even with these vagaries, the disposition of food references on the thematic arch reveals three significant implications otherwise easily overlooked: the absence of imagery is meaningful; the grouping of images parallels the development of the narrative, as in *Richard II*; and finally single words, such as "sweet," take on their full resonance only in the context of all other related imagery. (A solid line indicates the lack of any food images in the scene.)

	2.8 _____	
2.7 _____		2.9 _____
[2.5 & 2.6] shall not gourmandize (3), bid to supper (11), to feed on Christian (14–5), no mind of feasting (37), the patch a huge feeder (45), riseth from a feast (2.6.8) sweet friends (21) lovely garnish of a boy (45) feast (48).		3.1 old carrion (32), red wine (36), take his flesh, to bait fish, feed my revenge, feed with same food (47–54).
2.4 suppertime (1), Jew to sup with Christian (17–18).		3.2. gold hard food for Midas (102), surfeit [on love] (114), sugar breath, sweet (118), our feast … in your marriage (212), sweet Portia (249), to feed my means (262), [Antonio:] sweet Bassanio (315).
2.3 Launcelot robs house of "taste of tediousness" (3), at supper (5).		3.3 pound of flesh to bloody creditor (33–4).
2.2 smack taste (16), famished in his service (101), supper (109), cater-cousins (124), fructify & dish of doves (127), feast tonight (163), at supper-time (197).		3.4 _____
2.1 pluck young suckling cubs (29), lion roars for prey (30), after dinner (44).		3.5 pork-eaters (22), prepare for dinner (43), serve the meat (50 ff), good sweet Jessica (65), dinner table talk (80 ff).
1.3 dine with us (28), smell pork (29–30), feed fat grudge (42), goodly apple rotten at the core (96), pound of man's flesh not worth pound of mutton (161).		4.1 merchant's flesh (23), carrion flesh (41), gaping pig (47), palates seasoned with viands (96), pound of flesh (99), [Bass:] Jew will have my flesh (112), wolvish, starved (138), pound of flesh (303,312), dinner (397).
1.2 sweet madam (of Portia, 3), sick with surfeit (5), death's head with bone in mouth (49), sober … drunk (82–3), glass of Rhenish wine (92).		4.2 at dinner (8).
1.1 vinegar aspect (54), heat liver with wine (80), fish with melancholy bait (101), dinner (104, 105), a neat's tongue tied (112).		5.1 sweet soul [of Jessica] (49), sweet music (67, 100), sweet Portia (192), sweet doctor (284), manna for a starved people (293).

These "images," mostly literal references to foods and dinner,[3] keep the idea of feeding subliminally present. The three scenes at the center of the play are without food imagery, so that the "image plot" in the first half is clearly demarcated from that of the second half. It is worth noting that scene 3.4, in which Portia plans her disguised service, is the only other scene lacking food imagery; the implication is that her service is a spiritual action, anticipating the "spiritualization" of the play that occurs in the final scene. (*All's Well That Ends Well* similarly distinguishes bodily actions from spiritual actions, and similarly, if much more subtly and complexly, spiritualizes earlier food imagery in the last scene.)

As I've said, the play builds toward an uneasy community in Bassanio's feast at the end of the first half, in which Jew and Christian will eat together. The second half enacts the alternative feedings—Shylock's feast of revenge on Antonio's pound of flesh and the marriage feasts—precipitated causally by a change of wind but symbolically by Jessica's betrayal of her father. Both kinds of feasts are developed in the imagistic narrative of the second half, alternating revenge and marriage feasts through each section. They are referred to in order as soon as food imagery is resumed in 3.1, when Shylock wants to feed his revenge, and in 3.2, when the marriage feast is anticipated. Except for the reference to a pound of flesh in 3.3, the food imagery disappears until 3.5, in which the "saved" Jessica's praise of Portia prepares for her intended "praise" of Lorenzo as "table-talk" at dinner (19, 87–8). Next, the trial with its predatory imagery narrowly avoids the feast of revenge Shylock had anticipated. Finally, the food imagery is spiritualized in the final scene in "sweet" music and "manna" from heaven, a sublime realization of the nuptial feast (5.1.67, 100; 293). (See *Othello* for a similar contrast between a nuptial feast and a revenge feeding, Iago's "diet[ing]" of his "revenge" [2.1.294].)

We might also notice the precise use of "sweet" as it is disposed through the play. It is used only twice among the mostly unpleasant food images in the first half of the play, of Portia (1.2.3) and by Lorenzo of his friends immediately before Jessica appears dressed as a boy (2.6.45). Each time it is used in the second half of the play—of Portia in her own person and that of her disguised persona, the doctor (3.2.118, 249; 5.1.192, 284); of Jessica, as a person and as a "soul" (3.5.65; 5.1.49); and of music repeatedly in the last scene—it flavors a variant of the nuptial feast. The single other use of the word is in the salutation of Antonio's letter asking Bassanio to attend his friend's death (3.2.314). In isolation, the two applications of the word to males would hardly be noticed, but in the overall image pattern it delicately suggests a tinge of homoeroticism in both Lorenzo and in the melancholy merchant. (*As You Like It* and *All's Well That Ends Well* also use "sweet" in distinguishing heterosexual and homosexual desires.)

Finally, to return to the question of the traditional break between 2.5 and 2.6. It is true that more than the final rhyming couplet of 2.5 and the cleared stage seem to justify the break. Separate scenes emphasize Jessica's transformation from Jewish plainness to Christian masquing and heighten the contrast between Shylock's gloominess and the Christians' gayety. Separate scenes appear to tidily express a basic polarity of the play. At this point in the action, however, that polarity has not yet widened into a complete break. It is important to the balance and objectivity of the play that everyone—Jew and Christian alike—is departing to feed, ultimately, on Antonio, whose flesh is surety for the money that supplies the banquet. In all, a subtle violence is done in dividing by a scene break the trajectory of the single stage action of the various departures for Bassanio's feast, disrupting the lucid symmetry of the narrative and thematic design.

7

The Thematic Arch of *Julius Caesar*
Sacrifice

Perhaps no Shakespeare play has suffered as much distortion from deleted thematic actions as *Julius Caesar*. The play, of course, narrates a political conflict. Using Gustave Freytag's terms, Mark Rose succinctly expresses its narrative structure and its antagonists: "The central scene is the assassination (III.i), which comes exactly in the center of the play, dividing it into two movements, the conspirators' action and Antony's counter-action."[1] This neatly constructed story survives even extensive cutting. The proscription scene (4.1), showing the ruthlessness of Antony, seems not to have been staged at all during the Restoration. To allow time for such august spectacles as Caesar's entrance in a 71-person procession, John Philip Kemble's text, the standard acting text of the nineteenth century, cut over a quarter of the play's lines, as did Bernbohm Tree's similarly spectacular and similarly influential production at the end of the century. Cinna the poet was not killed onstage in America until a New York production in 1937.[2] Even since the twentieth century, with "full text" productions the norm, it is not unusual to find that the Poet who interrupts the quarrel of Brutus and Cassius has disappeared or, as in the Joseph Mankiewicz film, Lucilius's offer of his life has been cut. None of these scenes or episodes is necessary to the narrative; every one is crucial to the thematic design.

In the central lines of the keystone scene, Antony manipulates the commoners by presenting Caesar as a martyred saint, invoked in images recalling earlier references to sacrifice. Hearing Caesar's will, Antony tells the plebeians,

> ... they would go and kiss dead Caesar's wounds,
> And dip their napkins in his sacred blood;
> Yea, beg a hair of him for memory,
> And, dying, mention it within their wills,
> Bequeathing it as a rich legacy
> Unto their issue... [3.2.132–37 of 264].

The entire play is symmetrically disposed around this image of Caesar as a Christian saint whose blood and every hair are sacred relics. Antony's speech is the third in a series of more or less cynical invocations of sacrifice, all three of which contribute to "Caesar's spirit, ranging for revenge" (3.1.370), and all three of which, it should be noted, are additions by Shakespeare to his Plutarchan source. Though implicit from the opening scene in the mention of the Lupercal, sacrifice is first explicitly introduced by Brutus: "Let us be sacrificers but not butchers," he says to Cassius of the murder of Caesar (2.1.167). "Let's carve him as a dish fit for the gods" (174). To get Caesar to the Capitol, Decius seizes on similar sacrificial imagery in reinterpreting Calphurnia's dream of the bleeding statue. "From you," Decius tells Caesar, "great Rome shall suck / Reviving blood and ... great men shall press/ For tinctures, stains, relics" (2.2.87–9). In spite of the variously ironic uses to which the conspirators and Antony put these invocations of sacrifice, the play ratifies a view of Caesar as the self-sacrificing hero of a drama about "the holiness of friendship" (in North's translation via Jacques Amyot's French version of Plutarch's phrase).[3] All of the play's essential actions, not just these three speeches, are cast in the light of the central image of a saintly Caesar. Though the narrative action of the play presents Antony as the enemy of the conspirators, in the larger sacrificial action he is simply one more in a line of self-serving or self-deceiving manipulators who contribute to the release of Caesar's spirit, both a spirit of revenge that comes to be embodied in Octavius Caesar and a spirit of friendship that is finally recovered by Antony through the example of Lucilius.

Following is the thematic arch, including the number of lines in each scene, for the proportioning is significant.

3.2 Funeral orations; Antony on Caesar's will and "sacred blood" (133 of 264).	

3.1 Caesar killed. (Antony enters at 146 of 297.)	3.3 Cinna the poet killed (38).

2.4 Portia sends Lucius on errand (46).	4.1 Antony sends Lepidus on errand (51).

2.3 "Lover" Artemidorus reads warning he plans to present to Caesar (15).	4.2 [& 4.3] Poet advises Cassius and Brutus to "love, and be friends" (181 of 356).
2.2 Caesar weighs dreams and auguries presaging his death (129).	5.1 Cassius now "partly" believes auguries; omens of his death (126).

2.1 Brutus: "Let us be sacrificers" (167 of 335).	5.2 Brutus orders attack (6).

1.3 Cassius: "Cassius from bondage will deliver Cassius" (164).	5.3 Cassius kills himself; "I am free," says Pindarus (110).

1.2 Cassius, Brutus's "glass," reflects Brutus to himself: "A Brutus once... (159 of 319). Caesar offers his throat.	5.4 Lucilius, claiming to be Brutus, is captured and asks to be killed (32).
1.1 Flavius & Marcellus disperse workmen celebrating Caesar's triumph (75).	5.5 Brutus kills himself, confirming Caesar's triumph (86).

Though not immediately apparent, the segment of the arch containing the opening and closing scenes is fundamentally about Caesar, as we will see. The subject of the next segment is the conspirators, and the third segment compares Caesar with Cassius (2.2 & 5.1) and then with Brutus (2.3 & 4.2). The central segment enacts the public (3.1 & 3.3) and private (2.4 & 4.1) chaos the conspirators and Antony visit on Rome. The thematic arch is further patterned in its proportioning. Each segment contains a pair of balanced scenes with approximately the same number of lines and a pair of "unbalanced" scenes with widely differing numbers of lines.[4] Generally, the short scene of the unbalanced pair reflects the central lines of the long scene. The "lover" Artimedorus in the short 2.3 reflects the Poet in the center of 4.2, who is also an advocate of love. The obvious exception to this central reflection is the 3.1–3.3 pair. The short scene of Cinna's murder has a double reflection in the paired scene:

Caesar's murder and the central entrance of Antony. The vivid murders need no structural emphasis, but Antony's responsibility for the poet's murder warrants the subtle structural reflection.

The central flanking pair immediately locates Caesar's murder thematically by comparing it with Cinna's murder (3.1 & 3.3). Rene Girard makes the obvious point: "After listening to Brutus, then to Mark Antony, the crowd reacts by collectively putting to death an unfortunate bystander, Cinna, in a grotesque parody of what the conspirators themselves have done. The crowd becomes a mirror in which the murderers may contemplate the truth of their actions."[5] The death of Cinna is not only a mirror of the conspirator's action; it extends that "sacrifice," that butchery of perverted love, via Antony's speech, through the whole city. Indeed, Caesar's influence is not fully eradicated until Cinna's death. Cinna is not simply an "unfortunate bystander." He is a poet, a dreamer and a friend of Caesar. He is representative of all the poets, dreamers and lovers of the play—the Soothsayer, Calphurnia, Artimedorus and the Poet, all of whom, it bears emphasizing, are accurate in their dreams and warnings.

The symmetrical structure of the play and the centrality of Antony's funeral oration are additionally emphasized by the second pair of flanking scenes. By having both Portia and Antony send someone on an errand in these paired scenes (2.4 & 3.1), Shakespeare shifts the focus into the private realms of family and friends. Though both Portia and Antony perform the same action, clearly linking the scenes, beyond that the similarities end. Portia is near hysteria and too distraught to have a purpose for the errand she sends Lucius on. Her earlier claim to "constancy" (2.1.300) is completely overthrown when she exclaims, "O how weak a thing/ The heart of woman is" (2.4.39–40). Her love for Brutus, like the loves of Artimedorus for Caesar and the Poet for Brutus and Cassius, proves to be insufficient to the task at hand. Antony, by contrast, fired by the spirit of revenge and the desire for power, commands Lepidus, "like to the empty ass" (4.1.26), with supreme assurance and coolly plans the murders of many victims, including kin. The five central scenes, then, complete the destruction of the republic in both the public and private realms. The murder of Caesar and the release of his vengeful spirit by means of Antony's speech transform the citizens into a raging mob, burning the city and killing indiscriminately. Portia's weakness and Antony's ruthlessness between them signal the destruction of the bonds unifying the private realm of family and friends.

In its thematic actions the next segment compares Caesar with the two main conspirators. The comparison with Brutus in scenes 2.3 and 4.2 focuses the importance of love in the play.[6] In the central scenes, love has created chaos. "Ingrafted love" (2.1.186) moves Antony to give voice to Caesar's wounds, thereby freeing "Caesar's spirit" to go "ranging for revenge" (3.2.270); Shakespeare's "Antony is not Plutarch's ambitious rival of Brutus but the deeply moved lover of dead Caesar."[7] The loving Antony is the pivotal instance of Shakespeare's many introductions of the idea of love into his source, though it is certainly not the only instance. Brutus, too, acted out of love. As Antony loved Caesar more than the Republic and therefore destroyed the Republic, so Brutus loved the Republican ideal more than Caesar and therefore killed Caesar. And in this instance Artemidorus and the Poet are paired as ineffectual spokesmen of love. In the short scene (2.3), Artemidorus reads his letter warning of the conspiracy and signed "Your lover"; he plans to present it "like a suitor" to Caesar. The mirroring Poet appears centrally in the long 4.2 (181 of 356). His original in Plutarch is not a poet but a kind of madcap "counterfeit philosopher" who, entering to the squabbling Cassius and Brutus, "broke their strife" with levity by quoting Homer: "My lords, I pray you harken both to me, For I have seen moe years than suchie three."[8] Shakespeare, though, has the Poet say, "Love, and be friends, as two such men should be; For I have seen more years, I'm sure, than ye" (181–82). By changing the original designation of the character and his quote, Shakespeare creates an obvious resonance not only with Artemidorus, who expresses his love and is rejected by Caesar, but also with Cinna the poet, whose treatment by the mob for his "bad verses" faintly echoes Brutus's mockery and dismissal of the Poet. Caesar of course dismisses Artimedorus because "What touches us ourself will be last served." Brutus, by contrast, throws the jigging fool out of the tent because his apparent frivolity is intrusive and annoying. In fact, the poet is eminently serious, willing to give his life to advise the generals ("Nothing but death shall stay me" [179]); he is, in little, a self-sacrificing advocate of love and is thus, as discussed below, like Lucilius and Caesar. Brutus cannot even recognize such love and devotion.

In comparing Caesar and Cassius, the next pair, 2.2 and 5.1, addresses the supernatural dimension of the play. Both Caesar and Cassius, having come to confront their own deaths, accede to the unearthly stuff that, in Yeats's phrase, rounds out a mighty scene. As Caesar has grown superstitious, so too has Cassius in the later scene. The skeptical rationalist has softened toward Caesar-like superstition. As Caesar confronted his presaged death in Calpurnia's dream, Cassius sees in the scavenger birds that have replaced the eagles accompanying the army omens of his own death.

The next segment characterizes the two main conspirators, Brutus and Cassius. Scenes 2.1 and 5.2, focus on the failed violence of Brutus. His centrally placed invocation of ritual sacrifice (167 of 335), his aspiration to carve Caesar as a dish fit for the gods, is no more successful than the explicit command to violence given in the terse expediency of battle. As his earlier distinction between sacrifice and murder—"Let us be sacrificers and not butchers" (167)—collapsed in the act itself, so now his battle strategy proves to be disastrous. In the last of the six lines comprising the paired battle scene (5.2), Brutus gives Marcellus the attack order for the soldiers: "Let them all come down." The result is defeat: "Brutus gave the word [to attack] too early," Titinius says, in the opening lines of the scene in which both he and Cassius kill themselves (5.3.5). Neither as conspirator nor as military leader has Brutus added much to the preservation of the Republic.

While also concerned with violence like the Brutus pair, scenes 1.3 and 5.3 focus on Cassius's desire for liberty. Unlike the Brutus pair, however, the scene pair demonstrates that Cassius either changes or reveals his true nature. His boast that he will kill himself rather than remain in bondage, his conviction that his love of freedom would be the cause of his suicide, is belied in the actual event, when he kills himself partly out of shame at his cowardice and partly out of friendship. The freedom he desired is ironically attained by the servant who held the sword, and even for him it is a hollow liberty since he will not return to Rome.

In the Caesar segment the second and penultimate scenes are structured like the central flanking scenes in having a double reflection. The impersonation of Brutus by Lucilius reflects most obviously one "other" Brutus in Cassius's glass; but Lucilius's offer of his life also reflects, not any action by Brutus, but rather Caesar's offer of his life at the Lupercal. These identical actions cannot be distinguished solely on the basis of the thematic structure, of course, and Caesar's gesture at the Lupercal may be, as Casca thinks, merely political theater. I will examine Caesar's action in more detail below. For now, it is enough to see the mirroring episode of Lucilius's offer of his life in the penultimate scene. The other balanced pair of this segment, the first and last scenes, marks the beginning and the end of the single arch the play traces, the balked public celebration of Caesar's victory and the final triumph of Caesarism.

The play, then, though it narrates a political conflict, thematizes the action in the light of sacrifice, especially self-sacrifice, the ultimate expression of the holiness of friendship. The pervasive religious preoccupations—the omens, rituals and sacrifice that Shakespeare added to his source—are organized around the central image of Caesar as a saint. The first half of the play is devoted to the death of Caesar, not primarily as a murder or an assassination but as a "sacrifice" that is further extended in Antony's funeral oration and finally fulfilled in the death of Cinna. The second half of the play traces the perverted sacrifice's disordering consequences and the final restoration of a more than merely political order through the corrective self-sacrifice of Lucilius.

Most critics who address the subject of sacrifice in the play take the murder of Caesar as some version of "a parody of Christian sacrifice," in David Kaula's phrase, because the conspirators produce "a disastrous imitation of the true redemptive action" in the consequent chaos of Rome.[9] There are a few critics with a different perspective. Mark Rose says that the comparison "between Caesar and Christ may not be wholly ironic," that the play can be considered a kind of "political Mass," because of the continuation of Caesar's spirit and its final triumph in the person of Octavius.[10] Though he does not expand on the characterization, Harold Bloom calls Caesar a "willing sacrifice to the imperial ideal."[11] Only Rene Girard finds the idea of sacrifice compelling enough to treat at any length. But, reading the play anthropologically, he finds the "sacrificial-cathartic" reading of the play to be our evasion of Shakespeare's unique presentation of the "foundational murder" every society requires, the violence we will not see because we are complicitous in it. Girard's reading is full of brilliant insights into the nature of sacrifice, but his interest is in the play merely as an illustration of his theories. Caesar becomes a scapegoat, a victim defined by the needs of the "real subject" of the play, "the violent crowd," rather than as a character in a dramatic work. However, Girard locates what I take to be the most significant action in the play and almost asserts that it is a willed, voluntary gesture by Caesar in saying that he "offers his throat to the crowd in a gesture reminiscent of some sacred king volunteering for the role of sacrificial victim."[12] Given the contested nature of kingship in the play, this comment is far from the last word on Caesar's action; nevertheless, I want to demonstrate the way in which the play enforces a modified version of this observation.

It is indisputable that the murder of Caesar and its manipulation by Antony bring chaos, and by that measure sacrifice is not redemptive but disastrous. But what restores peace and order? Gerard puts it succinctly: "The return to peace seems rooted in a single death, the suicide of Brutus."[13] As in traditional superstition, it is suggested,[14] Brutus appeases by his death the spirit of the man he killed: "Caesar, now be still. I killed not thee with half so good a will" (5.5.51–2). The last proponent of republicanism submits in what is usually considered an act of heroic suicide. "Fulfilling once again the role of sacrificer, the role he himself chose, … he satisfies his conscience, political necessity, history … and Fate"[15]; or, as another critic puts it, more simply, "Brutus's suicide signifies his *virtus*."[16] The mere fact of his suicide is assumed to fulfill a Roman ideal. But there are three suicides and an offered suicide in the last scenes, and the differences in motive and method among them are instructive.

Cassius, Titinius and Brutus all succeed in killing themselves. Thinking that Titinius has been captured, Cassius says, "O coward that I am to live so long, To see my best friend ta'en before my face" (5.3.34–5). The supposed loss of his friend is one element of Cassius's despair, but the more emphatic reason for his suicide is a sense of shame over his cowardice. And if his motive is mixed, so too is his means. As the instrument of his suicide, he enlists his bondman Pindarus, who is sworn to do as ordered. After Cassius dies, Pindarus says, "So, I am free; yet would not so have been Durst I have done my will" (46–7). It is only out of obligation to a vow that Pindarus stabs Cassius. It is also worth noting that Pindarus then flees "where never Roman shall take note of him" (50); he will no longer be part of the community.

Titinius's motive for suicide is unmixed. He takes a "Roman's part" (89), killing himself solely out of friendship. In Plutarch the motive of Titinius is similar to Cassius's in the play: he curses himself for not returning sooner and hence preventing Cassius's death. In Shakespeare, by contrast, Titinius is the noble, traditional Roman, and he is later invoked as an example by Lucilius (though, of course, Lucilius cannot know of Titinius's motives; it is Shakespeare who wants to distinguish between the friends' suicides.) The purity of Titinius's death is also suggested by the coincidence of motive and instrument. In his last words Titinius says, "Come, Cassius' sword, and find Titinius' heart" (90). The sword is neither the sword that killed Caesar, as it was for Cassius at the moment of his death, nor the sword that Caesar turns into the conspirators, as Brutus characterizes the same weapon when he discovers Titinius. It is simply the sword of his lost friend, the fitting means of his own death, of demonstrating how highly he "regarded Caius Cassius" (88).

Coming upon the dead Titinius, Brutus says that Caesar's "spirit walks abroad and turns our swords In our own proper entrails" (95–6). But this diminution of Titinius's traditional Roman heroism only shows that Brutus completely misunderstands the nature of friendship, as is most obvious at his own death. After two friends refuse to assist his suicide, Brutus still persists and makes the same request of Volumnius. "Good Volumnius," Brutus says, "Thou know'st that we two went to school together. Even for that our love of old, I prithee Hold thou my sword-hilts whilst I run on it" (5.5.25–8). Shakespeare has changed Plutarch here, who has Brutus ask Volumnius "for the study's sake which brought them acquainted together."[17] By substituting love for the philosophy of his source, Shakespeare has again placed the suicide in the context of friendship. Making explicit what the other two friends did not articulate, Volumnius replies, "That's not an office for a friend, my lord" (5.5.29). Rebuffed for a third time, Brutus then says, "My heart doth joy that yet in all my life I found no man but he was true to me" (5.5.34–5). Like his vacillation about suicide earlier, this puzzling comment can only heighten doubts about Brutus, here regarding his notion of friendship. He must finally ask his servant Strato (who, in Plutarch, is a fellow student) to hold the sword.

As the instrument of Brutus's suicide clarifies the office of a friend, his motive, differing as it does from those of Cassius and Titinius, explains why he should need instruction in friendship. "I shall have glory by this losing day More than Octavius and Mark Antony By this vile conquest shall attain unto" (36–8). As Knight says, Brutus puts honor before love.[18] His self-confessed estrangement from friends at his entrance into the play persists until his death. His honor, his glory, his ideals are more important to him than the love of his wife and friends, including, of course, his friend Caesar.

The three suicides demonstrate that friends do not kill friends; only servants and bondmen stoop to such an office. The "Roman's part" is to die with one's friend as Titinius does, courageously taking one's own life. Brutus misconstrues friendship and seeks, primarily, his own glory by his death. Cassius both avoids shame and joins a friend in death and so dies for both honor and friend. Against this background Lucilius's offered suicide stands out as exemplary, outdoing even Titinius.

During the fighting, Lucilius says, "I am Brutus.... Brutus, my country's friend" (5.4.7–8), revealing Lucilius's misunderstanding of Brutus, who, we have seen, subordinates friendship to honor and therefore puts himself before Rome. Shakespeare shows that Lucilius, by contrast, relegates honor to a secondary place. After Cato falls, Lucilius says, "Why, now thy diest as bravely as Titinius And mayst be honored" (10–11). The suicide of Titinius (and I take it to be significant that Cassius is not mentioned here) is as honorable as death in battle, and Lucilius recognizes not only Cato's and Titinius's honorable actions but also a higher allegiance implied in his (mistaken) understanding of Brutus and confirmed when he is captured. "Yield, or thou diest," a soldier says, and Lucilius responds: "Only I yield to die. There is so much that thou wilt kill me straight. Kill Brutus and be honored in his death" (12–15). Whether or not Lucilius offers money, as some editors think, his offer of his life in place of Brutus's is clear. His willingness to die in place of Brutus is not merely a Roman's part; it is the Christian's part of a man who would lay down his life for his friends. It is not suicide but self-sacrifice.

Shakespeare renders this scene subtly. Not only does he precisely discriminate ideas of friendship and honor among the characters, he also understates, by condensing, what in Plutarch is a sequence of potentially big scenes: Brutus under pressure on the battlefield before Lucilius's intercession; Antony's whole camp turning out, amazed that "Brutus" has been taken alive; Antony lingering in his tent to ponder what he should do with the prisoner; the final scene between Lucilius and Antony, ending with an embrace by Antony. Shakespeare selectively conveys this entire sequence in 30 lines, radically muting the thematic resolution of the play, for in a few laconic statements and a (disputed) stage entrance the conspirators' party and the revengers' are reconciled. In the Folio Antony enters at line 15, one line after Lucilius's offer of his life, though he does not speak until line nineteen. Some editors, Humphreys among them, change Antony's entrance to coincide with his first words. But the earlier entrance creates the strong suggestion that Antony overhears Lucilius and that it is the self-sacrificial example of Lucilius that restores Antony at least to the Titinian ideal of friendship that he had expressed to the conspirators after Caesar's death, when he had invited them to kill him. With Lucilius, that sense of friendship is restored to Antony. "This is not Brutus, friend," Antony tells the soldier, "but, I assure you, A prize no less in worth. Keep this man safe; Give him all kindness. I had rather have Such men my friends than enemies" (26–9). "Then he embraced Lucilius," Plutarch's account continues, "...and Lucilius ever after served him faithfullie, even to his death."[19] The Antony who loosed the mob on Rome, ruthlessly marked for death the names of friends and kin, and clashed with Octavius is once again the generous friend he was to Caesar. Shakespeare's rendering of this restoration and reconciliation is notable chiefly for its lack of histrionics, its almost willful refusal to hit the high notes. Spare as it is, the scene has the weight of the whole play behind it, not only in its diction and characterization but in its architecture as well, for the symmetrical structure indicates that the offered self-sacrifice of Lucilius reconciles the camps in the spirit of the loving Caesar.

*

That the pseudo-sacrificers invoke ritual either consciously or half-consciously for their own ends is obvious. But how does Caesar understand sacrifice? What does his death mean to him? We can infer his attitude from his responses to the interpretations of Calpurnia's dream. When the dream is understood as signifying mere murder, he decides for Calpurnia's sake that he will not go to the Capitol. However, when Decius re-interprets the dream of the statue spouting blood as indicating Rome will "suck reviving blood" from him (2.2.87–8), Caesar changes his mind. It is an odd moment. As Girard points out, Decius has chosen an unusual way of reassuring Caesar. Why not make up an interpretation of the dream that did not involve Caesar's death, since the whole point is to get Caesar to the Capitol? In notes to these lines both the Arden and the Oxford editions quote J. Dover Wilson's note to explain this strange choice and the effect of Decius's re-interpretation: "Caesar, taken with the notion of his blood being sacred, doesn't notice that it implies his death no less than Calpurnia's interpretation."[20] Caesar doesn't notice? What characterization of Caesar could produce a man who doesn't notice that his own death is being presaged by either interpretation of the dream? Nor can we say that Caesar changes his mind only when Decius mentions that the Senate intends to confer the crown, as though Caesar's ambition and lust for the crown make him feeble-minded enough to forget the portent of his death. The paired scene confirms that Caesar realizes the meaning of the dream. As Cassius in 5.1 understands and "partly" believes, even after his earlier skepticism, the omens of his own death, Caesar too understands the import of Decius's interpretation.

Why then does Caesar go to the Capitol? Because Decius has shrewdly appealed to the most fundamental strain in Caesar's character; Caesar believes that ruling Rome entails his figurative and perhaps even his literal death, his self-sacrifice. This belief is repeatedly suggested. In spite of the common critical perception of Caesar as arrogant, he is, in fact, in all things but one, not merely "urbanely friendly to his fellows,"[21] as is often grudgingly conceded, but surprisingly humble. His graciousness to his friends (as he thinks them) includes his gratitude for their least service, as when he says to the group come to escort him to the Capitol, "I thank you for your pains and courtesy" (2.2.114). As both the Arden and Oxford note, his apology for having delayed things is certainly not necessary, but nevertheless he says, "I am to blame to be thus waited for" (119). This sounds like genuine concern for either the servants or the Senators whom he has kept waiting, not "simply gracious good manners," as Daniell says,[22] but true consideration, even humility.

That Caesar sees himself as one among many equals, that he locates his place as among friends rather than among underlings, is also clear from a remark that is often turned against him. His refusal to repeal the banishment of Cimber is usually taken as a sign of extreme arrogance. "If I could pray to move," Caesar says in refusing Cassius's plea, "prayers would move me" (3.1.59). Editorial comment on this line again seems to derive from J. Dover Wilson, whose note to it is quoted in the Arden edition: "This is to claim super-divinity, since even the gods are moved by prayer."[23] In his note to the line Humphreys restates as "Caesar's pose raises him virtually above godhead, since the gods are moved by prayer."[24] Daniell also makes the same comment, interpreting the opening clause as meaning "If like you I were in the low position of expecting change..."; and, finally, the Riverside interprets "pray to move" as "beg favors of a superior (as you do)."[25] Why can't Caesar "pray to move"? Because he thinks himself above the gods? Surely this is not the implied reason. Rather, he cannot *justify* praying to move because the state depends upon his fixity. There is no measure of high and low implied here, as each of the quoted editors thinks, only the contrast of constancy versus change, as the whole speech makes clear. "The skies are painted with unnumbered sparks, They are all fire, and every one doth shine; But there's but one in all doth hold its place" (63–66). The only distinction among the stars, as among men, is that one remains constant. His "rank" is not measured by above and below but by constancy.[26] And this constancy is maintained only by means of self-sacrifice. When Artimedorus presses his letter upon Caesar by saying that it "touches Caesar nearer" than the other suits, Caesar replies, "What touches us ourself shall be last served" (3.1.7–8).

Caesar is not less aware than his critics of the infirm man and the Olympian ruler; he wills his immovability at the conscious expense of his private person. And that this continuous act of will is not without effort, we have his repeated overcompensatory insistencies as proof. What critics condemn as imperiousness and inflated self-love is often, it seems to me, a way of bucking himself up, of reminding himself of what he is in continual danger of losing: "always I am Caesar" (1.2.212). As Derek Traversi says of the northern star speech, it is almost "a plea, an appeal to the world to support him in his self-estimate."[27] The more pressing the requests for change, the more insistent on his fixity Caesar becomes. With so many friends pleading their suit for Publius Cimber, Caesar is forced to his most extreme self-presentations, as the north star and Olympus. "I am constant as the northern star" may sound like unmixed "hubristic arrogance,"[28] but it may also sound the note of a hard-pressed determination that is threatened with wavering. It might be the voice of a man who loves his friends and who would like more than anything to grant their request. As a friend he would be moved; as the foundation of Rome he must remain fixed.

The most explicit though elliptically presented action of self-sacrifice by Caesar is his offering of his throat at the Lupercal. Told, as it is, by a dismissive Casca, with plenty of editorializing and out of chronological order, Caesar's action comes across as a merely theatrical gesture of refusing the coronet for the commoners' approval. In Plutarch the gesture is even more damning, for Caesar has previously arranged the offer of the crown in order to test the response of the populace. When they cheer his refusal of the crown, he becomes angry, and "in a rage" he showed his neck, "bidding any man strike off his head that would."[29] But Shakespeare's Caesar is not Plutarch's. In the play there is no evidence that the offer of the crown was previously arranged; it seems perfectly in keeping with Antony's sportive ways. It is true that in Shakespeare Caesar, according to Brutus, has a "spot" (1.2.183) of anger on his brow when returning from the marketplace, but this could easily be attributed to the embarrassment of falling down. Caesar's predominant mood seems rather to be "sad," (i.e., serious or grave) than angry, as Brutus twice remarks (217 & 273). And one additional change to Plutarch by Shakespeare seems to decisively remove the whole gestural conversation with the populace from the "mere foolery" (235) Casca finds in it: the epileptic fit.

In Plutarch the swoon occurs after Caesar has come home from insulting the Senators and, by way of apology, bared his neck to anyone who would cut it. He then falls into an epileptic swoon, later excusing his excessive gesture as due to his infirmity. For some critics, the infirmity is the whole point of the incident Casca relates. McCallum argues that the physical infirmities of Caesar are introduced in such a way that they "almost make the Emperor ridiculous. At the great moment when he is putting by the coronet tendered him by Antony that he may take with the more security and dignity the crown which the Senate will vote him, precisely then he falls down in a fit."[30] McCallum expresses here what is essentially the combined view of Casca and Cassius: the play-acting ends in a kind of pratfall. However, McCallum's summary omits Caesar's critical act of offering his throat after refusing the coronet and points up the crucial difference Shakespeare's change to Plutarch makes. Only after offering his throat, signaling to the crowd that he will sacrifice everything for the people of Rome, does Caesar fall down. The offering may be merely a theatrical gesture, the empty fakery of an ambitious demagogue, but the immediate swoon fits the gesture so aptly that rather than being ridiculous the epileptic fit has the momentary effect of realizing the death the gesture signals. Had it been planned, it could not have gone better. Certainly, the crowd is sympathetic and, Casca reports, "forgave him with all their hearts" (1.2.269–70). McCallum has taken the view of the cynical republicans, also expressed, evidently, by Cicero, who elicits smiles and head shaking from his companions. But, assuming for the moment the perspective of a commoner, the epileptic fit, the fall, rather than undercutting a pretense of magnanimity and fake self-sacrifice, gesturally confirms the fact of Caesar's little death, as it might be called, his offer of his own life in the service of Rome.

Rather than read Caesar's motive as Casca, Cicero and Decius do, all of whom express cynicism about ritual and self-sacrifice, we can read Caesar's offering of his throat to be consistent with his response to Decius's interpretation of Calpurnia's dream and to Artimedorus's proffering of his "suit." Here, too, Caesar puts himself last and makes a difficult but sincere response to the request of the people. After refusing the crown three times, each time more feebly (if Casca is to be believed), not because of his impending epileptic fit but because of his undisputed desire for kingship, Caesar offers his throat to signify the death of his personal ambitions, his private self, for love of Rome. He then falls in a swoon. We can read back from his last words—"*Et tu, Brute?* Then fall, Caesar"(3.1.77)—to see the epileptic fall as a little death, an involuntary sacrifice of himself, which will become "voluntary," consciously accepted, at the moment of his actual death. As before his assassination, wavering when pressed by his friends, Caesar resorted to grandiloquent but sincere imagery, so, too, wavering when pressed by the populace to refuse the crown, he resorts to grandiloquent but sincere body language. To quote Girard's words again, Caesar "offers his throat to the crowd in a gesture reminiscent of some sacred king volunteering for the role of sacrificial victim." Caesar, however, has met his "death" in *giving up* kingship, in retaining the fixity of purpose rule requires without the personal aggrandizement. Far from being, as Girard suggests, a passive victim in the sacrificial process, Caesar is a knowing participant, indisputably putting himself in the context of willing self-sacrifice.

The function of the Lupercal celebration at the beginning of the play, then, is not simply for the purposes of dramatic economy that have been praised so often by critics. In a play permeated by rituals and ceremony, the Lupercal festival is the one instance of authentic religious observance, for Caesar's offered self-sacrifice makes him not merely the scapegoat, as Girard suggests, but the willing victim of the Lupercal ritual. It has been shown by Naomi Liebler that Shakespeare read the *Life* of Romulus, the first of Plutarch's Roman *Lives*, which contains the following account of the Lupercal:

> Howbeit many things are done, whereof the original cause were hard now to be conjectured. For goates ... are killed, then they bring two young boyes ... whose foreheads they touch with the knife bebloudied with the bloude of the goates that are sacrificed.... They cut the goates skinnes, and make thongs of them, which they take in their hands and ronne with them all about the cittie.

The play's core preoccupation with sacrifice derives from this originary Roman custom, which Shakespeare has transposed into a context of Christian morality. Though Liebler suggests only that this might be a source or inspiration for the bloody hand-washing after Caesar's murder and that Antony is "the official Lupercus,"[31] Shakespeare has modeled the first two scenes to indicate that Caesar is the sacrifice of the Lupercal.

Furthermore, the sacrificial nature of Caesar's action is confirmed, as I have already indicated, by the pairing of this scene (1.2) with that of Lucilius's offer of self-sacrifice (5.4). The pairing epitomizes the kind of ironies that pervade the play. I have said earlier that the Lucilius scene focuses the "other Brutuses" in the mirror Cassius holds up to Brutus and that Lucilius, like most of the other characters in the play, has an inflated estimation of Brutus. Ironically, then, in offering his own life, Lucilius is imitating not his hero, Brutus, but the opposition's hero, Caesar, and, further, restoring the spirit of Caesar to Antony. Brutus is not the redeemer of Rome, the savior he envisions in the central lines of the paired scene, Caesar is, not as Brutus's victim but as a self-sacrificer whose spirit lives on in Lucilius.

In *Julius Caesar* the political community is thought of largely in terms of friendship. Almost all of the characters profess love for one another and act, or claim to act, out of love. The murder of Caesar and the chaos Antony instigates are both perversions of love and are both presented as perverted versions of sacrifice. The disorder that results—in the mob, in Antony's ruthlessness, in the quarrel between Cassius and Brutus, in the confused fighting, in the power struggle between Octavius and Antony—can be set right only by an act of proper sacrifice, an act of corrective self-sacrifice. The highest ideal of friendship must be restored. The offered self-sacrifice of Lucilius re-establishes the holiness of friendship; Antony accepts Lucilius as a friend, righting the blasphemous earlier invocation of sacrifice. The fact that Octavius accepts Strato, a servant who has done merely a necessary "service" in killing Brutus, points up the difference between Octavius and Antony and signals what has become secondary in the change from Caesar to Caesarism—the self-sacrificial love symmetrically enacted by Lucilius and by Caesar.

8

The Construction
(and Catholicism) of *King John*

Most critics agree that *King John* post-dates an anonymous play, *The Troublesome Reign of King John* (*TR*), published in 1591, and that Shakespeare drew on the earlier play as his primary source,[1] not so much verbally—there are only a handful of parallel sentences and phrases—but structurally. "The selection and compression of historical material and the sequence of events are sometimes extremely close [between the two plays].... With minor variations between events dramatized and narrated, and with some significant differences in emphasis, the actions ... are closely parallel up to the end of Act 3" of *King John*[2]; and even after this point all but one of Shakespeare's scenes is based on a corresponding scene in *TR*. With so much of his plot borrowed directly, Shakespeare's "wrighting" of *King John*, his construction and shaping of the play, might not seem to offer much in the way of interest or illumination. "To praise the contrivance of a play which deviates very little from its 'source-play' would be dangerous," E. A. J. Honigmann, the editor of the Arden edition, writes (who believes that the influence went from *King John* to *TR*, and therefore uses quotes around "source-play")[3]; and in commenting on Honigmann's judgment, the editor of the Oxford Classics edition, A. R. Braunmuller, implicitly agrees: "Praise-for-contrivance need not be the end-all of critical response."[4] Shakespeare's genius in *King John*, critics agree, is most evident in his characterizations and dramatic verse rather than the plotting, in the writing rather than the wrighting of the play.

But the structure of *King John* is much disputed (and often denigrated), and we can hardly judge the merits of its plotting without understanding its design. While the narrative of *King John* largely follows that of *The Troublesome Reign*, Shakespeare subordinates the temporal narrative sequence to a chiastic thematic design totally absent from his primary source (and from the ultimate source of both plays, Raphael Holinshed's *Chronicles of England, Scotland and Wales* [1587], which provided Shakespeare with some additional or corrective details). By slightly altering the sequence of the events economically selected from the earlier play, Shakespeare creates structural configurations, "patterns," that are not simply confluences of meaning (as in the common phrase "image pattern") but that also establish positional connections and thematic emphasis. It is not only verbal elaboration or dramatic heightening, the usual tools of narrative emphasis, that Shakespeare wields; significant thematic elements are pointed spatially, by their relative positions on the structural arch, most especially the keystone position, and by their reflections in actions of corresponding scenes across the arch.

The patterned construction of the play, the arrangement of its scenes and of episodes within scenes, constitutes a syntax of its own, a meaningful spatial configuration that also organizes the disposition of the imagery. In this way, with an extraordinary economy of structural means, Shakespeare transformed a comparatively rambling, propagandistic, anti–Catholic chronicle play into a tightly focused, subtly shaded pro–Catholic drama.

Critics disagree as to the play's structure and find fault especially with its concluding scenes. The bluntest critic is E. M. Tillyard, who says the play is "badly proportioned" and "lacks unity": "Shakespeare has huddled together and failed to motivate properly the events of the last third [by line count] of the play."[5] (The play's unsatisfactory ending, universally remarked, is variously interpreted and explained.[6]) Tillyard refers here to the evident imbalance between the action before and after Arthur's death, generally considered the first and second halves of the play, which Geoffrey Bullough tallies as containing 1,987 and 728 lines respectively. Bullough's division into halves is itself problematic since it defers to *TR*, which was published in these same two parts, "quite unnecessarily," Bullough comments, "for it was obviously written as one piece."[7] However, attempts to divide Shakespeare's play based on its own articulations yield divergent conclusions. Honigmann considers 4.1, the scene of Arthur's intended blinding, to be the center of the play.[8] Adrien Bonjour, the one critic who thinks the play "remarkably balanced," finds the turning point to be 3.1, the scene in which John commands Hubert to kill Arthur.[9] This division restores some line proportion to the play, but Braunmuller effectively refutes it by demonstrating a number of weighty changes occurring later (the change in Hubert, the revolt of the nobles, the deaths of Constance, Eleanor and Arthur, and the change in the Bastard). He locates a rather diffuse midpoint at 4.1 and 4.2.[10] It appears then that the structure fails or is intentionally indeterminate, for there is no consensus on what the structure is, not even on the simple designation of the turning point and, consequently, of the first and second halves of the play.

Before turning to the overall structure, I would like to suggest some of the other differences between *King John* and its source. The opening and closing lines of the respective plays illustrate their divergent purposes. In keeping with the promise of its title, *The Troublesome Reign of King John* begins with John's ascension to the throne of England. Eleanor, John's mother, expresses the hope to the assembled lords of the realm that her son will "in rule and vertue both Succeed his brother," Richard I, and John, with suitable humility, says he "Will (as he may) sustaine the heavie yoke Of pressing cares, that hang upon a Crowne" (I, 7–8, 13–14). John's subsequent spiritual and political troubles may be hinted in these speeches, but only faintly. The main point is to dramatize, however briefly, the beginning of John's rule, as the final lines of the play fittingly signal its end with the dramatized crowning of Henry. In true chronicle form, *TR* treats, however selectively, the historical period of a monarch's reign and, further, makes that historical period structurally determinative. By contrast, Shakespeare (in spite of his play's full Folio title, *The Life and Death of King John*)[11] starts not with John's ascension but with the second incident in *TR*, the French challenge delivered by Chatillon, to which Shakespeare adds a short conversation between John and his mother that establishes the theme. When Eleanor anticipates the "bloody issue" necessary to arbitrate the contested claim to the throne, John answers, "Our strong possession and our right for us," and Eleanor replies,

> Your strong possession much more than your right,
> Or else it must go wrong with you and me;

So much my conscience whispers in your ear,
Which none but heaven, and you, and I, shall hear [1.1.38–43].

The French challenge in Arthur's name is not simply a military threat by a rival with a persuasive claim to the throne, as it is in *TR* and Holinshed's *Chronicles*.[12] Shakespeare has emphatically presented John's rule as illegitimate and has made its illegitimacy the essential question and organizing action of the play, which ends not with Henry's actual crowning but with the universal acceptance of Henry's right to rule, both in conscience and in temporal power, his right to succeed, that is to say, to a legitimate title. Shakespeare is thus Aristotelian in having a single action (of dual aspect) as his subject, not an historical period. The action of *King John* proceeds along two intertwined lines, the various political conflicts for possession of the crown of England and the less obvious determination of the moral and spiritual right to the crown.

The divergent purposes of the two plays are also signaled, much more subtly, in the second scene. After the issue of legitimacy—of both the king and the bastard Philip Falconbridge—is addressed in terms of possession in the first scene, the second scene turns briefly but importantly to the issue of right, of conscience, of spiritual influence rather than temporal power, and chiastically connects the right of (the unhistorically young) Arthur with the right of the young Henry. The symmetrically mirrored actions in the second and penultimate scenes are instances of forgiveness. Arthur forgives Austria for killing Richard I (2.1.12–14), and Henry, as reported by Hubert, persuades his father to pardon the rebellious nobles (5.6.34–5). Neither of these acts of forgiveness occurs in the source play, in which Pandulph persuades John to forgive the nobles and Arthur makes no comment at all on the killing of Richard. Indeed, Shakespeare has heightened the impact and resonance of Arthur's forgiveness of Austria by presenting Richard as the boy's father (2.1.6, 13). Though this "genealogical confusion"[13] is sometimes regarded as Shakespeare's error, it creates too artful a symmetry to be unintentional, for Arthur, as Honigmann puts it, is "resurrected" in Henry. Furthermore, the contrast between Arthur and his "brother," the vengeful Bastard, who decapitates Austria, is emphasized even to the very end of *King John*, when Falconbridge wants to take revenge for John's death. The two characters are early distinguished as spiritual and temporal forces in the play, indeed, as opposite moral agents.[14] The first two scene pairs then establish John and the Bastard as embodiments of power, embroiled in the struggle for territorial possession, and Arthur and Henry (via the reflected acts of forgiveness) as embodiments of "right" (1.1.40), what we might think of as spiritual rather than temporal agents in the play's overall enactment of legitimizing John's title. Shakespeare carefully disentangles the ethical muddle of *TR*, thematizing the political narrative on underlying moral issues, particularly on the opposition of vengeance and forgiveness, rather than on merely sectarian prejudices.

Shakespeare's Aristotelian plot and mirroring character actions suggest the economy and subtlety of his wrighting. Apparently small changes are transformed in the context of the overall structure, which, though elusive, can be recreated by building on the play's most evident characteristic, its instability, its "ever-shifting world … where what is done is undone only to be done again."[15] Virginia Mason Vaughan has listed some of the incidents creating this ever-shifting, "repeated pattern of reversals," which I quote here at some length and also number before rendering them more schematically in their spatial configuration:

[1] The audience—particularly if used to stories of John, the warlike Christian—may expect John to die fighting for his kingdom. Instead, John sickens with fever…. [2] We expect the

English nobles to continue their fight.... But after they learn of Lewis's plan to execute them—a reversal of expectations revealed by the dying Melun—they change sides and return to [John]. [3] Finally despite his proud boasts that he would pursue the conquest of England, Lewis meekly signs a peace. For all the talk of war deciding the fate of great nations, the battles in *King John* decide nothing" (418–19).[16]

In recreating the structure of the play we should first notice that these reversals are not merely reversals of "expectation." In the context of the drama, they constitute, in whole or in part, actions and their outcomes, more specifically, the early successes and later failures of the military conflicts. (*King John* thus resembles *Love's Labor's Lost* in its scaffolding of actions that become undone.) Furthermore, in keeping with the chiastic design, these successes and failures are arranged in pairs of corresponding scenes in the first and second half of the play (as determined not by line count but by number of scenes). The symmetrical arrangement of the actions Vaughan mentions can be sketched scene by scene as follows, reading up the left-hand column and down the right.

3.2 Victorious John to Bastard, who is carrying Austria's head.	5.3 Feverish, John leaves field.
3.1 Pandulph excommunicates John, blesses revolt & secret murder.	5.4 Melun convinces nobles of Louis's plan to murder them and ends their revolt.
[2.1.300–598] Hubert suggests marriage of Louis & Blanche: "at this match we fling ope wide and give you entrance."	5.5 Louis receives news of Melun's death, of defections, of lost ships.

The scene pairs each bookend one of the three main attempts to gain or hold the throne, actions sometimes more encompassing than Vaughan isolates. The early successes of Louis, Pandulph and John in scenes 2.1.300–598, 3.1 and 3.2, respectively, are paired with later failures. By means of his marriage to Blanche, Louis gains a foothold in John's possessions; in the paired scene, 5.5, Louis gets the news of Melun's death, of the defections of the nobles and of his lost ships, effectively ending his threat. In 3.1 Pandulph blesses revolt and secret murder, while in the paired scene, 5.4, Melun convinces the nobles that Louis secretly plans to kill them and thus ends their revolt. Most clearly and succinctly enacting early triumph and later collapse is the 3.2–5.3 pair, in which John, having captured Arthur, enters in victory to the Bastard and, in the later scene, abandons the field, feverish and defeated. In these symmetrical pairings we see that the "ever-shifting world of *King John*" has a solidly constructed foundation and that the incidents of the main actions are related spatially though they may appear episodic in their narrative sequencing. The spatial configuration demonstrates yet again, in Una Ellis-Fermor's phrase, Shakespeare's perfect hold on the Aristotelian action.

The symmetry is expressively varied to express two further "reversals of expectation" that Vaughan isolates:

> [1] When John decides he needs Arthur alive, he finds the boy is dead.... [2] After John has reconciled himself to the papacy, Pandulph assumes he can stop the war he so easily started [by inciting Lewis]; much to the Cardinal's chagrin, Lewis resolves to pursue the war anyway.[17]

These outcomes are unlike those of the three symmetrically paired military actions, for John and Pandulph do not so much fail as succeed too well. Intervening episodes highlight the apparent "success" of John in the continued life of Arthur and the success of Pandulph in gaining John's submission by means of Louis's threat. It is the continued "success" of their original intentions that ironically constitutes their failures. Shakespeare expresses the irony structurally by cross-relating the beginning and ending of the actions rather than directly pairing them. (The x's indicate this chiastic linking.)

3.4 [2] Pandulph incites Louis to invade England.	5.1 Bastard informs John that Arthur is dead.
XXX	XXX
3.3 [1] John orders Hubert to kill Arthur.	5.2 Louis refuses Pandulph's peace plan.

Not unexpectedly, this symmetrical pattern also supports more complex reflections in other scene pairings. The scenes flanking the central scene, 4.1 and 4.3, enact a more ambiguous variation of the mirroring of success and failure. At the center of 4.1 Hubert summons the executioners in preparation for blinding/killing Arthur. But Hubert is dissuaded from the murder; he fails in his task. He can then truthfully proclaim his innocence in the death of Arthur in the center of the paired scene, 4.3, when accused by the nobles. The 4.1–4.3 pair thus seems to reverse the order of victory/defeat we've seen elsewhere. Defeated in his initial task, Hubert can later claim a literally moral victory. The other important episodes of these scenes are also ambivalent. Arthur's success in softening Hubert in 4.1—his escape from death—is matched by his successful escape from prison in 4.3, but this results in his death. Both in rumor and in reality, though, Arthur's death, far from being a failure, stirs and inspires commoners, Bastard and (via Hubert and Melun) nobles alike. Ultimately, as Honigmann puts it, "a child-figure, Arthur, resurrected as Prince Henry, triumphs."[18] In outline the central flanking scenes contain the following incidents:

4.1 Hubert summons executioners, preparing to kill Arthur.	4.3 Hubert defends his innocence in Arthur's death.
Arthur, having touched Hubert's conscience, escapes death.	Arthur, escaping from prison, dies in leap from wall.
	(Bastard inspired by Arthur's body.)

It is worth noting that the initiation of the Bastard's "thousand businesses" at the end of 4.3, noted parenthetically in the outline, signals his psychological change and begins the new action of the second half of the play in Shakespeare's characteristic position, the scene immediately after the keystone. Thus the means of Arthur's subsequent spiritual and temporal influence in the play are neatly presented in the central flanking scenes: Hubert is changed by the spirit of Arthur in 4.1 (most notably his promised forgiveness of Hubert [81]); the Bastard is changed by the body of Arthur in 4.3

The following outline presents the reflecting pairs in the complete play and the central episode of the central scene. The outlined actions are located in the scene by their line number and the total number of lines in the scene. (This is a reliable measure of centrality since *King John* is written entirely in verse.) The outline also indicates both the degree of Shakespeare's indebtedness to his source and his transformation of it in carefully pairing actions in the first and second half and focusing the entire structure on the thematically crucial, though radically understated, keystone episode, Peter of Pomfret's prophecy. The bold number below the *King John* scene designation indicates the source scene in *TR*, which contains a total of 22 scenes[19]; if bracketed, the scene was not used by Shakespeare beyond providing suggestions for a scene of his own creation.

4.2 Bastard enters (132 of 269) to John with Peter, **13** who says John will lose crown by Ascension Day at noon.	

4.1 Hubert summons executioners, **12** preparing to kill Arthur (70 of 133).	4.3 Hubert defends his innocence in **14, 16** Arthur's death (81 of 159).

3.4 Pandulph incites Louis to invade **10** England (125 of 183).	5.1 Bastard informs John that Arthur **15, 17** is dead (39 of 79).
XXXXX	XXXXX
3.3 John commands Hubert to kill **9** Arthur (30–54 of 74).	5.2 Louis refuses Pandulph's **17** peace plan (78–108 of 180).

3.2 Victorious John to Bastard, who is **[6, 8]** carrying Austria's head (10).	5.3 Feverish, John leaves field (17). **19**
3.1 Pandulph excommunicates John, **5** blesses revolt & secret murder (172–79 of 347).	5.4 Melun convinces nobles of Louis's **18** plan to murder them and ends their revolt (30 of 61).
[2.1.300–598] Hubert suggests marriage of **4** Louis & Blanche: "at this match we fling ope wide and give you entrance" (448–51).	5.5 Louis receives news of Melun's **20** death, of defections, of lost ships (22).
[2.1.1–299] In Arthur's name Philip claims **2** John's lands (150–54). *Arthur forgives Austria for Richard's murder.*	5.6 Hubert tells Bastard that John has **[21]** been poisoned (23 of 44). *At Henry's urging, John pardons the nobles.*
1.1 Bastard chooses "shape" and "face" **1** over lands (138–47 of 276). *John's legitimacy challenged.*	5.7 John dies as Bastard tells of **21, 19** "devouring" flood (59 of 118). *Henry's legitimacy accepted.*

The outline provides a convenient way of comparing the overall scene dispositions of the two plays. We should first notice, however, the careful central positioning in each scene of the most significant narrative actions from the source. The crucial action of each scene, usually lifted from *TR*, is located exactly halfway through the scene. The only exception, 3.4, contains what are generally considered 47 interpolated lines between Philip's request to Constance to accompany him and her response; without these lines the center of the scene would be the resumption of the conversation between Pandulph and Louis summarized in the outline.[20] This central positioning is further evidence of Shakespeare's precise attention to the construction of *King John* and is, as we will see, a constructive principle Shakespeare applies to both the action within scenes and the imagery of the play. (In the first two scene pairs, those lowest on the outline, it is not the central narrative actions that most obviously reflect one another but the italicized actions of forgiveness original with Shakespeare, as explained above.[21])

At first glance it might appear that Honigmann's assessment is accurate, that there is very little difference in the construction of the two plays. Shakespeare has created only two scenes, one of which has only ten lines and is hardly more than the articulation of narrative facts from *TR*, and one other, also relatively short (44 lines). Furthermore, except for some shuffling of chronology in the second half of the play, the order of scenes is almost identical in both plays. But the symmetrical structure outlined already suggests how strikingly economical Shakespeare's wrighting is. Of the earlier play's 22 scenes Shakespeare uses only 15 as scenes. He omits the Bastard's pursuit and killing of Austria (3, 6), Eleanor's capture and rescue (7, 8), the Bastard's ransacking of the monasteries (11), the nobles' oath of fealty to Louis (16) and Louis's agreement to withdraw from England (22). Furthermore, scenes 19 and 21 are so sparingly used as to also be effectively deleted. Both are mainly concerned with the poisoning of John by a monk, continuing the anti–Catholic thrust initiated in the earlier scene in which the Bastard discovered the monks' lechery and greed. Shakespeare retains only the essential narrative facts from the later scenes—the Bastard's report to John of the loss of his forces in the Wash and the poisoning and death of John. Clearly Shakespeare was concerned to remove as much as possible of the anti–Catholic material and to mute the sensationalism of *TR*. Equally economical is the deft rearrangement of scenes. By slightly altering the sequence of only two scenes and shifting slightly the chronology of narrative facts within scenes, Shakespeare has created—as we will see—a structure whose "contrivance" is subtle but thematically transformative, changing the narrative of John's reign from its virulent anti–Catholic dramatization in *TR* into a more nuanced and subtle pro–Catholic play.[22]

The focus of Shakespeare's symmetrical structure is the Peter of Pomfret incident in the central scene, 4.2, a focus further emphasized by the design of the scene itself, which replicates the overall symmetrical balance of the play:

4.2.132–59 Bastard and Peter of Pomfret with Ascension Day prediction.	
109–32 Messenger with news of French invasion and deaths of Eleanor and Constance.	159–76 Bastard's news of French invasion & nobles' anger.
44–105 Nobles ask for Arthur's release. Hubert with news of Arthur's "death."	181–248 Hubert prods John to accept responsibility for Arthur's "death."
1–43 John & nobles on re-coronation.	248–69 Hubert informs John that Arthur is alive.

With Arthur's "death," the various crises of the realm are precipitated in the three central episodes of the scene. News comes of the French invasion and the deaths of Eleanor and Constance; and the Bastard arrives with news of the "strangely fantasied" populace (144), Peter's prophecy and the nobles' anger. John's unstated means of regaining the nobles' trust when he sends the Bastard to them must be considered, in light of the structure, a ploy to evade the Bastard's implied question about Arthur's death, for it is only when John accepts his part in the "death" of Arthur that the fortunes of England appear to change again. After attempting to evade responsibility for Arthur's death for some 40 lines, John finally accepts that he had ordered his rival claimant killed. Only then does Hubert tell John that Arthur still lives. John immediately exclaims to Hubert, "O, haste thee to the peers" (260). With the "resurrection" of Arthur the rift in the kingdom admits of possible healing. Thus, the pairing of the first and last episodes of this keystone scene indicates the success of the earlier "failed" re-coronation. What the re-coronation could not accomplish the symmetrically reflective "undoing" of Arthur's murder promises to achieve.

The Peter of Pomfret incident is thus the keystone of *King John*, positioned at the center of the central scene of the play. It is an odd focus. Most critics ignore it. The incident is almost completely irrelevant to the narrative and is sometimes deleted in performance, an excision that Braunmuller, for one, finds "more effective" than the uncut version because the incident is also "dramaturgically clumsy," interfering with the conversation between Hubert and John.[23] Why does such an unlikely incident occupy the most important structural position in the play?

Most obviously, Peter's prophecy refers to the sun, the traditional image of kingship. Compared to, say, *Richard II*, the sun imagery seems to have little importance in *King John*. Tillyard, for example, after noting how little sun imagery there is, says it is given a "new, ironic turn" for it is used merely in Act Five to indicate John's decline into sickness and death (218).[24] But few though they are, the sun images are arranged so as to gain significance by virtue of their place in the thematic arch, extending the keystone emphasis anticipating John's re-coronation by Pandulph. (The following outline merely positions the sun images; the commentary provides full quotes. A solid horizontal line in this and in subsequent outlines indicates the absence of relevant imagery.)

	4.2 "eye of heaven."
	Ascension Day at noon.
4.1 _____	4.3 _____
3.4 _____	5.1 Ascension Day at noon (3x).
XXX	XXX
3.3 John wishes the sun away.	5.2 _____
3.2 _____	5.3 _____
3.1 "the sun ... plays the alchemist." Constance prays: "ere sunset Set armed discord 'twixt these ... kings." "the sun's o'ercast with blood."	5.4 [Louis:] no "daybreak" for nobles. "day-wearied sun."
[2.1.300–599] "yon green boy [Arthur] shall have no sun to ripe [his] bloom." Louis's shadow "becomes a sun."	5.5 Louis: "the sun was loath to set."
[2.1.1–299] _____	5.6 "the black brow of night."
1.1 [day and night.]	5.7 [implied morning.]

The sun imagery is arranged in the same paired pattern as actions already considered. In the central scene the sun is explicitly compared to kingship, as it is in the same position though much more emphatically in *Richard II*. John's re-coronation, Salisbury says, is as taper light to the sun, "the eye of heaven" (4.2.14–15), establishing the sun as the symbol of monarchy, as in all the history plays, and additionally suggesting an all-seeing divinity. In Peter's prophecy of "Ascension Day at noon," John's loss of the crown is announced explicitly and his re-coronation hinted symbolically. In the cross-related pattern of 3.3 and 5.1, John's wooing of Hubert to kill Arthur renounces the crown in renouncing the sun:

> The sun is in the heaven and the proud day
> Attended with the pleasures of the world
> Is all too wanton and too full of gauds
> To give me audience [34–37].

It is only at an imagined "midnight bell," "in despite of brooded watchful day" (37, 52),[25] that John makes his proposition, lapsing from true majesty by the intended homicide. The re-coronation of John by Pandulph in the cross-related scene, 5.1, the submission of the English crown to the Papacy, occurs when the solar symbol of monarchy is at its height. The clear implication is that true majesty is attained by submitting the English crown to Papal authority, an implication confirmed by Shakespeare's handling of his source.

Shakespeare slightly rearranges some of the episodes in his source so that at the moment John yields his crown to Pandulph and is re-coronated by him John's conscience is clear and his will is unforced. At the time of his submission to Pandulph in *TR*, John has already been informed of Arthur's death, of the crowning of Louis, and of the advance of the rebellious nobles at Pandulph's prodding. John's attempt to dissemble with Pandulph has failed as well, and John then defiantly decides not to submit to the Pope. But at that moment news arrives of the imminence of the enemy forces, including the nobles, confirming that the Bastard's attempt at reconciliation has also failed. John has run out of options; he is forced to surrender the crown to Pandulph (not dramatized) and to receive it back from him. The sequence is clearly designed to mitigate John's responsibility for accepting Papal power, to effectively invalidate the coronation by Pandulph and to preserve John's image as a Protestant martyr. In *King John*, by contrast, John thinks that Arthur is alive and that Hubert's embassy to the nobles will therefore succeed; Louis's attack, should it come, would be meet by the full force of John's loyal followers. John's submission is not coerced but is, as he says, "voluntary" (5.1.29). Reminded that it is Ascension Day, John recalls Peter's prophecy (departing from *TR*) that he would give up the crown and muses, "I did suppose it would be on constraint, But, heaven be thanked, it is but voluntary" (5.1.28–29). With a clear conscience and an uncoerced will, he surrenders his crown to Pandulph and is re-coronated by the Papal representative. John's crown is "spiritually" validated, legitimizing its lineal descent to Henry.

Critics often question John's comment that his submission to Pandulph is voluntary. Honigmann calls it a "nominal submission" and attributes the use of the word "voluntary" to its appearance in the same narrative place in the *Chronicles*.[26] Braunmuller says of the lines just quoted: "An ironic comment, since John has been constrained by the French invasion and earlier (3.1.155–58) regarded his relation with heaven as requiring no mediation."[27] As I've said, without the support of the rebellious English nobles the French threat is greatly diminished and is certainly not determinative. As to John's idea of his relation to heaven, it changes in distinct stages through the course of the play.

John begins as a conscienceless political figure for whom "strong possession" is paramount; he ends enfeebled and tormented by his conscience.[28] The awakening and refinement of a conscience in the king is accomplished almost invisibly, by a series of actions often considered puzzling but which are clear in the full arc of John's career. After breaking from the guidance of the Roman church (when John makes the comment Braunmuller alludes to), John orders Arthur's murder and subsequently—to restore the felt loss of majesty—his own re-coronation. When the nobles nevertheless bolt at suspicion of Arthur's death, John "repent[s]" (4.2.103) the homicide (which he thinks accomplished) but only for purely political reasons, as his subsequent conversation with Hubert demonstrates. Finally admitting his guilt at Hubert's insistence, John articulates the essential dynamic of the play, the familiar connection between the conscience of the king and the temporal condition of the country:

> ... in the body of this fleshly land,
> This kingdom, this confine of blood and breath,
> Hostility and civil tumult reigns
> Between my conscience and my cousin's death [4.2.245–48].

Having awakened the king's conscience, Hubert then tells him that Arthur is alive. Thinking himself blameless, granted a reprieve of conscience, John expects that the political health of the country will be restored as well, that the nobles will resume their allegiance to him. In this state of mind, with a clear conscience and the expectation of restored political integrity, John gives up the crown to Pandulph and is re-coronated. Almost immediately the Bastard enters with news of Arthur's death, and John collapses, now understanding that he cannot escape the consequences of his intended homicide. His political and military might continue to crumble; his debility worsens, expressed in fever. At his son's urging, he manages a single Christian act, forgiving the nobles, and dies in the conviction that the intended homicide condemns his soul to hell—his now exquisite conscience accepting the doctrinal Christian belief that intentions are as damning as actions. (In *TR* the dying John says explicitly that "I must be damned for Arthur's sodaine death" [II, 1051].) So when, in the lines Braunmuller refers to, John repudiates mediation—"that great supremacy Where we do reign, we will alone uphold" (3.1.156–57)—he is expressing a defiance of the Church that is long behind him. There is no unintentional irony on John's part in saying that his re-coronation is voluntary, though there is certainly dramatic irony, for the audience knows that Arthur is dead and that the nobles have sworn allegiance to Louis and will learn subsequently that Pandulph is powerless to stop Louis's invasion. Nevertheless, when John is crowned by Pandulph, when the sun is at its height on Ascension Day at noon, John becomes a divinely ordained monarch with a clear conscience and the fitting submission of his power to the spiritual authority of the Catholic Church.

The remaining sun images are extended, as appropriate, to the other claimants to the throne. The sun imagery is never explicitly associated with the rightful kings, Arthur and Henry. Rather the pattern is initiated by Eleanor's insistence that "yon green boy [Arthur] shall have *no sun* to ripe The bloom that promiseth a mighty fruit" (2.1.473–74, italics added); this is true throughout the play since Arthur never ascends the throne, while Henry, not yet crowned, is accepted as John's successor in the merely implied morning of the last scene. It is Louis who is associated with the sun in the paired scenes of contestation, [2.1.300–599]-5.5 and 3.1–5.4. The association is complex and carefully hedged but unmistakable in the lines coming shortly after Eleanor's plan to deny Arthur the sun, when Louis says to his father of Blanche,

> The shadow of my self formed in her eye,
> Which, being but the shadow of your son,
> Becomes a sun and makes your son a shadow [499–501].

The various puns on son/sun and the various denotations of "shadow" create multiple meanings here, but Louis is certainly, in his anticipated marriage to Blanche, anticipating some new, enhanced and—the imagery suggests—regal stature in having a portion of John's territories, though it is notably the "shadow self" of the false claimant that "becomes a sun." As though conscious of Shakespeare's pattern, Louis in the paired scene, while celebrating the military advantage that will momentarily be dashed, uses sun imagery in a manner so as to suggest his reluctance to leave the field: "The sun was loath to set" (5.5.1).

The outline further demonstrates that the terse references to the sun in the later scenes are amplified by the mirroring use of the sun images in early scenes. Melun tells the nobles that Louis is "forsworn if e'er those eyes of yours Behold another day break in the east" (5.4.31–2). That daybreak arrives in the last scene with the ascension of Henry, which the nobles, of course, witness. The clipped news of a new king is thus linked to the much fuller response of Philip at the wedding of his son in the paired scene:

> To solemnize this day the glorious sun
> Stays in his course and plays the alchemist,
> Turning with splendor of his precious eye
> The meagre cloddy earth to glittering gold [3.1.77–80].

As Henry is to give shape to the "indigest" left by John (5.7.26), so too the new king will transmute the "clod" and "clay" of John's remains (5.7.57, 69). Henry fulfills Louis's failed aspiration. Finally the wearily setting sun, as Tillyard suggests, signals the end of John's reign; the end looks back to the beginning, the paired scene, 3.1, in which Constance and Blanche anticipate the coming struggle in sun imagery (110, 326). In general, the action of the play is reinforced by solar references appropriate to each stage of the plot. The three central scenes establish the ideal of kingship, the section of cross-related pairs expresses John's loss of the crown and his legitimate re-coronation by Pandulph, and the section of contestation traces Louis's attempt to displace John, while it also hints at the ascension of Henry III. Peter of Pomfret's prophetic invocation of Ascension Day at noon is fittingly positioned as the keystone both of the deft, subtle patterning of sun imagery and of the symmetrically reflecting actions issuing in the legitimate temporal and spiritual succession of Henry III.

Peter's prophecy, however, also connects with a much more evident and pervasive image pattern in the play—that of the body. Caroline Spurgeon has demonstrated that "the dominating symbol ... is the body and bodily action" and that "it is impossible ... entirely to separate images of body and bodily action from those of personification," a figure which constitutes by far the largest number of "images" in this play and exceeds that of any other in the canon. Indeed, the body references seem to recur almost obsessively, in large and small ways, from the preoccupation with the Bastard's bodily resemblance to his biological father in the first scene to the many "almost continuous" "little vignettes" involving bodily action, such as the Bastard's sketch of "that smooth-faced gentleman, tickling Commodity" (2.1.574).[29] This insistence on the body has an obvious connection to "the old commonplace of the identity of king and country."[30] But it is further associated with Peter's keystone reference to the bodily ascension of Christ into heaven, for Arthur, as the legitimate king, is "incorporated"—the food-related imagery insists on the etymology of the word—into England, as a land, a people and a new king who "ascends" the throne.

The following outline locates by means of abbreviated quotes the food and feeding imagery—the means of Arthur's incorporation into the "body" of England—on the symmetrical structure.

4.2 "sweet child's [Arthur's] death" (81).
    "men's mouths are full" of news of French (161).
    "Arthur's death is common in their mouths" (187).
    "A smith with open mouth swallowing a tailor's
    news" of Arthur's death (195).

4.1 _____	4.3 "ruin of [Arthur's] sweet life" (66). "sweet life's loss" (106). "slaughterhouse" (111). "sweet breath" of Arthur (136). "morsel of dead royalty" (143). dog feeding on "bones of majesty" (148 ff.).
3.4 "Now will canker-sorrow eat my bud" Arthur (82). Constance: Arthur is "my food" (104). "spoiled the sweet world's taste" (110).	5.1 "Flesh his [Louis's] spirit in warlike soil" of England (71).
3.3 John: "fat ribs of peace [must] be fed upon" (9).	5.2 Louis and nobles "took the sacrament" to confirm oath against John (6). Louis dismisses "feasts Full warm" in persuading Salisbury to revolt (58–9). "feed this fire" (85). "jaws of death" (116). "sweet safety" (142). "bare-ribbed death ... to feast..." (177).
3.2 _____	5.3 _____
3.1 "fasting tiger" John (26). "most sweet lout" Austria (220). "feast with slaughtered men" (302).	5.4 _____
[2.1.300–599] Death feasts... (352 ff.).	5.5 _____
[2.1.1–299] "fig" as poison to Arthur (162).	5.6 "sweet sir," Hubert of Bastard. "king poisoned" (43). "Who did taste to him?" "A monk... Whose bowels ... burst." (28–30). "Washes devoured them" (41).
1.1 Mocked "mess ... sweet sir ... sweet, sweet, sweet poison..." (190–216). "Sir Robert may have eat ... his part in me ... and ne'er broke his fast" (233–34).	5.7 "Death having preyed..." (15). John leaves "indigest" (26). John "ill fare" (34). "icy fingers in my maw" (37). Bastard's army "Devoured by the ... flood" (64). Henry's "sweet self" (101).

The prevalent image is of death feeding on men generally (2.1.352, 3.1.302, 5.2.116, 177, 5.7.15), but it is Arthur who is specifically and repeatedly imaged as "sweet" and wholesome food, figuratively ingested (3.4.104, 4.2.81, 4.3.66, 106, 136). He is first described as "sweet" in the keystone scene, when the nobles suspect the "sweet child's death" at the hands of Hubert (4.4.81). As the same suspicion spreads throughout the kingdom, words, both spoken and heard, become a means of incorporation. Arthur is "common in the mouths" of the tradesmen, "swallowing" the news of his rumored death (4.2. 187, 197). After his actual death in the next scene, 4.3, he is referred to by the Bastard as a "morsel" (143); associations of sweetness are repeated three times, and the site of his death is referred to by Salisbury as a "slaughterhouse"

(111). That is, the central scene and the following scene use feeding imagery to record metaphorically Arthur's incorporation into the imaginations of the commoners—who are not then any more "strangely fantasied" than Peter of Pomfret (4.2.144)—and into the political and historical awareness of the aristocracy.

The next section (3.3, 3.4, 5.1 and 5.2) emphasizes that John and Louis are both predatory feeders, in contrast to Arthur who, again in the paired scene 3.4, is ingested. John will feed on the "fat ribs of peace" (3.3.9); Louis will flesh his spirit in the soil of England (5.1.71)—which has become identified with Arthur himself in the preceding scene—will blasphemously take the sacrament as a pledge of regicide and will dismiss "feasts [f]ull warm" (5.2.58–9) for, presumably, a "feast with slaughtered men" (3.1.302). It is ironically fitting that in scene 5.6 the feeder John should suffer poisoning, since his mother's offer to Arthur in the paired scene ([2.1.1–299]) is, according to Constance, a "fig," figuratively poison (2.1.162). To the end John wishes to devour voraciously. Feverishly dying and disseuered from his kingdom, he wants "winter to thrust his icy fingers in my maw" and England's rivers to "take their course through my burned bosom" (5.7.39–42). The play's final imagistic comment on John further insists on his difference from the "sweet" ingested Arthur; John is "ill fare," and leaves "indigest" (5.7.26, 34).

The ingestion of Arthur as food figures his spiritual influence not only on the commoners but on Hubert, John (via Hubert), the Bastard, the nobles (via Hubert and Melun) and, we are to understand, Prince Henry. Arthur awakens Hubert's conscience in 4.1; Hubert in turn awakens the king's conscience in 4.2; the dead Arthur, "all England," inspires the Bastard to his "thousand businesses" (4.3.142, 158); partly out of love for Hubert, Melun informs the nobles of Louis's treachery; and finally, as the embodiment of the right and conscience that Arthur represents in the play, Prince Henry requests of the dying John forgiveness for the nobles (5.7.34–5). The ever-widening process of Arthur's incorporation into the land and people of England, the incorporation of the "morsel" that is "the life, the right, the truth of all this realm," is fulfilled in the ascension of Henry III (4.2.143–44).

Between the extremes of the ingested Arthur and the ingesting John is the Bastard. He begins at risk of becoming like John, a feeder who is himself corrupt food. He introduces the play's food imagery in the first scene, as, newly knighted, he mockingly imagines "my Worship's mess.'" "When my knightly stomach is sufficed," he says, he will "catechize" a pretentious traveler, a "sweet sir," in the empty "dialogue of compliment." However hypocritical such customs may be, the Bastard concludes that he must "deliver / Sweet, sweet, sweet poison for the age's tooth" (1.1.190–216). This is obviously not a "feast [f]ull warm." The Bastard's profound mistrust of the social order is epitomized in his sardonic eating and the "sweet poison" he plans to deliver. He is here allied both with the monk who poisons the king and the king himself as narcissistic feeder and as "ill fare" (5.7.34). But in the course of the play the Bastard is transformed by his travels through England, the death of Arthur and his own narrow escape from death in the Washes. He experiences how the unsettled populace, the revolted nobles, and the French invasion collectively threaten the social order to its foundations. Understanding at the sight of Arthur's body, "the morsel of dead royalty," that "the life, the right, the truth of all this realm Is fled to heaven," *ascended* to heaven, we might say, the Bastard begins his "thousand businesses" to save England, the social order he finally compares to the Ptolemaic universe (5.7.78). By the end of the play, the Bastard is not "sweet poison" any longer but is simply "sweet sir," in Hubert's vocative (5.6.19), and is thus allied with Arthur and recognizes in

Henry's "sweet self" the "lineal state" of legitimate dynastic succession. Unlike Arthur though, the Bastard is not incorporated into England—neither Sir Robert initially nor the flood finally will "eat" or "devour" him (1.1.233; 5.7.64); he maintains his integrity. He is also unlike John, for the Bastard will not narcissistically incorporate England into himself: he continues to serve a king he knows to be corrupt, acting courageously against Louis in spite of private misgivings, finally assuaged in service to Henry. Nor will he allow "invasive" attacks, the kind of violation imaged before Angiers as rape: his early shield of sarcasm against official rhetoric preserves his personal integrity, as his later determination—the fruit of a more capacious identity—to push "destruction and perpetual shame Out of the weak door of our fainting land" preserves a political territory (5.7.77–78). This bodily imagery extending from the individual body to the body politic and the body of the land allusively charges the Bastard's platitudinous speech ending the play:

> This England never did, nor never shall,
> Lie at the proud foot of a conqueror
> But when it first did help to wound itself [5.7.112–15].

Whatever the threats against them, Arthur literally and John in conscience "wounded" themselves to death. Because the Bastard has maintained and extended his own integrity, he can meaningfully, if not quite convincingly, articulate the proverbial integrity of England.

In fact, in the dark night after John's and Louis's sun has set, it is the Bastard and Hubert, the representatives of John and Arthur respectively, the arm and the conscience of England, who metaphorically uphold the realm, re-uniting it in re-establishing their identities in the questions opening the penultimate scene, 5.6, and in the news of spiritual and temporal reconciliation that Hubert brings. In entrusting to the Bastard and Hubert—both radically transformed from their original characters—a mutual recognition and muted reconciliation in the night, the scene ironically ends the action initiated in the paired scene ([2.1.1–299]), in which the struggle for the crown begins between the more obvious claimants, none of whom prevail:

[2.1.1–299] In Arthur's name Philip claims John's lands (150–54). *Arthur forgives Austria for Richard's murder.*	5.6 Hubert tells Bastard that the nobles have returned and that John has been poisoned (23 of 44). *At Henry's urging, John pardons the nobles.*

In the central incidents of this scene pair, the struggle for political power begins with two opposing armies confronting each other and ends with two benighted and uncertain characters, both prominently changed during the course of the play, who embody the reintegration of possession and right, of temporal and spiritual power in England.

This penultimate scene is particularly interesting not only because it is virtually the only scene of Shakespeare's devising in *King John* but also because in function and technique it accords with other penultimate scenes in the canon. In the previous chapter we have seen the same mirroring technique in scene 5.4 of *Julius Caesar* in which a similar reconciliation occurs between Antony and Lucilius, representatives of Caesar and Brutus, of Caesarism and republicanism, respectively.

The mirroring actions, the ironic reflection, the personal reconciliation epitomizing the larger political harmony—these are elements common to the penultimate scenes of both *King John* and *Julius Caesar*. In Folio *Measure for Measure* as well a reconciliation occurs in a short penultimate scene, though of a psychological rather than political nature.

1.2. Mistress Overdone with news of Claudio's arrest as fornicator.	4.6 Isabella, taking Mariana's "part," to "speak indirectly" against Angelo as fornicator (15).

In substituting for Mariana and claiming to have been seduced by Angelo and in (ironically) reflecting the action of Mistress Overdone in the paired scene,[31] the novice Isabella is clearly becoming reconciled to her own sexuality. It appears, then, that at least one of the last scenes of *King John* is characteristic of Shakespeare's usual practice and is no more rushed or abbreviated than those of some other plays. Short scenes of personal reconciliation epitomize and foreshadow the ceremonious public resolution that invariably (excepting *Troilus and Cressida*) ends the plays and also reflect actions in the chiastically paired second scenes. However understated, such scenes are thematically crucial.

In the case of *King John* at least, it seems that a solely verbal analysis does not fully encompass Shakespeare's art. The importance of Peter of Pomfret's prophecy and of the sun imagery are easily overlooked unless "read" positionally, as focused in the keystone episode and developed in chiastically reflecting scenes. The action and the imagery are configured in a meaningful spatial syntax. A plot that appears episodic, halting and derivative when viewed with ordinary narrative expectations of temporal sequencing turns out to be designed more fundamentally as a patterned arrangement of Shakespeare's characteristic thematic mirrorings. The action is spatially coherent and symmetrically balanced. The imagery is appropriately linked to the evolving action by its disposition on the arch-like construction. Seen on its own structural and thematic terms, the wrighting of *King John* is no less subtle and expressive than the poetry.

9

Henry IV
The Structural Similarity of Parts One and Two

In the Riverside introduction to *Henry IV*, Herschel Baker succinctly states the range of opinion regarding the relationship of its two parts:

> The precise connection between the two parts of *Henry IV* has long been and is likely to remain a matter of dispute. Although Johnson, with characteristic bluntness, said that the two plays are separated "only because they are too long to be one," modern scholars find the problem more complex. R. A. Law and M. A. Shaaber, for example, have argued strongly that neither in intention nor in design can the two parts be said to be connected; Harold Jenkins has suggested that Part 2 took shape in Shakespeare's mind while he composed Part 1, which was therefore altered to accommodate the new addition; E. M. W. Tillyard, J. Dover Wilson, and A. R. Humphreys have tried to show that the two plays, conceived and written as a unit, are so intimately related in action, characters and theme that neither can be fully understood without the other.[1]

These different views must be parsed more carefully than Baker finds necessary. In saying that the two plays are effectively "one," Johnson means only that Part Two is a "sequel" to Part One, for he did not hold Shakespeare's histories to any rigorous rule of unity:

> "His [Shakespeare's] histories, being neither tragedies nor comedies, are not subject to any of their laws; nothing more is necessary to all the praise which they expect than that the changes of action be so prepared as to be understood, that the incidents be various and affecting, and the characters consistent and distinct. No other unity is intended and therefore none is to be sought."[2]

Johnson is not to be taken, then, as holding the same view as Tillyard, Wilson or Humphreys but merely as asserting the obvious fact that the second play can conveniently be described as a sequel to the first. Wilson and Tillyard take the far more extreme position that *Henry IV* cannot be properly understood except as a ten-act unit, a single play, while A. R. Humphreys concludes after measured consideration, that "Shakespeare intended two plays from the outset, or very near it."[3] At the other extreme are those critics like M. A. Shaaber, who think that a second play was far from Shakespeare's mind as he composed *Henry IV*, and only after its success did the playwright return to the subject.[4]

The only evidence we have, the plays themselves, suggests to me that Humphreys' assessment is correct, that Shakespeare intended two separate plays from the time he first took up the subject of Hal's education. The "whole story" contained in the sources extends to Hal's coronation, and the fact that Part One ends with the battle of Shrewsbury indicates a craftsman's practiced eye for well-proportioned material. As Humphreys reminds us, Part One looks forward to the ascension of Henry V, to Falstaff's banishment, to further hostilities and to the further development of some characters, yet without requiring these events to conclude the action. In addition to these general narrative and characterological links the similar formal characteristics of the plays also suggest a diptych, to use G. K. Hunter's word of their relationship.[5] Both Hunter and Shaaber have explored these similarities, pointing out the types of incidents from Part One that recur in Part Two in the same order, quiet domestic scenes followed by scenes of tavern revelry, for example, and comparing the similar mix in the sequence of historical and comic scenes. The disposition of the source material and the formal similarities of Parts One and Two suggest, again, two plays intended from the outset.

My analysis extends the observations of formal similarities to a more abstract level, for their chiastic designs demonstrate that the plays are a uniquely matching pair. The fundamental and unique similarity between the two parts of *Henry IV* is that they have the same number of scenes, grouped in the same paired arrangement. None of Shakespeare's other mature plays has this degree of similarity in structure. The two plays also have matching keystone scenes, both of which epitomize the problems—different though they are—of state and succession in King Henry's dialogue. These similarities of scene arrangement and keystone scenes heighten the slightly different developments of the double plots, emphasizing and clarifying Hal's rejection of Falstaff in Part Two in a way that suggests purposeful parallels.

The usual editorial problems of scene designation have inflated the number of scenes in both plays. In the Riverside edition, as in most modern editions, both plays contain nineteen scenes, although Part Two also contains what is usually designated an Induction. In fact, though, as I will demonstrate, both plays contain 17 scenes, and what is considered an Induction by modern editors is, as in the Folio, simply the first scene of Part Two. Except for one change to the scene designations of the battle sequence in Part One, the Folio divisions of both plays should be retained.

The Folio divides Part One into 18 scenes, with the final battle sequence occupying three scenes. Capell further divided the battle sequence into four scenes, and his division has become traditional, although it is generally recognized to be incorrect. (See, for example, Humphreys' note on 5.3.) The division at scene 5.5 (Riverside; 5.4 Folio) is also incorrect. It is not only the symmetry of the play but the structure of the new scene that confirms Shakespeare's intention here. At the center of Folio [5.3–5.4] is Hal's soliloquy over the prone Falstaff and the extraordinary moment when "Falstaff riseth up" (SD 110 of 209). If any dramatic moment in Shakespeare deserves a central place in its scene, it is certainly this one. An argument might be made for the division at Riverside 5.5 because of the ending this provides for scene 5.4, Falstaff carrying off the body of Hotspur. A scene break might seem appropriate both as emphasizing this final appearance of Falstaff in the play and as a conclusive action for the scene itself (though Shakespeare rarely makes the ends of scenes emphatic). But Falstaff is, in effect, simply doing the kind of stage clearing necessary and familiar in most battle scenes, when a character exits bearing off a body; we don't have to go so far as to say that Falstaff disappears into the metatheatrical to appreciate his exit's recalling a bit of common stage management which is both folded into the larger action of the encompassing scene and emphatically central to it. The reflecting speeches by Henry and Hal in the first and last scenes (1.1 and

[5.3 & 5.4]), summing up the altered positions of Hal and Hotspur, also suggest, again, a thematic scene division. In sum, the battle in Act Five occupies only two scenes; Act Five has only three scenes, and the play has 17 scenes, one less than the Folio indicates. The outline, the skeletal author-plot, of Part One thus looks like this:

	3.1 Hal to his father: "I shall hereafter ... be more myself."

3.1 Hotspur quarrels with Glendower; squabbles with Lady Percy.	3.3 Falstaff humorously quarrels with Hal; and squabbles with Hostess.
2.4 Falstaff tells of fighting two ... four ... seven ... 11 assailants.	4.1 Hotspur undeterred by odds against his forces.
2.3 Hotspur defends the quality of his plot and his troops.	4.2 Falstaff "ashamed" of his ragged soldiers.
2.2 Falstaff robs and is robbed.	4.3 Hotspur on Henry as an outlaw who has robbed the crown.
2.1 Gadshill informed of his marks and boasts of his cohorts.	4.4 Archbishop & Sir Michael debate rebels' chances.
1.3 Hotspur is told that Mortimer was named heir to throne. The rebellion is initiated. (Hotspur on honor.)	5.1 Henry offers rebels pardon. (Falstaff on honor.)
1.2 Hal counterfeits riotous behavior in tavern. (Falstaff's time.)	5.2 Henry's counterfeit, Blunt killed. (Hotspur on time.)
1.1 Henry praises Hotspur and denigrates Hal.	[5.3 & 5.4] Hal eulogizes Hotspur and Falstaff.

The play is structured in three main sections. The two central scenes in each half of the play (2.1 & 2.2, 4.3 & 4.4) are devoted to the Gadshill robberies and the robberies of the crown; the pairing of 2.2 and 4.3 and of 2.1 and 4.4 structurally embeds the fundamental similarity of the comic and historical plots: the robber Falstaff robbed by Hal and the robber Henry robbed by Hotspur, in attempt, at any rate. The two three-pair sections link Falstaff and Hotspur. In the central section (2.3 through 3.1 and 3.3 through 4.2) they deliver analogous speeches on their troops and on fighting generally. In the opening and closing scenes they deliver rhetorical set pieces on time and honor, while the larger action of the scenes is devoted to other character comparisons: between Henry IV and Hotspur (1.3–5.1), and between Henry and Hal.(1.2 and 5.2). The play is fundamentally structured, then, around the contrast between the two characters who threaten the succession of Hal—Hotspur and Falstaff. The world of the court and the world of the tavern alternate sequentially as the play unfolds, while the structural pairing, scene by scene, of Falstaff and Hotspur allows a point-for-point comparison between the extremes of comic detachment and tragic self-absorption. Temporally and spatially, Hal moves between the two worlds. His transformation occurs in a single sentence in the middle of the central scene, when he says to his father: "I shall hereafter ... be more myself" (3.2.92–3 of 180). At this point he changes his relationship with Falstaff, a change signaled by the humorous quarrel in the next scene, and enters the chivalrous, military world of Hotspur.

The number and arrangement of scenes in Part Two is identical to that of Part One. Part Two is accurately divided in the Folio, but traditional and modern editors change the battle sequence in F 4.1 into three scenes and of F 4.2, in which the King changes location, into two scenes. Neither of these divisions is justified. The action is perfectly clear in the battle sequence, and there is no reason to override the Elizabethan convention. Furthermore, the thematic unity of the Folio scene is apparent by virtue of its contrast with the paired scene in which Hotspur's courageous action in battle is praised by his widow (2.3). The rebels, Falstaff and, most obviously, Prince John, on the other hand, all consider battle a matter of mere words, preferably deceitful words. The break between the traditional 4.4 and 4.5 (F 4.2) is also wrong. As Humphreys argues, the change of location should be indicated by lights, curtains or some other means short of interrupting the King's speech by taking him off and on again.[6] Thus the outline of Folio *Henry IV* Part Two:

3.1 Sick king momentarily despairs: "The happiest youth…"	

2.4 Tavern: Falstaff a hero in thrusting out Pistol.	3.2 Country: Falstaff a hero, a knight come to recruit.
2.3 Hotspur's valor & chivalry praised by Lady Percy.	4.1 [4.2 & 4.3] Gaultree Forest: war as mere words in rebels, John & Falstaff.
2.2 Hal and Poins plan to disguise themselves & visit "sick" Falstaff.	4.2 [4.3] Hal visits sick king, takes crown.

2.1 Chief Justice holds Falstaff liable for debt to Hostess.	5.1 Shallow lets Visor off at Davy's request.
1.3 Archbishop on Henry IV and the sick commonwealth.	5.2 Chief Justice on Henry IV as the image of law. Hal on the "great body of the state."

1.2 Falstaff told he'll be healed by the punishment imposed by Chief Justice.	5.3 Falstaff corrupts Shallow and threatens Chief Justice.
1.1 Northumberland: "Let order die!" "Shadows and shows of men."	5.4 Beadle arrests Hostess and Doll, who claims to be pregnant, for murder.
Induction. Rumor ("full of tongues"): Hal and Henry dead.	5.5 Henry V's coronation. Falstaff ("womb" of "tongues") rejected.

The play is pervasively concerned with what Hal calls toward the end of the action, when law and justice have been reasserted (if not yet completely re-established) "the great body of our state" (5.2.136), a body which, in the paired scene, the rebels refer to as the "sick" "commonwealth" (1.3.87). Symbolically, the King and Falstaff compete to make this body his own. Both sick, as the pairing of 2.2 and 4.2 indicates, the King attempts to cure it; Falstaff intends to spread the disease, to become the virtual king of a land of lawlessness. Hearing that Henry IV is dead, Falstaff says, "I know the young King is sick for me.… [T]he laws of England are at my commandment" (5.3.131–33). The structure expresses this threat from Falstaff in the two central flanking scenes. In Part One the keystone scene of the King's interview with Hal (3.2) is flanked on the one hand by a scene of the rebels (3.1) and on the other hand by a scene of Falstaff (3.3), the two dangers facing the kingdom; at the center of Part Two the diseased King is flanked on both sides by the bloated body of Falstaff (2.4, 3.2). He has come to represent the more proximate, if symbolic, threat to the King and kingdom. The overfed coward who thrusts Pistol out of the tavern (2.4) remains comic, but he nevertheless darkens what in *1 Henry IV* was hardly more than mischief, for Falstaff is now regarded as a hero; his values are coming to prevail. Traveling as a recruiter (3.2), he extends his bombast heroism beyond the tavern to the country, finally corrupting what precarious law exists there, in the person of Justice Shallow. All of the bodies of the play—the body of the King, the body of Falstaff, the body politic—are disordered.

Parts One and Two both arrange threats to the kingdom—the robberies and the attacks on law itself—at the center of each of their two movements. In the two mid-movement pairs of Part Two (1.3–5.2 and 2.1–5.1), the Chief Justice upholds the law against Falstaff and against Hal, that is, against both segments of society represented in the play. Justice prevails with Hal, but the movement of the play continues the corruption of the comic world almost to the last moment, to scenes 5.3 and 5.4. So, although the rebellious anarchy threatened in 1.3 has been overcome by the accord of Hal and the Chief Justice in the paired 5.2, Shallow betrays his office in 5.1; the upbraiding Falstaff received from the Chief Justice in 2.1 has not stemmed the riotous knight's influence. The four scenes thus enact a delicate imbalance of law and disorder.

The two other sections of Part Two differ in their internal organization from the simpler arrangement of Part One, comparing Falstaff and Hotspur. In Part Two the scene tercets are organized by the order of their subjects: Falstaff (1.2–5.3 and 2.4–3.2), anarchy/order (1.1–5.4 and 2.3–4.1) and Hal (Ind.-5.5 and 2.2–4.2). This arrangement keeps Hal and Falstaff mostly separate even at the structural level, obviously because their interests are now so divergent. The increased subtlety of Part Two can be glimpsed in the anarchy/order pairs, in which the apparent contrasts are ironically undercut. The chivalric order Hotspur represents (2.3) makes the paired Gaultree battle (4.1) seem comparatively shabby, but Hotspur was, after all, a rebel, and the duplicitous promise of Prince John does restore the law of the state. And the brilliant comic disorder of the penultimate scene (5.4) is brought into high relief by the paired scene of grandiloquent rebellion (1.1). The Beadle brings order to a sick society, to an unreal city of murder and false pregnancies, to a state of "shadows and shows of men" (1.1.193). But he is an unusual healer: an almost emaciated memento mori—"Goodman Death, goodman Bones" (5.4.28). (The dynamic by which the comic plot is resolved is thus analogous to that of the serious plot, in which Hal willingly accepts the crown that feeds on its wearer.)

The keystone scene of Part Two (3.1), like that of Part One (3.2), epitomizes in the King the troubles of the realm. In the earlier play the problems are serious but simple: a military threat which, in the King's mind, recapitulates his own seizure of the crown and which, along with Hal's own behavior, threatens succession. In Part Two the threat is almost metaphysical, for the rebellion represents not a new order but complete disorder. Law itself is under siege in all classes of society. The kingdom, the very ground, is threatened with dissolution, which, in the King's mind, has now become the principle he reads in the "book of fate":

> [to] see the revolution of the times
> Make mountains level, and the continent,
> Weary of solid firmness, melt itself
> Into the sea, and other times to see
> The beachy girdle of the ocean
> Too wide for Neptune's hips [45–51].

This view expresses the King's disorder, his sickness, as the sickness of the state and country. He says of "the body of our kingdom": "what rank diseases grow … near the heart of it" (38–40). A related disorder, rumor, grotesquely imaged elsewhere in the play as issuing from Falstaff's "womb" full of "tongues" (4.3.22, 18), also contributes to the King's despondency because it inflates the number of his enemies (96–8). The disorders of Part Two, then, are more varied and encompassing than those of Part One and momentarily undo kingship itself. The "sun-like majesty" Henry invoked in Part One (3.2.79) is darkened by the night in which scene II.3.1 takes place; the "sumptuous feast" (3.2.58) to which Henry compared his presence and monarchical state has become the feast shared by Richard and Northumberland that did not stave off betrayal (II.3.1.57–60).

The muted turning point of the play is the King's change from despair to hope, from sleeplessness to rest, at the "good advice" and "counsel" of Warwick (43, 106), who functions in this scene much as Hal did in the central scene of Part One. Warwick counters Rumor's numbers with an accurate assessment of the enemy forces; re-establishes, against Henry's vision of watery dissolution, the King himself as "ground" (91); and politely suggests that Henry "go to bed" (99) to find relief from his sickness and sleeplessness. The King accedes and—as at this same point in Part One—the play's fortunes turn. But this turn is, as yet, only in spirit. As Hal's promise to his father to be more himself was not realized until the Battle of Shrewsbury ending Part One, so too the King's revivified spirit is not fully realized in the "great body of our state" until law is re-affirmed in 5.2, in the interview between Hal and the Chief Justice, and re-established in the final rejection of Falstaff at Hal's coronation. Unlike Part One, however, in which the action of both the serious and comic plots was resolved only in the final scene, Part Two stages the rebels' defeat at Gaultree earlier, allowing the more insidious anarchy of the comic plot to persist and to be gathered up in the "surfeit-swell'd" old man Hal finally and fully rejects (5.5.50).

Did Shakespeare originally envision extending the significance of Falstaff's bulk so pervasively through Part Two or plan from the outset the identical structural features of both plays? Such questions are unanswerable. When the connections between the two plays were conceived is of less importance than the fact that they indubitably exist. The plays have matching keystone scenes and scene groupings that locate the threats to the realm in exactly the same position, midway through the two halves of each play. The structural variations from one play to another—the different arrangements within the scene tercets, the different emphases of the central flanking scenes, the early resolution of the serious plot in Part Two—these variations gain in expressiveness and significance when the plays are paired and seen as an intentionally matched set.

The structure of the plays bears on three problems of composition. Harold Jenkins has argued that Shakespeare originally intended to compass the matter of both plays in a single work, but half way through, finding the material too extensive, changed his plan. This hypothesis is untenable, as is the wide-spread assumption from which it arises and which Jenkins explicitly states: "I do not of course mean to imply that *Henry IV*, or indeed any other of Shakespeare's plays, ever had a plan precisely laid down in advance. But it had to be supposed that when Shakespeare began a play he had some idea of the general direction it would take."[7] As though in fear of impugning the playwright's genius, critics shy from treating him as a craftsman. A precise plan is exactly what Shakespeare had. Everything that symmetry reveals about Shakespeare's compositional practice indicates that he formulated an author plot at a very early stage of designing a play. Even a glance at the symmetrical outline of Part One confirms not only the foundational reflecting actions of paired scenes but the intricate intertwining of every aspect of narrative, character and theme at the skeletal level. Consider any scene pair. It is evident that the later scene cannot be changed without changing the earlier. (The revision to the second scene of *Measure for Measure*, which retained the original action of proclaiming a fornicator while changing the speaker from Pompey to Mistress Overdone, suggests the constraints within which Shakespeare altered his author-plot.) Shakespeare did not begin with line one and write his plays sequentially; he constructed a symmetrical foundation of mirroring halves, carefully balancing the two movements of the play as he built up scene by scene.

A second problem concerns Part Two. Jowett and Taylor would conclude from the fact that 3.1 is missing from Qa and supplied by Qb that the scene was added after Shakespeare wrote the play, and they link this supposed addition to a conjectured revision which included other passages found in the Folio but not in Qa. They suppose that the scene, which at 108 lines would have occupied both sides of a single manuscript leaf, was intended to be added to the completed play by insertion somewhere into an already written sheet.[8] However, the design of the play leaves no doubt that the scene was intended from the outset, or at least from the time of the author-plot. It is the crucial keystone scene of this play, as a keystone scene is essential to every other mature play (excepting *The Winter's Tale*, discussed in a later chapter). The single manuscript leaf was simply overlooked or unavailable when Qa was set.

A final interesting textual point concerning Part Two. The Folio, though it contains scene 3.1, missing from Qa and supplied by Qb, does not contain the central three lines of the scene and of the play, 3.1.53–56 (of 108) on the "happiest youth." Wells and Taylor, like Samuel Johnson, find the lines to be illogical and digressive and speculate that Shakespeare cut them.[9] The lines certainly appear to intrude oddly into King Henry's lament on inconstancy:

> O God that one might read the book of fate
> And see the revolution of the times
> Make mountains level, and the continent,
> Weary of solid firmness, melt itself
> Into the sea, and other times to see
> The beachy girdle of the ocean
> Too wide for Neptune's hips; how chance's
> Mocks and changes fill the cup of alteration
> With divers liquors! O if this were seen,
> The happiest youth, viewing his progress through
> What perils past, what crosses to ensue,
> Would shut the book and sit him down and die.
> 'Tis not ten years gone
> Since Richard and Northumberland, great friends,
> Did feast together, and in two years after
> Were they at wars [45–60].

Without the sentence on the happiest youth the passage is uniformly pentameter and the sense flows smoothly, evidence for Wells's and Taylor's view. But, far from thinking that Shakespeare cut the lines, Humphreys, undisturbed by the putative illogic of the passage, thinks that "Qb preserves an addition to the original draft (perhaps inserted marginally) while the MS behind F at this point simply followed the original lines, overlooking the addition."[10]

Humphreys' conjecture is given weight by the central position of the lines in the play and the correspondence between them and the centrally located lines in *1 Henry IV*. The pivotal interview between Henry and Hal in Part One is in Part Two very faintly reprised by the addition of the three lines on the happiest youth. Henry's momentary despair extends to the thought of even an ideal youth—never mind his actual son—being similarly despondent. The issue of succession, which pervades the first play of the tetralogy, *Richard II*, is literally central to both succeeding plays. It is easy to imagine Shakespeare, having completed the central scene or perhaps even the whole play, casting an eye back over the correspondences between Parts One and Two and marginally adding the lines on the happiest youth. The elliptical echo is exactly in keeping with the structural and other correspondences between Parts One and Two and the more subtle effects of Part Two.

10

The Thematic Arch
of *The Merry Wives of Windsor*
Role-Playing

Though always popular on stage in shortened or musical versions, *The Merry Wives of Windsor* has not been much esteemed by critics, who find the construction of the play, especially in its subsidiary actions, loose almost to the point of incomprehension. "The conduct of this drama is deficient," Samuel Johnson pronounced; "the action begins and ends often before the conclusion, and the different parts might change places without inconvenience."[1] In the most recent Arden edition Giorgio Melchiori makes essentially the same charge: "Its overall structure is peculiarly uncertain, presenting a number of unnecessary side-scenes that break up and at times confuse the development of its plot or plots."[2] Directors agree and revise the play accordingly, performing what is structurally closer to the Quarto than the Folio version. The Quarto cuts five scenes and reverses the order of two remaining scenes, paring the play to more economically express the two intricate courtships that constitute the main actions. In one, the merry wives trick Falstaff and disabuse Mr. Ford of his misogynistic suspicions. In the second plot, Anne Page, courted by two arranged suitors, tricks her parents and marries her own choice of husband.

Among the frequent cuts is the scene in which William Page is quizzed on his Latin by Parson Evans, for William does not appear again (except as an unindividuated fairy in the Herne the Hunter theatrical) and the scene has no apparent connection to any other narrative, though its importance for the play's concern with language is clear. The four short scenes 5.1–5.4 are also often cut, as being, superficially at least, merely recapitulative. Among the other "confusions, inconsistencies and loose ends," critics find in the play are the unexplained tricking of the Host out of his horses and inn fees; the subsequent disappearance of the deer episode made so much of in the first scene; and Caius's challenge to Evans rather than to Slender, who is, after all, the rival for Anne Page's hand.[3]

Though the play seems structurally halting, it is constructed in Shakespeare's invariable pattern, symmetrically around the thematically crucial central scene, in this case the Falstaff-Brooke/Ford conversation in 3.5. The two-part structure of the play is blurred by the large number of speaking characters (22), the many intrigues and the unusual grouping of the scenes within the thematic structure, but the design is basically familiar. (In the following outline I have included a full summary rather than only reflecting actions, which are in bold face.)

3.5 Falstaff agrees once again to visit Mistress Ford and informs "Brook" of the **buck-basket** incident and of Falstaff's plans for another assignation. "Brook" resolves to be **"horn-mad."**

3.4 Attempting to court Anne Page, Fenton is interrupted first by his rival **Slender**, who **is quizzed on "will" by Anne**, and then by a hostile Master and Mistress Page.	4.1 **William**, the young son of Master and Mistress Page, **is quizzed on his Latin by Sir Hugh.**
3.3 As Falstaff joins Mistress Ford, Mistress Page enters with news that Ford is approaching. **Falstaff is tricked into climbing into a large laundry basket** and is hidden under dirty clothes and then carried out by servants who throw the basket's contents into the river. As Ford searches in vain for Falstaff, the women plot further revenge on both men.	4.2 Visiting Mistress Ford, **Falstaff is** again interrupted by Mrs. Page, again with news of Ford's threatening approach, and is thus **tricked into dressing as an old woman** hated by Ford. The disguise gains Falstaff a beating by Ford.
3.2 **Ford**, knowing of Falstaff's visit to Mistress Ford, gathers a group of men to go with him to his house, promising them fine entertainment there, for he **is self-deceived about Falstaff's entrapment, as he is about his wife's infidelity and Fenton's hopes.**	4.3 **Host is deceived into hiring out his horses** to some German visitors (accomplices in the plot of revenge against the Host by Dr. Caius and Sir Hugh).
3.1 Page, Shallow, and Slender join Sir Hugh, who is waiting to fight Dr. Caius. When the Host brings **Dr. Caius and Sir Hugh** together, the two, prevented from dueling and angry at being mocked, **reconcile in plotting revenge against the Host.**	4.4 **Mistress Page and Mistress Ford**, having disclosed their dealings with Falstaff to their husbands, conspire with them and Sir Hugh in a **plot to humiliate Falstaff** publicly that night at Windsor Forest. Master and Mistress Page each plan to take advantage of the occasion to marry their daughter to the suitor of their choice.
2.3 Dr. Caius responds furiously when Sir Hugh fails to meet him for their duel. **The Host mocks Caius and deceives him** into visiting Anne Page, away from meeting Sir Hugh.	4.5 **The Host learns that his horses have been stolen.** Mistress Quickly brings Falstaff another invitation, this time to meet Mistress Ford and Mistress Page.
2.2 **Ford enlists Falstaff to seduce Mistress Ford.** Ford plans to trap Falstaff with Mistress Ford.	4.6 **Fenton enlists the Host to arrange for Vicar to marry Fenton and Anne** that night.
2.1 The wives compare Falstaff letters they have received. **Pistol and Nym inform Ford and Page of Falstaff's designs on their wives.** Ford, as "Brook," plans to approach Falstaff.	5.1 **Falstaff**, having agreed to meet Mistress Page and Mistress Ford, **informs "Brook" of new assignation.**
1.4 Delivering Sir Hugh's letter to Mistress Quickly, **Simple** is discovered by Dr. Caius (another of Anne's suitors) and **tells Caius of Slender's suit**, Furious with Sir Hugh for interfering, Dr. Caius writes to Sir Hugh challenging him to a duel.	5.2 **Slender prepares to elope with Anne Page**, explaining the "nay-word" and Anne's white dress that will allow them to recognize one another.

1.3 Falstaff, in desperate need of funds, dismisses his servant Bardolph, who enters the employ of the Host of the Garter. **Falstaff plans to seduce Mistress Ford and Mistress Page** to gain access to their husbands' wealth. When Pistol and Nym refuse to act as his go-between, he dismisses them from his service. They plot revenge against him.	5.3 Dr. Caius waits to elope with Anne Page. **Mistress Page and Mistress Ford assess the plans for Falstaff's humiliation.**
1.2 **Sir Hugh sends** Slender's servant Simple with **a letter to Mistress Quickly, asking her to intercede with Anne Page on Slender's behalf.**	5.4 **Sir Hugh, disguised as a satyr,** and his "fairies" approach.
1.1 Justice Shallow and his nephew Slender accompany Sir Hugh the parson to the Page's home. There they meet Sir John Falstaff, whom Shallow accuses of killing his deer, while Slender accuses Falstaff's men of robbing him. Falstaff meets Mistress Ford and Mistress Page, and **Slender** clumsily **attempts to court Anne Page.**	5.5 Falstaff as Herne is tormented by the "fairies" and then publicly humiliated. Slender and Dr. Caius enter in turn to report that each has been deceived into eloping with a disguised boy instead of Anne Page. Finally **Fenton and Anne Page enter, married.** Fenton and Falstaff are forgiven, and the party moves to the home of Master and Mistress Page.

The central scene features Falstaff and Ford, disguised as Brook, each passionately embracing his fantasy of himself as, respectively, cuckolder and cuckold. In relating the buck-basket incident, Falstaff describes how he and Mrs. Ford "had embraced, kissed, protested, and, as it were, spoke the prologue of our comedy" before Ford crashed in on the intimate moment (3.5.69–70). Hearing Falstaff's account, Ford determines to "proclaim myself what I am"; "I'll be horn-mad" (133; 141). In his acceptance of a cuckold's horns in this scene (he has resisted until now), Ford becomes Actaeon, as Falstaff, in his ultimate disguise in the Herne the Hunter theatrical and here in the proleptic pun on "buck-basket," is also Actaeon. And both figuratively suffer Actaeon's fate. By the time Ford beats, as he thinks, the old woman of Brentford, he is a "mad dog," not only in Evans' estimation but in his image of himself when asking his neighbors to continue the search for Falstaff: "If I cry out thus upon no trail, never trust me when I open again" (4.2.118, 186–7). There is, of course, no trail except that of his own "distempered" imagination. In the self-deception and self-torment of his sexual fantasies, that is to say, Ford is both Actaeon and the hound that attacks him. In the same scene (4.2) Falstaff is also figuratively devoured by a dog, according to his anticipatory comment in the central scene: "Well, if I be served such another trick, I'll have my brains ta'en out, and buttered, and give them to a dog for a New Year's gift" (3.5.6–8). In fact, such another trick is played on him in 4.2 when he is beaten by Ford. At the center of the play, then, are the two Actaeons indulging their sexual fantasies, both self-deceived, and both to be, in scene 4.2, figuratively devoured by a dog. In locating the two Actaeons in the central scene, Shakespeare has focused the structure on the distempered imaginings that epitomize the disorder of the first half of the play. The central scene is the turning point for Ford in that he willingly accepts the cuckold's horns. In consciously taking on a role, he initiates the remedy that in the second half of the play will deliver him from his suspicious fantasies. Acting out, being "horn-mad," i.e., both the stag and the hunting hound, returns Ford to sanity. Falstaff, on the other hand, while he plays the cuckolder, is a mere puppy

(3.5.10) in self-torment and requires the pinchings and punchings of fairies to be brought to his senses.

The remaining scenes are grouped in a pyramid-like arrangement, in two three-pair sections, two two-pair sections, and one one-pair section. This arrangement serves to distinguish the many subplots by grouping the scenes of each together. But it inordinately emphasizes an oddity of the structure. As we have repeatedly noticed, the central flanking scenes ordinarily exhibit a marked similarity. Though occupying a position that should be emphatically paired with a mirroring scene, the Latin lesson of *Merry Wives* is less strikingly connected to the quizzing of Slender in the paired scene than is usual. The passive action, the new character, William, introduced in scene 4.1 and the lack of narrative continuity weaken the reflection between the two scenes. Furthermore, scene 4.1 seems totally unconnected to any apparent plot development in the play; it is almost always cut in production. And there is yet another anomaly about the scene. As the first scene after the midpoint, the Latin quiz occupies the position at which the second movement of a Shakespearean play habitually begins. Some new action, some counter-action, begins after the keystone. In *Merry Wives*, however, no action of any kind springs from the quizzing of William Page; the scene is completely, emphatically, self-contained. Little wonder that the construction of the play has puzzled commentators. But before examining the function of this scene, we have to look at each of the segments of the play.

The first and last three scenes form a cohesive group enacting the original courtship and seduction plans and their ironic outcomes. Evans stirs Slender to plan his phlegmatic courting of Anne in 1.1, and in the paired final scene Anne's marriage is accomplished, though not to Slender. But the first and third scenes with their reflections more prominently concern Falstaff. We usually think of the last scene as delivering Falstaff's just punishment for his planned seductions of the wives, and indeed in the course of the play the stag's head he finally dons comes to symbolize Actaeon. But in *Merry Wives* the Ovidian story coalesces with and is rooted in the familiar country practice of deer hunting, which Shallow introduces in the first scene in accusing Falstaff. The deer, the hounds, the venison pie have, at this point, no sheen of Ovidian myth. So the mirroring aspect of the last scene is Falstaff's karmic transformation into the deer killed and eaten: "Divide me," he says, "like a bribed [i.e., stolen] buck, each a haunch" (5.5.24). Only in1.3 with Falstaff's planned seduction of the wives do his Ovidian sexual desires take center stage, as is made explicit in the paired scene when Mrs. Page confirms that the final hoax is ready "against such lewdsters and their lechery" (5.3.21). The extremely short scenes 1.2 and 5.4, in which Evans is the controlling character, structurally embed the fact of his importance both in the courting of Anne and in the Herne the Hunter trick on Falstaff. There is also a subtle structural comment on the character of Evans in the pairing of these scenes.

Like the other same-character pairs in the play, the Falstaff-Falstaff pair (3.3–4.2) and the Host-Host pair (2.3–4.5), the Evans-Evans pair suggests the pattern of trickster tricked, attenuated here to the revelation of questionable motives for a prior act. Why does Evans suggest that Slender court Anne and even involve himself in the courting? Though the Arden editor counts it among the confusions of the play that Caius should challenge Evans, not Slender, to a duel, Evans is clearly the "will" behind the courtship. Appropriately, the satyr disguise the Quarto gives him (or, alternately, his goatishness, as in the Folio dialogue) comments on his vicarious part in the courtship, the extent to which Anne's "pretty virginity" attracts him (1.1.42). Whatever his exact costume in the last scenes, Evans, like Falstaff and Ford, also wears horns. In emphasizing Anne's dowry as a reason for Slender to court her, Evans further clouds his character by suggesting the same motive for courting Anne as Falstaff advances for his planned seductions (and as Fenton admits to having overcome). The pairing of these scenes defines Evans as yet another "lover," though at one remove, "from afar," as Shallow puts it (1.1.191). In playing the satyr, Evans is, like Ford, acting out an earlier fantasy, his intrigue, his involvement in the courting of Anne.

In the section 1.4–5.2 through 2.2–4.6 the courtships are initiated and—all but Fenton's—effectively undone. Simple's message to further Slender's courtship goes amiss in 1.4, and in the paired 5.2 Slender is still without words, for his "nay-word" to Anne, "mum … budget," denotes silence in a children's game (5–6). Falstaff's letters, received in 2.1, have been answered with the beating he relates in 5.1, and he is now himself the dupe of the husband he had planned to cuckold. Scenes 2.2 and 4.6 express the central contrast underlying the two main plots in the play. Ford enlists Falstaff to seduce Mrs. Ford, conspiring in adultery and his own cuckolding; Fenton enlists the Host's help in marrying Anne. Each scene is at the center of its half of the play, structurally emphasizing the core contrast between illicit and licit imaginings their pairing contains. Scene 4.6 is the only scene in which Fenton is the main figure; its position reinforces his crucial place as the play's moral standard, made explicit in his upbraiding of the Pages in the last scene.

The next section of four scenes contains the Evans-Host conflict.

3.1 Evans and Caius plan revenge against Host.	4.4 Wives plot Herne the Hunter trick on Falstaff with husbands. Evans volunteers to participate.
2.3 Host dupes and insults Caius.	4.5 Host robbed of his horses.

The Host's insult in 2.3 is answered in the paired 4.5, when his horses are stolen. Though Evans' responsibility for the duping of the Host is not made explicit anywhere in the dialogue, the structure confirms a retaliatory satisfaction of some kind. This is an appropriate uncertainty, for Evans' place in the mock duel, like his place in Slender's courtship, is also "afar off." He is not directly insulted by the Host, Caius is. Evans is no more a fighter than he is a lover, but he seems to indulge fantasies of being both, as Shallow's awed remark about his ability suggests. It is only by consciously playing a part, by expressing his desires in a role that is explicitly imaginary, theatrical, that he overcomes his earlier feeble pretensions, his vicarious actions as lover and as fighter. So in 4.4, when the wives and husbands plan the Herne the Hunter trick, Evans volunteers to be the "jackanapes" he was accused of being in the paired scene, 3.1 (at 76). The wives' planned theatrical inspires his own role-playing and his "good will," the realization of his desire for revenge on the Host in the next scene. (As a drinking companion of Falstaff's, a dishonest innkeeper and a gratuitous mocker, the Host deserves his temporary come-uppance, before his loses are restored by Fenton.)

The next four-scene section groups the deceptions and self-deceptions operating against Falstaff, Ford and the Host. Falstaff is twice tricked in the paired scenes 3.3 and 4.2, containing the buck-basket and beating incidents. Ford's self-deceptions have multiplied beyond the suspicions of his wife to include his inaccurate assessment of Fenton's chances with Anne and his own chances of catching the "monster" Falstaff with Mrs. Ford (3.2). In 4.3 the Host shows a similar combination of naiveté and self-deception, allowing him to be robbed of his horses.

Overall, the pyramidal structure partitions the various narratives in a coherent pattern, section by section: the planning and exposure of the two main actions at the beginning and end of the play, the Slender courtship and Falstaff's attempt to seduce the wives; the initiation and undoing of both these actions in the next section; then the Evans-Host plot; and finally the tricks against Falstaff and the Host before the keystone confrontation of the self-deceived cuckolder and cuckold. In each section the disordered imaginings are paired with their consequences, thus forming complete actions. The chiastic design also pairs distempered actions or imaginings with their cures. Acting out his fantastical misogyny of 3.3 in the paired scene, 4.2, by beating the supposed old woman, Ford is liberated to play Brook one more time, now with complete self-control and self-reflection, in 5.1, resolving the jealousy initiated in the paired scene, 2.1, when Pistol informed him of the Falstaff letter. The stolen deer turned into a hot pastry in the first scene is matched by Falstaff's disguise and figurative consumption (as "hodge-pudding," etc.) in the last scene. Evans transforms his absurd tough talk and placating asides to Caius in 3.1 into the consciously chosen role of jackanapes in the paired scene 4.4, as his vicarious participation in the courting of Anne Page in 1.2 is resolved by his satyr disguise in the paired scene 5.4. In each case an action is transformed into acting, the playing of a role. The pattern of the play is as carefully constructed as any in the canon.

How do the central flanking scenes, 3.4, in which Anne expresses her opinion of her three suitors, and 4.1, in which her brother is quizzed on his Latin declensions, fit into this scheme? Though they have no apparent narrative similarity, the scenes have a clear thematic similarity and to that extent accord with Shakespeare's usual practice. Both scenes focus on language and will. Quizzed by Anne in 3.4, Slender mistakes "will" as "last will and testament," associating it with death (57). On the other hand, during Evans' quizzing of William Page in 4.1, Mistress Quickly misconstrues Latin words as sexual terms. Their language blunders are obviously appropriate to their characters, but in invoking death and sex Slender and Quickly articulate the extremes of desire in the play. Slender is will-less in his idiotic deference and lack of desire. When Anne asks, "What would you with me?" Slender answers "Little or nothing" (59–61). The embodiment of will, on the other hand, is Will Page.[4] As the names of many of the other characters—Ford, Brook, Simple—occasion quibbles, William Page is certainly intended to invite the same wordplay and to find his place in the range of meanings "will" has in *Merry Wives*. The word denotes both sexual desire—as in Evans' double entendre asking if Slender can "carry [his] good will" to Anne Page (1.1.241)—and hostile antipathy—as when both Evans and Caius sarcastically use the same phrase in telling the duped Host they are acting out of "good will" (4.5.79, 89). Will Page, though, is involved in neither sex nor aggression; like the scene in which he first appears he is detached, a student rather than a participant. Only in the last scenes of the play will he too become an "actor"—playing a fairy in the Herne the Hunter theatrical—and so in miniature enact the essential transformation of each of the other changed characters.

Will Page also demonstrates a relationship to language which sets him apart from most of the other characters. It is not merely that, as a student of language and the embodiment of his name, he would not misunderstand "will," as Slender does in the paired scene, but that Will is also free of the other characters' linguistic flaws. Pistol remarks that Falstaff has "studied" Mrs. Ford and "translated her will out of honesty into English" (1.3.49–50). Falstaff's vanity seriously distorts his English, and the verbal tics of the other characters are simply variations of a similarly motivated distortion—Pistol's attempted self-inflation by using tags from old plays, for example, or Caius' almost willful unintelligibility. William, by contrast, exemplifies a healthy realism in answering Evans' question, "What is a stone?" William's choices include "testicles" (as in Caius's usage) or "lapis," which Evans has in mind. By saying "a pebble," William demonstrates the literal-mindedness of a Perdita or Desdemona and his implied freedom from a merely self-serving idiom (4.1.31–35).

The scene of the Latin quiz is also characteristic of Shakespeare's structure in beginning a second, counter-movement in the play. It initiates the parson's liberation from inappropriate involvement in courting and fighting to the self-controlled detachment of acting and directing. In teaching the children and stage managing the Herne the Hunter theatrical, Evans finds a more fitting role for a "soul-curer" (3.1.88). Like Falstaff, Ford and Fenton, Evans also undergoes a change in the play. The scenes ordinarily thought to be irrelevant to the main action of *Merry Wives*—the mutual duping of Evans and the Host in the aborted duel and horse-stealing, the Latin lesson, and the appearance of Evans as a satyr—are part of a coherent if largely implied third plot. One "who makes fritters of English" (5.5.142), apparently nothing more than a comic butt, another virtuosic language display from Shakespeare's hand, is yet another variation of a redeemed imagination. Falstaff becomes the "theme" of the townspeople, Ford is delivered from his obsession, Fenton rises above his original rioting and mercenary designs on Anne, and Evans' sullied imagination is purged by his play-acting.

Evans' second success is even more muted than his revenge on the Host. It is his success in training William Page to take part in the amateur theatrical. With the end of Evans' project to marry off Slender—will-less and linguistically inept—a new project begins, the training of William Page, a boy of "will" and language aptitude. Evans' humiliation and failure in the first half of the play—his treatment by the Host and the failure of Slender's courtship—educate Evans, as defeat and humiliation so often educate Shakespeare's characters. Evans becomes effective through behind-the-scenes manipulation and disguise, methods that also bring him to a new degree of self-awareness. As already mentioned, in volunteering for the role of "jackanapes" he fulfills the epithet Caius has applied to him in the paired scene, and in finally appearing as a Welsh devil, a Welsh goat, and a satyr, variations of the horned creature Falstaff and Ford also embody, Evans explicitly plays out the vicarious sexuality he expressed in spurring on Slender's courtship.

The structure of the play is unusual in many ways: the diminishing number of scenes from section to section; the extraordinarily muted plot developments, more implied than enacted, in the case not only of Evans but of William Page; the marked separation of the subsidiary actions from the main plots; the many seemingly trivial incidents in each scene, blurring the focus; and the large number of speaking characters. In spite of these anomalies, however, the play is fundamentally structured as are Shakespeare's other mature plays, in a thematic arch symmetrically arranged around the central scene, in this case of the two horn-mad Actaeons, Brooke and Falstaff.

11

Instinct and Artifice
in *As You Like It*

If plot consists of action or suspense, then *As You Like It* has almost no plot. After an initial flurry of violence at court, the locale quickly shifts to the Forest of Arden and the desultory life of the country, where the requisite marriages occur as if by magic, the legerdemain of the "magician," Ganymede (5.2.71). The play "replaces a developing intrigue, of the kind exemplified by *Much Ado About Nothing* or *Twelfth Night*," Anne Barton writes in the Riverside edition, "with a structure of cunningly juxtaposed characters and attitudes which Shakespeare has elaborated until it becomes a substitute for plot."[1] That is to say, pattern largely replaces plot. Consequently, an awareness of the play's symmetry is particularly useful in highlighting the movement of what action there is.

The thematic arch structuring the play mirrors instinctive urges in the first half with analogous civilized behaviors in the second half; aggression and nurturance are presented in direct acts and literal language in the "rising action" and are reflected in variously figurative transformations in the "falling action." As a simple illustration of the play's technique, consider the transform of aggression in the paired first and last scenes. The fight between the brothers Orlando and Oliver, erupting only 50 lines into the play, is reflected in Touchstone's seven "degrees of the lie," his indefinitely deferred "quarrel ... by the book" (5.4.88, 90). Violent action is attenuated into an elaborate code of conduct, and hostility between males is thus civilized, or, in this case, comically over-civilized, until Touchstone's imaginary combatants "swore brothers" (105). Or, again, "feeding," a literal grievance of Orlando's in the first scene, mentioned three times, is metaphorical in the last scene: Hymen advises the assembly to "Feed yourselves with questioning" (138); Phebe tells Silvius, "I will not eat my word," her promise of marriage (149); and, finally, the "loving voyage" of Touchstone and Audrey is said to be "but two months victualled" (191–92). These examples give some sense of the play's transformative mirroring of the literal and the figurative in paired scenes across a symmetrical arch. Each scene of the second half of the play contains at least one emphatic artifice, beginning with the acting of "Ganymede" by Rosalind and developing through the hunting ritual (4.2), the emblematic tale of lion and snake (4.3), the mock-heroic threats of Touchstone against William (5.1), the lovers' litany (5.2), the song "sweet lovers" (5.3) and finally the masque of Hymen (5.4). The initial savagery of the court gives way to the simple courtesies of Arden and is then fully civilized in more artful elaborations of natural impulses.

The keystone of the play is the soliloquy Orlando delivers while hanging effusive tributes to his beloved Rosalind on the forest trees. Isolated by a momentarily cleared stage when Orlando exits, the first ten lines of 3.2 are pivotal in form, content and position. In form, they are a truncated sonnet to Rosalind, Diana's "huntress" (4). The sonnet form is fitting for Orlando's Petrarchan attitudes, and its incompleteness—it lacks one quatrain—fittingly expresses his lack of skill both as a poet and a lover. But it is in the reference to Rosalind as Diana's huntress that Orlando invokes the play's essential action and pervasive metaphor. The hunt for food, literal in the first half of the play, most vividly a hunt for the "fool" deer, is in the second half compared to courtship. Rosalind is the huntress and Orlando, the Petrarchan lover, is prey, capable of being killed by her glance, by "her frown" (4.1.105), (as Rosalind, hearing that Orlando is "furnished like a hunter," fears that he "comes to kill my heart" [3.2.241–2]). He has suppressed his aggressive impulses in the Dukes' cooperative forest society and become a "doe" (2.7.128). Initially speechless with Rosalind, he has yet to establish at the midpoint of the play a suitably aggressive attitude toward women, though he has found his first conventional lover's words.

The action of hanging verses on trees is itself central to the establishment of new values, as its position between the flanking "scenes" (as I will refer to structural units) makes clear.

3.2.1–10 Orlando: "O Rosalind, these trees shall be my books."	
3.1 Oliver's lands expropriated. "I never loved my brother."	3.2.11–420 Orlando's "civil sayings" appropriate the "desert," civilizing it with love poems. (Orlando meets Ganymede.)

As You Like It, in the words of Jonathon Bate, is "uncompromising in its confrontation of those twin phenomena from which the Golden Age was imagined to be free: property (linguistically synonymous with 'propriety') and alienation (legal exclusion from property)."[2] The play's uncompromising concern with property is embedded in the central flanking scenes. Orlando's verses will appropriate the desert, civilize the wilderness, with the name of his beloved. By contrast, his brother in the paired scene has had his lands expropriated and has stated, "I never loved my brother" (3.1.14). In the play's tympanum the loveless Oliver becomes landless and the lover Orlando appropriates land. For both brothers, property-less at the center of the play, love brings land even before the final distribution of property by the Dukes: Orlando is given Oliver's estate and Oliver, in marrying Celia, gains her property (5.2.10). In anticipating cultivated lands and expressing a sexual relationship, however immature, the keystone soliloquy and flanking scenes address the two major elements that constitute the marriage union, "blessed bond of board and bed" (5.4.142).

The rest of the play is arranged in three sections of mirroring pairs: a section of four scene pairs paralleling the search for food with the search for love; a three-pair section redirecting divisive violence into socially beneficent aggression; and a final three-pair section establishing heterosexual love in place of hostile, ineffectual and homoerotic relationships.

In the four-pair section "board and bed" are figuratively united in the play's comparison between the search for food and the wooing of a beloved. From the entry of Rosalind and Celia into the Forest of Arden (2.4) through the banquet of Duke Frederick in 2.7, the court exiles search for food; this search is analogously reflected in the courtships of scenes 3.3 through 4.1.

2.7 Orlando disarmed from stealing food by Duke's civility.	3.3 Touchstone deflected from invalid marriage by Jacques' insistence on church wedding.
2.6 Orlando carries Adam off to seek food.	3.4 Rosalind, doubting Orlando's love, exits to see Phebe & Silvius: "The sight of lovers feedeth those in love."
2.5 Song: "Seeking the food he eats/ And pleased with what he gets." Duke's banquet prepared.	3.5 Rosalind to love-struck Phebe: "thank heaven, fasting, for a good man's love."
2.4 Rosalind et. al., "travelers," meet love-lorn Silvius, ask Corin for food.	4.1 Rosalind mocks Jacques' travels and scolds late Orlando, who, after "marriage," goes to dinner with Duke.

The four-pair grouping mirrors the search for food with the courting of a lover. It dramatizes, in Touchstone's comic inversion of the analogy in the first food image of the earlier section, the "wooing of a peascod" (2.4.49). Orlando is deflected from stealing food by the Duke's civility (2.7), and Touchstone is analogously deflected from marrying "under a bush" by Jacques' insistence on a proper and binding church wedding (3.3.81). As Orlando carries Adam off to seek food in 2.6, Rosalind, doubting Orlando's love, exits to see Phebe and Silvius, for "the sight of lovers feedeth those in love" (3.4.53). Indeed, for Rosalind, love ultimately substitutes for food: lovers live on love (3.5), not on such banquets as those prepared for Duke Senior (2.5). The very game she is playing suggests that she thinks love can subsist on feigning. But, of course, this too is unrealistic, a version of Petrarchan love that Rosalind herself is seduced by. The fact that Orlando goes off to dinner with the Duke after marrying Ganymede-Rosalind confirms the insufficiency of her game (4.1). It is worth noting that Orlando's mention of dinner is the last of 17 food references in these four scenes (3.3 through 4.1) and is the only literal reference. The mirroring scenes, by contrast (2.4 through 2.7), contain 30 food references, all but five of which are literal. The "marriage" of Ganymede-Rosalind and Orlando has nothing to subsist on, neither board nor bed. Both Rosalind and Orlando, like Jacques and unlike Celia, are travelers, i.e., landless and without support, without "board" in the largest sense. Orlando is effectively like the hapless Silvius of the paired scene (2.4), in every substantive way deprived of his beloved. It is little wonder that, when next seen, Orlando is "Chewing the food of sweet and bitter fancy" (4.3.102); that is all Rosalind has provided him.

The next section of the play, a three-pair grouping, transforms in its reflections the divisive violence of the court into usefully directed aggression. In the early scenes the Duke has banished his brother; Orlando and Oliver fight on stage; and Charles breaks the ribs of two contenders before his match with Orlando. In this atmosphere, the women cling to one another, fearful of but fascinated by male aggression and drawn, therefore, to the wrestling match (and, in Rosalind's case, to male disguise). The Forest of Arden, by contrast, is sentimental about aggression. Jacques sobs with the sobbing deer, and the Duke indulges him, enjoying the "matter" of the fool's lamentations (2.1.68). In an all-male community repeatedly described as "sweet," the animals hunted for food are considered to be usurped "native burghers" (2.1.23), banished as Duke Senior has been. Like the two women, the men of the forest are ultimately narcissistic. The early scenes, then, present two opposite and equally unhealthy kinds of relationships, relationships that make marriage impossible: the open hostility of the male court or the homoerotic affection of the women and of Duke Senior's men. The distortions of aggression underlying both the hostility and the sentimentality are transformed in the mirroring pairs of the play's middle section.

2.3 Adam warns Orlando: "This house is but a butchery."	4.2 Jacques & Lord "sing ... home" deer slayer.
2.2 Duke sends for Orlando or, in his place, Oliver, to find Celia.	4.3 Oliver, sent by Orlando, to Rosalind, who swoons at tale of bloody napkin.
2.1 Lord tells of Jacques' sorrow at wounding of "fool" deer.	5.1 Touchstone's mock-heroic threat to kill the "fool" William.

The later scene of each pair dramatizes redirected aggression. The "butchery" of Oliver's house (2.3), the elder brother's plan to kill Orlando, is appropriately visited in 4.2 on the deer the lords "sing home," and the isolate critic Jacques is now a participant in the male comraderie, indicating that the successful hunt is itself a bonding through communal ritual. The hunt also makes an implicit comment on Orlando's keystone invocation of Rosalind as "huntress," and on Ganymede-Rosalind's aggression in threatening to cuckold Orlando. In the next pair the court hostility epitomized in 2.2 by the imperative Duke has been transformed by the imperative Orlando in 4.3, and the substitution of one brother for another is now in the service of consideration and friendship. The Duke's vehemence is supplanted by Orlando's forgiveness of Oliver and his redirection of aggression. The third pair showcases the two fools meeting their unrecognized reflections: Jacques, sobbing over the "fool" deer, the venison that will supply the Duke's table, and Touchstone, gleeful at the sight of the "fool" William, a figurative meal: "It is meat and drink to me to see a clown" (5.1.10). Touchstone has attained a threatening stance toward his rival—thus accepting, if comically, a necessary aggression—in contrast to Jacques' sentimental attitude toward violence in the paired scene. In the "deaths" of these three pairs of scenes—of the deer, of the swooning Ganymede and of William, in threat—the early divisive aggressions of the court are productively part of a new social cohesion. The change in the two fools is particularly evident. Jacques, after his losing encounters with Orlando and Rosalind, is now taking part in the group celebration of the hunt; and Touchstone, by virtue of his harmless threats, his adolescent male defense of his woman, is insinuated into the simple but fundamentally good-natured country scene: "God rest you merry, sir," William says to him in parting. Touchstone's threats against his rival bind the court fool to the rural community.

The central scene of these three (4.3) transforms the relationship between Orlando and Oliver. Seeing his brother sleeping in the forest, Orlando identifies himself with the threatened male; that is, the Duke's forest community has allowed Orlando to overcome his earlier male hostility and to see the threats against Oliver as threats against himself (as Jacques identified himself with the wounded deer). But Oliver is not just any threatened male. More than a narcissistic identification of himself with the sleeper is necessary if Orlando is to forgive his brother. Orlando must give up his desire for revenge and dominance. A certain self-sacrifice is necessary, a willingness to put himself in harm's way, to take a wound. This selfless act by Orlando, we are to understand, accounts for his brother's conversion.

This scene not only changes the relationship between the brothers, it simultaneously transforms the relationship between Orlando and Rosalind. To audiences and critics, Orlando is being tutored by a disguised Rosalind, but to Orlando, the "real" relationship is with Ganymede, a homosexual male, and the "marriage" of Orlando and Ganymede violates the necessary bond of board and bed. Nurturance is disordered in the androgyny of Rosalind-Ganymede, as is emblematically rendered in the encounter with the lioness and snake. The aggressive female, the lioness, is dry-dugged and hostile; the effeminate male, the snake of female gender, "consumed" (she "approached the opening of his [Oliver's] mouth") is emphatically not nurturance (4.3.110–11). Orlando chases off the snake and kills the lioness. As Orlando faints within Oliver's report of his adventure, Rosalind swoons on stage, returning her momentarily to her true identity. Orlando and Rosalind "die" together. Shakespeare has thus separated out the two meanings of the Elizabethan pun on "die." Ganymede and Ganymede's husband cease to exist: when he next sees "Ganymede," Orlando dismisses the whole imaginary courtship: "I can live no longer by thinking" (5.2.50); in a striking instance of dramatic irony, he cannot pretend that Ganymede is anything other than Ganymede. But in the deaths of the imaginary couple, Orlando and Rosalind are brought to the certainties of biological reality in losing consciousness, a "dying" that prefigures their marriage. Orlando's defeat of the snake and lioness in saving his brother is the crucial moment of transformation, restoring his aggressive impulses, deflecting violence from Oliver to the animals, symbolically freeing Orlando from Ganymede, and establishing a natural basis for the relationship with Rosalind.

Finally, the last section overcomes the hostility and the ineffectual and homoerotic affections of the opening scenes.

1.3 Rosalind, banished, plans male disguise. Celia to Rosalind: "Thou and I are one."	5.2 Rosalind, as Ganymede, gives riddling promise of marriage to Phebe. Oliver & Celia are in love. Rosalind promises marriage to Orlando.
1.2 Wrestling match. Orlando & Rosalind fall in love. Orlando speechless with her.	5.3 Song, "sweet lovers" of "no matter," says Touchstone.
1.1 Orlando & Oliver fight.	5.4 Touchstone on courtly fighting. Masque.

The homoeroticism of Celia and Rosalind has developed into the heterosexual relations of the mirror scene. Celia's girlish profession of love to Rosalind is paired with her adult affection for Oliver (1.3 and 5.2); in her male disguise Rosalind promises marriage to Orlando (5.2). (Rosalind's plan to don a male disguise in 1.3 is thus paired with her implicit plan to remove the disguise in 5.2.) And the penultimate scene indulges a charming sentimentality in the love song dismissed as "no matter" by Touchstone, aligning it in precise contrast to the actions of the paired scene in which Orlando had not only no matter but nothing at all to speak to Rosalind. The last scene reprises in Touchstone's comic vein the process of civilizing basic male aggression, as I have already noted, and caps the play with a final masque, the most imaginary, "unreal" and civilizing of the play's dramatic techniques.

By combining the play's four sections into a single outline, we can see at once the entire symmetrical arch of the play:

3.2.1–10 Orlando: "O Rosalind, these trees shall be my books."	
3.1 Oliver's lands expropriated. "I never loved my brother."	3.2.11–420 Orlando's "civil sayings" appropriate the "desert," civilizing it with love poems. (Orlando meets Ganymede.)

2.7 Orlando disarmed from stealing food by Duke's civility.	3.3 Touchstone deflected from invalid marriage by Jacques' insistence on church wedding.
2.6 Orlando carries Adam off to seek food.	3.4 Rosalind, doubting Orlando's love, exits to see Phebe & Silvius: "The sight of lovers feedeth those in love."
2.5 Song: "Seeking the food he eats/ And pleased with what he gets." Duke's banquet prepared.	3.5 Rosalind to love-struck Phebe: "thank heaven, fasting, for a good man's love."
2.4 Rosalind et. al., "travelers," meet love-lorn Silvius, ask Corin for food.	4.1 Rosalind mocks Jacques' travels and scolds late Orlando, who, after "marriage," goes to dinner with Duke.
2.3 Adam warns Orlando: "This house is but a butchery."	4.2 Jacques & Lord "sing … home" deer slayer.
2.2 Duke sends for Orlando or, in his place, Oliver, to find Celia.	4.3 Oliver, sent by Orlando, to Rosalind, who swoons at tale of bloody napkin.
2.1 Lord tells of Jacques' sorrow at wounding of "fool" deer.	5.1 Touchstone's mock-heroic threat to kill the "fool" William.
1.3 Rosalind, banished, plans male disguise. Celia to Rosalind: "Thou and I are one."	5.2 Rosalind, as Ganymede, gives riddling promise of marriage to Phebe. Oliver & Celia are in love. Rosalind promises marriage to Orlando.
1.2 Wrestling match. Orlando & Rosalind fall in love. Orlando speechless with her.	5.3 Song, "sweet lovers" of "no matter," says Touchstone.
1.1 Orlando & Oliver fight.	5.4 Touchstone on courtly fighting. Masque.

The tympanum enacts the final shift in locale from court to country. The accompanying shift in values is dramatized in the contrast between the loveless and landless Oliver and the loving, verse-writing Orlando in the central flanking scenes (3.1 and 3.2.11–420). The savage court has reduced not only Oliver but almost everyone to beggary; civilization will be restored by the re-education of basic impulses that takes place in Arden, love allowing cultivation in the largest sense. The natural drives toward food and sex are refined (though not yet fully civilized) in the four paired scenes of the next section, most obviously in Orlando's education by the Duke (2.7) and by Ganymede-Rosalind (3.2 through 4.1). The violence both of court and country in scenes 2.1 through 2.3 are redirected in the later scenes of the next section in which the ritualized death of the deer, the figurative death of Ganymede and the threatened death of William recover rather than destroy community (4.2 through 5.1). Finally, the three opening and closing scenes of the play transform hostility and misguided or ineffectual affections into the heterosexual bonds necessary to people every town.

The significance of the imagery is also clarified by its distribution on the thematic arch. I have already commented on the predominance of literal references to food in the first half of the play and of figurative uses in the second half of the play, initiated in 3.2. But the patterning is much more exquisite than that. Consider the apparently trivial word "sweet." It is carefully distributed in the play to trace the movement from variously inappropriate affections to heterosexual love. It is introduced in the second scene when it is used twice of Rosalind by Celia, expressing the sisterly affection of the two women. The repeated uses of the word to describe the life of the Duke's men in the forest (2.1.2, 12, 20) suggests that their affections, too, are essentially like those of Rosalind and Celia, if less specifically attached. The only other use of the word in the first half of the play (beside the pastoral note of "sweet" birds) is by Adam of his master (2.3), so that the first heterosexual application of the epithet is by Touchstone of Audrey early in the second half of the play (3.3); however comic, the relationship of fool and goatherd is the first appropriate gender pairing in the play and is the "natural" coupling that is the basis of the civilized marriages the play finally celebrates. That Rosalind calls Celia "sweet" in the previous scene (3.2.248) indicates the persistence of the affection between the two women; they are still, as Celia said earlier, "one" (1.3). When Celia in 4.3 addresses Rosalind for the only time as "sweet Ganymede," expressing affection for the homosexual male of the disguise, Celia has moved a step closer to heterosexual love. When next she appears, she is in love with Oliver. So the play's final use of the epithet, in designating the lad and lass of the song "sweet lovers" (5.3), answers the paired scene (1.2), notably lacking satisfactory food otherwise, in which Rosalind is twice called "sweet" by Celia; homoerotic affection has become heterosexual affection. In addition, the song comments on the initial meeting of Orlando and Rosalind, also in the paired scene, a relationship like those of Touchstone and Audrey and of Silvius and Phebe ("sweet" twice in 3.5) that is from the outset heterosexual, if problematically so.

The same connotations inform other uses of "sweet" in expressing the difficulties of Rosalind and Orlando in attaining heterosexual love. Touchstone compares the homosexually disguised Rosalind to the sweetest nut with the sourest rind (3.2.109); Orlando, struggling with the androgyny of Ganymede-Rosalind, paces the forest "Chewing the food of sweet and bitter fancy" (4.3.102). ("Bitter" is the homoerotic contrast to "sweet," as in the "bitter" relationship of Phebe and the "sweet youth" Ganymede-Rosalind [3.5 138, 64].) Like the scene mirrorings of the symmetrical arch, the embedded patterns of food imagery also demonstrate the play's intricate movement toward heterosexual relationships in a bond of board and bed.

Beside the "sweet bird's throat" (2.5.4) of Amien's song, striking the requisite pastoral note, there is one other occurrence of the word "sweet." When admitting that he is Orlando's brother, Oliver says, "I do not shame To tell you what I was, since my conversion So sweetly tastes, being the thing I am" (4.3.136–38). This single most important use of the word in the play does not have any gender relevance at all but picks up, in "conversion," the religious associations that Adam has brought to it. For the old servant, as for Corin, hospitality is the way to heaven (2.4.81): Adam offers Orlando a "foster nurse," his savings, and casts himself on the Providence that feeds sparrows (2.3.39, 43). In calling Orlando "sweet master" in this context (2.3.3), Adam is expressing not the homoerotic connotations of the word but rather the "sacred pity" also extended to Orlando in Duke Senior's forest society (2.7.123). Oliver's conversion reprises Orlando's conversion by the Duke in 2.7, transcending or underlying—in "being the thing I am"—gender identity.

As You Like It may not have a suspenseful plot but it has a persistent if diffuse movement from savagery to civilization. The first half moves from the physical violence at court to the peaceful feast of Duke Senior in Arden (which is, incidentally, in the same position as the cancelled feast in *The Merchant of Venice* and the celebratory feast in *Othello*); the second half moves from the merely physical relationship of Touchstone and Audrey to the commitments and the sophistication of the wedding scene. The meeting of Orlando and Ganymede in the scene following the keystone initiates the action of the second half; *As You Like It* thus begins its second movement at the same point as does *King John, Measure for Measure* and most other Shakespearean plays. The disordered relationships of the first half—the male violence, the stunted heterosexuality and the male and female homoeroticism—are educated into the civilized behaviors symmetrically expressed in the artifices of the second half, leading finally to the heterosexual bonds of board and bed necessary to people a renewed society.

12

The Thematic Arch of *Henry V*

Despite its loose-jointed appearance, *Henry V* is structurally among Shakespeare's most subtle and masterful achievements, particularly in its presentation of Henry. He is usually considered either an epic warrior king or a warmonger,[1] or the play itself is considered inconclusive because Shakespeare is either ambivalent or intentionally ambiguous.[2] All of these views have in common the notion that Henry "has no private, personal self, but only a public character"[3]; he "seems to be exempt from the condition of humanity,"[4] revealing no inner struggle, no change other than the seemingly miraculous change that occurs, according to the Bishops, before the play opens. However, the thematic structure belies this notion of a solely public character. *Henry V* disposes its symmetrical halves to reflect the two roles Henry undertakes in the play. The first half presents Henry aspiring to the role of warrior prince modeled by his ancestors, Edward and his son, and the second half presents Henry's personal struggle to create a role better fitted to his experience of war, the persona he finally elaborates for Katherine, that of the bluff, blunt king of the tradition. Henry is role-playing through the entire drama and in that regard can be said to have only a public character; however, his deliberate change of roles and the new role he creates express the character of the actor himself. Prince Hal played the wastrel ironically, indulging his witty detachment; Henry plays the *roi du soleil* earnestly, until it comes to seem no more than hollow ceremony and he must invent a different role for himself as king.

The keystone scene of the play is 3.6. It contains three incidents. Fluellen angrily denies Pistol's request that Bardolph be spared and sees through Pistol's earlier "prave words" (63); Fluellen informs Henry that Bardolph is to be hanged, and Henry agrees, re-affirming the order against pillaging; and Henry answers the French request for ransom brought by Montjoy. The scene is transformative for both Henry and Fluellen, who is so often in the play a surrogate for the king. It marks in both men the central turn from words to actions, from show to substance.

Fluellen learns the essential lesson of the play, the difference between words and actions, in discovering that Pistol is nothing more than bluster. Though Pistol has earlier "uttered as prave words at the pridge as you shall see in a summer's day," in asking that a breach of discipline be excused, Pistol reveals himself to Fluellen (with help from Gower) as "not the man that he would gladly make show to the world he is" (63–4, 83–4). Pistol goes "under the form of a soldier" (69), according to Gower, and "learn[s] … by rote" the details of battles, which he "con[s] perfectly in the phrase of war" (71, 75). Whatever the gravity of Pistol's offense, his windy braggadocio is no surprise to anyone but Fluellen, who is so taken with language that talk of the "disciplines of the war" (3.2.59) is of more pressing concern than the war itself. Until this pivotal moment he is an easy dupe for Pistol's grandiloquence.

It is also in this scene that Henry turns from being a man of words to being a man of action. Like Hamlet, Henry begins as a student and ends as a soldier. The change is most easily seen by comparing the first and last scenes. In the opening scene the churchmen are amazed that Henry has become a "sudden scholar" (1.1.32). Somehow he has acquired the fruits of contemplation and study. He speaks "sweet and honeyed sentences," discoursing on theology, politics, war and statecraft (50). His learning and his equally sudden lack of "will-fulness"—we see his pliability in the next scene when the Bishops argue his claim to France—constitute the nearly miraculous change in Henry (35). Though the bishops may be puzzled as to how he came to his amazing knowledge, its result—a man of taking eloquence—is confirmed by at least two of Henry's audiences in subsequent scenes, the French diplomat and the citizens of Harfleur. At the end of the play, by contrast, Henry characterizes himself as "plain soldier" (149), a man of action: "If I could win a lady at leapfrog, or by vaulting into my saddle.... I should quickly leap into a wife. Or if I might buffet for my love, or bound my horse for her favors, I could lay on like a butcher" (136–41). Not only does Henry have "neither the voice nor the heart of flattery," even in the appropriate circumstance for it, he energetically disparages precisely the kind of man the churchmen have described him to be, "fellows of infinite tongue" (156), and dismisses the eloquence he was earlier praised for: "a speaker is but a prater" (158). By positioning Henry's unsuccessful attempt at French in the center of the scene, Shakespeare further reinforces the pervasive point: Henry has changed from a man of words to a man of action.

This change in Henry occurs, like Fluellen's analogous insight, in the central scene and is given an explicitly religious cast. In responding to Montjoy's request for ransom, Henry says,

> My people are with sickness much enfeebled,
> My numbers lessened, and those few I have
> Almost no better than so many French;
> Who when they were in health, I tell thee, herald,
> I thought upon one pair of English legs
> Did march three Frenchmen. Yet forgive me, God,
> That I do brag thus! This your air of France
> Hath blown that vice in me. I must repent [3.6.145–52].

Despite his offhandedness here, Henry sees bragging as a vice that must be forgiven. As a form of pride, it must be repented. Which is exactly what Henry does. From this point, we hear nothing more that is inspired by a muse of fire, but only Henry's reiterated insistence on humility. The menacing, pietistic, self-inflating Henry of the first half of the play has been sobered by the sickness and starvation of his troops, the deaths of his friends and the imminent defeat he expects at the hands of the French.

In the keystone scene, then, the play turns from boastful words to committed action, from show to substance, from pride to humility, from the characteristic French vice to traditional English virtue. The other 22 scenes are symmetrically arranged around the keystone.[5]

3.6 Fluellen refuses Pistol's plea
to intercede for Bardolph.
Henry & Fluellen on hanging.
Henry answers Montjoy.

3.5 French send defiance to English.	3.7 French boast of their prowess.
3.4 Katherine shocked at English words for body parts.	4.1 Henry bristles when his words called "foolish saying."
3.3 Henry threatens Harfleur with rape and pillage.	4.2 French in "fair show" hope to "suck away" souls of English.
3.2 Fluellen chases soldiers into battle.	4.3 Henry inspires soldiers to battle by means of Crispin speech.
3.1 Henry rouses soldiers at Harfleur.	4.4 Pistol threatens Frenchman.
2.4 French receive Exeter with demands.	4.5 French routed & regroup.
2.3 Death of Falstaff.	4.6 Deaths of York & Suffolk.
2.2 Henry commands traitors' executions and army's departure for France.	4.7 Henry gets news of victory & gives Fluellen Williams' glove.
2.1 Bardolph stops quarrel between Nym & Pistol. News of Falstaff: "King has killed his heart."	4.8 Henry interrupts quarrel. Williams blames king for disguise. "All offenses come from the heart."
1.2 Henry responds to tennis ball mock.	5.1 Fluellen feeds Pistol mocked leek.
1.1 Bishops characterize Henry.	5.2 Henry characterizes himself.

The play is divided into four main sections by the two pairs of French scenes, one pair flanking the central scene (3.5–3.7) and one pair marking the narrative boundary between war and peace (2.4 & 4.5). The first section (1.2–2.4) concerns the breaking of bonds (of loyalty, friendship, and diplomatic relations) and the last section (4.5–5.1) the resolution of conflict. The coherence of this last section may not be immediately evident in the routed French, the deaths of the two English noblemen and the comic cudgeling of Pistol, but in each case the underlying theme is of reestablished bonds. The scenes portray the rekindled honor and regrouping of the French, the loyalty unto death of York and Suffolk, the resolution of Henry's quarrel with Williams, and Pistol's enforced change of diet from "unwholesome" blood to leek (2.3.57)—all occurring around the news of the Agincourt victory, the center of the central scene in this five-scene section; that is, the military victory is flanked by other, varied, instances of resolved conflict. The middle sections (3.1–3.5 and 3.7–4.4) concern not only the conflicts with the French but conflicts within the English forces—Fluellen and the other Captains, Henry and the common soldiers—and within Henry as well. The keystone scene and the first and last scenes are structurally separate from the main narrative. The keystone scene focuses the thematic concerns with words/actions and friendship/war; the first and last scenes emphatically focus on the character of Henry.

Each scene of the first half is mirrored by the corresponding scene in the second half. In the central flanking scenes the French indulge their windy boasting, the inflated rhetoric their actions will not be able to match. In 3.4 and 4.1 Katherine and Henry each receive "language instruction" from a social inferior, Henry's lesson from Williams being on the "word" of the king (196, 201, 202). In 4.2, going into battle, the French expect that their "fair show" will "suck away" the souls of the English (17); in the paired 3.3 before Harfleur Henry too depends on a show, of fierce rhetoric. Using their different means of coercion and persuasion,

Fluellen and Henry coax the soldiers into battle in 3.2 and 4.3. Henry exhorting his men into the breach at Harfleur and Pistol threatening his French prisoner are each in "full … voice" in 3.1 and 4.4 (67), acting the part of the soldier, imitating the tiger, as Henry advises. In 2.4 and 4.5 Exeter's threats to the French are made and fulfilled. Falstaff's death clearly contrasts with the battlefield deaths of York and Suffolk (2.3–4.6). Scenes 2.2 and 4.7 initiate and end the war. In 2.1 and 4.8, Bardolph quells the squabble between Pistol and Nym as Henry ends the quarrel between Williams and Fluellen, Henry's surrogate, and resolves his own quarrel with Williams. Similarly, Fluellen and Pistol function as surrogates for Henry and the Dauphin in resolving (for the audience), through a marvelous double indirection by Shakespeare, the insult of the tennis ball mock (1.2–5.1). Some analogous action or other essential element joins the two scenes of each chiastic pair.

   This structure clarifies and unobtrusively enlarges on the character of Henry. Notice the main characters in paired scenes:

3.6 Henry, Fluellen, Montjoy.	
3.5 French	3.7 French
3.4 Katherine	4.1 Henry
3.3 Henry	4.2 French
3.2 Fluellen	4.3 Henry
3.1 Henry	4.4 Pistol
2.4 French	4.5 French
2.3 Death of Falstaff	4.6 Deaths of York & Suffolk
2.2 Henry	4.7 Henry
2.1 Bardolph	4.8 Henry
1.2 Henry	5.1 Fluellen
1.1 Bishops on Henry	5.2 Henry on Henry

   Henry is paired with Katherine, the French, Fluellen and Pistol in the central sections and with Fluellen a second time (1.2 & 5.1) and with Bardolph in the other half of the play (2.1 & 4.8). In each case we are invited to remark the correspondences, as the brief summaries above suggest. Henry is like Katherine, though for different reasons, in his sensitivity to enumerated body parts (4.1.135–36); like the French in depending on "show"; like Fluellen in, among other things, his dependence on language; like Pistol in his full voice; and like Bardolph in his peacemaking. In the mirrored light of these scenes we can see, for example, Henry as an actor like Pistol and like the French when he rallies his soldiers and threatens the citizens of Harfleur. By matching Pistol's treatment of his French prisoner with Henry's acting lesson to the troops before Harfleur, Shakespeare accents that Henry is playing a similar role to Pistol's, the subtlety of the structural analogy exactly appropriate to the skill of Henry's acting. Or compare 2.1 and 4.8, Bardolph as peacemaker, deflecting the anger of Pistol and Nym toward the French, and Henry as peacemaker, taking to himself the truth of Williams' accusation about his disguise. Prince Hal's education among the citizenry was fully dramatized in the earlier plays of the sequence; King Henry's further education is implicit in the structure of this play.

Because Fluellen is literally a surrogate for Henry in the quarrel with Williams and is structurally a surrogate for Henry in retaliating for a mockery (scenes 1.2 and 5.1), we would expect Fluellen to clarify Henry's relationship with language. The comparison is embedded in the pair 3.2–4.3, which contain Fluellen's untimely request for disputations on the disciplines of war and Henry's speech to Montjoy on the brink of battle. MacMorris emphatically rejects Fluellen's request for talk. "It is no time to discourse," he tells Fluellen. "The town is beseiched, and the trumpet call us to the breach, and we talk, and, be Chrish, do nothing.... There is throats to be cut, and works to be done" (107–12). Henry's speech to Montjoy is a matching disputation on the disciplines of war. But Henry's speech is not a trivial discourse at an inappropriate time. On the discipline of "Dying like men" (99), Henry, anticipating the "day's work" (97), "speaks proudly": "We are but warriors for the working-day" (108–9); "Our hearts are in the trim" (115). The thesis of Henry's speech is that of MacMorris's rebuttal to Fluellen: there is work to be done, the work of fighting to the death. Of course, MacMorris's elevation of actions over words, of unconsidered action, issues in the much-remarked grotesquerie of his climactic threat to Fluellen: "So Chrish save me, I will cut off your head" (3.2.133). Henry is rather more reverently conscious that it may be his own "joints" that are dismembered (4.3.123).

In Henry's speech to Montjoy we see that the king in his emphasis on work has moved away from his inflated rhetoric and general dependence on language, effective as it was, before Harfleur. We see the same change in the dispute with Williams. When the disguised Henry says he will not trust the king's word again if the king is ransomed, Williams calls it a "foolish saying" (4.1.202). As many critics have noted, Henry's oath in prickly response, an oath to confront Williams should they meet after the battle, is broken at their next meeting. The breaking of the oath is emphasized by having Henry invite Fluellen's opinion on the matter, and the Welshman predictably insists that the oath must be kept under any circumstances. Henry, however, gives Williams a gloveful of crowns instead. "The King compounds his honor for crowns," one critic concludes.[6] But surely no one would expect Henry to act under the circumstances with Fluellen's rigidity. Though advising action, Fluellen is here constrained by words, as he was in wanting to discourse on the disciplines of war. By this time in the play Henry is no longer a man of mere words; a "foolish saying," even if it is an "oath," deserves no further action. Henry accedes to the truth of Williams's retort, even rewards the soldier for it and for his larger point that the disguised Henry deserved what he received. As I mentioned above, unlike Bardolph's peacemaking in the paired scene, which turned the anger of Pistol and Nym against the French, Henry's peacemaking defuses anger.

In addition to pairings with other characters, there is one Henry-Henry pair in the play, 2.2 and 4.7. It has, first, a narrative function: the war against France is initiated and ended. In the early scene, with the preliminaries over—the "justice" of the cause established, the message of defiance sent to France, the traitors taken off to be executed—Henry ends the scene by exhorting his countrymen, "Cheerly to sea! The signs of war advance! No king of England if not king of France!" (192–93). In the paired scene Henry is told of his victory and names the Battle of Agincourt. Whatever credit Henry insists on giving to God, the structure of the play situates Henry as the initiator and victor in the conflict with France. Secondly, this pair of scenes points up the difference between the initiator and victor, the inexperienced king and the war-hardened veteran. Henry is something of the cocky and self-righteous showman when toying with the traitors. Since the king knows "by interception all they do," Henry's thanks to God for bringing the betrayal to light seem disingenuous. Certainly, the veteran would not think of saying, "Let us deliver Our *puissance* into the hand of God" (189–90, italics added), or shouting quite so lustily to embark for France: "Cheerly to sea!" By comparison with the victorious but humbled veteran of war, the jingoistic young king seems brash; and, like his war chants, his piety seems studied in its clichéd formulations.

In its paired scenes, then, the chiastic structure of *Henry V* highlights the changes in Henry from the first to the second half of the play. The man of showy words becomes the man of work-a-day action; the inexperienced young king, aspiring to traditional military glory, becomes the realistic, humbled veteran; the actor casts off his glorious hereditary role for a role forged in his own dark hour. The extent to which Henry is an actor in the first half of the play is clear from the Bishops' characterization of him, from his speech to the French ambassador, his cat-and-mouse game with Scroop and the other traitors and the pairing of his Harfleur speeches with the obvious "shows" of both the French and Pistol. The role Henry is so earnestly acting is that of his valiant ancestors, Edward III and Edward the Black Prince. Henry is directed in this role by Canterbury, who advises him to take on their "warlike spirit" (104) and similarly overcome the French: "Edward the Black Prince ... on the French ground played a tragedy, Making defeat on the full power of France " (1.2.105–7). This is the script for Henry's victory at Harfleur. "O noble English," Canterbury continues,

> that could entertain
> With half their forces the full pride of France
> And let another half stand laughing by,
> All out of work and cold for action! [111–114]

War against the French is a play, an entertainment, as Canterbury describes it and as Henry initially wages it. Victory achieves the crowning of the *roi du soleil*, as the French king remembers well; for, while the Black Prince fought at Crecy, his father, "his mountain sire, On mountain standing ... crown'd with the golden sun ... smil'd to see him Mangle the work of nature and deface the patterns [made] by God and by French fathers" (2.4.57–66). Between them, Canterbury and the French king describe the ideal, the *roi du soleil*, the model to which Henry aspires in the first half of the play.

This ideal and its transformation are presented in the sun imagery Shakespeare had already deployed as symbolic of kingship in *Richard II*, *King John*, and the two parts of *Henry IV*. In *Henry V* the imagery does not so much comment on the shifting fortunes of kingship in the play as demonstrate Henry's re-interpretation of monarchy. Instead of the *roi du soleil*, a monarch of power, especially military power, Henry becomes, in the Chorus's famous phrase, "the mirror of all Christian kings" (2.0.6), discovering and enacting an appropriate reciprocity with his subjects and, ultimately, with the defeated French. The sun imagery is disposed on the framework of the thematic arch. (Solid line indicates a scene without sun imagery.)

3.6	
3.5 "the sun looks pale, killing [English] fruit with frowns" (16–7). "Rush" on Henry as "melted snow Upon the valleys" (50–1).	3.7 "stars or suns?" on armour (70). Henry "longs not for the dawning" (131).
3.4 _____	[4.0.43 Henry's eye "like the sun."]

	4.1 "Morning breaks" (89, 90). "turn the sun to ice with fanning" (198). Peasants "help Hyperion to his horse" (272).
3.3 _____	4.2 the sun (1). "high" (62).
3.2 _____	4.3 "The sun shall greet [the English] dead & draw their honours ... up to heaven" (99).
3.1 _____ [3.0.6 "the young Phoebus fanning." (Fleet embarks.)]	4.4 _____
2.4 Edward "crowned with the golden sun" (58).	4.5 _____
2.3 _____	4.6 _____
2.2 "sweet shade" of Henry's government (28).	4.7 _____
2.1 _____	4.8 _____
1.2 title "as clear as summer sun" (86). Henry "will rise with glory" to "blind" Dauphin (279–81).	5.1 _____
1.1 _____	5.2 "good heart is the sun" (162). "face not worth sunburning" (147). "hot summer" (and Katherine "blind") (310).

The imagery is disposed according to the four main sections of the play. The first section (1.2 through 2.4) begins and ends with the traditional notion of the *roi du soleil* embodied in the victorious Edward "crowned with the golden sun." Henry implies a similar military conquest in his promise to "rise with ... glory" to "blind" the Dauphin who has mocked the English monarch. (The "sweet shade" is Cambridge's ironically accurate comment on Henry's present government.) The second section, however, (3.0 through 3.5), though it begins with the embarking fleet "fanning young Phoebus," stirring hopes of another glorious victory like Edward's in which Henry would attain the stature of his ancestor, ends in Alpine cold and pale sun (3.5), the weakness and illness of the English force, the last stage on the way to Henry's "night" (3.6.169).

The third section contains Henry's transformation of the significance of the sun symbol, a transformation that grows out of his desperate military situation and his encounter with Williams. Before looking at the imagery, it is well to recall Henry's plight. In the central scene Henry has acceded to the execution of Bardolph, the third of his friends the king is to various degrees responsible for killing, and offers, for the ransom the French demand, only his own "frail and worthless trunk" (153). Far from going out into the camp to dispense "a largesse universal like the sun," as the Chorus thinks, the disheartened Henry comes among the soldiers like Antaeus to the earth to try to recover strength from the friendly comraderie that, with the deaths of Falstaff, Scroop and Bardolph, he no longer enjoys.

There are two strands to the sun images in the third section. One indicates the actual passage of the day from dawn to noon, when the sun is "high" (3.7.131; 4.1.86, 90; 4.2.1, 62), with a literalism that is itself, as I discuss below, significant. The second strand comments on the encounter with Williams and its consequences. When the soldiers express their disbelief in the king's refusal to be ransomed, Henry feebly says that, if the king is ransomed, Henry "would not trust his word after." Williams sensibly dismisses these "foolish words." "That's a perilous shot out of an elder-gun," he says, "that a poor and private displeasure can do against a monarch! You may as well go about to turn the sun to ice with fanning in his face with a peacock feather" (4.1.195–202). In remarking the gulf between a private subject and a monarch, Williams insists that the connection Henry had hoped to make with the soldiers is not possible. Henry has to confront the truth of his irrevocable distance from the common man. Furthermore, Williams accuses Henry of the windy inconsequentiality of the Chorus (3.0.6), the Dauphin and Pistol, a form of bragging that Henry has repented. The hyperbolic aspirations toward heaven of the Chorus (1.0.1–2) and the Dauphin (3.7.14–18, 4.2.5) are the foil for the literalism of the "high" sun in this scene, for in the last two sun images of this section Henry's "rise" is through a brutally clear-eyed view of the monarch's place and use.

In confronting Henry with the hard truth of his solitary position, Williams has, like the peasant Henry imagines, "helped Hyperion" to his horse, to rise to his true height. Testy as Henry is after his encounter with the soldiers, acerbic and condescending in tone, he is only being substantively truthful in thinking of the soldier as a "wretched slave" and describing him to be "like a lackey" who

> from the rise to the set
> Sweats in the eye of Phoebus, and all night
> Sleeps in Elysium; next day after dawn
> Doth rise and help Hyperion to his horse [265–72].

In the toils of the war under Henry's leadership this accurately relates the relationship of king and subject (though not the soldiers' sleeplessness), as it does the personal sense in which Williams has angered Henry into his present speech, limited, shortsighted and self-pitying though it is, which accedes to the distance between king and subject. Henry must abandon his egalitarian impulse and rise like Hyperion.

From that height he can reciprocate the support of the commoners:

> ... those [English] that leave their valiant bones in France,
> Dying like men, though buried in your dunghills,
> They shall be fam'd; for there the sun shall greet them,
> And draw their honors reeking up to heaven,
> Leaving their earthly parts to choke your clime,
> The smell whereof shall breed a plague in France [4.3.98–103].

This is the climactic sun image of the narrative proper—"singularly unpleasant," one critic calls it.[7] Henry's indebtedness to the peasant, the common man, the English soldiers, can only be repaid by "draw[ing] their honors reeking up to heaven." This image is a response to and contradiction of the Constable's prediction, conveyed by Montjoy, that the "souls" (85) of the English will "retire" (86); rather than retreating, the "honors"—both the souls and the reputations—of the soldiers will be drawn to heaven, according to Henry's preoccupation that his men make a good end. In this image Henry also accepts, elaborates and throws back in the Constable's face his prediction that the "poor bodies [of the English] will lie and fester" in the fields (87–8). Not only will they fester, they will spread contagion in what is presented as an afterlife of bodily corruption corresponding to the afterlife of the soul: "Killing in relapse of mortality" (107). Certainly, Henry's image has the virtue of seeing war for what it is, rather than as the glorious fantasy implied by the play's early images of the *roi du soleil*, the glorified killer, or the fantasy of the one other sun image in this section, the plural "suns" in 3.7, an unreality, a merely possible device on the Dauphin's shield. In this reply to Montjoy, made before the entire English host, Henry's awareness of death provides an example markedly different from the content of the blood-and-guts rhetoric flourished before Harfleur. Henry's view of war and of his place in it has changed markedly.

But the pattern of sun imagery is resolved only in the last scene. In the play the English war dead are epitomized in York and Suffolk, loyal and constant to an extent that modern critics mock. In their fidelity to cause and king, the play clearly sets them up as the opposites of Scroop, Bardolph and Pistol. When Henry says that Kate, in taking him, takes a soldier, it is the two noblemen that are his model. Their constancy is Henry's "plain and uncoined constancy," imaged in the most significant variation of the sun imagery: a "good heart ... is the sun." The king must be a good man, and, conversely, every man of good heart is a king. This is a far cry from Edward deriving his sun-crown from his military victory; constancy, particularly in defeat, has become the measure of royalty. It is also a far cry from Henry's initial threat to rise in military glory and blind the Dauphin. In the last scene it is Katherine and Henry himself who are repeatedly said to be "blind." While Henry's bantering with Burgundy in vulgar puns leaches any false sentimentality from the courting of Katherine, the imagery nevertheless insists that committed love not military conquest "blinds," i.e., consummates not only the relationship but the political peace as well. But otherwise, the generically comic ending of the play suggests, war and marriage require the same devotion to the death. Henry begins as a vainglorious sun-king playing a tragedy but ends as a plain soldier working a comedy.

13

The Anomalous Arch of *Hamlet*

Hamlet is so varied and full of incidents that its plot almost disappears into the intricate patterning of events and language, and the play has often been accused of lacking unity, indeed, of being plotless. "It is of no clear shape," Frank Kermode writes in the Riverside edition, and applies Harry Levin's estimate of Hamlet's character to "the play as a whole": "it is ... a state of perplexity ... into which we enter."[1] Even basic facts about the divisions of the play and the plot emphases are uncertain. Should the play be divided into 18, 19 or 20 scenes? Is the central scene the mousetrap scene, as Harold Jenkins and others suppose, or the prayer scene, as G. R. Hibbard thinks? Or perhaps the closet scene, a possibility Bernard Beckerman entertains.[2] The designation is not trivial, for it raises important questions about the play. Is the central thematic emphasis on art and acting, as the mousetrap scene would suggest; on the Christian view of revenge, as the prayer scene would suggest; or on the Oedipal psyche of Hamlet, as the closet scene would suggest? The thematic arch helps answer these questions.

The thematic arch also reveals that the chiastic structure of *Hamlet* is anomalous in two important respects. Most significantly (and unsurprisingly), speeches rather than actions are chiastically related across the arch. Moments of speculative rhetoric ("To be or not to be..."), general comment ("What piece of work is a man!") or other mere words are chiastically related rather than actions or performative speeches like Coriolanus's denunciations of the tribunes. Even the chiastic reflections in the central flanking scenes are, uniquely, inconsequent speeches, admonitions to memory and purpose by the Player King and the Ghost that are in the end ignored by Hamlet. This pervasive prolixity contributes to the enigmatic cast of the whole play, its protagonist's wavering between words and actions and the play's interrogation of action itself. Indeed, the basis of some pairings are much less certain in *Hamlet* than in the other plays, and I advance them tentatively. It is as though the very foundation of the play has an element of the speculative.

The second anomalous feature of *Hamlet* is the asymmetry of its five acts. Though the scene groupings retain the characteristic chiastic balance, the act divisions do not. Other plays with discernible five-act structures have the same number of scenes in acts one and five and in acts two and four, with a third act consisting of an odd number of scenes, maintaining the overall balance. (See, for example, *Much Ado* and *King John*.) *Hamlet's* act divisions violate the fundamental symmetry of Shakespeare's compositional practice both by extending the third act and by the consequent displacement of Act Four, which does not directly reflect the second act. This subtle skewering of the play's balance contributes, however faintly, to the general sense of the uniqueness of *Hamlet*.

The structure of the play has been obscured partly because of the traditional act-scene divisions.[3] Neither of the early quartos divides the play, and the Folio's erratic divisions end at 2.2. Traditionally, *Hamlet* has 20 scenes, but the break at 4.1, derived from a quarto of 1676, is universally recognized to be, in W. W. Greg's word, a "disaster."[4] The Queen should remain on stage after Hamlet drags off the body of Polonius and the King enter to her. Though most editions retain the break for convenience of reference, editors recognize that the traditional break occurs in the midst of a scene and should be ignored. Granville-Barker suggests a second departure from the traditional breaks.[5] He argues from the lack of a division in the Folio that the fourth and fifth scenes be combined, that Hamlet follow the Ghost onto the battlements in a "continuous action," that persistent rationale for overriding thematic distinctions. But the Folio does not mark the obvious break at 1.4 either, instead running the first Polonii scene into the Ghost scene. Such carelessness makes the Folio untrustworthy in these matters, and the definitely cleared stage is sufficient warrant for retaining the traditional division. The play has nineteen scenes.

The keystone scene is the prayer scene. It connects the play's two essential concerns: Christian forgiveness and mimetic theory. From a Christian point of view, Hamlet becomes a wholly diabolical avenger and Claudius an unredeemable murderer. The central lines of the scene, and thus of the play, assert, through heaven's example, the Christian answer to the bloodlust of revenge: forgiveness. Claudius reminds himself of the "mercy" of "sweet heaven" and of the efficacy of prayer:

> And what's in prayer but this twofold force,
> To be forestalled ere we come to fall
> Or pardoned being down? Then I'll look up [48–50 of 98].

While they affirm the Christian view at the heart of the play, finally attained in the mutual forgiveness of Hamlet and Laertes,[6] the lines are, of course, doubly or trebly ironic in their immediate context. It is the villain of the piece who expresses the redemptive Christian view, and he is incapable of acting on it. Moreover, Hamlet is "forestalled" from killing Claudius not through prayer but through his most diabolical moment. He has not only failed to forgive but has taken upon himself the prerogatives of God himself to condemn the soul of Claudius. Claudius's pious maxim has no relevance to the behavior of either man. The focal point of the play then is a deeply ironic tableaux of murderer and avenger, both of whom explicitly reject Christian redemption. The tableaux expresses, that is to say, the essence of revenge tragedy.

As yet another meta-dramatic moment in the play, the prayer scene also presents Hamlet with a dumb show that the deep thinker takes to be exactly what it seems: a man praying. It is, as many critics have noted, the only time in the play that dramatic irony is turned against Hamlet. In the focal scene the theoretician of drama, the amateur actor and lover of plays is exposed as a rather naive spectator, almost a rube, who might, at a later show, leap onto the stage to save Desdemona from Othello. I will return to this seeming lapse in Hamlet's mimetic sophistication. My intention here is to point out that the prayer scene is thematically as well as architecturally central, focusing the play's concerns with Christian forgiveness and with mimesis in the tableaux of Hamlet and Claudius.

The nineteen scenes of the play are disposed as follows:

3.3 Claudius tries to pray for pardon.

3.2 Player King: "Purpose is but the slave to memory" (174–203 of 382).	[3.4 & 4.1] Ghost: "Do not forget. This visitation is … to whet thy … purpose" (95–131 of 237).
3.1 Hamlet: "to be or not to be" (57–89 of 189).	4.2 Hamlet, asked about Polonius's body, calls Rosencrantz a sponge (14–19 of 28).
2.2 Hamlet: "quintessence of dust" (291–308 of 594).	4.3 Hamlet reveals location of body (35 of 70).
2.1 Polonius sends Reynaldo to spy on Laertes (53–67 of 120).	4.4 Fortinbras with army (8).
1.5 Hamlet to Ghost: "Remember thee?" (92–110 of 198).	4.5 Laertes demands of Claudius: "Give me my father" (109–54 of 219).
1.4 Hamlet questions Ghost (23–36 of 66).	4.6 Hamlet's letter to Horatio, promising "words … [that] will make thee dumb" (11–29 of 32).
1.3 Polonius's "few precepts" to Laertes (58–80 of 136).	4.7 Claudius spurs Laertes to "play" with Hamlet (84–115 of 169).
1.2 Hamlet: "too, too solid flesh would melt" (129–159 of 260).	5.1 Hamlet and Gravedigger: "the day…. Hamlet was born" (111–74 of 289).
1.1 Horatio relates combat of King Hamlet and old Fortinbras (79–95 of 157).	5.2 Hamlet and Laertes prepare to duel (172–200 of 356).

Granville-Barker has pointed out[7] the long temporal intervals that occur between 1.5 and 2.1, the Ghost's charge to Hamlet and Hamlet's mute appearance in Ophelia's closet, and between 4.4 and 4.5, an indefinite but lengthy interval in which Polonius is buried, Ophelia goes mad, Laertes returns from Paris and Hamlet returns from his adventure with the pirates. These intervals, indicated by the break in the outline, divide the play into three broad movements in each of which the action is completed in two or three days. The first and last movements of the play, each of five scenes, are structurally balanced, and the temporal breaks are reinforced by the narrative digressions in the first and last scenes of the central section—Polonius's and Reynaldo's conversation (2.1) and Fortinbras with his army (4.4). The balance of the first and last movements is also heightened by the similarity of scenes 1.5 and 4.5, in which Hamlet and Laertes are each initiated into avenging his father's death. As the Ghost informs Hamlet of his father's murder, so too Claudius informs Laertes of his father's murder. The other scene pairs linking the first and last movements are similarly reflective. Laertes receives advice from his father and from his surrogate father, Claudius, in the 1.3–4.7 pair. One locus of the often-expressed sense of young Hamlet as a ghost himself, haunting the play, is the 1.4–4.6 pair: like the Ghost Hamlet has harrowing words; his threaten to make Horatio dumb.[8] The central speeches of the 1.2–5.1 pair structurally embed the transformation in Hamlet from his earlier desire for death to his "birth" and subsequent sketched biography in the last act.[9] The combat reported in the first scene and the mirroring duel between Hamlet and Laertes in the last scene are the most vivid actions in the play and are the only actions (as distinct from speeches) structurally central in their respective scenes. In the duel and the murder of Claudius, Hamlet finally succeeds in emulating his warrior father. The scholar becomes a soldier.

The reflections in the mirroring scene pairs of the central movement are not nearly so evident. Broadly speaking, the 2.2–4.3 and 3.1–4.2 pairs link Hamlet's speculative speeches on death with his terse reactions to its reality. In revealing the location of Polonius's body by anticipating the smell of the decaying corpse, Hamlet is already the sardonic commentator of the graveyard scene; he has finally confronted the "quintessence of dust" that anticlimactically ended his paired speech on the wonders of man (2.2.306). The second pair, 3.1 and 4.2, seems to contrast Hamlet's excruciating consciousness of death with Rosencrantz's obliviousness, though this might not be immediately evident because of the unfamiliar image at the center of 4.2.

In calling Rosencrantz a sponge, Hamlet is using an image derived ultimately from Seutonius, "who tells how it was said of the emperor Vespasian that he used rapacious officials like sponges, advancing them to high positions so that they would be richer when he came to condemn them" and confiscate their wealth. A characteristic Elizabethan twist to this idea is contained in an emblem that pictures "a king squeezing a sponge and in the background the condemned hanging from a gallows."[10] For Shakespeare's audience, the sponge image would have included this inevitable association with death. Taunted with this image of himself and the death sentence awaiting obsequious hangers-on, Rosencrantz replies, "I understand you not, my lord" (4.2.20). The "sponge" confirms his complete lack of awareness, of nearly total unconsciousness. By contrast, Hamlet is painfully aware of death in the famous soliloquy of 3.1.[11]

Characteristically, each of the incidents in the outline is the central episode or speech in its scene.[12] The combat between King Hamlet and Fortinbras is the central of five incidents, flanked by the appearances of the Ghost, which are in turn flanked by the arrival and departure of the watch. Hamlet's soliloquy in 1.5 is the central panel of a triptych, located between his encounter with the Ghost and his insistence on secrecy from Horatio and the soldiers. Claudius's prayer in 3.3 is also at the center of three incidents, flanked by his conversations with his lackeys, Rosencrantz, Guildenstern and Polonius, and Hamlet's soliloquy. The conversation between Claudius and Laertes in 1.5 is flanked by the two appearances of Ophelia, and preparations for the duel between Laertes and Hamlet are located in the middle of the two-part last scene. In this respect *Hamlet* is typically Shakespearean in its structure.

The three broad movements of the play are further divided by the Ophelia plot, as can be seen by adding to the above outline the incidents (italicized) in which she appears.

3.3 Claudius tries to pray for pardon.	
3.2 Player King: "Purpose is but the slave to memory" (174–203 of 382). (*Ophelia questions dumb show.*)	[3.4 & 4.1] Ghost: "Do not forget. This visitation is ... to whet thy ... purpose" (95–131 of 237).
-----------------------------------	4.2 Hamlet, asked about Polonius's body, calls Rosencrantz a sponge (14–19 of 28).
3.1 Hamlet: "to be or not to be" (57–89 of 189). (*Hamlet & Ophelia: nunnery speech.*)	
2.2 Hamlet: "quintessence of dust" (291–308 of 594).	4.3 Hamlet reveals location of body (35 of 70).
2.1 Polonius sends Reynaldo to spy on Laertes (53–67 of 120). (*Ophelia on Hamlet's dumb show in her closet.*)	4.4 Fortinbras with army (8).

1.5 Hamlet to Ghost: "Remember thee?" (92–110 of 198).	4.5 Laertes demands of Claudius: "Give me my father" (109–54 of 219). (*Ophelia as dumb picture.*)
1.4 Hamlet questions Ghost (23–36 of 66).	4.6 Hamlet's letter to Horatio, promising "words ... [that] will make thee dumb" (11–29 of 32).
1.3 Polonius's "few precepts" to Laertes (58–80 of 136) *and admonitions to "green girl" Ophelia.*	4.7 Claudius spurs Laertes to "play" with Hamlet (84–115 of 169). (*Ophelia's garlanded drowning, singing.*)
1.2 Hamlet: "too, too solid flesh would melt" (129–159 of 260).	5.1 Hamlet and Gravedigger: "the day ... Hamlet was born" (111–74 of 289).
1.1 Horatio relates combat of King Hamlet and old Fortinbras (79–95 of 157).	5.2 Hamlet and Laertes prepare to duel (172–200 of 356).

Both the Ophelia sections, 2.1 through 3.1 and 4.5 through 4.7,[13] begin with a dumb show and end (as indicated by dotted lines) with its articulation. In his wildness Hamlet merely gesticulates in Ophelia's closet; his meaning is articulated in the nunnery speech. Ophelia in 4.5 is effectively a dumb show. Her "speech is nothing," Horatio says at the opening of the scene; it provides only "winks and nods and gestures" by which she can be understood (7, 11). Claudius further confirms her essential muteness by implicitly comparing her to a picture or "mere beast" (82). Her meaning is finally articulated in the "snatches of old tunes" she sings before drowning (4.7.152). This pattern of a dumb show later articulated repeats the structure of the first act, which begins with the dumb show of the Ghost and ends with his explanation to Hamlet. The thrice-repeated pattern invites the inclusion of other dumb shows from the central flanking scenes and the last two scenes. (The added dumb shows and their articulations are italicized.)

3.3 Claudius tries to pray for pardon.	
3.2 Player King: "Purpose is but the slave to memory." (Ophelia questions dumb show.) *Hamlet: "Lucianus, nephew to the king."*	[3.4 & 4.1] Ghost: "Do not forget. This visitation is ... to whet thy ... purpose." *Hamlet kills Polonius, thinking he is Claudius.*
3.1 Hamlet: "to be or not to be." (Hamlet & Ophelia: nunnery speech.)	4.2 Hamlet, asked about Polonius's body, calls Rosencrantz a sponge.
2.2 Hamlet: "quintessence of dust."	4.3 Hamlet reveals location of body.
2.1 Polonius sends Reynaldo to spy on Laertes. (Ophelia on Hamlet's dumb show in her closet.)	4.4 Fortinbras with army. [Q2: *Hamlet: "My thoughts be bloody..."*]
1.5 Hamlet to Ghost: "Remember thee?"	4.5 Laertes demands of Claudius: "Give me my father." (Ophelia as dumb picture.)
1.4 Hamlet questions Ghost.	4.6 Hamlet's letter to Horatio, promising "words ... [that] will make thee dumb."
1.3 Polonius's "few precepts" to Laertes and	4.7 Claudius spurs Laertes to "play" with

admonitions to "green girl" Ophelia.)	Hamlet. (Ophelia's garlanded drowning, singing.)
1.2 Hamlet: "too, too solid flesh would melt."	5.1 Hamlet and Gravedigger: "the day.... Hamlet was born." *Yorick's skull.*
1.1 Horatio relates combat of King Hamlet and old Fortinbras.	5.2 Hamlet and Laertes prepare to duel. *Fortinbras has Hamlet's "dying voice."*

I include Hamlet's comment during The Murder of Gonzago as retrospectively complicating the dumb show and pointing up the similarity between Hamlet and its murderer. In his soliloquy in Quarto 4.4 Hamlet articulates what it is to be the mimed murderer (as he has become, like Claudius and Lucianus): "My thoughts be bloody" (66). The soliloquy was presumably deleted from the Folio because to have bloody thoughts is yet to have thoughts; Polonius's murder is pure act, thoughtless, rash and sudden: a dumb show. Similarly, the skull of Yorick is a dumb show questioned, emblematically, by Hamlet and articulated finally in Hamlet's "dying voice." That is, Hamlet, preoccupied by death through the whole play and now "come back" from death, articulates his version of the message of a death's head. He commands Horatio to tell his story and, as Hamlet the Dane names the next king of Denmark.

With these related incidents and the Ophelia plot the play divides into five parts, each beginning with a dumb show and ending with its articulation. Part One, which coincides with Act One, begins with the appearance of the Ghost (1.1) and ends with his revelations (1.5). Part Two begins with Hamlet's dumb show in Ophelia's closet (2.1) and ends with the nunnery speech (3.1), in which he articulates the implicit message of his earlier visit. Part Three begins with the dumb show of the Mousetrap (3.2) and ends with Hamlet's resolve that thoughts be bloody (Q2, 4.4); that is, he articulates, after having killed Polonius, what it is to be a murderer like Lucianus/Claudius. Part Four begins with Ophelia's dumb show in 4.5 and ends with her final songs. The fact that these old tunes are hardly more than the tunes she sang earlier suggests the way in which articulations of the dumb shows are themselves puzzling, perhaps inexplicable. Part Five extends this indeterminacy in having Hamlet with his dying voice name Fortinbras as successor, a man who, in Quarto 4.4, is a dumb show to Hamlet, and who, with only 25 or so lines in the play, is himself a virtual dumb show for the audience.

Excepting Part Two, these Parts have been remarked by other commentators (for other reasons than those I adduce), who recognize them as essentially Act divisions.[14] If the dumb shows and their articulations do in fact constitute the boundaries of the Acts in *Hamlet*, the anomalous imbalance of the play is immediately evident. While Acts Two and Four are clearly reflections as "Ophelia" Acts, they are not chiastically related, and Act One is not equally balanced by Act Five as in all the other plays whose act divisions have been indicated by the thematic arch. Furthermore, Act Three, also uniquely, extends by three extra scenes into the second half of the play. This extended Act Three, of course, contributes to the play's emphatic focus on Hamlet, but the function of the other departures from Shakespeare's usual practice remains one more oddity of an eccentric play.

Hamlet's misinterpretation of Claudius at prayer is pivotal to the structurally defining yet ultimately "inexplicable" dumb shows. Why does Hamlet misread Claudius? Hamlet's theory of drama discounts dumb shows as suitable only for the groundlings. To Hamlet the action without the word admits of no speculation and is therefore "meaningless." Yet it is this very meaninglessness, this incapacity for reflection, that opens a way out of thinking too pre-cisely and into action. The sequence of three dumb shows in the central scenes is the pivot of the structure and of Hamlet's change.

The dumb show the Players unexpectedly include in their presentation before the court ironically traps Hamlet.[15] His response to it can be gauged retrospectively from his comments during the performance of The Murder of Gonzago. In identifying the murderer as Lucianus, "nephew to the King," Hamlet unstrategically interprets the play before the whole court as a threatened murder of Claudius and, further, conflates himself as Lucianus with Claudius, the murderer in the dumb show. That is to say, Hamlet acts as though the dumb show alone has achieved the purpose for which The Murder of Gonzago was intended—confirmed Claudius's guilt and justified Hamlet's vengeance. But, to the persistent vexation of critics, Claudius does not respond in any way to the dumb show (nor to the subsequent dialogue between the Player King and Queen). Only Hamlet's reaction to the mimed murder and incest explains his foolish, public threat against Claudius. Despite Hamlet's denigration of dumb shows, he responds to them spontaneously and unreflectively, as is again confirmed when he responds uncritically to Claudius's posture in the chapel. When the murder of his father is mimed in action, Hamlet responds instinctively and, before any response from Claudius, proclaims the "nephew to the king" to be a "murderer" bent on "revenge" (3.2.239, 246–7, 248). And he reacts similarly in the blind, rash action of murdering Polonius in the paired scene, another inexplicable dumb show.

While the murder of Polonius by Hamlet imitates the dumb show, for the audience the murder alludes to the staged assassination of Julius Caesar. When Polonius recalls playing Julius Caesar, killed by Brutus in the Capitol, Hamlet replies, "It was a brute part of him to kill so capital a calf there" (3.2.104–5). As a "calf," Polonius is a fool and perhaps an ironically sacrificial victim, and his killer is ambiguously brutish and heroic, for, as Harold Jenkins glosses, one meaning of "brute" refers to Brut(us) the legendary founder of Britain.[16] But "brute part" also refers to the actor's role, and extends the pun emphatically by making an in-joke on the recent play of Julius Caesar, in which the roles of Caesar and Brutus were taken by the actors playing Polonius and Hamlet, John Hemminges and Richard Burbage. Both in its rash, unseeing enactment and in its reflection in the paired scene, the murder of Polonius is presented as a play, a dumb show as staged by Hamlet and Julius Caesar by allusion for the audience.[17] The mode of Hamlet's long-delayed action is simple imitation. The three central dumb shows—the Players', Claudius's and Hamlet's—trace Hamlet's escape from his suffering mind and into action.

In addition to providing dumb shows as structural markers, the Ophelia incidents also extend the parallel between Hamlet and Laertes as revengers. For the Ghost is not only informer, exhorter and father to Hamlet, as Claudius is to Laertes, but the Ghost is dumb show and victim as well. These roles are filled for Laertes by Ophelia. The scene in which Laertes is informed of Polonius's murder opens with Horatio's description of Ophelia in her madness as a dumb show, as described above. Seeing her distributing flowers, Laertes says, "Has thou thy wits, and didst persuade revenge, It could not move thus" (4.5.170–1). Almost as though in response, she echoes the Ghost in giving Laertes rosemary—"that's for remem-brance. Pray, love, remember"—and pansies—"that's for thoughts" (4.5.176–8).[18] With the narrative of her garlanded death (4.7.139–59), which literalizes her father's paired character-ization of her as a "green girl" (1.3.101), Laertes is fully confirmed in his intended revenge, now for two victims. Between them Claudius and Ophelia function for Laertes as the Ghost does for Hamlet. Like parallels between Richard II and Bolingbroke or Romeo and Paris, though with much more intricacy, the mirroring of Hamlet and Laertes is embedded structurally in the symmetry of the play.

The pairing of the first and last five scenes not only parallels Hamlet and Laertes as revengers but also highlights the changes in Hamlet after his return from the sea voyage. That Hamlet now shares the victim's point of view—that he is now the object of revenge—and that some profound death-like transformation has occurred is suggested by the pairing of scenes1.4 and 4.6; as mentioned above, Hamlet is like the Ghost in having harrowing words, a tale to make Horatio dumbstruck. Between the soliloquy of 1.2 on the "too, too solid flesh" and the paired conversation with the Gravedigger (5.1), Hamlet's tedium vitae has moderated to mordant humor, and his desire for death, as already mentioned, gives way to the mention of his birth and subsequent sketched biography. Finally, in the duel of the last scene, the two avengers break the analogous cycle initiated by the combat of King Hamlet and King Fortinbras in the first scene: the revengers come to mutual forgiveness.

The traditional act division of *Hamlet* seriously distorts the underlying structure that pairs the revengers and highlights Hamlet's transformation. Though Act One accurately encompasses the initial action of the Ghost's revelation, Act Two, on the Hamlet-Ophelia relationship, should extend through 3.1. Act Three, on Hamlet's change into an avenger, should extend from 3.2 through 4.4, to the emphatic time interval ending the second of the larger movements of the play. Act Four should include 4.5 through 4.7, Ophelia's madness and death, which balances the three scenes of Act Two on the Hamlet-Ophelia relationship. The traditional designation of Act Five should be retained.

Underlying the skewed act divisions, however, is a typically Shakespearean symmetry based on a frequent structural unit, the scene triplet, revealed by creating breaks at the extended dotted lines in the outline immediately above.

3.3 Claudius tries to pray for pardon.	
3.2 Player King: "Purpose is but the slave to memory." (Ophelia questions dumb show.) Hamlet: "Lucianus, nephew to the king."	[3.4 & 4.1] Ghost: "Do not forget" Hamlet kills Polonius, thinking he is Claudius.
3.1 Hamlet & Ophelia: nunnery scene. (soliloquy: "to be or not to be.")	4.2 Hamlet, asked about Polonius's body, calls Rosencrantz a sponge.
2.2 Hamlet: "quintessence of dust."	4.3 Hamlet reveals location of body.
2.1 Polonius sends Reynaldo to spy on Laertes. (Ophelia on Hamlet's dumb show in her closet.)	4.4 Fortinbras [Q2: Hamlet: "My thoughts be bloody..."]
1.5 Ghost reveals murder to Hamlet.	4.5 Claudius to Laertes on death of Polonius. (Ophelia as dumb picture.)
1.4 Hamlet questions Ghost.	4.6 Hamlet's letter to Horatio, promising "words ... [that] will make thee dumb."
1.3 Polonius's advice to Laertes (and admonitions to "green girl" Ophelia).	4.7 Claudius plots with Laertes. (Ophelia's garlanded drowning, singing.)

1.2 Hamlet: "too, too solid flesh."	5.1 Hamlet and Gravedigger: "Hamlet born." Yorick's skull.
1.1 Horatio relates combat of King Hamlet and old Fortinbras.	5.2 Hamlet and Laertes duel. Fortinbras has Hamlet's "dying voice."

Hamlet's central transformation is itself rendered in three movements: the break from Ophelia (2.1–3.1), the enactments—staged and real—of murder in the central pinnacle (3.2 through [3.4 & 4.1]), and the response to Polonius's murder (4.2–Q 4.4). The first and last broad movements are subdivided to separate what Francis Fergusson has called ritual scenes at the beginning and end of the play (1.1, 1.2, 5.1 and 5.2)[19] from the group of three scene pairs in which sons engage with fathers, Hamlet with the Ghost and Laertes with Polonius and his surrogate, Claudius.

This, then, is the skeletal author-plot: a symmetrical arch with the prayer scene as keystone and with the focal incident of each scene of the first half mirroring—perhaps "echoing" is a better word in the case of the speechifying Hamlet—the corresponding incident of the second half. But unlike, say, *Much Ado About Nothing*, the symmetry of scene groupings does not coincide with the overlaid pattern of act divisions. Thus the "Ophelia acts," two and four, are not directly reflective, and the third act uncharacteristically extends three extra scenes into the second half of the play. These are perhaps not immediately perceptible departures from Shakespeare's usual practice, but it is possible that the skewed structure partly accounts for the play's felt unity and "poor ... plotting,"[20] for the fact that, as John Jones puts it, the play is "a miracle of seeming not to hang together."[21]

14

The Stories in *Troilus and Cressida*

Troilus and Cressida has no story, or is as near to having none as a Renaissance play can be. And it is the only one of Shakespeare's plays of which this can be said: no other, for instance, shares its notable lack of a formally structured ending, as of wedding or funeral. This absence of simple story-line in *Troilus and Cressida* is experienced by anyone who tries to remember the exact order of events, particularly in the middle of the play; and it is the source of most of the other problems that disturb the play's readers. No one finds it easy to describe how the action develops, if indeed it does develop, or to decide who its chief characters—its protagonists— actually are, as between Troilus and Cressida themselves, who hardly come in, Ulysses, who is a bore, Achilles, who is a thug, Hector, who is opaque, even Thersites, who does nothing: and all of them have decidedly little to do with one another. Since what characters have to do with one another is a basic part of the meaning of "story," this is what in the present case appears to be missing [Barbara Everett, *Young Hamlet: Essays on Shakespeare's Tragedies*, 165].

This accurately records the impression left by *Troilus and Cressida*. The play seems not to consist of intelligible and unified actions in the Aristotelian sense but rather of a confusing series of fragments from the two well-known stories of the death of Hector and the infidelity of Cressida. "*Troilus* does not cohere," John Jones writes and further remarks the play's "calculated obscurity."[1] Under these circumstances even a modest description of the two plots might be helpful, particularly as they are chiastically arranged, for the reflecting halves of the play clarify both the individual plots and the relationship between the war story and the love story. For, of course, the play does have stories, protagonists, relationships among the characters and all the elements we would expect in a narrative. It is only that coherence of action, consistency of character and loyalty of affection are not especially the hallmarks of Shakespeare's Trojan war, and they are not immediately evident in the surface of the play.

And therein lies the problem. We complete the story ourselves. The narrative is so muffled, fractured and indirect and our knowledge of the stories invoked is so unshakable that we don't see the extent of Shakespeare's revisionism. Without—I hope—being merely contrarian, I will dispute the commonly accepted reading of a high-principled Hector and a false Cressida. Rather, I will argue that his inflexible "honor" ultimately makes Hector (like the honorable Brutus in *Julius Caesar*) the villain of the piece and her regretted infidelity makes Cressida the only hope for constancy and love. This conclusion derives from examining the keystone issue of the play, the corruption of sacrifice. In *Troilus and Cressida* sacrifice is embedded figuratively in the central scene, so that the entire structure turns on the "exchange" of Cressida, imaged not as a commodity transaction but as an unacknowledged sacrificial offering. As Hector makes a "polluted off'ring" in his vow to fight (5.3.17), Troilus makes a similarly polluted offer of his "heart," for Cressida is the unacknowledged sacrifice who learns through her victimization the truth of love. Like the plays set wholly or partially in pagan Rome— *Julius Caesar, Coriolanus,* and *Cymbeline,* most obviously—a play set in the pagan Greek world also serves as an occasion to probe the nature of sacrifice.

The Love Story

The love story pivots on a quick sequence of three scenes at the center of the play when Cressida is given over to the Greeks.[2] The two scenes flanking the central sequence set up and complete the exchange.

4.3 Troilus and Paris on delivery of Cressida.	
4.2 Troilus learns from Aeneas and Cressida from Pandarus of impending exchange.	4.4 Troilus & Cressida's farewells; Cressida handed over to Diomedes.
4.1 Diomedes brings Antenor to Troy to exchange for Cressida.	4.5 Diomedes brings Cressida to Greek camp.

The central scene both of the sequence and of the entire play is the short scene in which Troilus and Paris discuss the delivery of Cressida. It might seem to be an odd focus for the play, but it is characteristic of Shakespeare's mature art that the interpretation of the event— here, the exchange—rather than the event itself should receive structural emphasis. As a comment on the larger narrative of the play, the central scene distills into 12 lines the essential irony in the juxtaposition of the two plots: Troilus gives up Cressida, while Paris keeps Helen. By ending the scene with Paris's oblivious, self-serving statement, "I know what 'tis to love; And would.... I could help" (4.3.10–11), Shakespeare makes the irony as obvious as it is pervasive throughout the play. The psychological and thematic relevance of the scene will be discussed later, but we might also notice here that the brevity of the scene contributes to the sense of callous negligence attendant on the exchange, for Cressida has no sooner consummated her love for Troilus than she is informed of her fate (by Pandarus, no less) and, almost as quickly, is handed over to Diomedes. The plot actions are disposed chiastically. The intelligence of the exchange and its accomplishment are paired (4.2 and 4.4), as are the delivery of Antenor to the Trojans and of Cressida to the Greeks (4.1 and 4.5). The rest of the love story proper is quickly told, again in paired scenes:

3.2 Troilus and Cressida pledge fidelity.	5.2 Cressida betrays Troilus with Diomedes.
3.1 Pandarus extracts promise from Paris to make excuse for Troilus who will be dining with Cressida.	5.3 Troilus tears up Cressida's letter.

The 3.1–5.3 pair in effect begins and ends the action of the love story (though not its preliminaries and consequences). The first and only assignation is finally arranged by Pandarus in 3.1, when we discover in the midst of Helen's and Paris's bantering that Troilus is to dine with Cressida; in 5.3 Troilus tears up Cressida's letter, the last communication between the lovers, and (in the Folio) dismisses Pandarus. Both scenes involve an excuse—the excuse for Troilus's absence (3.1) and Cressida's written excuse for betraying Troilus (5.3). In 3.2 and

the paired 5.2, the scenes of pledged fidelity and of betrayal, the lovers are both on stage for the first and last times. One of the most important similarities between the scenes is the psychological "division" of Cressida. "I have a kind of self resides with you," she tells Troilus, after admitting her love for him, "but an unkind self that itself will leave To be another's fool" (3.2.143–45). Watching the betrayal, Troilus seems to pick up on this notion of self-division in his various attempts to deny what he has witnessed. Cressida was not here, he insists; "This is and is not Cressida"; "This is Diomed's Cressida" not the Cressida Troilus loves. And Cressida herself extends the sense of self-division in her final speech: "Troilus, farewell. One eye yet looks on thee, But with my heart the other eye doth see" (113–14), where the pun on "I/eye" picks up exactly the comment already quoted from the paired scene. The apparent fragmentation of the play, we might say, is epitomized in this division within Cressida, which is highlighted in the most important of the love story's paired scenes.

   Combined in a single outline, the trajectory of the love story is relatively simple and straightforward. It is concentrated in the middle scenes of the play. Eight of the 11 central scenes are importantly concerned with Troilus and Cressida, (though neither lover appears in some of the eight, those bracketed in the following outline). The three central scenes are devoted exclusively to the love story and comprise a separate grouping. The scenes of the beginning and end of the affair, though not exclusively about the lovers, should also be viewed as a separate group.

4.3 Troilus and Paris on delivery of Cressida.	
4.2 Troilus learns from Aeneas and Cressida from Pandarus of impending exchange.	4.4 Troilus & Cressida's farewells; Cressida delivered to Diomedes.
4.1 [Diomedes brings Antenor to Troy to exchange for Cressida.]	4.5 Diomedes brings Cressida to Greek camp.
3.3 [Calchas granted request to exchange Antenor for Cressida.]	5.1 Troilus follows Diomedes to Calchas' tent.
3.2 Troilus and Cressida pledge fidelity.	5.2 Cressida betrays Troilus with Diomedes.
3.1 [Pandarus extracts promise from Paris to make excuse for Troilus who will be dining with Cressida.]	5.3 Troilus tears up Cressida's letter.

   The preliminaries of this action are presented in the first two scenes of the play. In the opening scene the moony Troilus unarms because he has no "heart" for fighting (1.1.4); his love for Cressida preoccupies him; his battle is within. Pandarus upbraids him for his impatience, for not tarrying to have "a cake out of the wheat" (1.1.15), and leaves. Frustrated in his hopes for love, Troilus then departs for the field with Aeneas. In the second scene, Pandarus sings Troilus's praises to Cressida by comparing him favorably to Hector, and Cressida admits in soliloquy that she loves Troilus. With the apparent exception of these two scenes, which I will return to, the love story is disposed in the shapely, symmetrical structure outlined above. Cressida's betrayal, however, both in the structural balance of its position and in its staging, is emphasized, while the shoddy treatment of Cressida by Troilus is more diffused, occurring over the three central scenes. On the morning after, Troilus is already impatient to go and, learning of the deal for Cressida's exchange, is so thoughtless or indifferent as to leave without telling her himself. In the short central scene he speaks hyperbolically and narcissistically of the sacrifice of his heart to Diomedes; and, finally, in his farewell to Cressida already doubts her fidelity, now indulging the misogynistic suspicions that he had earlier more tentatively expressed. The disposition of the narrative, that is to say, invites the traditional condemnation of Cressida as a false woman, while muting the part Troilus plays in undermining the relationship. As in the war plot, Shakespeare misleadingly invites a traditional judgment, here of Cressida's character, and inclines us to overlook her final reformation.

The War Story

The war story is more complex, halting and elliptical than the love story, and it helps to rigorously reduce it to the essential conflict between Achilles and Hector. Again, the narrative's answering moments are arranged in chiastically paired scenes from the first and second halves of the play. (The traditional scenes 5.5 and 5.6 are actually one scene as explained in note 1.)

4.1 Diomedes brings Antenor to Troy to exchange for Cressida with "despiteful gentle greetings."	4.5 Cressida brought to Greek camp. Hector ceases combat with Ajax: "the issue is embracement." Achilles: friend and "fell as death."
3.3 Achilles refuses to fight, sends invitation to Hector.	5.1 Initially bellicose, Achilles receives Polyxena's letter and will not fight; welcomes Hector to feast.
3.2	5.2
3.1 Paris, kept from field by Helen, promises to make excuse for Troilus' absence from supper (to dine with Cressida).	5.3 Hector refuses women's pleas to stay home; Troilus tears up Cressida's letter.
2.3 Thersites offers his services to Achilles, who has refused to fight.	5.4 Thersites watches Diomedes and Troilus fight; is spared by Hector.
2.2 Hector and Troilus argue the merits of returning Helen; Hector on honor.	[5.5 & 5.6] [Patroclus killed.] Hector and Troilus sought in battle by Greeks; Hector spares Achilles.
2.1 Thersites beaten by Ajax; Achilles tells of proclamation from Hector: "trash."	5.7 Achilles instructs Myrmidons to kill Hector; Thersites chorus to Paris-Menelaus fight.
1.3 Achilles accused of creating dissension; Hector's challenge brought by Aeneas.	5.8 Achilles and Myrmidons kill Hector.

In the central scenes of the war story, 4.1 and 4.5, the action teeters between love and war. Hector stops his fight with Ajax and accepts an invitation to feast; "the issue" of the combat, Hector says, "is embracement." Achilles is a friend today but a deadly foe, he says, tomorrow. And in the paired scene Diomedes greets the Trojans with "despiteful gentle greetings" when he brings Antenor for exchange, expressing the same apparently contradictory impulses toward doing battle and performing courtesies. The extremes of this ambivalence are enacted in abrupt reversals and significant offstage events in the second half of the play.

The war story proper begins with Hector's challenge to the Greeks (1.3) and ends with his death in the chiastically paired scene (5.8). Achilles' disdain for the conventional values of war is expressed in both scenes of the 2.1–5.7 pair. In the early scene Achilles dismisses Hector's challenge, which links the warrior's valor with his mistress's honor, as "trash" and in the later scene instructs the Myrmidons to surround and impale Hector "in fellest manner" (5.7.6), violating any chivalrous ideal of warfare. The 3.3–5.1 pair enacts the invitation and welcome of Hector to the feast and highlights the change in Achilles' motives that occurs between these two actions. In the first half of the play, to scene 3.3, Achilles is recalcitrant and dilatory. But, pressed by Patroclus and the other Greeks, by the opening of 5.1 Achilles is converted to Hector's idea of honor and is therefore determined to kill Hector. After reading the letter from Polyxena, however, he does an abrupt volte-face and by the end of scene 5.1 sincerely welcomes Hector to the feast. This seems to conclusively settle the narrative question of the first half: Achilles will not fight. It is only with the offstage killing of Patroclus that Achilles again changes his mind and returns to the battle, thus conforming to the storyline of the epic tradition.

In addition to the explicit reversals staged in Achilles' double volte-faces and Cressida's betrayal, there are also two implicit changes after the midpoint. One involves the "opaque" Hector. Even in his consistency, he seems to vacillate. After arguing persuasively that keeping Helen is immoral, he yet resolves on exactly that course. Though he has issued the challenge that initiates the war story, he breaks off fighting with his kinsman Ajax, commenting that "the issue is embracement"; he spares Theristes; and he spares Achilles. He seems to waver in his purposes and motives as much as Achilles does. But, of course, Hector is perfectly consistent throughout the play. He is motivated by "honor." Keeping Helen is a question of honor. Ajax is not the warrior Hector intended to face; his challenge, though generalized, was clearly intended to engage Achilles. He spares Thersites because he is an unworthy opponent. He spares Achilles for more nebulous reasons, perhaps because he himself is tired, perhaps because it is dishonorable to kill an unprepared man, perhaps out of a feeling of guilt at having killed Patroclus. He is not merciful on the battlefield, as Troilus suggests, but is instead vain of his reputation. While Hector's notion of honor is progressively dismantled in the play until it is revealed as mere lust for a superficial "value" that reduces to a glittering piece of armor, Hector does not deviate from his ideal. Unlike the other characters and in direct contrast to Achilles, he remains fixed in his devotion to his ultimate aim. Yet even his consistently motivated actions are presented so as to undermine any sense of consistency in the plot.

Therefore, it is easy to overlook the further turn after the midpoint: Hector's betrayal of Achilles in killing Patroclus. Within the ostensibly fractured narrative I have described, the almost ghostly presence of the traditional story is given body by our preconceptions. We know the story; we do not have to think about it. Yes, Hector kills Patroclus and the death of his friend brings Achilles back into battle. But why does Hector kill Patroclus? Why is Achilles so brutal in murdering Hector and defiling his body? As the betrayal by Cressida impels Troilus to bloodthirstiness, the betrayal by Hector drives Achilles to a mocking savagery. It is not the fact of his friend's death alone that spurs Achilles to such angry extremes, but the additional impetus provided by Hector's deceit as well. When Achilles welcomes Hector to the feast in 5.1, the Greek hero is no longer "fell as death" (4.5.269). The feast is no longer a chance to appraise an enemy's weaknesses—the motive for the original invitation— but is rather an offer of friendship and peace. The feast, that is to say, is a successful (so Achilles thinks) "seduction" of Hector occurring offstage at the same time as Diomedes "seduces" Cressida onstage.

Feasting and food imagery in general are one of the most important means by which the play suggests those relationships that, as Everett points out, are otherwise absent from the action. Both love and war are imaged as feeding. Pandarus compares Cressida to bread; Troilus anticipates with "imaginary relish.... Love's thrice-pured nectar" (3.2.17–20) and soothes Cressida's fears by saying, "Praise us as we are tasted" (87–88). Love is mutual sustenance: Troilus and Cressida "sup" together. War, on the other hand, is a predatory rather than a mutual feeding. Men are "consumed in the hot digestion of cormorant war" (2.2.5). Achilles says, "I have fed mine eye on [Hector] … joint by joint" (4.5.231) to determine how best to kill him, and Achilles' meal with Hector is at first also intended as part of hostilities:

> I'll heat his blood with Greekish wine tonight,
> Which with my scimitar I'll cool tomorrow.
> Patroclus, let us feast him to the height [5.1.1–3].

Both war and love, however, as has often been remarked of this play, can become self-cannibalism. The honor sought in battle can become merely narcissistic pride (3.2.152, 154, 182–5). Love can become mere lechery, and, as Thersites says, "lechery eats itself" (5.4.31–4). Ulysses sums up the workings of narcissistic desire:

> And appetite, an universal wolf,
> So doubly seconded with will and power,
> Must make perforce an universal prey
> And last eat up himself [1.3.120–24].

In both plots there is a trajectory of imagery coincident with the development of the story. Betrayed, Troilus rails against the "greasy relics" of Cressida's "o'ereaten faith" (5.2.166–67) and dismisses her letter in similar imagery: "My love with words and errors still she feeds" (5.3.110); she is no longer either bread or nectar. The "honey-sweet Helen" is also mere "lees," "dregs" and "carrion" after she is attained and lost (3.1 passim, 4.1.61, 64, 73). In the war story the trajectory of the imagery is, like the plot, halting and often deflected. Men are repeatedly imaged as food for war. The final occurrence of the image is in the scene in which Hector is killed, 5.8, when both he and Achilles talk of their swords feeding; they have both become mere engines of destruction. Hector: "Rest, sword, thou hast thy fill of blood and death" (4). Achilles: "My half-supped sword, that frankly would have fed, pleased with this dainty bait, thus goes to bed" (19–20).

But this inhuman butchery was not necessary, for, like the lovers, the warriors too, now literally, have fed together, and their feasts are ideally acts of friendship. Not that "factious feasts" (1.3.191) are not possible, or feasts in which the enemy is eyed "joint by joint" to find signs of weakness and ways of killing him. But like the figurative feast of lovemaking, the literal feast is ideally one of amity. The structure embeds the contrast. The scene of Hector's death, the scene in which Achilles' "half-supped sword" feeds on "this dainty bait," is paired with the scene in which Aeneas is invited to feast with the Greeks as a courtesy extended to a "noble foe" (1.3.308).[3] Achilles, having decided not to fight, entertains Hector in this same spirit. Hector's decision in 5.3 to return to the field, then, not only denies his wife, his father, and his prophetic sister; it also betrays Achilles's friendship and destroys the only hope of peace, the amity of the two heroes.

Fittingly, the scene of Hector's decision is paired with the Paris-Helen scene (3.1), the only time Helen appears in the play. This pair of scenes (3.1–5.3) enacts the essential contrast of the play as arming and "unarming" in the medieval sense of wearing armor.[4] Not only is Hector not persuaded by repeated pleas to "unarm" in 5.3 but Troilus is also unconvinced, both by Hector and by Cressida's letter, which, had it been better received, would have pacified him. In the paired scene, on the other hand, Paris has been kept home by Helen, who, as the scene ends, is exiting to "unarm" Hector (3.1.143–44); Troilus is absent from the battlefield because he is with Cressida; and Pandarus, subjected to Helen's charms in the scene's dominant action, capitulates, singing as she has requested. Hector, that is, is the one character so inflexible and fixed on his own aim, the attainment of a narcissistic honor, that he cannot be moved by love, filial devotion, prophecy or pleasure. His absolutism is the cause of his own death and the destruction of Troy. The two scenes also extend the play's essential contrasts by elaborately playing on "dying"—in love and in war: "Dying love lives still," as Pandarus sings (3.1.124), but Hector's death, in Cassandra's prescient description (5.3.80–87), admits no playful paradoxes. To oversimplify, these two scenes present the extreme values of the play—love and war, pleasure and honor, playfulness and predation.

Hector's absolute fixation on honor, then, adds to the three explicit reversals after the midpoint—Achilles' double volte face and Cressida's betrayal of Troilus—the implicit reversal by Hector in betraying the friendship of Achilles by killing Patroclus. The second implicit reversal occurs in the love plot, in Cressida's letter to Troilus. I will return to it after establishing a wider perspective.

Clearly, the problem is not that the play has "no story." It has in fact too much story. There are too many staged reversals in the action and too many important offstage events which are only elliptically presented for the play to be easily apprehended in a single narrative trajectory. But now that we have some sense of the structure of the separate stories, we can outline the entire play to see the overall structure and the mirroring, beyond the analogous betrayals by Cressida and Hector, of the love and war plots.

The structural groupings of two scene pairs each in the following outline are themselves expressive, since "couples" underlie both plots. Each group of two pairs, the scene couplets, devotes three of its four scenes to the same character(s), either as a dominant topic of conversation or as an onstage presence. In a characteristically logical arrangement, the first scene couplet, opening and closing the play, is on Hector; the second on Achilles; the third on Hector and Troilus; the fourth on the women; and the fifth on Achilles and Hector, their wavering relationship mingled in this ambivalent scene couplet with similarly wavering relations from the love story.

4.3 Troilus and Paris on delivery of Cressida.	
4.2 Troilus learns from Aeneas and Cressida from Pandarus of impending exchange.	4.4 Troilus & Cressida's farewells; Cressida delivered to Diomedes.
4.1 Diomedes brings Antenor to Troy to exchange for Cressida with "despiteful gentle greetings."	4.5 Cressida brought to Greek camp. Hector ceases combat with Ajax: "the issue is embracement." Achilles: friend and "fell as death."
3.3 Achilles refuses to fight, sends invitation to Hector. Calchas granted request to exchange Antenor for Cressida.	5.1 Initially bellicose, Achilles receives Polyxena's letter and will not fight; welcomes Hector to feast. Troilus exits after Diomedes to Calchas' tent.

3.2 Troilus and Cressida pledge fidelity.	5.2 Cressida betrays Troilus with Diomedes.
3.1 Paris, kept from field by Helen, promises to make excuse for Troilus' absence from supper (to dine with Cressida).	5.3 Hector refuses women's pleas to stay home; Troilus tears up Cressida's letter.
2.3 Thersites offers his services to Achilles, who has refused to fight.	5.4 Thersites watches Diomedes and Troilus fight; is spared by Hector.
2.2 Hector and Troilus argue the merits of returning Helen; Hector on honor.	[5.5 & 5.6] [Patroclus killed.] Hector and Troilus sought in battle by Greeks; Hector spares Achilles.
2.1 Thersites beaten by Ajax; Achilles tells of proclamation from Hector: "trash."	5.7 Achilles instructs Myrmidons to kill Hector; Thersites chorus to Paris-Menelaus fight.
1.3 Achilles accused of creating dissension; Hector's challenge brought by Aeneas.	5.8 Achilles and Myrmidons kill Hector.
1.2 Hector's anger with Ajax & superiority to Troilus talked of by Cressida and Pandarus; parade of warriors.	5.9 Greeks learn of Hector's death.
1.1 Troilus and Pandarus on courting Cressida; Aeneas & Troilus to field.	5.10 Troilus tells Aeneas of Hector's death. [Pandarus' epilogue.]

I have already mentioned the essential irony in the central scene, the juxtaposition of the two plots: Troilus gives up Cressida, while Paris keeps Helen. Less obvious is the scene's focus on what I take to be the play's essential target, the motive for its semi-satirical animus: the perversion of sacrifice. In the central image of the play Troilus says to Paris,

> And to his [Diomedes'] hand when I deliver her [Cressida],
> Think it an altar, and thy brother Troilus
> A priest there off'ring to it his own heart [4.3.7–9].

Like *Julius Caesar*, though perhaps more surprisingly, *Troilus and Cressida* has at its very center an invocation of sacrifice. Troilus's conventional lover's language, casting the beloved as his own heart, is of course perfectly in keeping with his sentimentally romantic attitude. Even more importantly, the speech distorts the true nature of the sacrifice that is being offered. In his self-pitying narcissism Troilus displaces the true victim, Cressida, with his own heart (which we will see he does not, in fact, give up). The extent of his posturing and self-deceit can be measured by his attitude in the previous scene. From the moment the lovers appear after their single night together, Troilus is already anxious to leave and lamely attempts to cover his flight with false solicitude towards Cressida, who realizes immediately that Troilus is, as she knew men were, hot in pursuit but cool in the winning. Troilus' lamentation the next time we see him, in the central scene, is of a piece with that of Shakespeare's other hyperbolic, self-indulgent lovers, with, for example, Romeo's initial self-conceit or the Duke of Orsino's self-infatuation. Troilus' vaunted sacrifice of his own heart is what Cassandra will later term, characterizing Hector's vow to fight, a "polluted off'ring" (5.3.17). The true sacrifice is of Cressida, an innocent victim.

At the center of the play, then, is the "exchange" of Cressida, now presented not as a commodity in a transaction but as a sacrificial offering unrecognized by Troilus. After her early, witty self-possession, she gives herself completely to Troilus. Her earlier reluctance to admit her feelings stems from her understanding of "love's full sacrifice" (1.2.282)—that she would have "no more kin," and that her love would be the center of the earth (4.2.99, 105). (It is worth noting, too, that in the previous scene, only about 50 lines earlier, Aeneas has mentioned that Cressida is to be delivered before "the first sacrifice" of the day; though referred to merely as a time marker, the mention of sacrifice nevertheless makes us aware that Cressida thus becomes the first sacrifice of the day.) Once having admitted her love for Troilus, Cressida feels a sense of acute distress and self-division; and, having made the "full sacrifice," her self-possession disappears.

If Cressida gives herself so completely, what happened to make her false? David Bevington wants to excuse her by saying that she "yields to Diomedes … through fear, susceptibility to male authority and hopelessness."[5] But this is not what she says in explaining her defection to herself:

> Troilus, farewell! One eye yet looks on thee,
> But with my heart the other eye doth see.
> Ah, poor our sex! This fault in us I find:
> The error of our [heart's] eye directs our mind.
> What error leads must err. O then conclude:
> Minds swayed by eyes are full of turpitude [5.2.113–18].

Cressida distinguishes between her mind's eye, which retains the image of Troilus, and the heart's eye, ruled by her passion of the moment for Diomedes. When she made this distinction earlier, planning for her love to remain unprofessed, she located love in the heart: "though my heart's contents firm love doth bear, Nothing of that shall from mine eyes appear" (1.2.285–86). This formulation indicates the source of the problem when the eye of her heart falls on Diomedes. Cressida is coming to realize that it is not the heart but the mind which sustains love.

Cressida's distinction between mind and heart accords not only with Hector's earlier distinction in justifying keeping Helen (2.2.163–89), when he ignored his logic in the interests of his honor, but also with Cassandra's distinction when attempting to persuade Hector to remain home from battle. In reply to Hector's claim that the gods have heard his vow, Cassandra says,

> The gods are deaf to hot and peevish vows.
> They are polluted off'rings, more abhorred
> Than spotted livers in the sacrifice [5.3.17–19].

Hector's vow has been made, it is well to remember, in despite of what his mind concluded was the truth. It is therefore in accord with the "heart," which also creates problems for Cressida. If the gods do not accept vows that are hot and peevish, then Cressida's betrayal of Troilus, prompted by her heart's eye and apparently regretted in her letter to him, is similarly to be excused and overlooked.

Cressida's letter (an incident of Shakespeare's invention) has a wide context, for the women, with varying degrees of success, always try to keep the men home from war. Helen keeps Paris back from the field on at least one occasion. At Polyxena's request Achilles declines to fight. Andromache, though unsuccessfully, pleads with Hector not to join the battle. When Troilus tears up Cressida's letter and goes to the field (as he did in the first scene when he despaired of her love), it suggests that her letter too was, indirectly, a plea for him to stay home. How could she have prevailed on him to stay home? By saying that she loved him, that her heart momentarily betrayed her but her mind remains committed to him. But Troilus dismisses the letter: "Words, words, mere words," he says, "no matter from the heart" (5.3.106). Like Hector, Troilus dismisses what is true in the interests of his "honor." In spite of his claim in the central scene, he has not sacrificed his heart, as Cressida's letter implies she has in admitting her "error" and giving up Diomedes.[6]

Troilus's dismissive comment upon receiving Cressida's letter has its appropriate place in the food imagery tracing the diminuendo of the love story, the denial of love and its replacement by hostilities. The unremarkable, apparently trivial use of the verb "feeds" as Troilus tears up Cressida's letter is best appreciated in the context of the feeding images of 5.2 and subsequent scenes. Troilus's anticipatory "relish" in the paired 3.2 finds in 5.2 only the "greasy relics" of Cressida's love, now belonging to Diomedes. In 5.3, after dismissing Cressida's letter, Troilus immediately devotes himself to "venomed vengeance," an image that turns the "biting" of both love and war into a wholly aggressive action, lacking the aspect of feeding altogether, and in the play's pervasive tone renders war as a snake attacking. In 5.4, in the fight between Troilus and Diomedes, "lechery eats itself": love is transmuted to war and devours itself. There is no further food imagery relating specifically to the love story, since love is now displaced by war, and the immediate result is the mechanical butchery of feeding swords wielded by Hector and Achilles. There follows the only scene in the play (5.9) without any food imagery and the natural consequence of such lack in the last scene (5.10): starvation. Aeneas, thinking the field is the Trojans', says, "Never go home; here starve we out the night" (1). The ironies in this the last food image in the play extend far beyond the simple dramatic irony of Aeneas's ignorance of the true state of the battle, particularly in light of the paired first scene in which Troilus found Helen "too starved a subject" for his sword[7] and was advised, in Pandarus's elaborate image, to think of Cressida as baked bread.

This is the context for Cressida's "words and [admissions of] error" as insufficient food for love in the letter Troilus dismisses: "Words, words, mere words, no matter from the heart.... My love with words and errors still she feeds" (5.3.107, 110). Troilus laments the lack of either deeds or substance in "mere words" that issue from the mind rather than from the heart. But in tearing up Cressida's letter and accusing her of inconstancy, he ends up starving. It is his insistence on heartfelt emotion that lacks substance. It is exactly words and repented errors that feed love. Her faithlessness has taught Cressida constancy. To persist in calling her false, as Troilus does, as history does, is, according to Shakespeare's revisionist rendering, to persist in scapegoating her.

Hector's betrayal of Achilles and Cressida's final reformation seem too subtle and elliptical to be easily understood even in reading and rereading the text, never mind in performance. But there can be no doubt of the "calculated obscurity," of this play, as John Jones has commented, and the playwright's general eschewal of the explicit, his creation of motive and meaning through interwoven plots, analogous characters, echoing actions and language, and other indirections.[8] And, I would argue, his use of "structural denotation," the meaning generated not merely semantically but by virtue of spatial positioning on a symmetrical arch. It is only the structure that signals, for example, the keystone importance of Troilus's invocation of sacrifice, the varying significance of the food imagery, or the precise resonance of Hector's refusal to unarm at Andromache's request. Indeed, it is only the symmetrical structure that tells the whole story.

15

The Thematic Arch
of *All's Well That Ends Well*
Hubris and Humiliation

The ground note of *All's Well That Ends Well* is sounded in the central scene of the play, in Helena's letter to the Countess. Repenting her "ambitious love," Helena explains that she is leaving on pilgrimage in order that Bertram might return from war to the safety of Rossillion: "He is too good and fair for death and me, Whom I myself embrace to set him free" (3.4.5, 16–17). This is the midpoint of Helena's education in humility. While no longer intent on forcing her will, via the King, on Bertram, she still has an insufficient idea of marital self-sacrifice. Her notion of embracing death is fittingly expressed as the final couplet of a sonnet because it is—as events will show—romanticized. She will learn true mortification in the bed trick, in embracing the Bertram who thinks she is someone else. This note of mortification pervades the play, for, like Helena, Bertram and Parolles are also mortified, each reduced to the thing he is, and the other prominent characters are also humbled, if not quite so drastically. Shakespeare's most astringent and Lenten play is structurally focused on Helena's keystone moment of self-abnegation.

The scenes flanking Helena's central sonnet preserve Shakespeare's usual practice in being linked by the same action, here the beginning and end of Bertram's military campaign. In 3.3 Bertram is installed as general of the horse, praying to be a "lover of [Mars's] drum," and in 3.5 he rides in military triumph through Florence after having fulfilled his aspiration by killing the opposing Duke's brother. Though Bertram would not act on the words of his marriage vow, he successfully unites his actions with the signs and trappings of war in these paired scenes. The three central scenes thus contrast Helena's self-abnegation with Bertram's self-assertion: Helena "kills" herself, Bertram kills others.

3.4 Helena's sonnet-letter to Countess.	
3.3 Bertram appointed general of cavalry.	3.5 Bertram with drums and colors in military triumph.

But these scenes do far more than structurally embed the basic contrast between Helena and Bertram. As so often in Shakespeare, the scene after the keystone initiates the change in the main character and the turn in the action of the play. As Duke Vincentio decides to save Claudio, as Othello succumbs to Iago's temptation, Helena, learning of Bertram's faithlessness,

135

plans the bed trick. Unlike Othello but again like the Duke, Helena's change—perhaps "intensification" is a better word—occurs without any explicit indication of it, but she obviously has a new understanding of Bertram and, consequently, of the self-sacrifice required of her. Furthermore, the scene includes the third focal action of the play, Parolles' loss of the drum.

	3.4 Helena's sonnet-letter to Countess.
3.3 Bertram appointed general of cavalry.	3.5 Bertram with drums and colors seen by Helena, who learns of his advances to Diana and plans bed trick. Parolles vexed by loss of drum.

In the structural time of the play the three tympanum actions—Helena's pilgrimage, Bertram's warring, and Parolles' loss of the drum—occur simultaneously, an overlap that emphasizes their analogous significance. Each entails a loss of honor, pretended and comic in the case of Parolles, unintended and subtle in the cases of Helena and Bertram.

On the face of it, Bertram has not lost honor in the war but has gained it. He courageously risks death; his procession through Florence is triumphal; he has the respect of his fellow soldiers; his commendations from the Duke are "sweet" (4.3.79). But the battlefield murders are committed in a war without principled cause, empty and vainglorious, undertaken only for a hollow honor. The King of France finds no reason to privilege one side over the other, yet the French Lord who responds to the Duke's offstage justification of the war almost parodically contrasts the Florentines' "holy" cause with the "black and fearful" opposition (3.1.4–5). On the other hand, Helena's justification of the bed trick as a strategy to thwart the "siege" of Diana confirms that it is "lawful meaning in a lawful act," both principled and courageous, and the Widow responds, "I have yielded" (3.7.46, 36). In contrast to Bertram's, Helena's victory is in a principled cause. Lacking her standards, the war is no more than murderous exercise for French youths, honorable only in the narrow sense of entailing personal risk and in creating a meaningful connection between the sign of war, the drum, and the action. Bertram succeeds in a superficially motivated action. The note of dishonor is more emphatic in the scene pairs flanking the justification scenes, which unflatteringly parallel Bertram with Parolles:

3.2 Clown on cowardly Bertram. Helena plans to leave Rossillion.	3.6 Lords on cowardly Parolles. Bertram & Lord to Diana.
3.1 Duke of Florence justifies war to Lord.	3.7 Helena justifies bed trick to Widow.
2.5 Bertram lies to Helena, saying "business" takes him from "ministrations."	4.1 Parolles considers various lies to excuse his failure to retrieve drum.

The manifest cowardice of Parolles commented on by the Lords in 3.6 is reflected in the cowardice noted by the Clown in the Bertram who "has run away" from marriage (3.2.43.). In scenes 2.5 and 4.1 Bertram's lie to Helena finds its equivalent in the lies Parolles entertains to cover his feigned retrieval of the drum. Like Parolles—obvious differences in degree granted—Bertram is a lying, unprincipled coward. His battlefield killing gains him worldly honor, but it also reveals the superficiality of his character. Lacking education, lacking words, he understands neither himself nor others. He acts—honorably, bravely—as directed by others' words and is a mere robot to Parolles' instructions to expand his farewell to the departing Lords, for example. Bertram is unthinking action to Parolles' empty words.

Scene 3.2 also hints at the insufficiency of Helena's initial response to being abandoned by Bertram. Though her pilgrimage is not an action tainted with a self-serving motive, as was the curing of the King, but rather intends to save Bertram's life, it nevertheless mirrors Bertram's actions in this scene and in the paired scene: Helena too runs away from the marriage. However altruistically motivated, her pilgrimage reflects Bertram's exit to Diana in 3.6. It should be noted, though, that this initial instance of self-sacrifice beneficially influences the Countess. Hearing Bertram's letter to Helena, the Countess disavows her son and takes Helena as her only child (3.2.66–8); but upon feeling the "sharp stings" of Helena's written words, the Countess cannot distinguish whether Bertram or Helena is dearest to her (3.4.18, 38–40). The honorable example of Helena's sacrifice softens Bertram's mother. Nevertheless, Helena in her pilgrimage is like Bertram in turning away from the union, at least until 3.5, when Helena discovers that Bertram is not quite so "good and fair" as she had thought and plans the bed trick.

The wedding and bedding of Helena by Bertram are paired as the central structural scenes of the first and second half of the play (2.3 and 4.3). Excepting the last scene these scenes are the play's longest and most complex. Notably, it is not the marriage and its consummation that are emphasized in them; it is the onstage exposure of Parolles. In 2.3 Parolles is found out by Lafew, and in 4.3 Parolles is exposed to Bertram, while the wedding ceremony takes place offstage, and the bedding of Helena as Diana is merely referred to by the French lords awaiting Bertram during his "dieted ... hour" (4.3.28). The onstage incidents exposing Parolles clarify the analogous actions of Bertram in the same scenes. Parolles, dependent on uncommitted words in threatening Lafew and in saving himself from the "enemy," is exposed as a coward and a traitor, incapable of action or loyalty. Bertram, the man of action, cannot be bound by the mere words of a marriage vow. Its violation (like the merely verbal charges against him in the last scene) counts as nothing with him. Only when bested in action, in giving up his ring and impregnating his wife, can he be sufficiently humiliated to change, to realize the need for action combined with meaning, to want to "know ... clearly" what has happened (5.3.309). Parolles is all bluster and no action when insulted by Lafew; Bertram is all (escapist) action and false words when forced into marriage. They have in common a belief that words entail no obligatory truth or commitment.

The chiastic structure of this section of the play expresses their shared disavowal of truth. Like the justification scenes, the wedding and bedding pair is flanked by commenting scene pairs, most conveniently summarized in outline:

2.4 Parolles brings promise of marriage "rite" from Bertram to Helena.	4.2 Diana takes ring from Bertram, promising to meet.
2.3 King cured. Bertram weds Helena. Parolles found out by Lafew. Bertram refuses to bed Helena.	4.3 News of Helena's death. Bertram beds Helena (as Diana). Parolles exposed as traitor.
2.2 Clown mocks service at court.	4.4 Widow and Diana pledge service to Helena.

In the flanking scenes Bertram's false promise to Helena is mirrored in the false promise of Diana to Bertram (2.4 and 4.2), and the shallow accommodations of court service—the answer that fits all occasions—are contrasted with the true service of Diana and her mother

(2.2 and 4.4). These implied corrections of the court's misuse of language are part of the knowledge that Bertram will come to after the last scene, after he asks to "know this clearly" (5.3.309).

The wedding and bedding scenes also reveal the change in Helena from her earlier insufficient selflessness to her later total self-abnegation. Her reported death in the bedding scene expresses her absolute mortification in the bed trick. Contrasted as it is with the cure of the King, it renders yet again the lesson of *Measure for Measure* and other Shakespeare comedies and romances that life is attained through death. Helena comes to embrace death in a way she had not earlier understood, and in this embrace conceives life. The difference between the metaphorical death of the bed trick and Helena's earlier form of self-denial through pilgrimage is clarified by the food imagery. The "solemn feast" (2.3.180) of the wedding is refused by Bertram, who wishes to remain, in the imagery of the paired scene, "a whale to virginity," one that "devours up all the fry it finds" (4.3.212–13). (Here, as throughout the play, Bertram is "highly fed and lowly taught" [2.2.3].) He "fleshes his will in the spoil" of Diana's honor (15), according to a Lord awaiting Bertram during his "dieted hour" (28). "Virginity," on the other hand, an aspect of Helena's self-denial, "consumes itself" (1.1.139–40). In going to bed with Bertram the devourer, Helena is not self-consumed by her virginity any longer. In embracing this form of death, Helena finds what "sweet use" can be made of her (4.4.22). She is no longer self-consumed for Bertram; she is a sacrifice to Bertram. As Parolles at the end of the scene expresses his acceptance of the thing he is by his simple confidence that he "will eat and drink," Helena and Bertram are to be understood through the food imagery as having enacted (though Bertram does not yet realize it) their humiliated and humbled selves.

Helena's humility is conveyed structurally in the final section of the play:

2.1 King promises husband if Helena cures him.	4.5 King promises Maudlin to Bertram.
1.3 Helena to travel to Paris to cure the King.	5.1 Helena, Widow & Diana to seek help of the King.
1.2 Bertram presents himself to King, who praises Bertram's father.	5.2 Parolles humbly presents himself to Lafew.

Central to this section is the scene pair contrasting Helena's early intention to cure the King with her later intention to seek his help (1.3 and 5.1). She becomes a pure supplicant with nothing to barter; she is reduced to the thing she is without her father's medicinal recipe. The 1.2 and 5.2 pair suggests that Parolles' humility has made him more like Bertram's father, for whom words and actions were in accord: his "tongue obeyed his hand" (41); this pair also suggests, because of the play's continuing analogies between Parolles and Bertram, the humility Bertram will realize post-play. In arranging yet another marriage for Bertram (2.1 and 4.5), the King is pointedly making the same mistake he made earlier; by the end of the last scene he will promise only to provide a dowry for Diana, not enforce her choice, and in the Epilogue invites the audience to a reciprocal beggary.

Combining the scenes outlined so far with the first and last scenes, we can see at a glance the overall structure of the play:

3.4 Helena's sonnet-letter to Countess.	
3.3 Bertram appointed general of cavalry.	3.5 Bertram with drums and colors in military triumph.

3.2 Clown on cowardly Bertram. Helena plans to leave Rossillion.	3.6 Lords on cowardly Parolles. Bertram & Lord to Diana.
3.1 Duke of Florence justifies war to Lord.	3.7 Helena justifies bed trick to Widow.
2.5 Bertram lies to Helena, saying "business" takes him from "ministrations."	4.1 Parolles considers various lies to excuse his failure to retrieve drum.
2.4 Parolles brings promise of marriage "rite" from Bertram to Helena.	4.2 Diana takes ring from Bertram, promising to meet.
2.3 King cured. Bertram weds Helena. Parolles found out by Lafew. Bertram refuses to bed Helena.	4.3 News of Helena's death. Bertram beds Helena (as Diana). Parolles exposed as traitor.
2.2 Clown mocks service at court.	4.4 Widow and Diana pledge service to Helena.
2.1 King promises husband if Helena cures him.	4.5 King promises Maudlin to Bertram.
1.3 Helena to travel to Paris to cure the King.	5.1 Helena, Widow & Diana to seek help of the King.
1.2 Bertram presents himself to King, who praises Bertram's father.	5.2 Parolles humbly presents himself to Lafew.
1.1 Bertram leaves for court. Helena & Parolles on virginity.	5.3 Bertram exposed by Diana & Helena.

Structurally, the play consists of a tympanum of three scenes that, like the corresponding scenes in *Measure for Measure*, focuses the essential issue of death for the three main characters. Helena metaphorically embraces death; Bertram kills in battle; Parolles is "mortified" by the loss of the drum. Again as in *Measure for Measure* the bed trick is initiated in the scene immediately following the keystone scene. Excepting the first and last scenes, the remaining 18 scenes are grouped in three sections of three pairs each. The central pair in each thematically unified section is its focal point: the justifications of the war and the bed trick (3.1–3.7), the wedding and bedding of Helena (2.3–4.3), and Helena's initial overreaching and final humility (1.3–5.1). In the achieved marriage of Helena and Bertram the last scene obviously resolves the issues Helena raised in the first scene, though not "to her own liking," which is the manner in which she had hoped to lose her virginity (1.1.147). She has instead, in her bed trick mortification, absolutely suppressed herself—her liking (i.e., her will) and her identity—in loving Bertram, embracing a figurative death to save her husband from dishonor and to conceive life.

The chiastic structure organizes not only the narrative but, as the wedding-bedding scene pair suggests, the food imagery as well. The first half of the play dramatizes a court that, eating only "as is fashionable," and certainly "none of this homely meat," is starving, anemic and sickly (2.1, 2.2). (Only the Clown uses imagery of robust feeding in the first half of the play.) In the only food references in the tympanum Diana and Helena re-establish the literal fact of eating in both its deadly and vitalizing extremes as poison or nutrition (3.5). The second half of the play, animated by the voracious appetite of Bertram, then enacts a kind of feeding frenzy in the imagery. The shift occurs in the seven central scenes. (Solid horizontal line indicates absence of feeding imagery.)

3.4 _____	

3.3 _____	3.5 Diana: I would poison Parolles. Helena: eat with us tonight.

3.2 Clown: old lings; love is without stomach at court.	3.6 Bertram to Parolles: if you have stomach to retrieve drum.
3.1 War thirsts for blood; surfeit of ease cured by fighting.	3.7 _____

The matching images just before and after the tympanum, in scenes 3.2 and 3.6, express the court's lack of "stomach" for either love or war. "I have no mind to Isbel since I was at court," the Clown says. "Our old lings and our Isbels of the country are nothing like your old ling and your Isbels of the court.... I begin to love as an old man loves money, with no stomach" (3.2.12–16). In the same scene the Countess reads Bertram's letter informing her that he has "run away" (22), and Helena, at the end of the scene, decides to leave Rossillion. This is the end of the play's first movement, the structural point at which the court's love relationships— if they can be called that—collapse. In matching images as the second part of the play begins, the court, epitomized by Parolles, is shown to lack stomach for war (3.6), and, as a "fish," an image also used of him twice in the penultimate scene, Parolles is the personification of an "old ling," thus the epitome of the court's desiccated love appetite as well. Bertram, by contrast, has fought bravely in the blood-thirsty war and is about to give up a symbol of family honor for Diana. His appetite ultimately regenerates the court, cures its surfeit of ease (3.1). A "highly fed, lowly taught" man of action is just what the effete court needs to regain the stomach for love and war, to be restored to desire, action and fecundity (2.2).

These central scenes also point out that, as we have seen in earlier plays, even the absence of food imagery is significant. Three of the four scenes without food imagery are included in the partial outline above: 3.3, in which Bertram is made general of the horse; 3.4, in which Helena's letter is read to the Countess; and 3.7, in which Helena justifies the bed trick to the Widow. The one other scene is 5.1, in which Helena, Diana and the Widow are on their way to seek the help of the King. Three of these scenes are exclusively or predominantly "women" scenes. In fact, aside from the first and last scenes, women do not "eat" at all, except for the literal meal Helena invites them to in 3.5. In the first scene Helena laments the absence of Bertram, who "cannot feed her eye" (1.1.) The overall pattern suggests that even this much feeding on the part of a woman is too much, too ambitious, for the woman is not to devour but to be devoured. The one other image in which women feed—Diana's dieting by Bertram (5.3)—refers not to sex but to expressions of love. Here as elsewhere in the play women are "spiritual," and the absence of food imagery suggests a scene of higher impulses. Hence, Bertram's tympanum scene is also without food imagery to suggest that his nobility of intention matches Helena's tympanum nobility of intention; his self-assertion like her self-denial is nobly motivated. The play distinguishes between the carnal and spiritual by the presence or absence of food imagery.

The most pervasive word characterizing Helena and Bertram is "sweet." It is used of Bertram, always by other men, particularly in the first half of the play (2.1.24, 2.3.264 and

267; also 4.3.79 of the duke's commendations of Bertram) and of Helena (and her proxy, Diana) predominantly in the second half of the play (4.2.10 and 5.3.137 of Diana; 4.4.22, 33; 5.3.67, 78). The exception in the first half of the play, when the King (who cannot himself "bring home honey") calls Helena a "sweet practitioner" in 2.1 (184), reinforces the note of (inappropriate) ambition in Helena's early love; her success lies in self-abnegation not self-assertion. That the epithet is transferred from Bertram to Helena as the play progresses traces a necessary adjustment in gender roles for a successful marriage. The sex act is itself "sweet": Parolles refers to its sweets (2.4.42); Lafew jocosely refers to his (sweet) tooth for maids when he was younger (2.3.42); Helena finds what "sweet use" can be made of her after her hour with Bertram (4.4.22). It is no stretch to interpret Helena's early mocking intonation of courtly love talk—"sweet disaster" (1.1)—as also applicable to the sex act, particularly considering the bed trick. The play's last line then has a more specific referent than might at first be apparent: "The bitter past, more welcome is the sweet." The play's food imagery figures a marriage act of mutual sweetness.

But Helena is also imaged as an "herb" (4.5), and Bertram as a carnivore and "whale to virginity" (4.3). Again, the figurative language must be finely parsed as it changes with the play's narrative and psychological development. By the end of the play, the insufficient actions of the tympanum—Helena's pilgrimage and Bertram's warring—have been refined to meaningful words. The last scene presents marriage as a mutually spiritual "consumption." Diana is dieted on Bertram's mere expressions of love, and Bertram, Lafew anticipates, will "digest" not flesh or fry but a "name," the name of his wife's family. Of course, it is Helena, not Maudlin or Diana, who is Bertram's proper wife, and these sustaining words are nurturing for the true partners in the marriage. In addition to presenting Helena as a sweet confection and an herb, then, the pattern of the food imagery ultimately figures the marriage relationship as mutual spiritual sustenance. Only against the chiastic structure do these delicate touches of characterization and imagery in the last scene become meaningful. *All's Well* is an intricately crafted arch, with its reflecting actions of hubris and humility perfectly balanced and its food images as carefully disposed and shaded as those of a lyric.

16

Act Division and
Feeding Actions in *Othello*

Some of the most meaningful actions in *Othello* are nearly invisible. This may seem a strange claim to make of what is generally regarded as Shakespeare's most exciting play, with its taut intrigue and frequent outbursts of emotional and physical violence. Indeed, the play is so violent that audiences and critics may find it hard to watch. "To some readers," A. C. Bradley comments, "parts of *Othello* appear shocking or even horrible. They think … that in these parts Shakespeare has sinned against the canons of art, by representing on the stage a violence or brutality the effect of which is unnecessarily painful and rather sensational than tragic." In particular, Bradley says that he cannot reconcile himself to Othello's striking Desdemona: "there is not a sufficiently tragic feeling in the passage to make it bearable."[1] Lest we think that this is merely a quaint reaction to the play, consider John Jones's more recent comment on the episode in scene 4.2 in which Desdemona kneels to ask Iago for his help. We "feel a chaotic dismay at Desdemona's spirit of pure trust. And an even more chaotic revulsion at the threatened fouling of what is clean…. The whole thing is almost not art. We almost want to look away, as from the deeply disquieting sights life subjects us to."[2] Even more than these or indeed any other incidents in the play, the murder of Desdemona has shocked generations of audiences by its mingled violence and eroticism, and many productions attempted to soften its effect in various ways, placing the bed far upstage, for example, or half concealing the brutality behind the bed curtains.[3] This is the most common complaint against *Othello*, that some of its violence is "almost not art"—that is to say, no evident context gives these actions a tragic significance. Without a larger significance, the violence seems gratuitous.

But the dramatist's exquisite sense of action is, unsurprisingly, less than fully engaged in the merely sensational plot, and the violent stage actions, like Othello's striking of Desdemona, erupt from deeply motivated subterranean currents. Though elusive, a paradigmatic action recurs through the play, providing the tragic dimension that otherwise seems to be lacking: the quotidian action of eating.

The meals in *Othello* have received only incidental critical attention. They are mentioned as contributing to the domestic atmosphere of the play, and individual food images are sometimes isolated in the service of character analysis, particularly of Iago.[4] Otherwise the meals are ignored, in spite of the fact that Shakespeare often develops character relationships figuratively by means of food images; intimate relationships in particular are frequently imaged in patterns built upon common metaphors of endearment such as "honey" and "sweet." This is certainly the case in *Othello*. When set in the context of the play's many feeding actions—its meals and the sequential actions leading up to them—the love of Desdemona and Othello is most fully revealed in the symbolic nuptial feast.

Though crucial to the domestic tragedy, the feeding actions in *Othello*, as I have suggested, are far from prominent. Shakespeare mutes, attenuates and deflects their Aristotelian development as he often strategically obscures significant actions of other plays. It takes an effort of synthesis in viewing *Julius Caesar*, for example, to grasp the titular hero's action at the Lupercal because it is reported in fragments, out of sequence and with much editorializing by Casca. In *Measure for Measure*, the audience must provide its own ending for the courtship of Duke Vincentio and Isabella, indeed, must recreate the whole course of their almost invisible relationship from mere hints. Shakespeare often requires us to seek out and piece together the action for ourselves.

The task is made more difficult in the case of *Othello* because the traditional act divisions are misleading. While the first two breaks are correct, allowing time for the voyage to Cyprus after Act One and the remainder of Othello's nuptial night after Act Two, the last two breaks are misplaced. Critics from A. C. Bradley to Emrys Jones have suggested the need for intervals "at about the end of Act Three" and "somewhere in the Fourth Act."[5] There is clearly a supper interval between scenes 4.2 and 4.3 during which Othello sups in company with Lodovico while Cassio takes the evening meal with Bianca. After this interval, in 4.3, later that night, Desdemona is preparing for sleep, and the subsequent action leading up to and accomplishing her murder unfolds without a temporal interval. Act Five then consists of scenes 4.3, 5.1 and 5.2. The break between the traditional Act Three and Act Four is also in error. The second of the clown episodes, which function as structural markers, locates the break between 3.3 and 3.4. In calling for the music to cease as 3.1 opens, the Clown is, in effect, calling a halt to the whole movement toward marital pleasure that impelled the first half of the play, Othello's movement from the flinty bed of war to the downy marriage bed[6]; in punning on "lies" to open 3.4, the Clown initiates in a lighter key the tragic deceptions of the second half of the play (and tunes our ears to the almost farcical later use of the word with another, sexual, meaning by Iago and Othello at 4.1.32–36). Act Three then consists of scenes 3.1, 3.2 and 3.3; Act Four consists of 3.4, 4.1 and 4.2. *Othello* is constructed in five acts of three scenes each. With intervals indicated and familiar actions, particularly those of the newly-married couple, included, the play can be sketched in an arch-like structure that reads up the left-hand column and down the right, a structure that functions significantly in the meal sequences:

3.2 Othello gives Iago orders before inspecting fortifications.	
3.1 Cassio asks admittance to Desdemona. *Clown: Stop the music.*	3.3 Cassio parts from Desdemona. "Seduction" of Othello.
------------[**Nuptial feast**]------------	------------[**Indefinite interval**]------------
2.3 Othello and Desdemona "away to bed."	3.4 *Clown puns on "lies."* Othello asks for handkerchief that "subdue[d]" his father's love.
2.2 Othello's Herald proclaims victory and nuptial feast.	4.1 Othello strikes Desdemona.

2.1 At Cyprus, Desdemona and Othello kiss.	4.2 Othello calls Desdemona "whore."
------------[Voyage]------------	------------[Supper]------------
1.3 Brabantio "gives" Desdemona to Othello.	4.3 Desdemona sings willow song: "Let nobody blame him."
1.2 Othello summoned to Senate.	5.1 Othello: "I come": to kill Desdemona.
1.1 Brabantio roused by Iago's obscenities.	5.2 Othello kills Desdemona; Emilia to Iago: "Your reports have set the murder on."

Outlined in this way parallels, contrasts and narrative development are more immediately evident. The keystone scene of Othello at his occupation and Cassio's visit to Desdemona, beginning in 3.1 and ending in 3.3, bridge the two halves of the play. In their broad movements the two columns mirror the courtship and consummation of Othello's and Desdemona's marriage in the first half with its destruction by revenge murder in the second half. Act One contains varying reports of the courtship and leads to the "giving away" of the bride by her father in 1.3; Act Two accomplishes the consummation of the marriage in 2.3. In Act Four (3.4 to 4.2), after Iago's successful seduction, Othello's jealousy undoes the intimacy that had been attained in the paired Act Two, turning love into magic and affection into prostitution; and the last Act (4.3, 5.1, 5.2) contrasts Othello's composure in Act One, his refusal to be incited into violence, with his gloating anticipations and ritualized enactment of revenge.[7]

The play's six analogous meal sequences, as we will see, are precisely fitted to this structure. Four of the feeding actions culminate in offstage meals—the nuptial feast, dinner with the Cyprians, Bianca's supper and the meal with Lodovico; the two additional feeding actions are initiated by Iago, the drinking party and, symbolically, the murder of Desdemona. Each sequence consists, first, of a designation of literal and/or figurative food; second, an invitation to the meal; and finally a summons to the meal, which is (when literal) then consumed offstage. In three of the feeding actions the meal itself is also either enacted or described as in two parts, a truth-telling and a physical consummation, corresponding to the conversation and eating that would occur at any shared meal. Shakespeare has infused these common steps of planning, anticipating and consuming a meal—the menu, invitation, summons, table-talk and eating—with a range of symbolic meanings for the relationships in the play.

When Othello greets Desdemona in Cyprus, he first associates sweetness with the "heavens"—"Amen to that, sweet powers" (2.1.191, 194)—and then with Desdemona: "Honey," he calls her, and "my sweet" (2.1.203, 4). After this figurative designation of food, the invitation to the feast is issued by the Herald, Othello's spokesman, in the next scene—"There will be full liberty of feasting" (2.2.9)—and the summons to the nuptial feast, both literal and figurative, is given by Othello himself, once at the beginning of the next scene—"Come, my dear love, the purchase made, the fruits are to ensue" (2.3.8)—and again toward the end, after the brawl has been quieted and Cassio cashiered: "All's well now, sweeting. Come away to bed" (2.3.248). Othello designates the figurative food, orders the invitation to be proclaimed and summons Desdemona to the "nuptial feast" (which is delicately revealed over the course of the whole play, rather than coarsened, as here, by an abrupt phrase.)

Bianca's supper is preceded by a similar pattern. Cassio first associates her with sweetness, calling her "Sweet love" (3.4.171) and "Sweet Bianca" (3.4.179), (endearments without a supernatural association like Othello's). In the next scene, after Cassio has again addressed her as "Sweet" (4.1.155), Bianca invites him to the evening meal: "Come to supper tonight" (4.1.157). We find out after the fact that the supper has taken place, but the summons to it is made to Roderigo by Iago as part of the plan to murder Cassio. "He sups tonight with a harlotry.... [B]etween twelve and one—you may take him at your pleasure.... It is now high supper time...: about it" (4.2.235, 244). To Iago suppertime is a time not for shared intimacy but for murder, though his language—"you may take him at your pleasure"—insinuates the equivalence between them in his mind. (As Desdemona ends professing her love for Othello, Bianca in Act Five, in admitting that she had supper with Cassio, also overcomes Iago's attempt to taint the relationship.) The meals taken by the two couples are "prepared" in three steps: the designation and significance of the figurative food, the invitation to the meal and the summons to the offstage meal itself. That Iago summons to Bianca's meal is typical of his modus operandi, insinuating his envious manipulations into the action. Though it is not unusual for Shakespeare's actions to shift agents and instruments along the way—the courtship of Ann Page in *Merry Wives* is a comic example—this sleight-of-hand may be one of the reasons the meals of the play have not been seen as part of a larger sequential action.

The supper with Lodovico is Othello's "nuptial fast." After having been seduced by Iago in 3.3, Othello undoes the loving meal of Act Two scene by scene in Act Four. He first denies Desdemona food at all—that is, withholds himself—saying of her moist hand that it requires "a sequester from liberty, fasting and prayer" (3.4.40). He then attributes love not to the "sweet powers" of divinity but to the magic in the web of the handkerchief. When Bianca enters at the center of 4.1 carrying the handkerchief, the sight further corrupts in Othello's mind the nuptial feast, so when, after striking Desdemona, he extends an invitation to dinner to Lodovico, it is immediately associated with Iago's imagery of lecherous beasts:

> And, sir, tonight,
> I do entreat that we may sup together.
> You are welcome, sir, to Cyprus. Goats and monkeys! [4.1.461–3]

Finally, the summons to that supper in the next scene is issued by Iago, again insinuating himself into the action, as he has into Bianca's supper. At the sound of trumpets, he says to Desdemona:

> Hark how these instruments summon to supper:
> The messengers of Venice stay the meat,
> Go in, and weep not [4.2.171–3].

Iago's "meat" is the final corrupting touch to what the heavenly (2.1.194), unrestrained (2.2.9) and fruit-sweet (2.3.8, 248) nuptial feast has become—not simply lecherous but carnivorous as well, which, in Shakespeare's frequent opposition to vegetarian,[8] suggests the bloody and predatory and, more proximately, recalls Othello's savage insult to Desdemona in saying that she is no more chaste than "summer flies in the shambles" (4.2.67), a slaughterhouse or meat market.

The preliminary actions, each specifying a different food, of the nuptial feast, Bianca's supper and the "nuptial fast" with Lodovico are fitted one to each scene in Acts Two and Four to lead to the offstage meals as follows:

2.3 Othello **summons** Desdemona.	3.4 Cassio: "**Sweet** Bianca."	3.4 Othello of Desdemona's hand: "requires ... **fasting** and prayer."
2.2 Othello's Herald **invites** to nuptial feast.	4.1 Bianca **invites** Cassio to supper.	4.1 Othello **invites** Lodovico to supper: "Goats and monkeys!"
2.1 After thanking the "sweet powers," Othello kisses "**sweet**" Desdemona.	4.2 Iago **summons** Roderigo to kill Cassio: "It is now high supper time ... about it."	4.2 Iago **summons** Desdemona and Emilia to supper with Lodovico and company.

    ----Voyage----   ----Supper----

    The meals themselves in these instances are not further described. For that we have to look first at Iago's drinking party. In the last scene of Act Two, Iago invites Cassio for a drink— "Come, lieutenant, I have a stoup of wine" (2.3.26–7)—and then manipulates the reluctant Cassio into summoning Montano and the other revelers:

> IAGO: ... 'tis a night of revels, the gallants desire it.
> CASSIO: Where are they?
> IAGO: Here, at the door, I pray you call them in.
> CASSIO: I'll do't but it dislikes me. *Exit* [2.3.40–44].

Cassio returns with the others, the onstage drinking begins, with songs and Cassio's drunken ramblings, and Roderigo assaults Cassio, causing the noisy brawl, the violence and chaos that Iago intended. In this variation the figurative description of the "food" comes after the "meal." Cassio calls wine "unblest" (302), a "devil" (279, 291, 303), an enemy men put in their mouths that transforms them into beasts (285–88). Iago blandly replies that wine is a "good familiar creature" (304). Though the sequence is altered, the drinking party has the same elements as the feeding actions—the figurative designation of the wine, an invitation and a summons. But in this case the consumption takes place on stage, revealing that the meal itself is in two parts—a truth-telling and a physical encounter. Cassio, *in vino veritas*, admits his snobbish view of religion—"the lieutenant is to be saved before the ancient" (105–6)—exits and then re-enters pursuing Roderigo as the fight starts. Both the truth-telling and the physical alter-cation are couched in religious terms.

    Cassio's admission occurs in his conversation with Iago:

> CASSIO: Well, God's above all, and there be souls must be saved, and there be souls must not be saved.
> IAGO: It's true, good lieutenant.
> CASSIO: For mine own part, no offense to the general nor any man of quality, I hope to be saved.
> IAGO: And so do I too, lieutenant.
> CASSIO: Ay, but, by your leave, not before me. The lieutenant is to be saved before the ensign. Let's have no more of this, let's to our affairs. God forgive us our sins! [98–107]

In asking, however comically, for absolution from his sins after admitting his pride, Cassio's truth-telling amounts to an unintentional confession, a parodic sacrament of Penance. The brawl is similarly presented with a religious note. Pursuing Roderigo, Cassio re-enters, crying "Zounds, you rogue!" (141). The fight begins with an exclamation, a contraction of "God's wounds," recalling the suffering of Christ. The exclamation is also used in this scene by Montano—"Zounds, I bleed still; I am hurt to the death. He dies! (160–61)—and by Othello when he begins to lose his temper:

> Now, by Heaven
> My blood begins my safer guides to rule
> And passion, having my best judgement collied,
> Assays to lead the way. Zounds, if once I stir,
> Or do but lift this arm, the best of you
> Shall sink in my rebuke [200–205].

The three uses of the exclamation provide the moral standard by which to judge the speakers' actions. Cassio, in an Iago-like inversion, invokes the wounds of Christ, voluntarily and self-sacrificially suffered, while hoping to inflict wounds on Roderigo; Montano is similarly self-centered and aggressive, now toward Cassio. And Othello exhibits the same moral failing. He reacts not as an executive officer but, like Cassio and Montano, as though he has been personally affronted and turns on Cassio with an excessive vehemence, born of temper not of justice. He acts out of personal vanity, so that the best of the men there do indeed sink in his rebuke.[9]

There is also a certain apt applicability of the exclamation "Zounds" in that Iago has succeeded in causing not only the moral failures but also a distinct hurt to each of the men— Cassio in his honor and position, Montano physically and Othello in his relationship with Desdemona. Obviously, their hurts are not voluntarily undergone, as Christ's were, but the association holds at least in so far as the wounds were prompted by the devil Iago, as he calls himself when, after sending Roderigo to sound the alarm, he asks: "Who's that which rings the bell? Diablo, ho!" (157). It is Iago, through his instrument Roderigo, who rings the bell. In Iago's drinking party then we see a complete feeding action—a literal and figurative designation of the food, an invitation, a summons and the meal itself as both an (unintentional) truth-telling confession and a physical encounter that is, in this instance, diabolically violent.

The wounds that Iago inflicts are in keeping with his characteristic "eating habits" as they are revealed figuratively in this scene as well. Feeling expansive as Cassio succumbs to the wine, Iago expresses his delight by using, for one of only two times in his own voice (as distinct from fictitious quotes attributed to Cassio), the same endearment expressing the mutual sustenance of the play's lovers; he exclaims "O sweet England!" (84). England elicits a lover's pleasure from Iago because it is a narcissistic image of the man himself. Asked by Cassio if an Englishman is "so exquisite in his drinking," Iago responds: "Why, he drinks you with facility your Dane dead drunk; he sweats not to overthrow your Almain; he gives your Hollander a vomit before the next pottle can be filled" (76–80). The "good familiar creature," ingested, induces vomiting and a form of death. This physiological process is Iago's model of human relationships. When Desdemona is "sated" with Othello's body (1.3.351), she will "heave the gorge" (2.1.230); at first Othello finds Desdemona to be a "luscious" "food" (1.3.348), but she will become "acerb as coloquintida," an emetic (1.3.350). Iago has apparently convinced Emilia of his view; men, she says, "are all stomachs, and we all but food; They eat us hungerly, and when they are full, They belch us" (3.4.105–107). In physical violence, Iago, "cast" by Othello as Cassio is also "cast" (2.3.14, 269), engineers the inverse of nourishment, particularly, in the second half of the play, the inverse of mutual sustenance between lovers.[10]

The meal with the Cyprians can be thought of as Desdemona's meal, which, like the drinking party, illuminates the full feeding action, including both the preliminaries and the meal itself. It is actually characterized by means of two meals—the hoped-for meal with Cassio and the offstage meal with the Cyprians. The composite meal is defined in response to Cassio's cashiering, an overreaction by Othello, a vanity of his public persona, that Desdemona is anxious to remedy, as much for Othello's moral well-being as for Cassio's sake. In assuring Cassio that she will press Othello to reinstate him, Desdemona says, "His bed shall seem a school, his board a shrift" (3.3.24). She invokes the essential rituals of marriage in describing a meal that is the opposite of Iago's drinking party, though it contains the same two elements. Othello's table can be seen as a place of confession, of truth-telling, and the marital act, the physical consummation, a lesson in love. And when Othello only reluctantly agrees to her invitations to sup with Cassio, Desdemona retorts that in attempting to heal the rift between her husband and his lieutenant she is doing no more than encouraging Othello to have nourishing food. That is, his moral health is incorporated with his physical health. Desdemona's view of the meal is sacramental. Everyday actions have a spiritual dimension. Divinity is not transcendent, as it is for Othello, but immanent. The sacramental meal that Desdemona defines in saying that Othello's board will seem a shrift is further clarified in her summons to dinner: "Your dinner, and the generous islanders By you invited, do attend your presence" (3.3.284–85). This summons suggests the shared action of husband and wife—he invites, she summons—and "generous islanders" further suggests the reciprocity of the meal, in which Othello's hospitality is prompted or answered by the islanders' benevolence. Desdemona's meal is then a physical nourishment, an invitation to moral health and a mutual giving that is at least potentially sacramental.

The following outline includes the five feeding actions considered so far: Othello's nuptial feast and Iago's "anti-nuptial feast" in Act Two (the brawlers are "like bride and groom Divesting them for bed" [2.3.176–77]); Desdemona's meal in Act Three; and the two meals in Act Four, Bianca's meal and Othello's meal with Lodovico that undoes the nuptial feast.

3.2 Othello gives Iago orders before inspecting fortifications.		
3.1 Cassio asks admittance to Desdemona.	3.3 Cassio parts from Desdemona. Desdemona: Othello's "**bed** shall seem a school, his **board a** shrift." Desdemona: "nourishing **food.**" Desdemona **invites** Othello to supper with Cassio. Desdemona **summons** Othello to dinner. with Cyprians.	
------------[Nuptial feast]------------	------------[Indefinite interval]------------	
2.3 Othello **summons** Desdemona.	2.3 Iago **invites** Cassio to drink. Cassio **summons** revelers. "Forgive our sins." *Brawl.* Cassio calls **wine "devil."**	3.4 Cassio: "**Sweet** Bianca." 3.4 Othello of Desdemona's hand: "requires ... **fasting** and prayer."
2.2 Othello's Herald	4.1 Bianca **invites** 4.1 Othello **invites**	

invites to nuptial feast.	Cassio to supper.	Lodovico to supper: "Goats and monkeys!"
2.1 After thanking the "sweet powers," Othello kisses "**sweet**" Desdemona.	4.2 Iago **summons** Roderigo to kill Cassio: "It is now high supper time … about it."	4.2 Iago **summons** Desdemona and Emilia to supper with Lodovico and company.

------------[Voyage]------------   ------------[Supper]------------

The architecture and actions of *Othello* are precisely fitted. The traditional Act divisions obscure the careful construction and fragment the feeding actions in the second half of the play, so that the already subtle sequences are almost impossible to discern. Once isolated, however, the ordinary actions attendant on a meal—choice of menu, invitation, summons, table-talk and eating—turn out to carry much of the burden of the domestic tragedy.

In addition to these feeding actions there is Iago's final meal, extending over the whole second half of the play. While Othello is offstage at dinner with the Cyprians, Iago accurately describes Othello's contamination: "The Moor already changes with my poison; Dangerous conceits … are at the first scarce found to distaste" (3.3.328–30). Othello has not partaken of the meal Desdemona described and summoned him to; instead he brings his poisoned mind to it and re-enters already sick with Iago's "medicine" (4.1.45). Iago then presents the figurative food of his own meal, in an order exactly paralleling Othello's earlier endearments of Desdemona. In relating the fictitious dream, Iago has Cassio say "sweet Desdemona" and "o sweet creature" (421, 424) and then introduces the handkerchief "spotted with strawberries" (438), the food of the meal he is cooking up. The handkerchief is the symbol of Othello's sweet giving of himself to "sweet" Desdemona: "Come, my dear love," he says, as quoted earlier, inviting Desdemona to bed, "the purchase made, the fruits are to ensue" (2.3.8). Othello's "first gift" expressed a mutuality that is not yet completely assured (439)[11]; it represents Othello at his most vulnerable. Manipulated by Iago's keen if corrupt sense of mutual love, Othello feels devastatingly betrayed.

The handkerchief with embroidered strawberries has occasioned such varied comment that an imagistic reading might seem too simple. It has been taken as a fetish, a pledge of love or a "floating signifier,"[12] and strawberries in Renaissance iconography "might suggest a hidden evil, or the purity of the Virgin."[13] Most commonly, though, the strawberries are taken to represent drops of blood and the handkerchief to refer to bridal sheets, and "to the practice of proving purity by staining." "[T]his provides a satisfactory weight for the importance Othello attaches to his charmed (or farcical) handkerchief, the fact that it is spotted, spotted with strawberries."[14] This interpretation seems to me very distant from the text. In the first place, "spotted" is Iago's word of the handkerchief, and his "only joy is in spoiling good objects," as Adelman argues.[15] The handkerchief is a "good object" Iago is particularly anxious to spoil, just as he attempts to soil the similar expression of "sweet" mutuality between Cassio and Bianca (discussed below). And if the handkerchief is a proof of purity, would it not be a gift from Desdemona to Othello, the offer of her virginity? Rather than adopt Iago's view, it seems we might better understand the handkerchief as Othello's reciprocal gift to Desdemona, among the "fruits" of marriage, a gift of something in himself as intimate as blood. True, Othello himself thinks of blood-spotted sheets while on his way to murder Desdemona; the association with the handkerchief is impossible *not* to make. But the association has no force in establishing the meaning of the handkerchief for Othello when it was first given. It seems more likely that the later association registers one more inversion Iago has succeeded in implanting in Othello's mind, suggesting the corruption of the nuptial night into a night of murder, of the nuptial feast into "sweet revenge" (5.2.114). The attribution of magic to the handkerchief is similarly a result of Iago's influence, not an association that Othello initially wove into the web of his gift, as Desdemona's horrified reaction to the tale of magic confirms.[16]

That the handkerchief is a symbol of Othello's sweet self-giving is supported by the attendant food imagery, especially as it characterizes Othello and Cassio and their relationships with Desdemona and Bianca. Though the nuptial feast and Bianca's supper portray Othello and Cassio as consuming and consumed, there is a significant degree of difference. Both men, of course, find their women to be "sweet," and both are addressed once (and only once) as "sweet" by their partners (4.1.238, 5.1.76). With that one exception, however, Cassio's imagery of ingesting is not balanced by images of being ingested; that is, the mutuality of love is entirely absent from his relationship with Bianca until after their supper together. His few food images show him to be a feeder, though one who consumes only in moderation. His extreme boundaries of food-related activity are surfeiting to death (2.1.50) and starving to death (3.3.15); he imbibes sparingly, as we know from Iago's drinking party, and "relish[es]" daintily (2.1.165). By contrast, Othello's hyperbole extends to extremities of both ingesting and being ingested that are beyond Cassio's imagining. He has an insatiable appetite for revenge; of Cassio he says, "Had all his hairs been lives my great revenge had stomach for them all" (5.2.73). And in his remorse, in his final food image, he gives himself wholly to being consumed in a kind of hellish oven: "Roast me in sulfur, wash me in steep-down gulfs of liquid fire" (271–72). This boundless capacity for consuming and being consumed is characteristic of him in love as in revenge. His frequent use of "sweet" of Desdemona is matched by references to his being consumed by her. His first delight in Desdemona consists at least partly in the fact that she "with a greedy ear Devoured up my discourse" (1.3.150). He speaks of Desdemona as the place where he "has garnered up [his] heart" (4.2.58). While Cassio speaks only of eating, Othello speaks also of being eaten, of a reciprocal relationship.

Othello's sweet self-giving represented by the embroidered handkerchief also illuminates one incident of violence toward Desdemona. The one word "sweet" explains Othello's state of mind when he strikes her. Though he frequently calls her "sweet," she uses the word of Othello only at this climactic moment. The exchange occurs with the news that Cassio will become governor of Cyprus.

> DESDEMONA: By my troth, I am glad on't.
> OTHELLO: Indeed!
> DESDEMONA: My lord?
> OTHELLO: I am glad ... to see you mad.
> DESDEMONA: Why, sweet Othello!
> OTHELLO: Devil! [*Striking her*] [4.1.237–39][17]

Othello's echoing mockery (of "I am glad") and charge of madness (as he thinks, based on her public expression of fondness for Cassio) surprises Desdemona, and her exclamation attempts to recall him to their shared intimacy, to the "sweet" self-giving represented by the embroidered strawberries. But it is exactly those sweetest moments that Othello now thinks constitute the most profound betrayal. Furthermore, part of her hold on him has been her moral authority, her "sweet soul," which explains the slight tone of remonstrance in her exclamation. For her to use such a tone now, when she herself has been exposed—so her husband thinks—as an adulteress, is particularly galling to Othello, exacerbating his rage. His angelic wife becomes a devil.

Further evidence for an imagistic reading of the embroidered strawberries lies in a parallel use of the endearment "sweet" by Bianca of Cassio. As I've mentioned, Bianca, like Desdemona, uses the word only once, also in a moment of extremity. When, after supping with Cassio, she comes upon him wounded, she exclaims, "O my dear Cassio! My sweet Cassio!" (5.1.75–6). Ordinarily, in the atmosphere of military machismo defined by Iago, neither women would express such unguarded affection publicly, for it suggests the emotional vulnerability of their men. The epithet provides a glimpse of Bianca's and Cassio's intimate relationship, their achieved mutual affection, after their supper together. Hence Iago's immediate reaction, motivated by his instinctively corrosive envy: "O notable strumpet!" (77). The implicit violence of Iago's response is like Othello's response to the same word and to the same suggestion of a loving mutual relationship.

The "food" of Iago's final meal then is the strawberry-embroidered handkerchief that he has for so long pestered his wife to steal, for he understands its symbolic value for Othello. Its supposed gifting to Cassio goads Othello into suggesting that he will poison Desdemona as a fitting rejoinder to her fatal sweetness. But Iago intervenes to invite Othello to Iago's own more erotically charged plan: "Do it not with poison, strangle her in her bed" (4.1.205). Iago's invitation conforms to the sequence of the other eating actions and to the positions of the other invitations in the central scenes of Acts Two and Four, but Iago issues not so much a request as an imperative. He almost orders Othello to the method that will "diet" Iago's "revenge" (2.1.292), not least in commanding his commander, in reversing the relationship that is so emphatic in the six-line keystone scene in which Othello gives Iago three orders. In this as in other ways, Iago becomes his general's general.

After this invitation/command, Othello is finally summoned to murder Desdemona by the Iago-induced cries of Cassio in the central scene of Act Five.

Hearing the outcries of the wounded Cassio, Othello says,

> 'Tis he. O brave Iago, honest and just,
> Thou hast such noble sense of thy friend's wrong!
> Thou teachest me. Minion, your dear lies dead,
> And your unblest fate hies; strumpet, I come.
> Forth of my heart those charms, thine eyes, are blotted,
> Thy bed, lust-stained, shall with lust's blood be spotted [5.1.31–36].

Othello rejects Desdemona, who would make "his bed ... a school," as a teacher of love and instead takes as his teacher Iago, who has changed in Othello's mind the strawberry-spotted handkerchief into blood-spotted sheets.[18] In responding with such alacrity to a summons to murder—"strumpet, I come"—Othello is like Roderigo, the most easily gulled of the play's dupes. But the summoning of Othello is not even articulate; it is instead merely the (half-misapprehended) cries of the wounded Cassio, Iago's instrument here as he was at the drinking party and as Brabantio was in the paired scene, 1.2, when Othello responded so differently to offered violence. After the deceptive food, the invitation to violence and the violent summons, the preliminaries of Iago's final meal are complete. The murder/suicide in the last scene is its consummation, as the violent brawl in 2.3 is the consummation of Iago's drinking party and as the marriage bed is the consummation of Desdemona's meal. The "tragic loading" of that bed finally and fully "diet[s]" Iago's "revenge" (2.1.292).

The murder is preceded by the confession Othello bullies from his wife. "Think on thy sins," he says, and, after Desdemona's reply—"They are loves I bear to you" (5.2.40)—he insists again, refusing to believe the truth, "Confess thee freely of thy sin" (53). He finally smothers her. By this point in the action Othello's "eating habits" match Iago's. Like Iago, whose suspicions, he says, "gnaw my innards" (2.1.295), Othello is consuming himself. "Why gnaw you your nether lip?" Desdemona asks. He is eaten up with passion, as Iago noted earlier (3.3.394), now to the extent of self-cannibalism. In this violence toward himself, Othello diets Iago's characteristically mediated revenge. And in his violence toward others, Othello also diets his own revenge. In his final food image before killing Desdemona, Othello gloats over Cassio's supposed death by saying, as quoted earlier, "Had all his hairs been lives my great revenge had stomach for them all" (5.5.73). This is the Othello new-created by Iago; the general has become a mirror image of his ensign, both self-consumed and predatory.

After the murder, however, Othello is again transformed. The change in Othello is intimated even before he learns that Desdemona is innocent, when he says that as a consequence of her extinguished light the earth should "yawn" (98). And after he learns the truth, the change is made explicit in his final food image, quoted earlier: "Roast me in sulphur, wash me in steep-down gulfs of liquid fire" (271–72). In unreservedly casting himself as roasted and completely engulfed, Othello has broken from the Iago who would not wear his heart upon his sleeve "for daws to peck at" (1.1.63) and returned to Desdemona's influence, at least in the dynamic of total self-giving, the capacity in him that partially explains Desdemona's love for "sweet," "kind" Othello.

The following outline includes the six feeding actions of the play. The stages of the Iago meal in the second half are capitalized, and the consummations of Iago's and Desdemona's meals are italicized.

3.2 Othello gives Iago orders before inspecting fortifications.			
3.1 Cassio asks admittance to Desdemona.		3.3 Cassio parts from Desdemona. Desdemona: Othello's *"bed* will seem a school, his **board a** shrift." Desdemona: "nourishing **food.**" Desdemona **invites** Othello to supper with Cassio. Desdemona **summons** Othello to dine with Cyprians. IAGO FOOD: "spotted with **strawberries.**"	
----------[Nuptial feast]----------		----------[Indefinite interval]----------	
2.3 Othello **summons** Desdemona.	2.3 Iago **invites** Cassio to drink. Iago via Cassio **summons** revelers. "Forgive us our sins." *Brawl.* Cassio calls **wine "devil."**	3.4 Cassio: **"Sweet** Bianca."	3.4 Othello of Desdemona's hand: "requires ... **fasting** and prayer."

2.2 Othello's Herald **invites** to nuptial feast.	4.1 Bianca **invites** Cassio to supper.	4.1 Othello **invites** Lodovico to supper: "Goats and monkeys!" **IAGO "INVITES"** Othello: "strangle her."
2.1 After thanking the "sweet powers," Othello kisses "**sweet**" Desdemona.	4.2 Iago **summons** Roderigo to kill Cassio: "It is now high supper time … about it."	4.2 Iago **summons** Desdemona and Emilia to supper with Lodovico and company.
------------[Voyage]------------	------------[Supper]------------	
1.3 Brabantio "gives" Desdemona to Othello.	4.3 Desdemona: "Let nobody blame him."	
1.2 Othello **summoned** to Senate by Senators and by Brabantio.	5.1 **IAGO SUMMONS** Othello via Cassio's cries. Othello: "I come": to kill Desdemona.	
1.1 Brabantio roused by Iago's obscenities.	5.2 Desdemona: my sins "are loves I bear to you." *Othello kills Desdemona*; Emilia to Iago: "Your reports have set the murder on."	

It is a commonplace that *Othello* recalls medieval morality plays in which Everyman is drawn to an angel on one side and a devil on the other. The starkly contradictory siren voices of such a medieval "fable," as Othello alludes to it (5.2.283), are more variously and realistically suggested in the repeated summonings and meals of Shakespeare's play. But ultimately *Othello* too dramatizes diabolical and angelic extremes in the food-related imagery of Iago and Desdemona. Iago's repulsive nature is vividly apparent in his food references. He mentions only unappetizing or unhealthy foods, and instead of nourishing eating he repeatedly invokes both literal and figurative vomiting. As an image of human relationships, emesis, the opposite of mutual sustenance, is the most visceral and profound rejection possible. Hence the consummation of Iago's meal is the opposite of the loving communion of the marital act; it is instead predatory violence that diets his revenge. Desdemona's much less evident feeding is in every way a contrast to Iago's. She is first and foremost associated with ordinary, healthy eating; she both feeds well (3.3.187) and provides nourishing meals (78). Furthermore, Desdemona's meals are reciprocal; the generous Cyprians receive Othello's hospitality. As imaged by feeding, love is similarly, if more intimately, reciprocal and is pleasurable as well, hence the mutual "sweetness" of Othello and Desdemona and of Cassio and Bianca. Beyond its pleasurable, mutual intimacy, love also has a spiritual dimension for Othello and for Desdemona. In thanking the higher powers for his safe voyage, Othello expresses a belief in the supernatural that he also associates with Desdemona. She, on the other hand, has a sacramental view: the spiritual is immanent in the ordinary. Having "consecrate[d]" herself to Othello (1.3.255), she can invest his board and bed with spiritual meaning: his board shall seem a shrift and his bed a school of Christian love. In Desdemona's view the essential actions of marriage are also, simultaneously, the spiritual actions of confession and communion. The nuptial feast images a mutual Eucharistic self-giving. The lovers offer themselves to each other: This is my body, and (bearing in mind the association between handkerchief and wedding sheets) this is my blood.

In thus symbolizing the love of Othello and Desdemona, Shakespeare draws on the Catholic rather than the Anglican view of the communion service. Jeffrey Knapp puts the doctrinal difference succinctly.

> Catholics claimed that Christ's body was physically present in the consecrated host and that the priest in breaking the holy bread thus re-created Christ's sacrifice; the majority of English Protestant writers argued that Christ's sacrifice could only be remembered and imitated, not repeated and that Christ was spiritually, not physically present in the Eucharist

The Catholic Eucharist, like marriage, necessarily entails physical consummation. It is this doctrinal insistence on both the spiritual and the physical presence that makes the Catholic ritual an apt symbol of marital love, cohering Shakespeare's subtle, resonant analogies among the nuptial feast, the Eucharistic meal and the marriage act.

17

The Chiastic Design
of Folio *King Lear*
Evidence for the Quarto as a Draft

The provenance of the early texts of *King Lear*—the Quarto of 1608 and the Folio text of 1623—present especially difficult problems.[1] The Quarto is thought to have been printed from Shakespeare's foul papers. Misreadings, insufficient stage directions and inconsistent character designations suggest that the quarto "may reproduce certain features of such manuscripts more faithfully than any other Shakespeare quarto."[2] Or, to put it another way, the manuscript source may have been the most corrupt of all printer's copies for the quartos, increasing the possibility for error, even significant error. In spite of the title page, which states "As it was played before the Kings Maiestie," the Quarto may represent—to name only the fewest options—a draft of the play performed in 1606, a complete version as acted in 1606, or a draft of the Folio *Lear*.

The Folio deletes approximately three hundred lines from the Quarto, including an entire scene, 4.3, and adds about a hundred lines which do not appear in the Quarto.[3] Though as a performance text it is thought to have an authoritative derivation, substantially involving a promptbook, the Folio, too, is suspect. It includes passages often considered to be non-Shakespearean, particularly Merlin's prophecy and Kent's speech in 3.1, and deletes at least one passage directors find almost impossible to cut, the so-called mock trial. And in the minds of some editors, at least, Folio revisions are occasionally inferior to the Quarto lines they replace.

The differences between the two texts are variously explained. Summing up the views of the contributors to the influential *The Division of the Kingdoms*, Gary Taylor concludes his essay, "*King Lear*: The Date and Authorship of the Folio Version," by saying, "We are thus faced … with two *King Lears*, both representing what the author regarded, at the time, as the play's final form, and both of which presumably received full theatrical production by Shakespeare's company in Shakespeare's lifetime."[4] This "two-text theory" represents one extreme of current views. At the other extreme are critics like Sidney Thomas who dispute that the revising hand was Shakespeare's and explain many of the differences between Folio and Quarto as mistakes in the printing of the Quarto or theatrical cuts which could have been made by anyone.[5] Between these extremes critics weight the proportion of corruption to revision, sometimes finding the differences between the texts largely attributable to Shakespeare but not worthy of being considered two plays, rather reflecting successive drafts of a single play,[6] other times concluding that "no verdict should yet be given" as to the ratio of corruption to revision.[7]

Out of this range of views have come a similar range of editions. Taylor's view is the rationale for the Oxford edition's separate texts of Quarto (*The History of King Lear*) and Folio (*The Tragedy of King Lear*) and influences parallel-text editions. The Riverside and Arden editions are traditional conflated texts, though they carefully distinguish Folio and Quarto material. The Folio is now often regarded as the superior play (largely because of the work on the two-text problem), and recent editions, such as the New Cambridge edition, have been based on it.[8]

I hope to demonstrate that, in one respect at least, the Quarto cannot be a "final form" of the play, but is instead a draft revised by Shakespeare toward the structurally superior version printed in the Folio. The evidence is simple. The 23 scenes of the Folio *Lear* are chiastically disposed around the central scene, 3.5, in which Edmond betrays his father. As in all the other mature plays, each scene of the first half of the play mirrors the corresponding scene in the second half. This pattern cannot have been discovered in a late revision but must have been planned from an early stage of composition, presumably when the author-plot was formulated. The Quarto contains 24 scenes, destroying the symmetry of the play's design. The scene that editors usually designate as 4.3 in conflated editions and that I will refer to as Scene 17 (of *The History of King Lear*) was an early version, effectively a draft, and therefore deleted in the Folio. The 24-scene Quarto includes two versions of one scene. Scene 17, in which Kent and the Gentleman discuss Cordelia's pity and Lear's shame, is a draft of Scene 18, in which Cordelia herself expresses her compassion for her father.

This fact invites renewed speculation about the date and nature of the play's revision. The excision of Sc. 17, it has been argued, particularly by Taylor and the other contributors to *The Division of the Kingdoms*, is an important part of larger patterns of revision, most notably the diminished role of Kent, the changed characterization of Cordelia and the presentation of the war. If so, those changes must have been made before 1608, when the Quarto was printed. And if we are to posit two "final forms" of the text, the first final form would have to be the Quarto minus Sc.18. While this extends the differences between Q-minus-18 and Folio—between first and second versions, in the two-text theory—and therefore supports the changes as a "major revision," it also results in an appreciably weaker first final version, one Shakespeare would have been less likely to let stand. Moreover, the inclusion of an "extra" scene in the Quarto reinforces the idea that the printer's copy was exceptionally corrupt, lending support to those critics who maintain that some, at least, of the apparent Folio additions are in fact Quarto omissions. In our present state of ignorance not all of these questions can be definitively resolved. However, the symmetrical structure of the play conclusively demonstrates that Quarto and conflated texts include two versions of the same scene and strongly suggests that the major revisions to *King Lear* were completed by Shakespeare before 1608.

A skeletal author-plot of the Folio *Lear*,[9] arranged in the familiar chiastic design, looks like this:

3.5 Edmond betrays his father, becomes Earl of Gloucester.	
3.4 Lear & Poor Tom (Lear strips).	3.6 Lear ("wits gone") & Poor Tom.

3.3 Gloucester tells Edmond of letter.	3.7 Gloucester blinded by Cornwall.
3.2 Kent leads Lear from heath.	4.1 Edgar leads Gloucester to Dover.
3.1 Gentleman trusts Kent.	4.2 Albany quarrels with Gonerill.
2.2 Fool to Kent on Lear's fortunes.	4.3 Cordelia to Gent on Lear's madness.
2.1 Edmond describes "fight" with Edgar.	4.4 Regan asks Oswald for Gonerill letter.
1.5 Fool & Lear.	4.5 Gloucester & Lear.
1.4 Gonerill turns Lear out.	4.6 Cordelia with Lear, awakening.
1.3 Gonerill to Oswald: neglect Lear.	5.1 Edmond's precedence argued.
1.2 Edmond cons father with letter.	5.2 Edgar guides Gloucester from battle.
1.1 Lear ceremony, gives up kingdom.	5.3 Edmond's precedence, combat.

Except in the first and last scenes and in 5.1, the episodes chosen for inclusion in the outline are those at the center of long scenes. For example, the exceptionally long 2.2 contains 481 lines; the conversation between the Fool and Kent, a mere 22 lines, is included in the outline because of its positional emphasis at the center of the scene (238–260). Each "scene triplet," the groups of three pairs of scenes, is organized around the central scene pair in a manner similar to *The Merchant of Venice* and *All's Well That Ends Well*. In *Lear* though, the central pair of each triplet is devoted to the same characters, the villains, with Edmond, as the essential contrast to Lear, appearing in each of these pairs, somewhat as Iago is central to all but two scenes of *Othello*. The siblings are the main characters in the flanking scene pairs of the first triplet; the "fools" are the main characters in the flanking scene pairs of the next triplet; and Lear and Gloucester are the focus of the central triplet. The 3.1–4.2 pair is isolated because each of these transitional scenes functions as a prologue to the larger dramatic movement which follows.[10]

The outline reveals that the structural principle of the play's architecture is the often-remarked division of the characters into good guys and bad guys. Five of the 11 symmetrical pairs link good guys (1.5 & 4.5, 2.2 & 4.3, 3.1 & 4.2, 3.2 & 4.1. 3.4 & 3.6) and three of the pairs link bad guys (1.3 & 5.1, 2.1 & 4.4, 3.3 & 3.7). The important exceptions to this structural segregation of the two camps are 1.2–5.2 and 1.4–4.6 which link the good and bad siblings— only, however, to contrast them. Edmond's duping of his father in 1.2 is contrasted with Edgar's leading Gloucester to safety from the battle of 5.2; Gonerill's expulsion of her father in 1.4 is contrasted with Cordelia's kindness at Lear's awakening in 4.6. The pairing of these opposite treatments of fathers further heightens the moral contrasts between the two camps.

The three central scenes point up the opposite directions of Lear and Edmond along the same trajectory. King Lear's announced decision to give up his lands is matched by the bastard Edmond's contrasting desire to "have lands by wit" (1.2.172). At the exact center Edmond the natural himself becomes Earl of Gloucester, becomes "legitimate," by betraying his father. Immediately after Edmond's change in 3.5, Lear goes mad in 3.6; that is—as we see from his next appearance, in weeds—Lear becomes a natural as Edmond becomes "legitimate." Lear and Edmond follow the same trajectory from power and position to "nature" (in all its various meanings) in opposite directions. The King Lear of the first scene finally attains his desire in the last scene, happily renouncing the world and going "away to prison" (5.3.8) with Cordelia; in the same scene the natural Edmond briefly attains his long-sought dominance. King Lear is almost succeeded by King Edmond.

The thematic essence of the play is expressed in the contrast between the central scene of Edmond's treachery (3.5) and the flanking scenes of Lear's exposure (3.4 & 3.6). In gaining his father's title in the central scene Edmond also gets, so Cornwall thinks, a "dear father" in Cornwall's "love" (25).[11] This offer of fatherhood is an ironic emphasis to Edmond's isolation here, the fact that he is self-conceived, self-made, his own father, the epitome of dissociation from others. The flanking scenes focus on the imaginative empathy which is the counterforce to Edmond's isolation. Lear identifies himself with Poor Tom, first as a beggar and then as a madman. At the moment that Edmond is solidifying his isolation, Lear is breaking out of his.[12]

The other paired scenes of the central grouping emphasize the similarities between Lear and Gloucester. The betrayal of Gloucester and his blinding, the physical equivalent of Lear's folly and madness,[13] are accomplished in the tight causality of 3.3, 3.5 and 3.7, with the pair of Gloucester scenes (3.3 & 3.7) following immediately on the scenes of Lear's transformation (3.4 & 3.6). The pair of scenes in which Lear and Gloucester are led off (3.2 & 4.1) also contain their first moments of compassion. With the Fool "Lear becomes for the first time in the storm 'aware of the sufferings of others.'"[14] In 4.1 Gloucester expresses his concern for the Old Man's safety and gives a purse to Poor Tom, extending the charity he refused his disguised son in the storm earlier.

In the scenic triplet encompassing the early and late scenes of the play the good and bad siblings are contrasted. The 1.4–4.6 pair enacts the contrast between Gonerill and Cordelia. In the early scene Gonerill turns Lear out into the storm, and in the paired scene Lear awakens with Cordelia. The apparently neat contrast between ungrateful child and loving child, however, also places Lear deeper in his suffering. With Cordelia he is, after all, "upon a wheel of fire" he says (4.6.40), which allows him to answer his own anguished question in the paired scene: "Who ... can tell me who I am?" (1.4.212). From across the great divide of his sufferings he himself can tell: "I am a foolish, fond old man" (4.6.53). The expected narrative contrast is provided in the paired scenes, but the comfort we might take in it is seriously undercut. There is a similar irony to the pairing of the Edmond-Edgar scenes, 1.2 and 5.2. We would expect Edmond's villainy to be undone in a paired scene of Edgar's care for his father, and so it is. In 1.2 Edmond entices his father into hearing the forged letter, setting the plot against Edgar and ultimately against Gloucester himself into motion; in the paired scene Edgar leads Gloucester away from the scene of battle, presumably to safety. The irony here is, of course, that Gloucester is suicidal again and must be encouraged by the rather bleak observation that "ripeness is all" (5.2.11). In the central pair of this triplet, 1.3 & 5.1, Gonerill and Edmond hatch villainies. The betrayal initiated by Gonerill in the early scene by ordering Oswald to neglect Lear has flourished into near chaos in the paired scene—the quarrel over Edmond's precedence and his plans to take one or both of the sisters and to kill Lear and Cordelia. (As mentioned above, the central episode of this scene is not these actions of Edmond's but Edgar's delivery to Albany of the intercepted letter. In 12 lines at the center of this 60-line scene Edgar provides the kernel of hope that Edmond will be overcome, but Edgar's brief appearance does not override the dominant tone and narrative consequence of the scene as a betrayal parallel to Gonerill's in 1.3.)

In the Fool triplet the compassionate merging of one character into another that was initiated in the central flanking scenes is further extended. The pairing of 2.2 and 4.3 adds to other suggestions in the play of the linking of Cordelia and the Fool. In these scenes they both express concern for Lear; the Fool laments Lear's lack of wisdom and Cordelia laments the insufficiences of "man's wisdom" generally in effecting cures (2.2.241–60 and 4.3.8–18). As is often remarked, scene 4.5, in which the mad Lear meets the blind Gloucester, is an analogue of the paired 1.5, in which the Fool mocks Lear.[15] The central lines in each scene play on the sight imagery. The Fool asks Lear "why one's nose stands i'th'middle on's face?" and answers himself, so that "What a man cannot smell out he may spy into" (1.5.20–24). In the paired scene Lear answers the blind Gloucester's question, "Dost thou know me?" by saying, "I remember thine eyes well enough" and continues with a dozen lines needling Gloucester's "heavy case" (4.5.131–32, 142–43). The central pair of this triplet, 2.1 & 4.4, is linked by the common betrayal of a sibling. Edmond stages the incriminating "fight" with Edgar, and Regan betrays her sister by trying to turn Oswald, these cold treacheries appearing that much worse for being sandwiched between the two "foolish" pairs of commiseration.

Overall, then, the play is carefully, even exquisitely, constructed in an arch-like symmetry with Edmond's betrayal of his father the keystone scene and his continuing villainies central to each of the play's scenic triplets. The countervailing charities of the good characters, the subtle ways in which they identify themselves with each other, find their own fitted places within this architecture. This structural pattern refutes the theory that the Quarto *Lear* is an early but final version of the play and that it was performed as printed. The Quarto *Lear* with its 24 scenes skews the symmetry evident in the Folio *Lear*. The early-version theory would require that Shakespeare in the course of his later revisions came upon the structure here outlined, rather than having this author-plot in mind as he wrote the play initially, or at least very early.

The chiastic design confirms that Scene 17 can only have been a draft that was intended by Shakespeare to be replaced by Scene 18. The conversation between Kent and the Gentleman that comprises Scene 17 has always struck critics and directors as problematic. The weakest objection against it is that it has no connection to the plot; it is among the first cuts directors make to the play.[16] The poetry, too, with its "slightly contorted ingenuity," in John Jones phrase,[17] has seemed out of place with the taut verse of the rest of the play. But the scene mars the play more seriously, as Stephen Urkowitz has argued, in that it introduces contradictions. Kent asks about "Albany's and Cornwall's powers" and is told they "are afoot" (49–50); but Cornwall is dead and Albany has just been heard vowing revenge on Gloucester's tormentors. Kent informs the Gentleman that Lear is "in the town" (39), but in the next scene Cordelia orders a search for him in the "field" (7). Lear is said to feel such shame that he will not meet with Cordelia, but he seems not to know of Cordelia's presence in England when he awakens with her. Kent says that a French general, Monsieur Le Far, has been put in charge of the French army; in the next scene Cordelia appears to lead the army. In sum, the scene is, as Urkowitz concludes, "at best forgettable and at worst seriously misleading."[18]

Deserving of excision it may be, but at first glance Sc. 17 hardly looks like an earlier version of Sc. 18. A closer look, however, reveals the continuities in the three main topics of both scenes: Cordelia's pity, Lear's distraction and the leadership of the army. The central focus in both scenes is Cordelia. She is the dominant subject of conversation in the earlier scene, occupying 23 of the 56 lines, and a stage presence in the later. The change from her merely verbal presence to her physical presence onstage accords with the major difference in the imagery of the two scenes. The enskyed Cordelia of Sc. 17 is brought down to earth, to nature, in Sc. 18. Though the emphasis in both scenes is on her pity for her father, expressed in her tears, the transcendent, spiritual associations of the early scene are discarded in favor of more "mundane" associations in her physical presence and the imagery of her speeches. In Sc. 17 the Gentleman describes the "sunshine and rain" of Cordelia's smiles and tears, and says her tears are "holy water from her heavenly eyes" (31); in the revised scene her tears of pity would elicit from the earth itself the means for her father's cure:

> All blest secrets,
> All you unpublished virtues of the earth,
> Spring with my tears; be aidant and remediate
> In the good man's distress [Sc. 18, 15–18].

This change situates Cordelia within the play's varying ideas of nature, particularly after the scene's opening description of Lear in weeds (1–7). Sc. 18 also continues the concerns of Sc. 17 in making Lear a topic of conversation in both. Where Kent elaborates on Lear's sense of shame, Cordelia laments the "good man's distress" (18), continuing the note of Lear's suffering in madness rather than in consciousness of shame. A third topic common to both scenes is the presentation of the war. In Sc. 17 we are told explicitly that the King of France has returned home and left a Monsieur Le Far to command. In Sc. 18 Cordelia commands a "century" to seek her father (6); receives news of the British army and responds, "Our preparation stands In expectation of them (22–23); and refers to "our arms" (27)—all indicating that she is in command of the army. Though not literally paraded before us *with drum and colours*, as in the stage directions of the Folio, Cordelia's military command is implicit both in her stage presence and in the dialogue of Sc. 18. Though superficially unlike, largely because of Kent's absence from Sc. 18, the two scenes are variations on the same three subjects.

The replacement of Sc. 17 by Sc. 18 is importantly involved in at least three larger patterns of revision—affecting Kent, the characterization of Cordelia and the war. Because these three patterns of revision are all of a piece, it is unlikely that Sc. 18 replaced Sc. 17 without some additional revisions occurring at the same time. In fact, most of the arguments advanced for Shakespeare's revisions between the Quarto and the Folio apply equally to the differences that can be conjectured as consequent on the replacement of Sc. 17 by Sc. 18.

The absence of Kent from Sc. 18 is part of Michael Warren's larger consideration of "The Diminution of Kent."[19] Warren tabulates the number of Kent cues and words in the Quarto and Folio to suggest the extent to which the Kent role was cut. Most of the cuts are in act 4. (Warren does not record the differences by scene.) In the Quarto Act Four (Sc. 15–21) Kent has 19 cues and 304 words, whereas in the Folio he has only 4 cues and 56 words. This difference accounts for almost the entire change in the Kent role, for the total number of cues in the quarto is 124 and in the Folio 107, and the word count is 2512 and 2176, respectively. But with the deletion of Sc. 17 there are in Act Four only 8 cues for Kent, not 19, and 102 words not 304. Most of the cuts to Kent's role occurred between Q-minus-18 and Q-minus-17 simply by virtue of deleting Sc. 17, a change so consequential for the role that the other deletions would easily and immediately follow upon it. The most significant, Edgar's speech describing Kent's heartbreak at Lear's distress (Sc. 24, 201–18), depends for its effect partly on a narrative and emotional connection to the concerned Kent of Sc. 17. Without the earlier service expressed by Kent, the continuity is weakened; the deletion of Edgar's description from Act Five might easily fit into a larger coherent and single plan of revision.

In arguing that the change in Kent's role affects other parts of the play, Warren says, "The absence of [Q] 4.3 [Sc. 17] from the Folio is ... part of a profound difference in the presentation of Cordelia." In making this judgment Warren is, of course, considering not the bald contrast between *History* Sc. 17 and Folio 4.3, but that contrast mediated by the presence of Sc. 18. In Q-minus-18, the Cordelia of Act Four is almost an allegorical embodiment of pity, strikingly, even startlingly, different from the military commander of the Folio. But it is the mere replacement of Sc. 17 with Sc.18 that accomplishes most of the "profound difference in the presentation of Cordelia." Beside the stage direction for Cordelia to enter with soldiers, *drums and colours*, the only change between Sc. 18 and Folio 4.3 is the replacement of the Doctor by the Gentleman. Though Gary Taylor considers this substitution as more in keeping with a military scene, he does not examine the dialogue as replacing that of Sc. 17 and therefore does not consider whether Cordelia, even if in an "intimate scene," might not nevertheless be the head of the army.[20] In tracing the changes from Sc. 17 through Sc.18 to Folio 4.3, it is apparent that the first revision intended primarily to capture an "earthly" compassion in Cordelia, but included as well an implication of leadership. The difference between Sc. 18 and Folio 4.3 is a matter of emphasis, not a re-conception of Cordelia; that was accomplished between Sc. 17 and Sc. 18.

Consequently, it seems that Taylor's wider claims for the difference between Quarto and Folio as regards the war are true of the revision from Sc. 17 to Sc. 18. "Who leads the invasion army," Taylor says, "is a crucial issue, as a number of other Folio alterations make clear."[21] He then considers changes at SD 5.2.0, 4.2.56 and 5.1.25, all of which omit references to a French invasion. Again, Sc. 17 is, if not pivotal, certainly important to the changes Taylor demonstrates and seems to be of a piece with both the new conception of Cordelia and the changed presentation of the war. And, again, since Sc. 17 is draft material, it seems entirely possible that the changed conception of the war was worked into the play in Q-minus-17.[22]

Two final, more tentative, points. Because the deletions of the mock trial and Edgar's soliloquy from 3.6 bring the play more closely into line with a customary structural practice of Shakespeare's, I suspect that this too was an early revision. Invariably, as we have seen repeatedly, the scenes of the central flanking pair in Shakespeare's plays exhibit a stronger similarity than that of any other pair. This pattern is also evident in the Folio *Lear*. As I've shown, the disposition of scenes and the overall structure are based on which characters appear within scenes. The same characters appear centrally in paired scenes only when Lear and Poor Tom are together in 3.4 and 3.6. This basic similarity is further emphasized by the revisions to 3.6. Cutting the mock trial of the Quarto (Sc. 13, 13–51) and Edgar's soliloquy ending the scene (95–108) reduces the scene to 55 lines, throwing the focus almost exclusively on the 35-line interchange between Lear and Edgar, in which Edgar chases the dogs Lear has hallucinated (sometimes taken to symbolize the three daughters) and is then taken into Lear's imagined retinue of one hundred knights. These mutual charities provide the link with the paired scene, 3.6. Before the hovel Edgar asked for charity but would have been left behind by Gloucester except for Lear's and Kent's interventions. The structural pairing of the two scenes is heightened by the cuts to the Quarto, which give Poor Tom prominence and heighten the reflecting acts of charity. The deletion of the mock trial not only removes a duplicate fixation on justice which is more effectively conveyed in 4.5[23] but also and more appropriately focuses the scene on the issue of charity. And the deletion of Edgar's final soliloquy from the Quarto allows Poor Tom the madman predominance rather than the reasonable Edgar, thus heightening the madness of Lear and his identification of himself with Poor Tom. In the Quarto *Lear* the dazzle of the mock trial in 3.6 threatens to overwhelm the subtle mutual charities of the scene. The Folio version is structurally superior and, being closer to the customary architecture of the plays, suggests an early, Shakespearean revision.

This leads us circuitously to another crux, Folio 3.1, in which Kent inconclusively, confusingly, tells the Gentleman of division between Albany and Cornwall and sends the Gentleman on a mission he "knows not whither," as Samuel Johnson complained. In the Quarto Kent reveals news of the French invasion and specifies the Gentleman's Dover destination (Sc. 8, 21–32). Because this information has been replaced in the Folio by a far more hesitant and indefinite speech (*Tragedy* 3.1, 13–20), the passage is notoriously unsatisfying, but the conflated text[24] is hardly less so, its length alone enough to confirm its forced joinery. Impossible as it is to make any case for an authorial intention to create uncertainty, I will nevertheless try to indicate why such uncertainty is consistent with other changes in the revision.

First and most obviously, the deleted reference to the French invasion in 3.1 is consistent with the excision of Sc. 17 and the other changes to the presentation of the war. Why, then, conflate the texts to include information consistently deleted elsewhere? The evidence that I find most suggestive, however, follows from the structural pairing of 3.1 and 4.2. The essential action that links these two scenes is an assertion of loyalty to the Lear cause—in the one case by the Gentleman and in the other by Albany—in the midst of an uncertain, unstable situation. The revisions heighten the sense of instability by making two similar kinds of changes to each scene: both delete passages of animal imagery, and both diminish the grounds for conviction.

The animal imagery occurs in 3.1 among the eight-and-a-half lines deleted from the Gentleman's speech. It is reported that Lear is out "unbonneted" in a night when even famished beasts—the "cub-drawn bear and ... belly-pinched wolf"—find cover (Sc. 8, 13, 11–12). In 4.2, from which 28 lines are deleted (Sc. 16, mainly 31–49, 52–8), Albany condemns Gonerill and her sister as "Tigers," for their treatment of their father, "Whose reverence even the head-lugged bear would lick" (41, 43), and ends by characterizing the sisters' behavior apocalyptically: "Humanity must perforce prey on itself, Like monsters of the deep" (50–51). In both cases, the imagery has the obvious effect of emotional conviction and of moral summing up. Though the bond of loyalty asserted or implied by Albany and the Gentleman in each of these scenes does not change, the situation in which they make their choices is much more ambiguous. The other changes have the same effect. Albany's long passages condemning Gonerill in Sc. 16 forcefully convey his firm moral judgment amidst the series of changed loyalties which comprise the rest of the scene—the shift in Albany's loyalties as reported by Oswald, Gonerill's fear that Edmond will be lost to her, the news that the servant killed Cornwall and that Edmond betrayed his father. Cutting Albany's speeches to a minimum has the inevitable consequence of heightening the changes reported seriatim through the rest of the scene. Similarly, in the paired scene the French invasion and the Gentleman's Dover destination have been deleted, and the syntax of the Folio lines is tortured and fragmentary, leaving the scene, many commentators have found, maddeningly inconclusive. The revisions to both scenes seem intended to reinforce exactly what is conveyed by both their positions and their isolation in the symmetrical structure, a sense of transition and uncertainty. In both cases a good character turns to the right cause in the midst of confused and shifting circumstances. It seems that in spelling out Kent's message for the Gentleman conflated editions destroy the very effect the revision is intended to enhance, an indeterminacy which is also characteristic of the whole play.

Against the *textual* indeterminacy argued for the last two decades, however, we can definitely isolate three stages in the revisions to *King Lear* attributable to Shakespeare: the Quarto-minus-Sc. 18, the Quarto-minus-Sc. 17 and the Folio. The replacement of Sc. 17 by Sc. 18 plausibly entails the larger revisions to Kent's role, Cordelia's characterization and the presentation of the war. More speculatively, the deletion of the mock trial is a Shakespearean change in keeping with a customary structural practice, and the changes in 3.1 are in keeping with the overall strategy of the play, which is hindered by attempts to make the scene unambiguously conclusive. In more than printing an "extra" scene and destroying the symmetry, then, Quarto and conflated texts appear to fall short of a "final form" and to obscure the achieved masterpiece, the Folio *King Lear*.

18

The Thematic Arch of *Macbeth*
Reconsidering Hecate

Most modern productions of *Macbeth* entirely omit Hecate, the goddess of the witches, on the commonly accepted ground that she is a spurious later addition to the play. Without disputing the accuracy of that consensus, I will nevertheless argue for the retention of the first 33 lines of 3.5, in which Hecate prophesies that Macbeth will come to the "pit of Acheron … to know his destiny," as he in fact does in 4.1. Besides the obvious narrative link that Hecate's speech provides to the subsequent apparitions scene, her appearance also serves three other distinctly Shakespearean purposes. First, it fulfills the number of scenes required by the evident author-plot; second, it detaches the audience from its intimate engagement with Macbeth's illusions, altering—chastening—our relation to the continuing fantasies in the second half of the play; and third, it preserves Shakespeare's characteristic structural chiasmus in which each scene of the first half of the play reflects the corresponding scene in the second half.

Hecate is suspect for a number of dramatic and textual reasons. As a new character introduced late in the play, with no further plot connections and speaking in a different verse than the witches, she lacks any apparent organic ties to the rest of the drama. Furthermore, because two songs whose titles appear in the Hecate scene and the apparition scene (3.5 and 4.1) are known to be by Thomas Middleton and are thought to date from sometime between 1609 and 1615, later than the accepted date of *Macbeth*, critics almost universally suspect the whole of the Hecate scene (3.5) to be spurious. None of these objections are conclusive though. It is not unusual for gods from machines to appear late in Shakespeare's plays—Jupiter in *Cymbeline* and Ceres in *The Tempest*—and speak in jingling verse. And the fact that the songs are by Middleton does not necessarily mean that he wrote all of both scenes (3.5 and 4.1). As Gary Taylor has noted,[1] the suspicions of non-Shakespearean authorship rest on no more than the "felt inferiority" of the Hecate lines, and there have been critics—J. M. Nosworthy, Nicholas Brooke and Kenneth Muir, for example—who do not share the sense of the lines' inferiority (though their conclusions about the authenticity of the scene differ).[2] While the authorship of the scene remains in question, there is no definitive reason to remove Hecate from the cast of characters, and no fatal objection to the verse of 3.5.1–33, the portion of the suspect text that I hope to resuscitate.

Because I am arguing for the structural necessity of the scene as well as its thematic relevance, I must address the problematic question: How many scenes has *Macbeth*? Editors disagree about the Folio's last scene, the battle of 5.7. In keeping with its usual practice, the Folio does not mark a new scene at each cleared stage in the battle sequence, as antagonists exit and re-enter. Modern editors, with varying degrees of scrupulousness about a cleared stage, divide the scene further. The Riverside edition divides 5.7 into three scenes; the Oxford divides it into five scenes. But, however we imagine battle sequences to have been staged, (probably without the few seconds' pause at the cleared stage between designated scenes), the Folio 5.7 is perfectly coherent and structurally sound. The midpoint of the scene is the confrontation between Macbeth and Macduff, which has been anticipated through the second half of the play. The central speech expresses Macbeth's despair upon learning that Macduff was "from his mother's womb Untimely ripped" (5.7.45–46). Macbeth replies:

> Accursed be the tongue that tells me so,
> For it hath cowed my better part of man!
> And be these juggling fiends no more believed
> That palter with us in a double sense [47–50 of 104].

This is Macbeth's moment of climactic awareness. His manhood lost, the witches' equivocations revealed, in the last lines of the speech even his valorous warrior identity collapses: "I'll not fight with thee." This climactic moment is fittingly positioned at the midpoint of the scene's three broad panels: first, a flurry of fighting in which young Siward is killed; then the confrontation between Macduff and Macbeth; and finally Malcolm's forces in victory. There is no compelling reason to change the Folio scene and plenty of reason not to, for additional scene designations would encourage directors to break up what is clearly intended to be fast-paced action and, as we'll see, would also destroy the symmetry of the overall design.

There are, then, a total of 27 scenes in the play, a number which, given the proliferation of threes in the play and the traditional proclivity of witches for multiples of three and nine, seems perfectly apt: 3 × 3 × 3. The number of scenes provides a neat variation of "Thrice to thine, and thrice to mine, And thrice again" (1.3.35–6), suggesting that the play itself is a kind of charm like the one the witches wind up.[3] The central scene is the murder of Banquo, and the other scenes are symmetrically arranged around it. An outline of the play's chiastically related, reflecting actions follows:

3.3 Banquo murdered.	
3.2 Macbeth tells Lady Macbeth of his "terrible dreams" and fear of Banquo.	3.4 Macbeth sees Banquo's ghost at the banquet.
3.1 Macbeth: "To be thus is nothing, but to be safely thus."	3.5.1–33 Hecate: "security is mortals' chiefest enemy."
2.4 Old Father on unnatural things; Macduff to Fife.	3.6 Lennox and a lord on Macduff's visit to Edward Confessor.
2.3 Porter at (hell's) gate; discovery of murdered king.	4.1 Macbeth sees apparitions and show of kings.
2.2 Macbeth murders Duncan.	4.2 Macduff's family murdered.
2.1 Macbeth: "Is this a dagger..."	4.3 Macduff and Malcolm, in test of loyalty, restore trust.

1.7 Lady Macbeth persuades Macbeth to kill Duncan; she plans to drug grooms into "swinish sleep."	5.1 Lady Macbeth sleepwalks.
1.6 Duncan welcomed to the castle by Lady Macbeth and conducted to meet his host.	5.2 Scottish soldiers, marching to join English forces, discuss Macbeth's "distempered cause."
1.5 Lady Macbeth, "transported beyond this ignorant present," welcomes Macbeth.	5.3 Macbeth informed of opposing forces and Lady Macbeth's "thick-coming fancies."
1.4 Duncan commends Macbeth ("I have begun to plant you") and Banquo.	5.4 Soldiers cut camouflaging branches.
1.3 Macbeth and Banquo meet the Weird Sisters.	5.5 At news of Birnam Wood advancing, Macbeth suspects "equivocation of the fiend."
1.2 Duncan: "No more that thane of Cawdor shall deceive Our bosom interest"; confers title on Macbeth.	5.6 Macduff orders soldiers to throw down their branches, "show like those you are."
1.1 Weird Sisters plan to meet Macbeth.	5.7 Macbeth—"fiends no more believed"—killed by Macduff.

Each "scene triplet," the groups of three pairs of scenes, devotes two of its three early scenes to the same main character. So scenes 1.2, 1.3 and 1.4, with their corresponding scenes of the soldiery, form a Duncan triplet; the next three pairs comprise a Lady Macbeth triplet; and the next a Macbeth triplet. The central grouping of five scenes is devoted to the murder of Banquo. The first and last scenes, as frequently in Shakespeare (e.g., *Henry V* and *King Lear*), occupy a separate place, here as the most encompassing of the narrative and metaphoric links between paired scenes, the initiation and final disclosure to Macbeth of the Weird Sisters' equivocations. The scenes of the last remaining pair, 2.4 and 3.6, are transitional, choral scenes focusing on Macduff the deliverer and function much as the choral scenes in *Richard II*.

The murder of Banquo is the turning point in Macbeth's fortunes, the pivot which was perhaps suggested to Shakespeare by his source in Holinshed: "after the contrived murder of Banquho, nothing prospered with…. Makbeth."[4] In the source, though, Banquo is complicitous in the murder of Duncan, and Macbeth's fear for his own safety as well as of Banquo's progeny motivates the murder. By transforming Banquo into a man of conscience, Shakespeare has signaled in Banquo's murder the death of trust and of natural bonds under Macbeth. The depth of fear and depravity to which Macbeth has descended is conveyed in the unexpected presence of the third murderer and the plunge into total darkness (in imagery if not in the Globe staging) when the torch is extinguished at Banquo's death.

The central flanking scenes contain hallucinatory fears of Banquo. Both 3.2 and 3.4 demonstrate the workings of diseased imagination, the "terrible dreams" of Macbeth and the appearance of Banquo's ghost. The crucial difference between the two scenes is the fact that Lady Macbeth, while sharing the fears of the earlier scene, cannot see the ghost at the banquet. The murder of the central scene has opened a chasm between husband and wife. Only Macbeth (and the audience) sees the ghost; he and Lady Macbeth will now each be isolated in their own guilty imaginings.

I will defer discussion of the 3.1–3.5 pair, containing Macbeth's meeting with the murderers and the appearance of Hecate, until I have sketched the overall symmetry. It is enough here to note that the pair completes the group of five scenes centrally devoted to the murder of Banquo, a group set off by the transitional pair, 2.4 and 3.6, both of which introduce the hope Macduff represents at two important junctions in the action. After the murder of Duncan, Macduff refuses to attend the coronation; and after the murder of Banquo, Macduff, we learn, is attempting to persuade Malcolm to return to Scotland.

Excepting the first and last scenes, the rest of the play is structured in the three scene triplets already mentioned. Central to the first triplet is Macbeth's meeting with the three sisters (1.3) and, in the paired scene (5.5), his first suspicions of the "equivocation of the fiend" (43). This pair introduces and ends the complex pattern of illusions in the play, and their fleeting insubstantiality is suggested at the midpoint of each scene. The witches vanish at the center of 1.3, and Macbeth enters a purely illusory state of mind. With the news that he is in fact Thane of Cawdor, Macbeth muses, ironically enough in theater imagery, on the "happy prologues to the swelling act Of the imperial theme" (129–30). From this point until the paired scene Macbeth is more or less "rapt," enveloped in illusions, living in a play. By the time of the paired "epilogue" in 5.5 Macbeth has concluded that all of life is a theater illusion. Upon hearing of his wife's death and the advance of Birnam Wood, he says, "Life's but a walking shadow, a poor player That struts and frets his hour upon the stage And then is heard no more" (24–6).

The Duncan scenes of the first triplet further the king's associations with nature by twice pairing his presence with the short scenes devoted to cutting and dropping the branches of Birnam Wood (1.2–5.6 and 1.4–5.4). These scenes also signal the beginning and ending of the play's deceits, that is, the moral dimension of the play's illusions. Duncan ends 1.2 by saying: "No more that Thane of Cawdor shall deceive Our bosom interest." He then gives the title to Macbeth, who, of course, exactly repeats and fatally extends the original Thane's deceit. In throwing down the branches in the paired scene (5.6), the soldiers further the successive casting off of disguise and move closer to the revelation of the truth in the final scenes of the play.

The central of the three triplets is devoted to Lady Macbeth. The first and last of her "fancies" are rendered in the pair 1.5 and 5.3; she is transported beyond the "ignorant present" by Macbeth's letter in the early scene (56) and is sick with "thick-coming fancies" in the later scene (37). Her early fierce mockery of Macbeth's fears (1.7) is countered by her pathetic sleepwalking (5.1). The center of this triplet, the 1.6–5.2 pair, contrasts Duncan's rule with Macbeth's loveless command, but Lady Macbeth's place in that loveless scheme is suggested by her resonant central lines to Duncan in the scene: "All our service, in every point twice done and then done double, were poor and single business…" (14–16 of 31). We hear in these lines the repeated "done" of Macbeth's soliloquy, the "double, double" of the Sisters' chant, and the many euphemistic references to the "business" of killing Duncan. These prophetic echoes (or perhaps germinating words) reinforce the structural expression of Lady Macbeth's central influence in the play.

In the Macbeth triplet the murder of Duncan is paired with the murder of Macduff's family (2.2 and 4.2),[5] and the Porter's fantasy of opening hell's gate is paired with the apparitions the Weird Sisters conjure from their cauldron (2.3 and 4.1). The initiation and resolution of the play's hallucinations occur in the 2.1–4.3 pair, the imagined dagger and the loyalty test. In his brilliant discussion of *Macbeth* as a baroque drama, Nicholas Brooke points out that the dagger first initiates the audience into "seeing" what is not present on stage. In the depths of the play's inferno, when Banquo is killed, we (or at least the Globe audience) plunge into darkness at midday; and our imaginations become identical with Macbeth's when Banquo's ghost appears only to us and to Macbeth. This sequence of hallucinations, this tyranny of the imagination, is undone by Malcom's laborious exercise of duplicity with Macduff, in which reason and trust are reestablished. The significant work of the loyalty test in righting the impetuous, hallucinatory and diabolical impact of imagination, signaled by the pairing of 2.1 and 4.3, justifies the seemingly excessive length of the scene and its central lines: "God above Deal between thee and me" (4.3.120–21 of 240). As Muir says of the Malcolm-Macduff scene, "For the first time their [the audience's] moral sentiments and aesthetic responses are able to coincide."[6]

Macbeth is carefully structured to usher the audience into and out of the hellish imaginings which lead to bloody executions. The scenes are paired and organized into triplets in large measure to accomplish and to comment on this trajectory of illusory experience in which, as Brent Stirling puts it, "Macbeth's abstraction ["raptness"] gives way to awareness of reality, while Lady Macbeth's early command of pseudo-reality advances into the guilty raptness of walking sleep."[7] Let me recap briefly this trajectory in terms of the paired scenes.

The central scene requires that the audience in an open air theater imagine total darkness during full daylight. The Globe audience has now become like Macbeth. The darkness in the minds of the audience at Banquo's death is the essential Macbeth condition. Like Macbeth they and only they see Banquo's ghost. The symmetrical pairing of the play's scenes leads the audience into and out of that Macbeth moment. So the first and last scenes introduce the witches and reveal to Macbeth their equivocations. The initial meeting with the weird sisters, stirring Macbeth's first fantasies, is paired with the news of Birnam Wood, which creates Macbeth's first suspicions of equivocation. Lady Macbeth's initial fantasies of the future are paired with news of her final "thick-coming fancies." And her mockery of painted devils is paired with the sleepwalking scene. The dagger and the loyalty test are paired, as are the apparitions and the porter at Hell gate.

This journey into and out of the central darkness of Banquo's murder is experienced differently by Macbeth and by the audience. Macbeth is not freed of his illusions until just before his death; the audience is abruptly jolted from its deepest participation in Macbeth's feverous mind by the appearance of Hecate in 3.5. We are confronted by the banality of evil. In its scolding of the Weird Sisters, its insistently iambic octosyllabic couplets and its mingling of slight fancies and fatal matter, the Hecate speech alters the audience's relationship to the hallucinations of the play. When Macbeth subsequently meets the witches, his intensity is no longer shared by the audience; the apparitions seem relatively inconsequential to us. Certainly, they have nothing like the hold on our imaginations of the murder of Banquo or the appearance of Banquo's ghost. Hecate is a deus ex machina who saves not the characters from the circumstances of the drama but the audience from the play itself. We are freed from the arc of illusion we have until this point travelled with Macbeth. In the opening scene we have no idea of the status of the Weird Sisters; are they real or illusory? How are we to take them? Gradually, as Banquo comments on them, as the fantastic future begins to corrupt the minds of Macbeth and Lady Macbeth, as the hallucinatory dagger becomes "seen," as we are invited to imagine varieties of darkness in light, as Banquo's murder puts out the torch and the ghost appears, we come to know not what the witches are but exactly what they have done to Macbeth, for we have experienced the deepening of imagination's darkness. With the appearance of Hecate the illusory nature of what has motivated Macbeth becomes trivially clear. If the Weird Sisters remain ambiguous, except as part of a play, the illusion we have been ushered into and out of, their effect in Macbeth's hallucinatory and unnatural imaginings, is not at all ambiguous.

The Hecate speech not only fits the arc of illusion the play traces but also answers to Macbeth's central soliloquy in the paired scene, 3.1. The trivial cause is paired with the terrible consequence for Macbeth: His "eternal jewel" he has "Given to the common enemy of man" (3.1.68–9). Something ultimately as unreal as a stage play, a mere fantasy, has cost Macbeth his soul. Fittingly, Hecate provides a comment on Macbeth's state almost point for point. Macbeth begins by, again, invoking his desire for safety: "To be thus is nothing, but to be safely thus." (48). Hecate, in the penultimate couplet of her speech says, "And you all know security Is mortals' chiefest enemy" (32–3). In the equivocal pronouncements of the apparitions she will provide Macbeth with exactly the safety he desires. Hecate also says that Macbeth shall be drawn on by "illusion" to "spurn fate, scorn death, and bear His hopes 'bove wisdom, grace and fear" (28, 30–31). This couplet is essentially a text that Macbeth elaborates in the paired scene. He says his "fears in Banquo stick deep, and in his royalty of nature Reigns that which would be feared" (48–50); and, almost obsessively, "there is none but he Whose being I do fear." As Hecate says, Macbeth overrides that fear. In killing Banquo Macbeth kills exactly those qualities of wisdom and security that he so much lacks: "to that dauntless temper of his mind He hath a wisdom that doth guide his valour To act in safety" (51–53). Finally, Macbeth resolves to "scorn fate." Rather than have the crown descend to Banquo's heirs, Macbeth says, "come fate into the list, And champion me to th' utterance."[8] Scenes 3.1 and 3.5.1–33 are paired both structurally and verbally.

It may well be then that Brooke is correct in supposing a revision for the Blackfriar's theater. The baroque play of imagination that *Macbeth* enacts at the Globe in, for example, the moment of darkness at full day, loses some force if presented in a darkened indoor theater. The original 3.5 may have also been defective in this way, and the Hecate material substituted to address the deficiency. Though the bulk of the scene is almost certainly non-Shakespearean, Hecate's opening speech fits the plan and topics of the play perfectly. It maintains the number and order of scenes of the evident author-plot and preserves the play's arc of illusion as well as its symmetrical structure in pairing the Hecate speech with Macbeth's soliloquy.

19

The Triple Arch
of *Antony and Cleopatra*

In the *Riverside Shakespeare* Frank Kermode sums up the changing critical attitudes toward the structure of *Antony and Cleopatra*:

> From Johnson to Bradley (who called it "the most faultily constructed of all the tragedies") critics have censured its apparently loose construction—the rapid alternation of short scenes in places remote from one another, which characterizes the third and fourth act in particular. This has not prevented others from applying Coleridge's famous encomium of the "happy valiancy" of the style to the play as a whole; the bold scene changes from Rome to Alexandria are now understood as a reflection of a basic thematic opposition. Consequently, and rightly, the play is now considered to be among Shakespeare's supreme achievements…. [T]he sustained interplay of theme and poetry … makes this one of the most highly wrought of all the tragedies.[1]

In his *Prefaces to Shakespeare* Harley Granville-Barker similarly rebuts Samuel Johnson's complaint that the play is "without any art of connection" by detailing the links and contrasts from one scene to the next as the play unfolds in performance.[2] But invoking the play's admittedly brilliant "interplay of theme and poetry" or its colorful weaving of one scene to the next does not answer Bradley's objection; it simply changes the ground of the argument, shifting from the question of construction to other more nebulous matters. In fact, Granville-Barker, though a man of the theater and a playwright himself, says explicitly, "We should never, probably, think of Shakespeare as sitting down to construct a play as an architect must build a house…. He is liker to a musician, who takes a theme and … improvises."[3] There is then no point in seeking a blueprint; *Antony and Cleopatra* is pure poetry.

The complexity of the play's construction makes such critical dodges easily understandable. It has more scenes by far than any other mature play in the canon—the 29 scenes of *Cymbeline* and *Coriolanus* are the nearest approach to the 43 scenes of *Antony and Cleopatra*—and its wavering, often anticlimactic action and not infrequently tangential episodes justify Bradley's exasperated remark that the play "bewilders … the mind."[4] It may have a "vestigial" narrative structure, as Mark Rose thinks, which conforms to Shakespeare's customary practice in having two broad movements, preparations for war in the first movement and the war and its aftermath in the second movement with the midpoint, the last scene of the first movement, at 3.6, the scene in which Caesar attacks Antony's insolence, informs Octavia of Antony's faithlessness and resolves upon war. Or the midpoint might be 3.2, as Bradley thinks, the scene in which Antony marries Octavia. Or, as Mark Van Doren thinks, the play may not have a plot at all in the Aristotelian sense.[5]

I would suggest that far from being faultily constructed *Antony and Cleopatra* is exactingly crafted. As in the other plays we have seen, the skeletal structure of *Antony and Cleopatra* is spatial not temporal, a visual shape rather than a narrative sequence. *Antony and Cleopatra* can be visualized in the shape of an "M," divided horizontally through the middle. Its 43 scenes thus form a triple arch, one inverted, on two supporting "columns," with a "keystone scene" at each of the three angles. The structure is based on the relative positions of characters and actions. Following is the shaped outline containing the main character(s) in each scene, excepting the keystone scenes (2.6, 3.10 and 4.7.4–13):

2.6 Triumvirs' agreement		[4.7.4–13] Alexandria victory	
2.5 Cleopatra	2.7 Antony, Caesar, et. al.	[4.7.1–3] Agrippa	4.8 Antony & Cleopatra
2.4 Lepidus	3.1 Ventidius	4.6 Enobarbus	4.9 Enobarbus
2.3 **Antony**	3.2 **Antony**	4.5 **Antony**	4.10 **Antony**
2.2 Antony & Cleopatra	3.3 Cleopatra	4.4 Antony & Cleopatra	4.11 Caesar
2.1 *Pompey*	3.4 Antony	4.3 *Soldiers*	4.12 Antony
------------		------------	
1.5 Cleopatra	3.5 *Enobarbus*	4.2 Antony & Cleopatra	4.13 Cleopatra
1.4 Caesar	3.6 Caesar	4.1 Caesar	4.14 Antony
1.3 **Antony & Cleopatra**	3.7 **Antony & Cleopatra**	3.13 **Antony & Cleopatra**	4.15 **Antony & Cleopatra**
1.2 Antony	3.8 Caesar	3.12 Caesar	5.1 Caesar
1.1 Antony & Cleopatra	3.9 Antony	3.11 Antony & Cleopatra	5.2 Cleopatra
		3.10 Actium defeat	

The upper half of the play has a central Antony row beginning at 2.3, in which Antony is prominently onstage in each of the four scenes, and the lower half has a central Antony and Cleopatra row beginning at 1.3. These repeated appearances help both to establish the basic structural division of the play and to knit together its various parts. The three principal characters, Antony, Cleopatra and Caesar, are dominant in all but two scenes of the bottom half of the outline, 3.5 and 3.10, (exceptions I will return to), while the upper half includes scenes showcasing the various secondary characters as well. Scenes of secondary characters (italicized) initiate the three arches—a Roman arch (2.1), an Actium arch (3.5) and an Alexandrian arch (4.3), each with a separate action as detailed below. There is other evidence of suggestive patterning even with so little information. Antony is entirely absent from only one row, beginning with 2.4, a row including, as the full outline will make clear, the qualified loyalties of Agrippa and Ventidius and Enobarbus's ultimate desertion and death. The two rows flanking the central Antony and Cleopatra row, each with three Caesar scenes and one significant Antony scene, already suggest the conflict between them.

A fuller outline demonstrates the spatial patterning of the play's actions.

ROMAN ARCH		ALEXANDRIAN ARCH	
2.6 Triumvirate and Pompey seal agreement.		4.7.4–16 Antony, Scarus, Eros in victory.	
2.5 Cleopatra would kill messenger.	2.7 Antony et. al. at feast. Menas wants Pompey to kill triumvirs.	4.7.1–3 "Retire" ordered by Agrippa.	4.8 Antony, Cleopatra, Scarus rejoice at "beating them to bed."
2.4 Lepidus to war (if Antony "kiss Octavia we'll follow").	3.1 Ventidius with body of Pacorus; will do no more for Antony.	4.6 Enobarbus learns his treasure has been sent; regrets betrayal.	4.9 Enobarbus dies.
2.3 *Antony* resolves to return to Cleopatra.	3.2 *Antony* marries Octavia.	4.5 *Antony* sends Enobarbus's treasure.	4.10 *Antony* with army.
2.2 Antony accepts Octavia as wife from Caesar.	3.3 Cleopatra asks Messenger about Octavia.	4.4 Cleopatra & Eros help put on Antony's armor.	4.11 Caesar with army.
2.1 *Pompey on uncertain relation between Antony & Caesar.*	3.4 Antony with Octavia, leaving as "reconciler" with Caesar.	4.3 *Soldiers say Hercules has left Antony.*	4.12 Antony defeated ("betrayed" by Cleopatra).
------------	------------	------------	------------
1.5 Cleopatra, given pearl by Antony's messenger, sends messages of love.	3.5 *Enobarbus. & Eros on triumvirs' conflicts and upcoming battle.*	4.2 Antony orders feast (as of farewell).	4.13 Cleopatra to monument; sends word she's dead.
1.4 Caesar on Antony's past valor & present laxity.	3.6 Caesar tells his sister of Antony's adultery.	4.1 Caesar laughs at Antony's challenge to fight one on one.	4.14 Antony falls on sword, Eros dies.
1.3 *Antony* leaves **Cleopatra.**	3.7 *Antony* to fight by sea with **Cleopatra.**	3.13 *Antony* whips messenger who kissed **Cleopatra's** hand.	4.15 *Antony* dies in **Cleopatra's** arms.
1.2 Antony hears of reverses & Fulvia's death.	3.8 Caesar with army.	3.12 Caesar receives Antony's ambassador.	5.1 Caesar eulogizes Antony.
1.1 Antony & Cleopatra in procession embrace.	3.9 Antony views Caesar's ships, planning battle.	3.11 Defeated Antony. Cleopatra's kiss "repays" him.	5.2 Cleopatra dies: "Husband, I come!"
	3.10 Enobarbus, Scarus, Candidus on loyalty, after defeat of "doting mallard," Antony.		

ACTIUM ARCH

Antony's decline is in three stages, each dramatized in a separate action that is contained in an arch of 11 scenes. A Roman arch dramatizes Antony's failure as a politician (2.1–3.4), an (inverted) Actium arch dramatizes his failure as a military commander (3.5–4.2), and an Alexandrian arch dramatizes his failure as a soldier (4.3–4.12). As already indicated, each arch is initiated by a scene (italicized) in which a secondary character anticipates the ensuing action. Pompey worries Antony's relationship with Caesar (2.1), Enobarbus predicts the battle of Actium will come to "naught" (3.5), and the soldiers, hearing strange music, predict Antony's failure as a soldier (4.3). Each of the three actions ends with the departure of a figure important to Antony: Octavia, at the end of the Roman arch (3.4); Enobarbus, who voices his intent to leave in 3.13 and last appears with Antony at the "farewell dinner" in the final scene of the Actium arch (4.2); and Hercules, whose departure is confirmed by Antony's defeat in the last scene of the Alexandrian arch, 4.12, when his soldiers, in yet another of the play's conflations of war and love, "melt their sweets On blossoming Caesar" (22–23).

The first and last five scenes present Antony and Cleopatra's initial separation and final reunion as well as Antony's relationship with Caesar. These scenes, particularly those concerning the lovers, are suggestively paired. Cleopatra sends a message of love in the opening section of the play (1.5) and sends a false message of her death in the corresponding scene of the last section (4.13); Antony leaves Cleopatra in 1.3 and dies in her arms in 4.15; and their embrace in the opening scene finds its fulfillment in Cleopatra's orgasmic outcry in the last scene. The other two pairs bookend the relationship between Antony and Caesar, ending in Antony's bungled suicide (4.14) and Caesar's eulogy (5.1).

The divisions between the five sections of the play are welded together by subsidiary narratives. Antony's journey from Egypt to Rome, repeatedly alluded to by other characters during his travels, extends from 1.3 until he finally arrives in 2.2. Octavia's journey to visit her brother, extending from 3.4 to 3.6, joins the Roman and Actium arches. The Actium arch is narratively joined to the Alexandrian arch by the battle, first mentioned by Antony in 4.2 and extending intermittently until 4.8. The final section of five scenes is joined to the Egypt arch by Antony's plan in 4.12 to kill Cleopatra and himself. These varying narrative continuities veil the basic thematic divisions.

If the thematic breaks are welded by subsidiary narratives, they are further smoothed by retrospective dialogues in the first scene of each arch. The introductory scenes of the arches are Janus-faced, looking ahead to the coming action and also looking back toward the preceding action. Pompey both anticipates the tensions between Caesar and Antony and excoriates the Egyptian Antony (2.1); Enobarbus looks ahead to Actium and also sums up the offstage power struggles among the triumvirs (3.5); the soldiers predict Hercules's departure and allude to Antony's defeat at Actium (4.3). The momentum that carries the action through from Antony's final defeat in the Alexandrian arch to the last section of the play is not retarded by any retrospective dialogue. When Cleopatra sends Antony the false message of her death (4.13), there is only the forward-moving narrative leading to the deaths of the lovers. Otherwise Shakespeare is at pains to join the parts of the play almost invisibly, by subsidiary narratives to carry the audience over the breaks and by retrospective dialogue to further mute the points of demarcation.

The central scene, 3.10, contains the nadir of Antony's worldly fortunes, his defeat at Actium, and epitomizes in its shifting allegiances a major concern of the play. With Caesar's victory, Enobarbus, Scarus and Candidus consider whether to remain with Antony. Candidus decides to leave and join Caesar's forces; Scarus suggests he will remain with Antony conditionally, depending on "what further comes" (32); and Enobarbus emphatically reaffirms his loyalty though it flies in the face of reason. In the event, of course, Enobarbus abandons Antony and Scarus fights valiantly. In contrast to the wavering of his soldiers, Antony is described as a "doting mallard" (19), fulfilling in action the uxoriousness Philo condemned him for in the opening line of the play and losing himself in dotage, as he feared, but bound to Cleopatra with what amounts to instinct, a natural force. In its various responses to the defeat, the central scene expresses the play's pervasive dilemma: Rome or Egypt, policy or loyalty. For the off-stage Antony, it is a turning point whose effect is dramatized in the next scene (3.11); after this, he has no more Roman thoughts.

Because this scene is the nadir of Antony's fortunes, the "Actium" arch of which it is the "keystone"—scenes 3.5 to 4.2—is inverted.

3.5 Enobarbus and Eros on Caesar's treatment of Lepidus and the murder of Pompey. Upcoming action "'Twill be naught," Enobarbus says.	4.2 Antony orders feast (as of farewell). (Enobarbus's last appearance with Antony.)
3.6 Caesar tells Octavia of Antony's adultery and of need for war.	4.1 Caesar laughs at Antony's challenge to fight one on one.
3.7 Antony to fight by sea with Cleopatra.	3.13 Antony whips messenger who has kissed Cleopatra's hand. (Enobarbus resolves to leave Antony.)
3.8 Caesar with army.	3.12 Caesar receives Antony's ambassador, denies Antony's requests.
3.9 Antony views Caesar's ships before Actium.	3.11 Antony in despair over defeat; Cleo's kiss "repays" him.
3.10 Enobarbus, Scarus and Candidus on loyalty after defeat of "doting mallard" Antony.	

Scene 3.5 initiates this arch, summarizing the events that have occurred offstage and anticipating the disastrous military action to come. Enobarbus predicts, "'Twill be naught" (21), which he emphatically repeats in the opening line of the keystone scene after the defeat at Actium: "Naught, naught, all naught!" (3.10.1). The arch ends with the scene (4.2) in which Antony and Enboarbus, who has already resolved to leave Antony, are together for the last time; the feast Antony orders in this scene is fittingly taken as a farewell dinner. The counterpointing of Antony's "farewell" feast with the victory feast Caesar ordered in the preceding scene is, of course, lost on Enobarbus (ironically enough since Enobarbus so frequently deploys the play's feeding imagery). Caesar says his soldiers have "earned" the "waste" (4.1.16). At his "bounteous" feast, by contrast, Antony's self-annihilating generosity wishes that he could be made "so many men" as serve him and that all of his servitors could be "clapped up together in an Antony" that he might reciprocate their attendance on him (4.2.17–19). Enobarbus, characteristically misreading Antony, takes his fulsome treatment of his servants as mere theatrics, providing yet another reason to abandon his general.

Excepting the first, last and keystone scenes, the Actium arch contains Antony scene pairs and Caesar scene pairs. (In performance, of course, in temporal rather than spatial order, this arrangement yields alternating Antony and Caesar scenes in the preparations for Actium and its consequences.) The pairs contrast Caesar's strategy with Antony's passion and poor judgment. The later scenes of the Antony pairs (3.11 and 3.13), in which Antony is so emotional as to be out of control, simply confirm by their excess the identical basis of the decision to fight by sea, made and confirmed in the earlier scenes (3.7 and 3.9). Similarly with the Caesar pairs (3.6 & 4.1, 3.8 & 3.12), which show his cool demeanor and manipulative tactics under all circumstances. The central flanking scenes (3.9 & 3.11) show Antony preparing for the battle and reacting to his defeat, after he has "lost command" (3.11.23) and sits down in despair. After this, Antony's "low point," the turn in the action occurs when Cleopatra's kiss "repays" him for his loss (3.11.71), starting Antony toward his final ambiguous "high point," the Monument. This turn occurs in the usual position, in the scene immediately after the keystone.

Antony's wave-like progress toward dissolution and death includes moments of victory as well as those of defeat. Those victories are celebrated in the keystones of the other two arches. The keystone of the first arch, the Roman arch, is 2.6, in which the triumvirs and Pompey agree to the quadripartite rule of the world:

2.6 Triumvirate and Pompey seal agreement.	
2.5 Cleopatra would kill messenger bringing news of Antony's marriage.	2.7 Antony and other triumvirs at feast; Menas wants Pompey to kill other triumvirs.
2.4 Lepidus to war (if Antony "kiss Octavia we'll follow").	3.1 Ventidius with body of Pacorus; will do no more for Antony.
2.3 Antony resolves to return to Cleopatra.	3.2 Antony marries Octavia.
2.2 Antony agrees to accept Octavia as wife from Caesar.	3.3 Cleopatra asks messenger about Octavia.
2.1 Pompey on uncertain relationship between Antony and Caesar.	3.4 Antony with Octavia, leaving as "reconciler" with Caesar.

The Roman arch focuses on Antony's political relationship with Caesar, as suggested in its first scene by Pompey. After commenting extensively on the "amorous surfeiter" Antony (33), Pompey addresses the differences between Antony and Caesar and concludes uncertainly: "how the fear of us will cement their divisions … we yet not know" (47–49). The bond is cemented by Antony's marriage to Octavia and is implicitly severed in the last scene when Octavia and Antony are seen together for the last time and she leaves on a doomed mission of reconciliation (3.4). The compromised bond is highlighted in the 2.3–3.2 pair, in which Antony, having resolved to return to Cleopatra in the early scene, accepts Octavia from Caesar with promises of fidelity in the later scene. That Octavia, the pawn in the political game, is treated with such bad faith by Antony and possibly by Caesar as well is symptomatic of the "policy" that is the theme of this arch. The central flanking scenes (2.5 and 2.7) reflect murderous impulses common to Rome and Egypt, highlighting the difference between Egyptian passion and Roman calculation: on the one hand, Cleopatra's emotional outburst against the messenger who brings news of Antony's marriage to Octavia and, on the other, Menas's calculating offer to murder Pompey's rivals. Similarly scenes 2.4 and 3.1 present "political" (that is, conditional and limited) loyalties to Antony. Agrippa, leaving to join the army, conditions his service on the political marriage; Ventidius expresses the subordinate's fear of outdoing his superior and falling out of favor. (By virtue of being in the row including Enobarbus's desertion, these scenes take on a thematic significance that redeems their apparently tangential place in the narrative.) Finally, scenes 2.2 and 3.3 pair the rationalizations of Antony and of Cleopatra with regard to the marriage with Octavia. As the Actium arch showed Antony's failure as a military commander, the Roman arch shows his failure as a politician, his failure to attain the "peace" he sought through the marriage. There remains only the third arch, the Alexandrian arch, to complete the destruction of Antony's worldly identity.

The keystone of the Alexandrian arch is 4.7.4–16, in which Antony and Scarus receive from Eros news of their victory. (The traditional 4.7 is actually two scenes, as in the Oxford edition.)

4 .7.4–16 Antony, Scarus, Eros in victory.	
4.7.1–3 "Retire" ordered by Agrippa.	4.8 Antony, Cleopatra, Scarus rejoice at "beating them to bed."
4.6 Enobarbus learns his treasure has been sent; regrets his disloyalty.	4.9 Enobarbus dies.
4.5 Antony sends Enobarbus's treasure.	4.10 Antony and Scarus with army.
4.4 Cleopatra helps put on Antony's armor.	4.11 Caesar with army.
4.3 Soldiers say Hercules has left Antony.	4.12 Antony defeated, blames "Triple- turned whore," Cleopatra.

After having failed as a politician and as a military commander because of Cleopatra, Antony in the Alexandrian arch loses the last vestige of his worldly self, his warrior identity, again, as he thinks, because of Cleopatra. Shakespeare alters Plutarch significantly to focus on Antony as a soldier. The battle that Plutarch refers to as a "skirmish" seems in the theater to be as important as Actium itself because Shakespeare has made the victory the keystone of the arch (4.7.4–16). Furthermore, in the opening scene (4.3) the soldiers anticipate the losing military action, and their prediction is fulfilled in the defeat of the final scene (4.12): Hercules, ironically embodied in the soldiers themselves, has indeed left Antony. In this way the first, last and keystone scenes emphasize Antony as a soldier. And elsewhere in the arch his love of fighting is repeatedly stressed. He is "a workman" in "a royal occupation," "a business that we love" (4.4.15–17, 20). Cumulatively, however, the scenes of the arch characterize an elusive and curious kind of soldier. In the first place, scene 4.4, the armoring scene, as the Oxford editor notes, reverses the usual image of Mars and Venus:

> Shakespeare found the name of Antony's servant, Eros, in Plutarch, but makes metaphoric capital of it: here the spectacle of the hero armed by Eros and a mortal Venus recalls and reverses the iconography of Mars and Venus, in which the love-goddess and her cupids strip Mars of his armor.[6]

Though both Cleopatra and Eros fumble at the task of arming Antony, love is nevertheless in the service of war here, however ineptly. Indeed, love and war are often ambivalently interfused, as when Antony says "We have beat them to their beds" (4.8.19), a metaphor reflecting, however tenuously, Agrippa's "Retire" (4.7.1) in the other central flanking scene. Most significantly complicating Antony's soldiership in this arch, however, is the Enobarbus narrative. Shakespeare has altered Plutarch's chronology and moved Antony's treatment of Enobarbus from prior to Actium to after it, to a segment of the play portraying Antony as a soldier. His treatment of Enobarbus scants the usual martial virtues of bravery, valor, and courage and stresses instead generosity, magnanimity and fellowship. Victory gains, not the exercise of power or the humiliation of the enemy, as it does for Caesar, but celebratory feasts, a form of communion entailing the embraces and joyful tears of family and friends, who "kiss ... honored gashes whole" (4.8.20–21). When "All is lost" (4.12.9) Antony most laments the fact that "the hearts that spanielled me at heels ... do discandy, and melt their sweets on blossoming

Caesar" (4.12.20–23). That war entails affection as well as hostility—that, indeed, "both Antony and Cleopatra …minimize the distinctions between warring, loving and death"[7]—is suggested in the keystone scene itself. Antony enters accompanied by Scarus, who "fought…. As if a god, in hate of mankind, had Destroyed in such a shape" (4.8.24–26), but it is Eros who brings the news of victory. Antony's sole companions in this scene are almost emblematically representative of hate and love.

The opening and closing five scenes of the play, the two columns supporting the triple arch, reflect the lovers' early separation and final union in death. In the central focal scenes of the two columns, 1.3 and 4.15, Antony leaves Cleopatra for Rome and dies in her arms, the simple action of departure and return reaching across the whole play. Cleopatra's contrasting messages of love and death in 1.5 and 4.13 and the fulfillment of the lovers' opening kiss in Cleopatra's orgiastic death (1.1 and 5.2) complete the enveloping action of separation and union. The other two pairs of scenes address, once again, the conflict between Antony and Caesar, in which Caesar has the last historical word, the eulogy of 5.1, a fitting reevaluation of his earlier judgment of Antony as "the abstract of all faults" (1.4.9).

The main parts of the construction, then, dramatize an initial separation between Antony and Cleopatra and a final union attained only after Antony has, somewhat like Othello, lost his occupation, indeed, his entire worldly identity. In the three arches Antony fails as a politician, as a general and as a soldier. Only when "All is lost" and even Cleopatra has, as he thinks, betrayed him and sent false word of her death does Antony fully accede to his "sweet queen" (4.15.45), the serpent of old Nile, as the asp brings "sweet … balm" to Cleopatra at her death (5.2.311). The play has a five part structure that accords not with the traditional act divisions but with these three arches and two end columns.

As a postscript, it is interesting to note the cluster of late plays written in an unusually large number of scenes. Through *King Lear* no play exceeded 23 scenes. With *Macbeth*, in 27 scenes, Shakespeare began a series of plays with significantly more scenes than he had used previously—*Antony and Cleopatra* (43 scenes), *Coriolanus* (29 scenes) and *Cymbeline* (29 scenes). Since *Pericles* lacks the chiastic design of the other mature plays in the canon, I conclude that it was not plotted by Shakespeare and that, consequently, the final six plays of his sole authorship consist of the structural experiments in the plays just mentioned and the two dazzling variations of earlier scene structures—*The Winter's Tale*, which in its jealous protagonist and 15 scenes reprises *Othello* (the only other play of 15 scenes), and *The Tempest*, which in so many ways reprises *Love's Labor's Lost* and *A Midsummer Night's Dream*, most pertinently in its nine scenes. After a period of expansive new designs, that is to say, Shakespeare returned to plays with the fewest scenes, coming full circle in re-imagining and deepening in *The Tempest* his first use of the chiastic design, in *Love's Labor's Lost*.

20

The Thematic Arch of *Coriolanus*
Action and Eloquence

In the keystone scene of *Coriolanus* Volumnia introduces her idea of "action" as acting. The structural and thematic hinge of the play is her ambivalent statement in the central speech of the scene that "action is eloquence" (3.2.76).[1] The first half of the play develops what we might think of as Coriolanus's version of Volumnia's statement, the notion that action speaks for itself; indeed, that action *is* speech. Dominating the first half of the play is the scene in which Coriolanus is alone within the gates of Corioles "to answer all the city" (1.4.52). In the paired scene in the second half of the play Coriolanus is silent before Volumnia's eloquence, her "action" of defending Rome (5.3). To Volumnia eloquence is action; to Coriolanus action is eloquence. The differences between mother and son, and the principle of the play's organization, are contained in the two versions of action; and the nature of Coriolanus's tragedy—i.e., of specifically *sacrificial* action—is clarified by the play's detailed, chiastic contrast of action and acting.

The scenes of the first half of the play, tracing Coriolanus's rise by means of military action to the brink of a consulship, are exactly mirrored by the scenes of the second half, which trace his fall by means of a sequence of acting performances brought against him. The overall disposition of scenes is as follows:

3.2 Volumnia: "action is eloquence."	
3.1 Coriolanus denounces Tribunes and people.	3.3 Tribunes manipulate Coriolanus into denouncing them and people; he is banished.
2.3 Coriolanus receives the "voice" of the commoners for consulship.	4.1 Coriolanus parts from family, friends and city.
2.2 Coriolanus stands for consul and deeds told.	4.2 Volumnia curses the "brave deed" of the Tribunes.
2.1 Coriolanus welcomed into Rome.	4.3 Roman spy tells Volsce that Coriolanus has been banished from Rome.
1.10 Defeated Aufidius resolves to use "wrath or craft" against Coriolanus.	4.4. Disguised Coriolanus before house of Aufidius.
1.9 Victorious Coriolanus doesn't want to be "dieted in praises sauced with lies."	4.5 Servingmen narrate Coriolanus's feast with Aufidius.

1.8 Coriolanus and Aufidius fight.	4.6 Cominius brings news that Coriolanus and Aufidius, allied, are advancing against Rome.
1.7 Titus Lartius sets guard on city and goes to Romans in field.	4.7 Aufidius and Lt. discuss how men "fly to the Roman."
1.6 Coriolanus embraces Cominius.	5.1 Cominius tells of being rebuffed by Coriolanus.
1.5 Coriolanus leaves Corioles to help Cominius against Aufidius.	5.2 Coriolanus rebuffs Menenius before Aufidius.
1.4 Coriolanus alone within Corioles's gates "to answer all the city."	5.3 Coriolanus silent with Volumnia.
1.3 Virgilia refuses to go out until Coriolanus returns from war.	5.4 News of returning ladies' success spreads through city.
1.2 Aufidius and Senators hear that Rome has "circumvention."	5.5 Ladies in triumph—"the life of Rome."
1.1 Coriolanus refuses food to citizens.	5.6 Coriolanus: "cut me to pieces."

In the central scene acting imagery abruptly increases, initiated by Coriolanus's refusal to take on a role to placate the plebeians, his insistence that "I play the man I am" (15–16). Scripting her son's prospective behavior, Volumnia expresses an exactly opposite view in the central lines of the scene:

> Go to them with this bonnet in thy hand,
> And thus far having stretched it—here be with them—
> Thy knee bussing the stones—for in such business
> Action is eloquence, and the eyes of the ignorant
> More learned than the ears—waving thy head,
> Which often, thus, correcting thy stout heart,
> Now humble as the ripest mulberry
> That will not hold the handling... [73–80 of 145].

Given the stakes, Volumnia wouldn't hesitate to "dissemble with [her] nature" in the manner described here and asks Coriolanus to do the same, to "perform a part thou hast not done before" (62, 108–9). Coriolanus, however, feels that his very identity would collapse, and he would become a harlot, a eunuch, a virgin, a tearful schoolboy, a beggar—the degrading characters multiply almost hysterically in his imagination. He fears that "my body's action [would] teach my mind a most inherent baseness" (122–23). Though he agrees to act the part he is prompted to, he fails when confronted by the staged accusations of the Tribunes. When accused of being a traitor, he reverts to his usual anger. The tribunes' manipulation of him is simply the first of the "actings" that repeatedly overcome Coriolanus in the second half of the play. Scene 3.2 is literally pivotal. It introduces the alien (to Coriolanus) idea of action on which that the play turns and which ultimately destroys him. The first half of the play develops the successful, heroic action of Coriolanus, briefly earning the "voice" of the people; the second half is devoted to versions of "eloquence," acting, which baffle and finally defeat Coriolanus.

The narrative contrasts are fairly evident from the outline. The scenes flanking the central scene, 3.1 and 3.3, contrast Coriolanus's spontaneous outburst and his outburst manipulated by the tribunes, his first defeat by acting, which causes his banishment (the narrative turn, positioned, as usual, in the scene immediately after the keystone). The rest of the play, excepting the first and last scenes, is set out in four sections of three pairs each, enacting Coriolanus' welcome/banishment, Aufidius as enemy/ally, Coriolanus as friend/enemy to Rome and Coriolanus' victory/defeat. Each of these topics is detailed in the individual pairs of scenes. His acceptance into the full community of Rome in 3.2 is contrasted with his solitary exodus into the wilderness in 4.1. The heroic deeds of Coriolanus lauded by Cominius in 2.2 are contrasted with the sarcastically "brave deed" of the Tribunes that banished Coriolanus (4.2). Coriolanus's victorious entry into Rome is set against a traitorous Roman's gleeful telling of the hero's banishment (2.1 and 4.3). In the next section, in which Aufidius is an early enemy and later ally, the feast provided by Aufidius (4.5) ironically diets Coriolanus in exactly the sauce of lies that in the paired scene (1.9) he had rejected. The other two pairs of this section suggest Coriolanus's increasing similarity to his old enemy, as discussed below.

The sequence of battle scenes in the first half of the play (1.5, 1.6 & 1.7) establishes the bonds among the Roman warriors, while the contrasting pairs (5.2, 5.1 & 4.7) detail the breaking of those bonds and the treacherous nature of the new allegiance Coriolanus forms. This contrast is most vividly evident in the changed relationship with Cominius: the bloody embrace of the war scene (1.6) is paired with his report of being dismissed by Coriolanus (5.1). On the merely narrative level Titus Lartius and the Volscian soldiers both "fly to" Coriolanus in the pair 1.7 & 4.7; and in the pair 1.5 and 5.2, Coriolanus sacrifices his "father," Menenius, to Aufidius, "the man" Coriolanus says in the paired scene, "of my soul's hate." This sequence presenting Coriolanus's shift in loyalty is epitomized by the contrast of 1.8 and 4.6, Coriolanus fighting against Aufidius and Coriolanus in league with Aufidius against Rome. It is worth noting that the scenes of the second half of the play are usually conversations, narrations or other variants of "eloquence," often signaling the undoing of some corresponding direct action in the first half of the play, as Coriolanus's embrace of Cominius is paired with his narration of being rejected. (This technique is a variation of the contrast between instinct and artifice in *As You Like It*.)

The final three-pair segment comparing Coriolanus's victory at Corioles with his defeat before Rome is fittingly dominated by women and is largely ironic in its pairings. The "circumvention" that Aufidius and the Volscian Senators fear turns out to be the triumphant women of Rome (1.2 and 5.5); it is not Coriolanus who returns from victory, as expected in 1.3, but the women of 5.4; and heroic action such as Coriolanus's at Corioles is impotent against the "action," the eloquence, of Volumnia.

There are three critically important scene pairs: the pair contrasting Coriolanus's victory at Corioles with his defeat before Rome (1.4 and 5.3); the pair comparing his disguised entrance into Antium with the defeated and similarly changed Aufidius (1.10 and 4.4); and the pair contrasting the victorious Coriolanus after Corioles with his metaphorical defeat at Aufidius's banquet (1.9 and 4.5). The second half of the play thus sequences Coriolanus's repeated defeats by "acting," that of the Tribunes, of Aufidius and finally of Volumnia. The last is, of course, the "mortal" blow, structurally emphasized by the crucial symmetrical pairing of 1.4 and 5.3.

As is clear from 1.4, the action of fighting is Coriolanus's version of speech. The scene opens with a wager between Coriolanus and Lartius as to whether the Roman and Volscian armies have "met" and "spoke" (4); and, when Lartius later asks for Coriolanus, a soldier says that within the gates Coriolanus "is himself alone To answer all the city" (52). The equivalence of action and speech, of blood and words, for Coriolanus is also expressed in his later comment that "as for my country I have shed blood, ... so shall my lungs coin words" (3.1.75–7). For Coriolanus the action at Corioles is eloquent in and of itself, requiring no flattery to make its point, deserving no superfluous praise afterwards. He "rewards his deeds with doing them" (2.2.127–8). The action speaks for itself; it is itself an "answer." And as action is speech, speech is itself action. Coriolanus speaks a "gestural language"[2]; his speech acts are produced as are unmediated physical actions. "His heart's his mouth," Menenius says (3.1.259).

Volumnia, on the other hand, exercises a censoring brain. She describes her own more politic control of her anger in contrast to her son's:

> I have a heart as little apt as yours [to fawn to the plebeians],
> But yet a brain that leads my use of anger
> To better vantage [3.2.30–32].

She insists that the same anger Coriolanus feels can be transformed into acting, as she so successfully does. For Volumnia action and speech are both subsumed in "acting," though she is particularly savvy about the effects of gesture, posture and other physical means of expression. The calculated gestures of the orator or actor are "action" and "eloquence." Mere rote mouthings, words of the tongue alone, and histrionic gestures are as efficacious as the actions of the battlefield. This is the essential contrast underlying the victory of Coriolanus at Corioles and his defeat before Rome: action is defeated by acting.

The emphatic contrast between the "action" of mother and of son is also expressed in the structures and the images of the two scenes. Scenes 1.4 and 5.3 are similar battle narratives; their episodes mirror each other in content, sequence and proportions. Though the scene of Volumnia's eloquence is appropriately about three times longer than the scene of action at Corioles (209 vs. 64 lines), the two scenes are identically structured. Both scenes open before the gates of a city with a battlefield conversation about the opposing forces—that between Coriolanus and Lartius regarding the Volscians and that between Coriolanus and Aufidius regarding the Roman spokesman, Menenius. Coriolanus is then occupied with assessing the advancing enemy—the Volscians and his mother's party—and the attack follows—the attack of the Volscians and the attack of Volumnia's rhetoric, her first countering speech. Coriolanus's charge on Corioles and his retreat from his mother, the core contrast not only of these two scenes but of the whole play, also occur at the same proportionate point in each scene (lines 42 and 131). His mother, now like Coriolanus at Corioles, presses the issue and, in Coriolanus's silence, his inability to "answer" as he did earlier, she is victorious. Ironically enough, at a corresponding earlier moment Lartius has already delivered the appropriate elegy for an imagined death of Coriolanus; when he capitulates before Volumnia though, a moment he considers "most mortal," she comments only by her conspicuous silence. Point for point the episodes of Coriolanus's victory are paralleled with those of his defeat by his mother.

In deft touches all the significant imagery of the play is also contained in the action of 1.4 and matched in the acting of 5.3, so that the pressure of the imagery developed elsewhere is almost subliminally felt behind these two crucial scenes. While the fight is essentially seen as Coriolanus's version of speech, it is also seen as food ("to the pot" [50]), as burning (invoking the "fires of heaven" [40]; feeling the "sweat of wrath" [28]), as posture (he "outdares his sense-less sword, and when it bows, stand'st up" [58–9]) and as bloody (in the stage direction describing Coriolanus when he emerges from the gates [65]). The image of the bloody Coriolanus emerging from the gates further suggests his birth,[3] confirmed by his new name, and, in the later descriptions of his covering of blood as a mask (1.8.10) and a mantle (1.6.29), his role as warrior, that he is acting the man he is. The paired scene of his defeat has matching imagery, in each case suggesting the opposite of the use to which Coriolanus put the same figures. Rather than the warrior's glory of going "to the pot," Coriolanus envisions the cosmic chaos of "pebbles on the hungry beach fillip[ing] the stars," that is, a base hunger touching the fires of heaven (58–9). Where Coriolanus finds speech in the heat of violent action itself, Volumnia says, "I am husht until our city be afire And then I'll speak a little" (5.3.183–83), suggesting that her language is in response to action such as Coriolanus's. The "sweat of wrath" is answered by tears: "make mine eyes to sweat compassion" (195–96). The posture of the upright, unbowed Coriolanus celebrated in 1.4 is contrasted with his kneeling in 5.3. The mantle and mask of blood is no longer a costume—the perfect actor in his sword-like role is now a "dull actor" (40)—for blood now establishes his profound bond with his son and his mother. The bloody Coriolanus birthed from Corioles's gates immediately after his eulogy is insistently birthed again in 5.3 from his mother's body and the body politic of Rome. And his birth is finally matched by a perception of his death; he eulogizes himself as "most mortal" in this defeat (190).

Each of these images is elaborated and developed elsewhere in the play; but the images of hunger have deservedly received the most attention, since they brilliantly integrate the body politic and the body, both psychological and physical, of Coriolanus, dependent, in turn, on the relationship with Volumnia. To Coriolanus the action of fighting is feeding, in the sense that Adelman points out[4] and in the meaning that Cavell finds,[5] both giving and taking nourishment. Coriolanus alone within the gates of Corioles has gone "to the pot" ambiguously, both to be cut up as food to be cooked and to feed on the Volscians. Anger is not only Volumnia's meat. It is also the meat of Coriolanus and Aufidius. Unlike Volumnia however they do not have to feed on themselves; they feed on each other in fighting. Volumnia has only the power to nourish not to take nourishment, therefore she must feed on herself and consequently starve. Her hunger is sublimated[6] into her maternal care and expectation for her son; to nurse is to bleed, as is clear from her famous comparison of Hecuba's breast milk with blood from Hector's head wound. From the male view of a literal battle, however, the two men, Hector and the unnamed Greek, are both spouting blood like mother's milk, symmetrically engaged in feeding on each other's anger.

In the word "consuming" the images of feeding and of fire overlap.[7] As Coriolanus feeds and is fed in fighting, he can both consume and be consumed in the fire of Rome. It has often been remarked that Volumnia is Rome, but the fact that Coriolanus is also Rome has not received a similar emphasis. The maternal Rome, the nurse, Volumnia, has its counterpart in the masculine warrior. As Joyce Van Dyke says, "Coriolanus defines his identity by Rome and Rome's ideals, as he conceives them…. For Coriolanus, to be Coriolanus requires the existence and co-operation of a viable Roman state; it is only bravado which declares that there is a world elsewhere."[8] In burning Rome then Coriolanus would himself be consumed, as his "red eye" itself suggests. Rome's destruction in flames would be a noble suicide for Coriolanus and for the city itself. It is not mere revenge that Coriolanus seeks, for he loves what he fights, as with Aufidius, as the images of nuptial embraces between warring enemies repeatedly suggest. It is a Roman suicide, the ultimate Roman suicide. In that fire he will be completely identified with Rome, even gaining, as Kenneth Burke has suggested, the new name "Romanus."[9] He will be born into immortality, not the immortality of fame, of Jove's book or the "annals" he will later appreciate; but the immortality of the instant, the phoenix-moment of consummation.

In this contrast between mother and son, focused in the paired scenes of victory and defeat, we see the extremes of action in the play. In battle Coriolanus "being angry, does forget That ever he heard the name of death" (3.1.261–2). In taking revenge on Rome he aspires to becoming pure fire, the anger of the gods and the valor of Rome at once, and thereby to shed every vestige of mortality. Volumnia enacts the body politic of Rome with her own body, her eloquent words and gestures reinforcing the physical reality of life and death. If Volumnia is the life of Rome, the hero of a Roman comedy, Coriolanus means to be the death of Rome, the hero of a Roman tragedy. Volumnia is scripting and directing a comedy with her son as sole audience, based on kinship, ending in triumphal fires (rather than Rome afire), in life and the celebration of women. Coriolanus lives in a tragedy performed before the gods, in which he is the heroic victim, committed to his single role, playing the man he is. He would be the author of himself, making a new name for himself in the fire of Rome. The play's movement toward this stark confrontation of action as either fighting or eloquence, tragedy or comedy, proceeds through other variations of action, particularly in the scenes that compare Coriolanus and Aufidius: 1.10 & 4.4 and 1.9 & 4.5.

Coriolanus is transformed in 4.4 when he appears before the house of Aufidius in beggar's clothes. He is completely unlike his former self. What has caused this change? We know only that he has been "under the canopy … in the city of kites and crows" (4.5.39, 43), that is to say, under heaven, among scavengers. We know from elsewhere in the play how much Coriolanus despises carrion, how the smell of decaying flesh appalls him. We know too his joy in being, as his most ecstatic moment has it, a sword, how he is often described as metallic and almost mechanical. And, too, consider his immediate mention of his marital chastity when he meets Virgilia, "best of [his] flesh," and his praise of Valeria as an icicle in her chastity (5.3.42, 65). The body that the gourmand Menenius so deftly and humorously details in the first scene is, in its potential corruption, repulsive to Coriolanus. It stinks of death. Under heaven, among scavengers, the stark options are clear, and Coriolanus makes his choice: he plans a purifying conflagration.

This change in him is structurally reinforced by the pairing of 4.4 with 1.10. The disguised Coriolanus is parallel to the defeated Aufidius who, after wishing he were a Roman so that he could be himself, says that he will depend on "wrath or craft" (16) to overcome his hated enemy. Aufidius's phrase is a re-wording of the central contrast between action and acting: "craft" as acting and "wrath" meaning anger unchecked by any nice consideration of custom or religion; no "embarquements … of fury" would stop him (22). The choice Aufidius makes, however, is clearly of craft, of acting, rather than of action, while the Coriolanus in beggar's clothes outside the house of Aufidius has chosen wrath. In burning Rome Coriolanus will allow no check to his furious vengeance, whereas Aufidius has abandoned martial anger for expedient deception and dissembling and, like Volumnia, finally stands triumphant in his city. Thus the pairing of 1.9 and 4.5 is bitterly ironic. In his disguise and his platitudinous, superficial soliloquy on the inevitability of shifting loyalties, Coriolanus is a man whose body's actions have not yet taught his mind anything. He seems not to recognize that his determination to adhere to the highest standards, to remain a Mars, requires the kind of dissembling he could not pull off to avoid his banishment earlier. Furthermore, though himself disguised, Coriolanus does not admit the possibility that Aufidius might be acting.

After his victory at Corioles Coriolanus protests that he does not want to be "dieted in praises sauced with lies" (1.9.51–2). In the paired scene, however, that is exactly the treatment he receives from Aufidius; the feast is sauced with flattery and lies, as though Aufidius had taken Volumnia's advice on eloquent action. He "makes a mistress of [Coriolanus], sanctifies himself with's hand, and turns up the white o'th'eye to his discourse" (200–202). This feigned, soldierly courtship is simultaneously another fight between Aufidius and Coriolanus, conducted via feeding; the earlier metaphor of fighting as feeding has been reversed, as the Servingmen's commentary confirms.

While the warriors are dining, the Servingmen, in describing the meal, have their own parallel feast, a feast of words. Their conversation is laced with food metaphors that are sequenced like the courses of the offstage feast. The Third Servingman enters with "news." "Let's partake," says another (168–9). They then describe the previous defeat of Aufidius by Coriolanus: "He scotched him and notched him like a carbonado," says one. "And had he been cannibally given," adds another, "he might have boiled and eaten him too" (181–4). A similar food preparation is apparently being repeated in the warriors' present feast: "The bottom of the news is, our general is cut in the middle and but one half of what he was" (because Coriolanus has been given half of Aufidius's forces) (190–92). Finally, the planned attack on Rome is rendered by the Servingman "as it were a parcel of their feast, and to be executed ere they wipe their lips" (208–9). The news of the feast is itself a meal in which the Servingmen verbally enact what they think is occurring offstage, the "cutting" of their master, Aufidius. The food, alike in the present conversation, the present offstage feast and the past battles, according to the Servingmen, is Aufidius. But the irony is that Coriolanus is being sauced in exactly the lies he had denounced in the paired scene. Aufidius is not being prepared for the feast-killing, Coriolanus is: he is Rome, a parcel of the feast, a negligible morsel disposed of in the final scene. Aufidius's flattery of Coriolanus is war by means of word and gesture, a war that Coriolanus does not even know is occurring. He is the lamb to Aufidius's eloquence.

Coriolanus's essential failure is demonstrated in this pair of scenes as a failure of naming, the fundamental act of language. In 1.9 Coriolanus forgets the name of the poor man who has helped him: "By Jupiter, forgot," he exclaims (89), ironically enough, since Jove and language are linked in this play as in *Cymbeline*. In 4.5 Coriolanus withholds his own name, as though he thinks he should be recognized without it, that a name is not essential to who he is.[10] It is because he does not think a social tag of any value that he thinks he can create for himself a new name, author himself, in the fire of Rome. The deed itself speaks. In this, Coriolanus suffers a misconception similar to that of Brutus, who thought that the act of killing Caesar could be a sacrifice when it is only the interpretation of the act that redeems it from mere butchery, that makes it a ritual; Antony gives Caesar's dumb wounds tongue as the shedding of "sacred blood." The act must have words if it is to be efficacious. Similarly, in an image critics find grotesque, the tongues of the plebeians must give Coriolanus's wounds "voice." "If he show us his wounds and tell us his deeds, we are to put our tongues into those wounds and speak for them. So if he tell us his noble deeds, we must also tell him our noble acceptance of them. Ingratitude is monstrous" (2.3.5–9). The process is further elaborated by Menenius:

> Now the gods forbid
> That our renowned Rome, whose gratitude
> Toward her deserved children is enroll'd
> In Jove's own book, like an unnatural dam
> Should now eat up her own [3.1.287–91].

Through the voice of the people valorous deeds enter Jove's book, and the city thus maintains both its ideals and its life; the unnatural dam doesn't devour her own. Sustenance is in words. By denying the commoners the chance to put their tongues into his wounds, Coriolanus disallows the process of his apotheosis: he must be spiritual food for the people by having his deeds spoken of by them. This is the implicit success he attains among the Volscian soldiers, who "use him as the grace 'fore meat, their talk at table and their thanks at end" (4.7.3–4).

The Coriolanus of the last scene, however, has fallen from that Jovian ideal. Humanized by the encounter with his mother, Coriolanus among the Volscians is now contrasted with the Coriolanus of the opening scene, among the Romans. His refusal to participate in the stratified political life of Rome has mellowed; he enters the last scene, according to the stage direction, *"the commoners being with him"* (70). Instead of the insults heaped on Roman plebeians or the refusal to relate his deeds, Coriolanus here enters recapping his achievements in what sounds like a politician's speech. Even after Aufidius's first accusation, he remains conciliatory, at least toward the Senators, and only at the last does he revert to the simple gestural language of anger with which he greeted the plebeians in the paired scene. He has learned something of his mother's eloquence. In fact, one of the ironies of his penultimate speech is that, though it finally preserves his defining action in words, they are the words of the Volscians: "If you have writ your annals true, 'tis there, That like an eagle in a dovecote, I Fluttered your Volscians in Corioles" (5.6.113–15). The most evident contrast however is again rendered in the imagery of feeding. The Coriolanus who has withheld food from the people of Rome cries out, "Cut me to pieces, Volsces, men and lads, Stain all your edges on me" (111–12). This death by the sword and its implied sacrificial feeding is followed by his reference to the annals, as though at some level, Coriolanus now understands the translation of action into words, that wounds must be given tongue. Though he can not now be the spiritual food of the Romans, he seems to intuit something of the sacrificial method that will give him the only immortality remaining to him, in the Volscian annals. But even that compensation is denied him in the Volscians' response: "Tear him to pieces!" (123). If we remember Brutus's desire to "carve" Caesar as a dish fit for the gods and recall the careful ritualistic knife work a sacrifice demands,[11] the Volscians' cry takes on its full measure of savagery. It is the Coriolanus of the last scene, the Coriolanus who attempts the sacrificial action of eloquence, whose failure is tragic.

21

The Thematic Arch of *Cymbeline*
Sacrifice

The plot of *Cymbeline* has seldom been praised. In a tone of strenuous understatement, Hallett Smith writes, "The play is not tightly constructed,"[1] and J. M. Nosworthy, one of *Cymbeline*'s most appreciative critics, who finds the play to be a "supreme utterance," qualifies his praise by saying that "Shakespeare ... was prepared, in the interests of the characteristic diffuseness of romance, to let even unity of action fend for itself in *Cymbeline*."[2] Unity of action is precisely what the play seems to lack. Its subplots, though deftly resolved in the last scene, are, critics agree, ineptly integrated elsewhere in the play, and Nosworthy's demurral is more forcefully expressed by other commentators; a psychoanalytic critic, for example, thinks that *Cymbeline* is "a radically incoherent play."[3] Misunderstood, certainly, but as the chiastic structure reveals, far from incoherent.

The late, complex *Cymbeline* includes a number of different reflecting elements in its chiastic structure, as well as unusual pairings of various symbolic stage props[4]:

3.3 Belarius, Guiderius, and Arviragus to the hunt.	
3.2 Pisanio gives Imogen *her* letter from Posthumus.	3.4 Pisanio gives Imogen *his* letter from Posthumus; plans male disguise for her.
3.1 Cymbeline, Queen, Cloten receive Lucius.	3.5 Cymbeline, Queen, Cloten see Lucius off.
2.5 Posthumus on women (soliloquy).	3.6 Imogen (as Fidele) on men (soliloquy).
2.4 Iachimo with bracelet (as token of Imogen).	3.7 Belarius & princes with deer (as symbol of Imogen).
2.3 Imogen courted by Cloten; loss of bracelet; Lucius arrives.	3.8 Roman emperor's writ of war.
2.2 Iachimo's voyeuristic violation of Imogen (soliloquy).	4.1 Cloten plans violation of Imogen (soliloquy).
2.1 "Cock" Cloten denied the satisfaction of a fight.	4.2 Cloten (as Posthumus) fights with Guiderius and is killed; body is Imogen's "bedfellow."
1.7 Iachimo feigns distraction, "assaults" Imogen and retreats.	4.3 Cymbeline, distracted with worry, threatens Pisanio and then relents.

1.6 Queen secures "poison" and gives it to Pisanio as medicine.	4.4 Princes convince Belarius to fight, to let their "blood … fly out."
1.5 Posthumus wagers with Iachimo.	5.1 Posthumus resolves to die for Imogen (soliloquy).
1.4 Posthumus' departure narrated ("flier").	5.2 Posthumus ("stander") defeats Iachimo.
1.3 Cloten on duel with Posthumus, who "rather played than fought."	5.3 Posthumus on battle in which he sought death; imprisoned as Roman.
1.2 Posthumus banished from adoptive family; given Imogen's mother's ring.	5.4 Posthumus' vision of biological family; receives book from Jupiter.
1.1 Family losses of Cymbeline.	5.5 Cymbeline's family reunited.

Cymbeline is structured with three main sections of chiastically mirroring pairs, one primarily devoted to Imogen (2.5–3.6 through 2.3–3.8), one to her suitors (2.2–4.1 through 1.7–4.3), and one to her husband (1.5–5.1 through 1.3–5.3). In the second half of the play the central scene in each of these three segments contains a violent encounter: Guiderius kills the deer; Guiderius kills Cloten; and Posthumus defeats Iachimo. The deep association of sex and violence in the play is structurally embedded in Imogen/Fidele's embrace of Cloten's decapitated body in the central scene of the central segment (and structurally echoed by the blow Posthumus gives the "page," the disguised Imogen, in the central episode of the final scene [5.5.228–48 of 485]). The thematic focus of the play is the appearance of the Mountaineers in the central scene. The princes and Belarius are the saviors of Britain not merely as courageous soldiers but also as reverent practitioners of a sacrificial ritual (discussed below) that is paradigmatic in the play. Their appearance at the focal point of the structure, the keystone of the arch-like design, introduces the values of the hard life under the "holy sun" that finally reinvigorates Cymbeline and Britain (4.4.41). In the two scene pairs at the beginning and end of the play, blood ties are re-established: Posthumus with his biological family and Cymbeline with his.

The five central scenes encompass all three plots, Cymbeline's war with the Romans, Posthumus and Imogen's separation and the princes' exile. Belarius and the princes, structurally like Dogberry and the Watch in *Much Ado*, are the pivot of the play. They are the vigorous noble blood that has escaped the decadence of Cymbeline's court and will redeem it. In the central flanking scenes Imogen reads the letters addressed to her (3.2) and to Pisanio (3.4), the latter initiating the violence between husband and wife: "the paper hath cut her throat," Pisanio remarks, watching Imogen read the order to kill her (33–4). Similarly, the departure of Lucius initiates the war between Britain and Rome (3.5). After the appearance of the hunting party, that is to say, open hostilities—potential bloodlettings—begin in the other plots.

The play is often faulted for the absence of Posthumus from many of its scenes, 20, in fact, 12 of them in succession, the entire third and fourth acts, restricting his presence onstage almost entirely to the beginning and end of the play. If we compare these chiastically related scenes, however, Shakespeare's deft handling of the psychological changes to Posthumus become evident. As the first and last scenes address Cymbeline's family, fractured and reunited, the second and penultimate scenes address Posthumus' families, adoptive and biological. Though physically absent from 1.3 and 1.4, Posthumus is the subject of both scenes, which comment on his early avoidance of conflict and contrast with his later immersion in battle. The diffident, effeminate, and affected Posthumus of the opening scenes becomes the committed soldier and husband of the last scenes, restored to his biological family and its martial tradition. He no longer "play-fights," as he did with Cloten (1.3), but engages in battle to the death (5.3). He no longer "flies" from trouble, as he does in 1.4, but instead "stands" courageously in defeating Iachimo (5.2). He no longer gambles over Imogen's chastity, risking mere trinkets (1.5); he commits his life to expiate his faithlessness (5.1).

Other scenes crucial to the Posthumus-Imogen plot are handled with equal dexterity. Though Posthumus himself does not appear through the long central part of the play, his letters figure importantly, and they are given an equivalent structural importance. Given his character, he is as present in his letters as in his person. As the "theme" of the First Gentleman's gossip, Posthumus is first described as taking "learnings" "as we do air." (1.1.39, 43, 45). He asks that Imogen write to him in Rome, promising that "with mine eyes I'll drink the words you send" (1.2.31). He lives and breathes learning and drinks words. When the Queen, gleeful at his banishment says, "His name is at last gasp," equating his life and his name, she is doing no more (or less) than Posthumus does in comparing himself to a trifle (1.2.50–51). In his anger he threatens to "write" against women. That mere words, mere signs, constitute Posthumus' reality is confirmed when he accepts Iachimo's word as proof of Imogen's infidelity. (The bracelet is a superfluous proof, offered after Posthumus has already conceded.) Similarly, Posthumus' value consists solely in the fact that he is loved by Imogen. The ambiguous praise by the First Gentleman—Posthumus is compared to spring and to a child as well as to a mirror of the "more mature" and comes off as both juvenile and old, never vigorously manly (1.1.45–50)—culminates in deferral to Imogen's judgment: "his virtue By her election may be read What kind of man he is" (1.1.52–4). This is the Posthumus structurally enacted, even in his absence, at the center of the play, by his letters and, equally importantly, in Imogen/Fidele's soliloquy mirroring his.

The chiastically related soliloquies of Posthumus and Imogen in 2.5 and 3.6 focus the gender roles of the play. Imogen as Fidele has followed Pisanio's advice: "You must forget to be a woman," he tells her (3.4.136) and further specifies that role as it is enacted in Cymbeline's court:

> change
> Command into obedience; fear and niceness
> (The handmaids of all women, or, more truly,
> Woman it pretty self) into a waggish courage.
> ... nay, you must
> Forget that rarest treasure of your cheek,
> Exposing it (but, O, the harder heart!
> Alack no remedy) to the greedy touch
> Of common-kissing Titan: and forget
> Your laborsome and dainty trims [156–66].

Standing before the cave of Belarius and the princes, Imogen/Fidele meditates on "a man's life" (3.6.1) and finds it to be exactly as Pisanio has described, a life exposed and lacking the delicate niceties of the court, a life of "hardness": sleeping on the ground, enduring hunger, witnessing poverty, facing the enemy with drawn sword, entering the "rock" in which her brothers live. She now understands that "plenty and peace breeds cowards" (21), and that courage comes of tribulations: "hardness ever of hardiness is mother" (21–22). In the paired scene in which Posthumus, too, is hoping to reject the "woman's part" in him, his effeminacy ironically persists (2.4.172). Rather than hardness, he seeks "pleasure" (2.4.161). Far from embracing poverty, he identifies himself with money, fittingly, a counterfeit coin. Instead of wielding a sword, Posthumus almost comically threatens "to write against" women, "Detest them, curse them" (183–84). Consequently, when Imogen says in her soliloquy that Posthumus is "one of the false ones" (3.6.15), turning his accusation of her against him, she not only denies his charges against her and against women generally but reverses their gender roles. She is now the male and he the false female he describes, false in his letter to her and guilty of betrayal in wagering with Iachimo.

Somewhat more circuitously, sexuality is also touched on in two further details of the paired soliloquies, in images of feeding and of the sun. The food imagery contrasts Imogen's delicate sexuality (or asexuality) with the repressed violence of Posthumus. His gross image of Iachimo as a "full-acorned boar" mounting Imogen (168) is paired with the famished Imogen deriving sustenance from the mere thought of her husband:

> Now I think on thee,
> My hunger's gone; but even before, I was
> At point to sink for food [3.6.15–17].

A similar delicacy is suggested in the sun images. Perhaps the fundamental difference between Cymbeline's court early in the play and Belarius's rustic society lies in their attitudes toward the sun. For Belarius and the princes it is the "holy sun" (4.4.41); to Cymbeline's court it is, in Pisanio's phrase, "common-kissing Titan," a vulgar threat to the complexion of women and, as is also stated in Posthumus' tirade, to their chastity: Posthumus thought Imogen "as chaste as unsunned snow" (2.4.165). In entering the life of her brothers, Imogen/Fidele is introduced to a sexuality that requires as much courage as fighting does, a violent, senseless (i.e., "headless") instinctual force.

Finally, these paired soliloquies address the corruption of power that attends the confusion of sexual roles in Cymbeline's court. As part of her sexual transformation from a woman to a man, Imogen must "Change command into obedience," Pisanio advises. Like the Queen, if to a lesser extent, Imogen is in charge; she dominates Posthumus as the Queen manipulates Cymbeline. "Me of my lawful pleasure she restrained And prayed me oft forebearance," Posthumus complains (2.4.161–62). "Forebearance" from his advances is exactly what Imogen also asked of Cloten (2.3.97). Imogen's request of Posthumus expresses the "fear and niceness" Pisanio sees, through the distorting lens of the court, as "woman it pretty self" (3.4.160). In approaching the cave, Imogen takes her first steps in overcoming her fear of the "savage" (3.6.23) and therefore her first steps in relinquishing the need to command.

The various soliloquies, so often derided, are in fact critical not only to the structure of the play but to the character of Posthumus. Beyond their local significance, they mark the three main sections of the play. The paired soliloquies of Posthumus and Imogen delimit the Imogen section; the paired soliloquies of Iachimo and Cloten delimit the suitors' section; and the expressively varied 1.5–5.1 pair, containing only one soliloquy and the wager, delimits the Posthumus section. The pair in which Iachimo and Cloten accomplish or intend their violations of Imogen elaborates Posthumus' similarly violent soliloquy on women in 2.5. But in attaining his soliloquy in 5.1, holding the cloth stained with what he thinks is Imogen's blood,

Posthumus rights his effete response to Iachimo's insult of Imogen in 1.5 by vowing to die for her. In the international social setting of 1.5, with various Europeans as mute onstage personae, Posthumus is the pliable, over-civilized defender of his lady's honor. By contrast, when he expresses his resolve to die—indeed, when he lives in "every breath a death" (27)—he is alone, soliloquizing. This pair, and particularly Posthumus' soliloquy, gains force by its expressive structural variation from the two other pairs of soliloquies.

Posthumus appears in one other scene of the play, 2.4, in which Iachimo convinces him of Imogen's infidelity. It is paired with scene 3.7, in which Belarius and the princes return to the cave with the dead deer and find Imogen/Fidele. In these scenes of mistaken divorce and unknowing reunion, Posthumus is contrasted with Belarius and the princes. Posthumus' low valuation of Imogen as a whore is contrasted with the awe in which Belarius and the princes hold her: she is "an angel" (15). The briefly imagined wooing of Imogen/Fidele by Guiderius— her "[bride]groom in honesty" (42)—is contrasted with Posthumus' paired faithlessness and the recollection of him by Imogen as "false" (61). Gold and money, the pervasive standards of valuation by Iachimo and Posthumus, are angrily dismissed by the brothers when Imogen/Fidele offers to pay for her food:

> Guiderius. Money, youth?
> Arviragus. All gold and silver rather turn to dirt,
>   As 'tis no better reckoned but of those
>   Who worship dirty gods [25–28].

Beyond these obvious contrasts, the scenes contrasting Posthumus and the princes more subtly and importantly symbolize Imogen as the essential sacrificial victim of the play.

Sacrifice in *Cymbeline* is ritually enacted in its simplest form by Belarius and the princes. Beyond fulfilling the natural need to provide food, they formalize the actions of the "morning's holy office" (3.3.4): the hunting, killing, cooking and eating of the deer. The kill is the culmination of a "sport" (10) or contest whose winner is formally recognized at a ceremony sharing the cooked meat: "He who strikes the venison first shall be lord o' the feast, To him the other two shall minister" (74–76). The ritual is re-affirmed after the hunt. Returning with the deer, Belarius proclaims Guiderius "master of the feast," and says that himself and Arviragus "will play the cook and servant, 'tis our match ... now peace be here" (3.6.2–3, 8). The Mountaineers' society is structured around an explicitly religious routine containing an agon, a kill, a cooking and a communion: a ritual that insures peace.

The sacrificial ritual that seals the peace between Britain and Rome contains the same elements of killing, cooking and eating, though it is more emphatically religious and mutes the violence. Cymbeline proposes to "smoke the temple with our sacrifices" (5.5.399), and in the final speech of the play he commands,

> "Laud we the gods
> And let our crooked smokes climb to their nostrils
> From our blest altars....
>   In the temple of great Jupiter
> Our peace we'll ratify, seal it with feasts.
>   ...Never was a war did cease
> (Ere bloody hands were washed) with such a peace [477–86].

Cymbeline emphasizes the smoke of the cooking sacrifice and the communal feast; he doesn't mention the central action of this pious ceremony, the slaughter of the victims, and he is mute as to their identity. The unspecified victims are scapegoats for the Roman soldiers Cymbeline had intended to kill until he was moved to follow the example of Posthumus' forgiveness of Iachimo. The bloody hands also suggest that the dead soldiers of both sides are symbolically among the sacrifices, that the battle is the agon and that the ritual is expiatory. Already bloody hands draw further blood reverently, as naturally and blamelessly as in killing a deer. The Mountaineer's simple hunting ritual is extended in the scope of its agon and the number of its victims to become symbolically cosmic. The ritual that coheres and sanctifies the small self-sufficient community in Wales has been extended to cohere the universal peace.

This paradigmatic action introduced at the center of the play (3.3) is variously repeated. The Mountaineers' ritual is the seed that grows through elemental blood sacrifices to the final ritual in which the sacrifice is once again sustenance, now symbolically. Cloten is the most vivid sacrifice of the play, a blood sacrifice introduced, though comically, with a foreshadowing of his fate: "The violence of action hath made you reek as a sacrifice," the First Lord tells him (1.3.3). His decapitation by Guiderius provides the blood that restores Imogen/Fidele, as Arviragus anticipates: "Poor sick Fidele! ... to[re]gain his colour I'ld let a parish of such Clotens blood, and praise myself for charity" (4.2.166–69). Thinking Cloten to be Posthumus, the "dead" Imogen/Fidele comes to life apostrophizing the headless corpse: "Give color to my pale cheek with your blood" (330). Instead of food as restorative and feasting as a form of communion, staining with blood serves these purposes in the more primitive sacrifice. (It is also worth remembering the Aristotelian notion of sexual intercourse as "mingling bloods," a phrase Shakespeare uses in this sense in *The Winter's Tale* [1.2.109].) And as Imogen/Fidele is restored by the blood of Cloten, (thinking it to be that of her husband), Posthumus, too, is restored by blood, the blood—as he thinks—of Imogen on the cloth Pisanio has provided. After his long absence from the play Posthumus returns apostrophizing the bloody cloth, having forgiven Imogen and determined to die for her.

As described by Posthumus, the battle in the narrow pass is another variant of the paradigmatic action. The noble-blooded princes, who have the blood of the deer and of Cloten already on their hands, are joined by Posthumus, who thinks he has Imogen's blood on his hands. These then infuse the "dead" soldiers with blood and color, resurrecting them. The same imagery that expressed Fidele's rebirth is now used of the soldiers' faces. The princes have "faces fit for masks, or rather fairer than those for preservation cased, or shame" (5.3.21–22). That "fairer" does not mean "paler" is evident from the succeeding lines: "These three [the princes and Belarius] gilded pale looks ... [so] that some [soldiers], turned coward but by example ... 'gan to look the way they did, and to grin like lions Upon the pikes of the hunters" (28–39). When the British soldiers witness the "stand" of the three, the soldiers' pale faces are "gilded" (34), changed to resemble the faces of the Mountaineers, "fair" from long exposure to the sun and from the blood flowing in and perhaps on their cheeks. The color in the Standers' faces and the blood they drew, that is to say, reinvigorated the Britains, putting blood into their cheeks and giving them the courage of lions, of Leo, the sign of the sun, and they become "leo-natus," (re)born of the sun: "some slain before ... are now each one the slaughter-man of twenty. Those that would die or ere resist are grown the mortal bugs of the field" (5.3.47–51). The bloody battle also brings the action closer to the paradigm in that the soldiers are compared to food: they are "like fragments in hard voyages become the life of the need" (5.3.44–45).

Posthumus' maturation requires that he too become sustaining food, a sacrificial repast.

After offering his life for Imogen's life and awakening from his vision of a sulfurous descent by Jupiter, Posthumus is asked if he is ready for death and replies "Over-roasted rather," initiating a series of quibbles in which he is "well-cooked food," "a good repast," and the "dish" that "pays the shot" (5.4.153–56). (Imogen also occasions the elliptically sacrificial moments finally experienced by Iachimo when, recalling his wager at the feast, he wishes had been poisoned—"my heart drops blood.... I faint" [5.5.147–48]—and by Cymbeline, burning with impatience to hear news of his daughter's fate—"I stand on fire" [168]).

Imogen is the essential sacrifice of the play, symbolically killed by most of the major characters. She is so rare, so spiritual, that mere words affect her as physical actions do the other characters. To her "words are strokes and strokes death" (3.5.40–41), and she is therefore murdered by the mere words of Posthumus' letter, which "cut her throat." (She is, of course, transformed by the end of the play, and her final "death" is physically caused—"You never killed Imogen til now," Pisanio tells Posthumus after he has struck the "page" [5.5.231].) As the dead (Arabian) bird, her voyeuristic violation by Iachimo is imaged as it will later be judged, a murder, and as Fidele she is poisoned by the Queen. In the central line of a central flanking scene she describes herself using a traditional symbol of the essential historical victim, Christ: "the lamb entreats the butcher" to kill her (3.4.98 of 195). One of the most elusive of her deaths occurs, symbolically, in the central sacrificial action of the play, the killing of the deer.

Imogen is twice referred to as a deer. While musing on gold as the means to attain Imogen, Cloten says it "makes Diana's rangers false themselves, yield up their deer to the stand of the stealer (2.3.70). ("Stand" puns on "erection" and thus, with its more common battle usage, has reference to sex, war/dueling and hunting/gaming.) The deer image is also used as a self-designation by Imogen, with a religious qualifier rather than a sexual pun, when asking Pisanio to kill her: "Why has thou gone so far to be unbent when thou hast taken thy stand, the elected deer before thee?" (3.4.110). At the moment of Imogen's question, Guiderius is killing the deer, and when Imogen next appears it is as Fidele. As the "elected deer" Imogen's death first becomes transformative, for she dies into a new identity, casting off the "fear and niceness" of a woman and becoming a man. The central action of the play, a "natural" sacrificial ritual for the Mountaineers, is also a symbolic sacrifice of Imogen. With exquisite delicacy Shakespeare has suggested both a sexual conquest and a spiritual awakening in the death. When Fidele is revealed as Imogen, restored to being Imogen, by Posthumus' blow in the last scene, these subtle suggestions become overt.

This background explains the chiastic pairing of the scene in which Posthumus is convinced of Imogen's betrayal (2.4) with the scene of the Mountaineers' return to the cave (3.7). Both are focused on Imogen, each with its appropriate representation of her. Iachimo displays the bracelet as a token of Imogen, a reductive sign; her brothers return with the deer, a rare symbol in keeping with the pervasive "tender air" of Imogen's nature (5.5.452) and explicitly interpreted for the audience in the Mountaineers' awed reactions to Fidele.

There is one other pair in the Imogen section of the play. In 2.3 Imogen is courted by Cloten and discovers the loss of her bracelet; in 3.8 a Roman Senator summarizes the "emperor's writ" regarding the war:

2.5 Posthumus on women (soliloquy).	3.6 Imogen (as Fidele) on men (soliloquy).
2.4 Iachimo with bracelet (as token of Imogen).	3.7 Belarius & boys with deer (as symbol of Imogen).

2.3 Imogen courted by Cloten; loss of bracelet; Lucius' arrival.	3.8 Roman emperor's writ of war.

As the central scenes encompass all three plots, so the Imogen section locates her in the three worlds of the play. The paired soliloquies link her with Posthumus; the representations of her as bracelet and deer locate her in the "Renaissance Italian" world of Iachimo and the rustic world of the princes; and the 2.3–3.8 pair mirrors the threats against her by Cloten and Iachimo with the threat of war by the classical Romans, embedding in the structure the association between sex and violence that pervades the language and action of the play.

Three of the four remaining pairs in the play enact threats or assaults against Imogen, by Iachimo and Cloten.

2.2 Iachimo's voyeuristic violation of Imogen (soliloquy).	4.1 Cloten plans violation of Imogen (soliloquy).
2.1 "Cock" Cloten denied the satisfaction of a fight. (Second Lord's soliloquy.)	4.2 Cloten (as Posthumus) fights and is killed by Guiderius; body is Imogen's "bed-fellow."
1.7 Iachimo feigns distraction, "assaults" Imogen and retreats.	4.3 Cymbeline, distracted with worry, threatens Pisanio and then relents.

Iachimo and Cloten are linked in their actual or planned violations of Imogen (2.2–4.1). The self-controlled strategies of Iachimo in his "assault" of Imogen (1.7) are contrasted with Cymbeline's martial and marital helplessness (4.3). The difficult and bizarre central pair of this scene triplet (2.1–4.2) is, in one of its narrative aspects at least, a comic, almost surreal fulfillment of Cloten's desires to fight and to rape Imogen. It is worth noting that scene 2.1 also contains the Second Lord's summarizing soliloquy. As the play unfolds in performance, it seems merely stilted and unnecessary, but in the context of the spatial structure, paired with Imogen's awakening on the headless body of Cloten, the speech has an ironic, comic applicability. "The heavens hold firm," the Lord prays for Imogen,

> The walls of thy dear honour, keep unshaked
> That temple, thy fair mind, that thou mayst stand
> T' enjoy thy banished lord and this great land! [61–64]

Fidele's rebirth from the blood of Cloten makes this speech one more example of the decadence of Cymbeline's court, praying for an inviolate Imogen. In the event, her mind is deeply shaken, her honor is symbolically compromised, and she certainly does not "stand" (either beside Cloten's body or when struck by Posthumus), a posture in war and in sex, the play makes abundantly clear, inherently male.

There is one other scene pair to be considered, 1.6, in which the Queen secures the "poison" that will ultimately "kill" Imogen/Fidele, and 4.4, in which Guiderius and Arviragus convince Belarius that they should join the battle, that he should allow their "blood … to fly out" (53–54). These scenes embody the essential contrast of the play: the Queen as representative of all that is decadent, the princes as representative of all that is, in the Roman sense, virtuous: moral, vigorous and manly. Like the bracelet and deer earlier, the poison and blood express the differences of the two cultures. The poison is concocted from flowers, "the pleasures of this world" (4.2.296), Imogen says, awakening on Cloten's headless body, and epitomize the soft life that breeds cowardice and death-in-life (3.6.21; 5.3.69–72). Blood is restorative, the elixir of (the hard) life, in which it is both expressed and drawn in sacrificial action. Imogen, Posthumus, the soldiers, and ultimately Britain itself (5.5.15) are restored to life by it. We might even think of the play as moving from an easy misreading of its two opening lines—"our bloods No more obey the heavens"—to the ensanguined celebration of its last two: "Never was a war did cease, Ere bloody hands were washed, with such a peace." In flying out, the blood of the princes obeys the heavens and furthers the sacrificial blood-letting that redeems the court from the Queen's poisonous pleasures. This pair of scenes, because it embodies the fundamental contrast in the play, occupies a section of its own in the complex elegance of the chiastic design.

22

The Parallel Plays
of *The Winter's Tale*
Entertainment

It is a critical commonplace that *The Winter's Tale* is structured in two parts: the tragic enactment of Leontes' jealousy in the Sicilian first half and the restoration of Perdita and Hermione to Leontes in the comic, largely pastoral, second half.[1] These disjunct halves—the tragedy of Mamillius and the comedy of Perdita—are joined in the single overriding action which encompasses both: the destruction and re-creation of a culture. With the death of Mamillius, the exposure of Perdita and the supposed death of Hermione, the Sicilian court is left without an heir or potential heir. The culture, epitomized in its consummate art, Hermione's entertainment, is destroyed by Leontes' savage "dreams" (3.2.79).[2] The second half of the play trains Perdita to take her "part" (4.4.651) in the restored culture, the art, finally recognized as "lawful" (5.3.105, 111) of the "resurrected" Hermione.

The two main actions of the play, the tragic and comic halves, may be thought of as, first, the enactment of Leontes' "fancies" (3.2.179), which in "killing" Hermione destroy the arts of culture, and, second, the gradual recovery of those arts in the person of Perdita and the "statue" of Hermione. These main actions are paralleled in the virtuoso structures of the play, both in the Sicilian and Bohemian halves and, in smaller compass, in the cameo dramas of the court and country scenes. The overall structure varies Shakespeare's usual practice. Instead of "rising" to a central turn, third-act climax, and "falling" to the denouement, *The Winter's Tale* "falls" to the destruction of Antigonus and the ship and begins again after the Shepherd finds the abandoned Perdita. We have, in effect, two plays. Each scene of the tragic first action is paired with the corresponding scene of the comic second action to form parallel dramas, one ending in Hermione's apparent death and the other in her restoration. A skeletal author-plot looks like this:

	3.3 (cont.) … things new born": Perdita and gold found.
1.1 Camillo and Archidamus on the promising Prince.	4.1 Time on Prince Florizel & Perdita.
1.2 Polixenes asks to leave court, but remains. Leontes "wears" his face like a mask.	4.2 Camillo asks to leave court, remains. Polixenes puts on disguise.

195

2.1 Leontes takes child from Hermione.	4.3 Autolycus takes money from Clown.
2.2 Birth of Perdita ("Freed" by Nature from the womb).	4.4 Pastoral: Perdita's nature freed by art.
2.3 Perdita brought before Leontes and taken off.	5.1 Perdita brought before Leontes and taken off.
3.1 The oracle.	5.2 The oracle fulfilled.
3.2 The "death" of Hermione.	5.3 The "resurrection" of Hermione.
3.3 Antigonus killed; ship destroyed: "things dying…	

With two exceptions the parallels between the story of destruction and that of re-creation are mostly obvious. Scenes 1.1 and 4.1, both addressing the promise of royal children, function as prologues to the two parallel plays. The paired court scenes in Sicilia and Bohemia (1.2 & 4.2) suggest the habitual duplicity of both and the relative lack of sophistication in Bohemia. The identical action of bringing Perdita before Leontes is repeated in 2.3 and 5.1, and the last two scenes of the first half—the oracle and the loss of Hermione—are resolved in the paired scenes of the second half, the fulfillment of the oracle and the restoration of Hermione. Only the pairing of 2.1 and 4.3 seems to have no particular force. But in fact it "stabs the center" of the play's concerns. Autolycus is a surrogate for Leontes, and money has replaced children. To demonstrate how these two central metaphorical substitutions take place, we have to take a long run at them. In doing so, the second rather obscure pairing, between 2.2 and 4.4, will also be clarified.

Because the play traces the destruction and re-creation of a cultural tradition, the examples of art range from the naïve to the most sophisticated. The comic second half, the re-creation, starts with the Clown's obsessive eating metaphors and moves on through the Shepherd's folk superstitions and Autolycus's ballads, through the dances, songs and costumes of the sheep shearing feast and Paulina's sustained, intricate performance to culminate in the "statue" of Hermione. Given this range of artifice, it is initially helpful to classify the art as Hermione does the truths, the "verities,"[3] of the play: into men's art and women's art. There are three pivotal instances of women's art in the play, the entertainments by the three most prominent women in their roles as hostesses: Perdita's reluctant hostessing of the sheep shearing feast, Hermione's entertainment of Polixenes and Paulina's guided tour through her gallery to the chapel. All the other art in the play is clarified by comparison with these entertainments.

In the course of the play Perdita goes from a simple-minded insistence on the complete separation of art and nature to a mature, though reluctant, acceptance of the necessity of art. The sheep shearing reveals her initial attitude. At first she resists the costumes she and Florizel are wearing because they are deceptive; the prince becomes a mere swain and a lowly maid resembles a goddess. To Perdita, costumes are analogous to hybrid flowers and painted women, departures from nature. She consents to being "pranked up" for the sheep shearing only because "our feasts in every mess have folly and our feeders digest it with a custom" (4.4.10–12). Perdita accepts her inevitable role as hostess, required to provide both food and, as she thinks, foolish pretendings, but she is careful to maintain a distinction between them. Compare the Shepherd's description of his wife as hostess:

> When my old wife lived, upon
> This day she was both pantler, butler, cook,
> Both dame and servant; welcomed all, served all;
> Would sing her song and dance her turn; now here,
> At the upper end o' the table, now i' the middle;
> On his shoulder and his; her face afire
> With labor, and the thing she took to quench it
> She would to each one sip [55–62].

Here the distinction between food and folly is blurred. The wife's provisions of both food and art come increasingly to seem one nourishment, and the "sip" she gives seems equally a toast and a drink (and perhaps even a kiss). This drift from the association of food and folly to the identification of nourishment for the body with nourishment for the imagination culminates in Camillo's substitution of beauty for food when he says to Perdita, "I would leave grazing, were I of your flock, And only live by gazing" (108–9). But Perdita, insistent as always on the literal truth, chides him, "You'd be so lean that blasts of January Would blow you through and through" (111–12). While she understands the connection, she is careful to maintain the distinction between food and folly—or, more broadly, between biological processes and art—the two provisions that together make up female entertainment.

At least, these are the two provisions of the simplest entertainment, for Perdita discovers that being pranked up also encourages spontaneous expression of her feelings. It is love as well as food that Perdita's costume prompts her to provide when she wishes Florizel "quick and in mine arms," a desire she excuses by saying that "this robe of mine Does change my disposition" (4.4.132, 133–34). Her disposition may be changed, but it is certainly not falsified by her "acting." In fact, the scene gradually reveals that it is only in necessary folly, in art, that she truly reveals herself, as the initial distinction between doing and acting blurs and finally disappears.

Commenting on Perdita, Polixenes maintains the distinction, however unemphatically: "Nothing she does or seems but smacks of something greater than herself" (156–57). Florizel's lovely praises erode the distinction between "does and seems" further:

> What you do
> Still betters what is done. When you speak, sweet
> I'd have you do it ever. When you sing,
> I'd have you buy and sell so, so give alms,
> Pray so, and for the ord'ring your affairs,
> To sing them too. When you do dance, I wish you
> A wave o' the sea, that you might ever do
> Nothing but that, move still, still so,
> And own no other function. Each your doing
> So singular in each particular
> Crowns what you are doing in the present deeds
> That all your acts are queens [135–46].

Perdita replies, "Your praises are too large" (147), her "acting" having again taken on uncomfortable implications of social class.

But after Polixenes' threats, to preserve her relationship with Florizel, Perdita finally accepts art. In a comment which beautifully establishes the seamless connection of female entertainment with a nature only expressible through art, Camillo says, instructing Perdita, already costumed like Flora, to disguise herself: "Disliken The truth of your own seeming" (646–47). "I see the play so lies," Perdita responds, "that I must bear a part" (4.4.650–51). In discarding the Flora costume, Perdita leaves nature (which is, again, known only through art) and assumes a role which will grant her entrance into society. In accepting not merely a costume but a disguise, Perdita fully accepts art, (though the disguise is like the Flora costume in truly expressing Perdita's identity, now as a princess [541, 543–44]). Perdita is on her way to the perfection of Hermione; Florizel's praise will come to be true of the daughter as it has been of the mother: "all your acts are queens" (146). The long pastoral scene, 4.4, that is to say, trains Perdita in a necessary acceptance of art. Her love for Florizel, in particular, requires her disguise and her acting. In the paired scene, 2.2, Paulina described Perdita's birth as a liberation from the womb: "This child was prisoner to the womb, and is By law and process of great nature thence Freed" (58–60). In 4.4 art similarly frees Perdita from nature.

Polixenes' reaction to the feast clarifies the male notion of entertainment, which is inextricably connected not with food or love but with money, a connection that ultimately explains the pairing of Autolycus and Leontes in 2.1 and 4.3. Polixenes demonstrates the incipient confusion of money and love in his speech to Florizel.

> Your heart is full of something that does take
> Your mind from feasting. Sooth, when I was young
> And handed love as you do, I was wont
> To load my she with knacks. I would have ransacked
> The peddler's silken treasury and have poured it
> To her acceptance; you have let him go,
> And nothing marted with him. If your lass
> Interpretation should abuse and call this
> Your lack of love or bounty, you were straited
> For a reply [341–350].

Polixenes' idea of feasting has nothing at all to do with food or nurturance; it consists of buying presents for the woman. Florizel tells his disguised father that Perdita has no interest in the "trifles" of the peddler: "The gifts she looks from me are packed and locked Up in my heart" (353–54). Measured against this standard, Polixenes' view comes dangerously close to equating the expression of love with the love itself and the object of love with the objects used to express love; women thus become things. And in fact that is exactly the transformation Polixenes imposes on Perdita; he reduces her to a trinket by calling her a "knack" (425). Once the woman is made a mere object, the process proliferates; Perdita is called a "sheephook" and is said to "hoop" Florizel with her embraces (417, 436). Polixenes' attitude is given its ultimate and most vulgar expression when the Clown, ironically auguring his own imminent escapade with two country lasses, accusingly asks of maids, "Will they wear their plackets where they should bear their faces?" (241–42). All individuality is lost in the literal transformation into a sex object. Women themselves become the "thing" bought, the prostitutes of Autolycus's entrance song.

If women are objects to be bought, it follows that male potency will be equated with money. Hence Autolycus's "to geld a codpiece of a purse" (606–7). And if money is male potency, insemination and pregnancy become a kind of financial transaction: "He hath paid

you all he promised you," Mopsa says in taunting Dorca about the nature of the Clown's atten-
tions; "Maybe he hath paid you more, which will shame you to give him again" (238–40). The
issue therefore will be not children but money; all men are like the usurer whose "wife was
brought to bed of twenty money-bags at a burden" (261–62). This confusion of value, of
money as maleness and ultimately of the preciousness of life for the preciousness of money,
is succinctly expressed in the personification ending Autolycus's gleeful, greedy summing-up,
when he says that except for the Shepherd's intervention he "had not left a purse alive in the
whole army" (613–14). For Autolycus, at least, money is not simply male genitals, as in his
earlier metaphor, but is now the whole man, a soldier. In stealing money from the Clown
Autolycus is, by a kind of inverse metaphor, taking a child, as Leontes is doing in the paired
scene.

Polixenes' dehumanization of Perdita and Autolycus's personification of money inevitably
distort nurturance and love. The entertainments of Perdita and the Shepherd's wife, which
include both food and amusement, collapse for the men into the one provision: art of whatever
kind becomes food, as in Camillo's compliment that he "would live by gazing" (4.4.109) and
in Autolycus's estimation of his trinkets, which, he says, "keep my pack from fasting" (596–
97). Unlike Florizel, who has had a "worthy feeding" (171), Autolycus has "eaten ballads" (187).
In this context of male entertainments, of money and trinkets replacing food, Mamillius's
negative answer to the proverbial "Will you take eggs for money?" (1.2.159) suggests the reason
for the paucity of food imagery in the Sicilian court. Court entertainment is refined beyond
the vulgarity of "lower messes" (1.2.224). Like Autolycus, Sicilia feeds on art, a sophisticated
diet that finally results in one hungry bear.

Sex and love are similarly problematic, as the Clown suggests in enacting Polixenes'
courtship strategy of buying trinkets. At the entrance of Autolycus as a peddler, the Clown
says, "If I were not in love with Mopsa, thou should'st take no money of me; but being
enthralled as I am, it will also be the bondage of certain ribbons and gloves" (4.4.231–33). It
is only a short step from this romantic enthrallment to the sinister "enchantment" that Polixenes finds Perdita to be, personified "witchcraft." And this explains the male fear of women
and the fear of being mocked by art. Love is a form of enthrallment, of enchantment, of aesthetic experience, which puts men at risk of losing their money and of being mocked, of being
like the rustics at the ballad-singing, "admiring the nothing" (4.4.609) of duplicitous art and
being taken, having one's maleness, one's purse, stolen, of being gelded.

Leontes is the epitome of male values in the play. Like Autolycus, the connoisseur believes
that art is "nothing" (4.4.609). It is because Hermione's entertainment of Polixenes is not
nothing that Leontes becomes jealously enraged:

> Is whispering nothing?
> Is leaning cheek to cheek? Is meeting noses?
> Kissing with inside lip?...............
> ....
> Is this nothing?
> Why then the world and all that's in't is nothing [1.2.282–3, 289–90].

After years of penance Leontes learns that art—at least the female art of Paulina and
Hermione—is not nothing; the statue is not nothing. Hermione's entertainment of Polixenes
is not nothing; it is real, with just so much love for her husband's friend as she claims at her
trial. In his earlier mistaken aesthetics, in his ironically self-reflective idea that "affections ...

fellow'st nothing" (1.2.137–41), Leontes is a match with Autolycus, and the paired scenes, 2.1 and 4.3, structurally enforce the connection.[4]

The identical aesthetics of Leontes and Autolycus are embedded in another structural tour de force, the parallels between 1.2, the court scene, and 4.4, the country scene. Though the country scene is about twice as long as the court scene, both are cameo dramas built on the traditional five-act structure,[5] with a typically Shakespearean turn in the middle of the third "act," when in both scenes father reveals himself to son.

1. Hermione's entertainment (to 108).	1. Perdita's hostessing (to 182).
2. Leontes, aside and deceiving Hermione & Polixenes (to 183).	2. (Disguised) Autolycus (to 338).
3. Leontes & Mamillius (to 208).	3. Polixenes discovers himself to Florizel (to 459).
4. Leontes' plan (to 346).	4. Camillo's plan (to 665).
5. Camillo's plan (to 460).	5. Autolycus's plan (to 835).

In the "third act" turn of the court scene, Leontes drops his pretense of cordiality before Hermione and Polixenes and tells Mamillius just how his mother "plays" (1.2.185). At the corresponding moment in the country scene, Polixenes removes his disguise to inform Florizel of the true nature of his Shepherdess, a "[master]piece Of ... witchcraft," an "enchantment" (4.4.419–20, 431). It is not only in their misogynistic aesthetic, the idea that women's arts, especially acting, are dangerous beguilements that Leontes and Polixenes are linked. They are also both disguised, though in a different manner. Leontes is disguised in the sophisticated way of the Sicilian court. In duplicitously counseling duplicity, Camillo tells Leontes to approach Polixenes "with a countenance As clear as friendship wears at feasts" (1.2.339–40); this wearing of his face like a mask is exactly what Leontes does in deflecting Hermione's and Polixenes' concern. Hence, the pairing of Leontes and the disguised Autolycus in "act 2" of the court and country scenes.[6] The disguised men—the "masked" Leontes, the bearded Autolycus and the "old" Polixenes—live in a world of deracinated fantasy, in a savage dream.

Deceptive as they are, Camillo's plans in each of these scenes succeed where the plan of Leontes to kill Polixenes and the plan of Autolycus to reveal Perdita's origins both fail. For Camillo practices a female art. In Camillo's motives, Shakespeare demonstrates that "male" and "female" art is not a sex-based distinction. Camillo deceives Perdita and Florizel because, the cupbearer says, he "so much thirst[s] to see" Leontes (4.4.510); Camillo has "a woman's longing" for Sicilia (663). Like Paulina, he indulges a "male" deception out of "female" motives of love and affection. The marriage of the two virtuoso playwrights (4.4.590, 5.3.153–54), Camillo and Paulina, usually said to be abrupt, is an inevitability of the play's aesthetics. Indeed, Leontes's recognition of Paulina's "worth and honesty" (5.3.144) after being taken in by her ruse for 16 years demonstrates his changed aesthetic; he now realizes that there is "an art lawful as eating" (110–11), not only in the "statue" but in Paulina's long deception (5.3.153–54).

Hermione, of course, is the perfect embodiment of female art, at the opposite extreme from the nihilistic aesthetic of Leontes and Autolycus, resolving the main concerns of the play in her "play," her acting, her entertainment. In fact, we might think of the whole of *The Winter's Tale* as a lesson in appreciating the Hermione of the second scene as analogous to the "statue" of the last scene at the moment when, for Leontes and the audience, the woman and the statue cannot be distinguished, when nature and art are one. Like the structurally parallel entertainment by Perdita at the sheep shearing, Hermione's entertainment of Polixenes also renders the play's concern with aesthetics in images of food, sex and money, consummately expressed in the speech that sets off Leontes' first explosion of jealousy.

At Hermione's entreaty Polixenes has agreed to prolong his visit, and Leontes says that his wife has "never spok'st To better purpose ... but once" (1.2.87–88). Hermione replies:

> What! Have I twice said well? When was't before?
> I prithee tell me. Cram's with praise, and make's
> As fat as tame things. One good deed, dying tongueless,
> Slaughters a thousand waiting upon that.
> Our praises are our wages. You may ride's
> With one soft kiss a thousand furlongs ere
> With spur we heat an acre. But to th'goal:
> My last good deed was to entreat his stay.
> What was my first? It has an elder sister
> Or I mistake you. O would her name were Grace!
> But once before I spoke to th'purpose? When?
> Nay, let me have't, I long! [89–100]

Leontes finds his wife's entertainment to be "too hot" (107), too real, beyond the bounds of mere social interaction, beyond the "nothing" of courtesy and public affection. He takes the speech to be Hermione's mockery of him for the benefit of her lover and not an expression of sexual, familial and spiritual love and a bantering plea for a responsive love from him. (It is amusing to see critics, too, fairly shuffling their feet and blushing at the frank sexuality of Hermione's speech.[7]) But, grown in her art beyond the Perdita of the feast, Hermione is not dismayed in her entertainment nor does she find any "praises ... too large" (4.4.147). Praise is the food that makes her fat; praise is, the nine-months-pregnant Hermione suggests, the love that impregnated her. Praise is money (and horsemanship, with its own sporting transform of intercourse). As love, food and money inclusively, praise issues in the family relationships she embodies and invokes, even to that of Grace.[8] All of these associations find summation in the wonderfully broad reference of her last pronoun: "Let me have't, I long!"

The tone of the speech is playful, delicate, bawdy and spiritual almost all at once. It is so lightly allusive that its glances at the main images of the play almost elude us. It not only resolves all the play's main images of food, sex and money, it reaches beyond them to the source of poetry and of courtesy in its classical allusion to "Grace," and to a spiritual realm in its Christian meaning. It is not the statue of the final scene that deserves Leontes' awed response and awakened faith, but the Hermione of this speech, the Hermione in whom nature and art, doing and acting, are passionately at one.

23

The Thematic Arch of *The Tempest*
A Hand for Prospero

In the Epilogue of *The Tempest* Prospero addresses us, the audience, as our Ariel asking to be released:

> Now my charms are all o'erthrown
> And what strength I have 's mine own,
> Which is most faint. Now, 'tis true
> I must be here confined by you
> Or sent to Naples. Let me not
> Since I have my dukedom got
> And pardoned the deceiver, dwell
> In this bare island by your spell
> But release me from my bands
> With the help of your good hands [1–10].[1]

The conventional request for applause is here transformed into the last of the play's hinted metamorphoses. It is not only Prospero who shimmers briefly with another identity but, if we respond to his invitation, ourselves as audience who change as well. The omniscient and nearly omnipotent charmer, whose magic has been worked to "please," requests his freedom of us as Ariel has repeatedly asked his of Prospero. We are Prospero to his Ariel.[2] In effect, our parting from the play, our retrospective glance, is through the lens of the relationship between Prospero and Ariel, perhaps the most elusive relationship in the play. If our release of Prospero is to re-enact the full significance of his release of Ariel, we have to understand the whole course of the relationship of the magus and his "chick," from Prospero's initial bookworming to his final fare-thee-well.

Because of the extraordinarily interwoven texture of *The Tempest*, this understanding requires a consideration of the entire play. Shakespeare's usual art of analogy is heightened to such an extent that neither Ariel nor Prospero can be understood except in terms of the other characters and incidents. In fact, Prospero exists almost wholly by analogy. His inner life must be inferred by analogies between his abrupt and often enigmatic actions and the more expansively developed actions of the other characters. Similarly, Ariel is intelligible only as the most visible portion of a much wider spectrum of spirits in the play, ranging from the alcoholic spirits of Stephano to the "solemn air" which finally restores the Italians to their senses. Furthermore, the weave of the play is so subtle that the correspondences between Prospero's relation to Ariel and the relation of the other islanders to yet other spirits is demonstrable only if we locate the play's language within the play's thematic arch. It is not only analogies of language but analogies of structure that create the play's extraordinary self-referentiality. An understanding of Prospero and Ariel requires an investigation of both the recurring paradigm, the tempest, which affects all of the characters, including Prospero, in the same way, and the chiastic design of the play in order to provide a framework for examining Prospero's major speeches of the final two acts.

The Thematic Arch of the Play

Prospero's labor throughout the play derives from the legendary Hermes Trismegistus' succinct statement of cosmic correspondence: as above, so below. "A scientist [i.e., a magician]" Pico della Mirandola writes, "unites heaven and earth and makes the lower world join the powers of the higher world."[3] The magus of the tarot gestures upward with one hand and earthward with the other to signify just this yoking together of the divine and the mundane. In courting the influence of an "auspicious star" (1.2.182) Prospero is laboring at the magician's usual task of joining above with below, of making the protean sublunar world correspond to the immutable translunar realm of the stars. Prospero's metaphor of courtship is not adventitious. In the hermetic tradition the conjunction of above with below is called the Nuptial. Fortune is now Prospero's "dear lady" (1.2.179), and in courting the influence of an auspicious star Prospero is attempting to achieve a union between the celestial and earthly realms, both within himself and in the universe of the play. The marriage of the magus is twofold. It is first the attainment of an inner harmony, the well-ordered microcosm reflecting the order of the Ptolemaic universe. This achievement allows the second, ultimate, work, the consummate nuptial: "To perform magic is nothing other than to marry the world."[4]

With this nuptial of Prospero's in mind we can see the symmetry of the basic plot conception. The present action of the play consists of two courtships and two conspiracies. Prospero's laborious courtship of stellar influence is parallel to Ferdinand's laborious courtship of Miranda; and Antonio's conspiracy with Sebastian against the King parallels Caliban's plot against Prospero. The symmetry of the plot conception is reflected in the symmetry of the play's architecture, outlined in an earlier chapter, but repeated here for convenience of reference.

	3.1 The marriage agreement between Miranda and Ferdinand.	
2.2 Caliban's party.	3.2 Caliban's party.	
2.1 King's men.	3.3 King's men.	
1.2 Prospero, his people & spirits.	4.1 Prospero, his people & spirits.	
1.1 The storm.	5.1 Spell-stopped tableaux.	

Within scenes, as diagrammed below, the character groupings continue the mirror symmetry around the marriage agreement (3.1). The scenes of Caliban's crew (2.2 and 3.2) and of the King's party (2.1 and 3.3) are followed by mirroring episodes of Miranda and Ferdinand, meeting and watching the masque performed for them (1.2.375–506 and 4.1.1–164); Prospero with Caliban in the first and fourth acts (1.2.305–374 and 4.1.165–266); and with Ariel in the first and fifth act (1.2.187–304 and 5.1.1–57). The final pairings are cross-related rather than directly paired (indicated by "x'"s in the following outline). The opening scene, the storm (1.1), balances not with the end of the play but with the penultimate action of the play, the spell-stopped tableau that is the storm's resolution (5.1.58–165); and the conversation with Miranda in which Prospero explains their past (1.2.1–186) is paired not with the next-to-last but with the last incident resolving Prospero's initial narrative—the gathering of the Italians. The final incidents of the play, occurring after Prospero's charms have ended, are situated outside the arch to indicate the return to reality. The diagram below makes these pairings conveniently visual. Excepting Ferdinand, the visitors to the island are segregated in their own section, as are Prospero and his companions, until the groups are cross-related in the final section. Like a nesting toy in the center of the play or a jewel in a symmetrical but intricately worked setting, the marriage agreement of Ferdinand and Miranda enacts in small the more encompassing marriage with his fortune that Prospero accomplishes.

3.1 Ferdinand and Miranda agree to marry.	
2.2 Caliban's party.	3.2 Caliban's party.
2.1 King's men.	3.3 King's men.
1.2.378–506 Prospero and meeting of Miranda & Ferdinand.	4.1.1–163 Prospero and masque for Miranda & Ferdinand.
1.2.308–377 Prospero & Caliban.	4.1.164–264 Prospero and Caliban.
1.2.190–307 Prospero & Ariel.	5.1.1–57 Prospero & Ariel.
1.2.1–189 Prospero tells Miranda of Milanese.	5.1.58–100 Spell-stopped tableaux.
X X X	X X X
1.1 The storm.	5.1.100–171 Recognition of Prospero & Milanese.
	(Coda: return to reality). Discovery of Miranda & Ferdinand. Enter ship's crew. Enter Caliban's party. Epilogue.

The pair of speeches between Ferdinand and Miranda in the keystone scene achieves the harmony that is the play's ideal, a love free of illusions, one that finds divinity to be of the earth. At first sight Ferdinand mistook Miranda for a goddess and she mistook him for a "thing divine" (1.2.419). By the central scene of the play each justly appraises the other, if not in fine gradations of practicality, at least as between real and illusory. After the discipline of carrying logs, Ferdinand can perceive Miranda accurately. She tells him her name (3.1.37), simultaneously creating her separate identity by breaking her father's command and identifying herself to Ferdinand. Ferdinand now sees her as "the top of admiration, worth what's dearest to the world" and "created of every creature's best" (3.1.38–39; 47–48). However hyperbolic, this is sober compared to his earlier view of Miranda as a goddess, for it locates her in the world, as a created being. And Miranda similarly:

> I would not wish
> Any companion in the world but you;
> Nor can imagination form a shape,
> Beside yourself, to like of [3.1.54–57].

Miranda is now clearly distinguishing between human being and imaginary being, between a companion in the world and the shapes imagination creates. Significantly, Ferdinand then identifies himself as a "prince" (3.1.60), retreating from the certainty of his earlier claim to being "Naples" (1.2.435). This central conversation demonstrates the realism of the lovers' self-knowledge and of their mutual appraisal. They have overcome the illusory shimmer the spirit cast over them.

A second important element in the marriage agreement, an essential distinction between the courtships and conspiracies of the play, is the willing self-sacrifice of both Miranda and Ferdinand. Her offer to carry the logs and to serve him is outdone by his sacrifice. Ordinarily, he says, "I … would no more endure This wooden slavery than to suffer The fleshfly blow my mouth" (3.1.61–63). Metaphorically such drudgery is death to Ferdinand, but he willingly undergoes it. The love of the couple is thus marked by its freedom from illusion, their accurate identification of themselves and each other, and their willing self-sacrifice, which is presented in Ferdinand's case as an acceptance of death.

A glance at the parallel moments in the conspiracies demonstrates the essential contrasts. Like the lovers sealing the marriage agreement, the would-be murderers also express their love for each other. But in their delusions, mistaking both their circumstances and their own identities, they plan to realize "love" not by self-sacrifice but by homicide. As they are about to—as they think—do the deed, Sebastian says to Antonio, "One stroke … and I the king will love you." "Draw together," Antonio responds, "And when I rear my hand do you the like" (2.1.292–295). At the mouth of Prospero's cell Stephano says, "Give me your hand" to Caliban, accepting his "suit" to his "king" and imitating the gesture sealing the marriage agreement, here turned to grotesque parodic effect: "I do begin to have bloody thoughts" (4.1.220–21). Thinking to be kings and to consummate their "love" with murder, the conspirators invert the central stage image of harmony, the lovers' marriage agreement in self-knowledge and self-sacrifice.

In the last act the dialogue between Ferdinand and Miranda over the chess game—"not for the world"; "Yes, for a score of kingdoms" (5.1.173–74)—extends the marriage agreement symbolically into the world, so that the lovers' anticipated nuptial and Prospero's coincide. Prospero's nuptial, however, being so much more encompassing, requires the action of most of the play before it can be realized.

The Paradigm of The Tempest

To achieve his nuptial, Prospero has the magician's traditional power to bind and loose spirits.[5] The figure of the magus is ultimately derived from Hermes, able to put even the hundred-eyed Argus to sleep; similarly Prospero puts Miranda to sleep or charms Ferdinand so that his "spirits, as in a dream, are all bound up" (1.2.487). On the other hand the various illusions enacted by Ariel and his fellows are instances of loosed spirits; Prospero describes the masque, for example, as being performed by "spirits … from their confines called" (4.1.120–

21). These illusions of loosed spirits are manifested as storms. The title of *The Tempest* names its recurring paradigmatic action: the play is a sequence of metaphorical storms, and storms are, most simply, a perturbation of spirits manifested as an illusion. The illusions of the play are all paired within scenes, generally along lines suggestive of conspiracy or courtship, hellish or heavenly promptings; additionally, some tempestuous element is embedded between the illusions of each pair, marking them as analogous to the opening storm. This structure is most evident in the second half of the play where the storm references are more obvious, both in their content and in their positioning, for each is centrally located in the scene. Between the illusory banquet spread for the Italians and Ariel's impersonation of a harpy there is thunder and lightning (stage direction after 3.3.52 of 109); between the masque and the hunt of act four is a strange noise (stage direction after 138 of 266) and the subsequent "vexed" speeches of Prospero. Between the paired illusions provided by Ariel for Caliban's crew, the mimicked voice and the mimicked song, Trinculo is beaten (3.2.76 of 152), the stage action "punning" on the various beatings of the storm, as in the "beating" minds of Prospero and Miranda.

The pattern is also evident in the three pairs of illusions in the first half of the play: Miranda's vision of Ferdinand as divine and Ferdinand's vision of Miranda as a goddess; Gonzalo's vision of the Golden Age and Antonio's vision of a descending crown; Trinculo's "vision" of Caliban as a monster and Caliban's vision of Stephano as a god. The tempestuous element between each of these pairs of illusions, however, is much less obvious than in the second half of the play. The illusions are not recognized as "storms" except in retrospect, by comparison with the later explicitly marked psychic disturbances. Nevertheless there is an active or invoked storm/spirit between each of the early illusions. Between Miranda's and Ferdinand's expressions of infatuation Prospero praises Ariel: "Fine spirit" (1.2.421). Between Gonzalo's and Antonio's visions, the courtiers mock Gonzalo's angry retort as a feeble "blow" (2.1.180), the violence fittingly verbal among these men of words. Between the two "visions" of Trinculo and Caliban, the spirits of alcohol are imbibed. Though the storm-related language or action varies from scene to scene, the structural position of each metaphorical tempest makes the analogy clear.

As we have seen so often before, the individual scenes of the play are thus miniature versions of the overall symmetrical design in having thematically crucial centers. Of the first four acts (excepting 3.1) only the second scene of the first act is without a prominent, "stormy" center, and in that case Prospero is berating Ariel for requesting his liberty. Most emphatically, in the center of the opening scene, between the pair of encounters with the Boatswain—the search for the Master and the cursing of the "cur"—is the thing itself: the storm, raging on an otherwise cleared stage. And some variant of it occurs in the center of each of the succeeding scenes until all tempests are calmed. At that time, after the spell-stopped tableau, at the exact center of act five, Prospero recovers his identity.

Not only the central storm but an explicit or metaphoric designation marks even the early illusions as the work of spirits. The plotting of Antonio and Sebastian is a clear instance. Though the King, Gonzalo and others of the party are falling asleep (charmed by Ariel), Sebastian says he does not feel drowsy. Antonio answers,

> Nor I; my spirits are nimble.
>   ....
> They dropped, as by a thunderstroke. What might,
> Worthy Sebastian, O, what might—? No more.

Yet…
My strong imagination sees a crown
Dropping upon thy head [2.1.202–209].

The nimble spirits, the thunderstroke simile (i.e., Antonio's perception of the others falling asleep as by a thunderstroke indicates his state of mind), the broken sentence and the elevated imaginings mark this as a lesser version of the opening tempest, a moral disorder, a storm of ambition in Antonio. The paired illusion, Gonzalo's vision of the Golden Age, is explicitly also a storm of spirits. Called a "spirit of persuasion" (2.1.235) by Antonio, Gonzalo mentions his inner storm to Alonso: "It is foul weather in us all, good sir, When you are cloudy" (142–43). Gonzalo then describes his visionary paradise.

The spirits of alcohol cause the illusions of Trinculo and Caliban. "Another storm brewing" (2.2.19), Trinculo says, using a metaphor so common as to be overlooked until he then compares a cloud to "a foul bombard about to shed his liquor" (21) and waits for "the dregs of the storm" (40). It is the storm as metaphoric alcoholic spirits that cause Trinculo's brief comic categorization of Caliban as a monster. (He realizes almost immediately that Caliban is a man, i.e., "an islander"; it is only after Trinculo actually drinks the sack that his mistake hardens into conviction.) Stephano then enters with his spirits, the sack, and thus becomes a kind of Prospero through the association of his alcoholic spirits and the spirits of the magus. The bottle, being "made of the bark of a tree" (123), is like the pine that contained Ariel. As a "book," the bottle is further associated with Prospero; in ordering Caliban to "kiss the book" (130) Stephano is joking about the practice of kissing the Bible in swearing an oath, but the more proximate reference is Prospero's book. Book and bottle are also associated as the only true "drownings" in the play. And like the imaginary crown Antonio sees descending from heaven, like the divine creatures Miranda and Ferdinand think each other to be, Caliban finds the liquor to be celestial. Thus drunkenness is another storm, another disordered imagining, another transport by the agency of spirits, now physical spirits.

The spirits are further clarified by noticing the analogies among these incidents. In the prologue of each incident a spirit comforts a "king" who is grieving a "death." The nearly literal rendition of this pattern occurs when the spirit of persuasion, Gonzalo, tries to comfort the grieving Alonso: "weigh Our sorrow with our comfort." (2.1.8–9). Ferdinand, who supposes his father dead and himself king, is also comforted in his grief by a spirit, the singing Ariel:

This music crept by me upon the waters,
Allaying both their fury and my passion
With its sweet air [1.2.392–94].

More circuitously, in presenting his plot to Sebastian, Antonio is also a spirit comforting a king in grief. As I've already shown, Antonio's "nimble spirits" are stormy. In speaking "out of his sleep" (2.1.212) Antonio is "a comforter," according to the logic of the comment Sebastian has just made to Alonso: "[Sleep] seldom visits sorrow; when it doth it is a comforter." (195–96). And according to Antonio, Sebastian, who will call himself king before the end of the scene, should be grieving a death, the death of his fortune: "Thou let'st thy fortune sleep— die, rather" (216). So Antonio is a nimble spirit comforting "King" Sebastian for the death of his fortune.

Stephano, singing and slugging away at the liquor, enacts the pattern as well, now solipsistically. The "king o' the isle," as Prospero will later call him (5.1.288), projects his fear of death in his song—"here shall I die ashore"—and turns to the spirits of the bottle: "Well, here's my comfort" (2.2.43 and 44). The analogies among each of these incidents helps to explain the attraction of spirits: they are taken or administered as a comfort against the knowledge of death.

Comfort seems otherwise to be given by a beloved. When not directly or indirectly referring to spirits, the word is most frequently used of solace from a loved one. Miranda tries to "comfort" Ferdinand against the harshness of Prospero (1.2.496), and Sebastian says that "Milan and Naples have Moe widows in them of this business' making Than we bring men to comfort them" (2.1.133–35). Toward the end of the play, when hot brains have cooled, comfort against death is provided not by spirits but by "Patience"; Prospero claims to have successfully "sought her help" "to comfort" him for the "loss" of his daughter (5.1.140,142,147). Of whatever physical, abstract or illusory nature, comfort seems to be provided by the opposite sex. Lacking that comfort there is again the comfort of spirits. Even a song about rejection by a sharp-tongued Kate gives Stephano a second excuse to turn to the bottle (2.2.55). For Prospero especially, I will argue, spirits, Ariel in particular, are a solace as of a beloved against death.

Not only are illusions paired within scenes, but the mirror symmetry of the two halves of the drama pairs illusions of the first half of the play with those of the second. We might think of the former illusions as caused by "natural" spirits and the latter as created by "artful" spirits, dramatizations by Prospero's spirit-actors. In a manner reminiscent of the transformation of instincts into artifice in *As You Like It*, the art illusion elaborates the corresponding natural illusion. The banquet spread in the second half of the play, for example, answers Gonzalo's earlier spontaneous fantasy of natural abundance "to feed my innocent people" (2.1.165); Ariel's harpy speaks to Antonio's conspiratorial vision of a descending crown. Ariel's mimicry of Trinculo's voice (3.2) dramatizes the mistaken identities in the paired earlier scene of drunkenness (2.2), and the mimicked song reprises the paired exit, an insurrectionary advance now become a parade led by "the picture of Nobody." The masque of act four dramatizes an infatuation with goddesses— Ferdinand's in the paired scene (1.2.375–506) and Prospero's in his relationship with spirits; the hunt acts out Prospero's anger toward Caliban in the paired scene. In the fully staged illusion each character can see his own guilt or desire, which was only implicit in the paired earlier illusion. In typically Shakespearean fashion the performance functions as a mirror and thus allows (though it does not necessitate) catharsis. The following diagram sets out the central storms and the reflecting illusions (except Ferdinand's) in the two halves of the play.

Caliban mistaken for a monster.	Mimicked voice.
2.2. *Caliban drinks spirits of alcohol* (86 & 93 of 188).	3.2. *Beating of Trinculo* (76 of 152).
Stephano mistaken for a god.	Mimicked song.
Golden Age.	Banquet.
2.1 *"It is foul weather in us all"* (142–84 of 327).	3.3 *Thunder and storm sounds* (53 of 110).
Descending crown.	Harpy.
	Masque.
1.2. *Prospero berates Ariel* (245–96 of 502).	4.1. *Storm and strange noises* (137 of 266).
	Hound hunt.
1.1. *The storm on empty deck* (33 of 68).	5.1. *"I am Prospero"* (159 of 320).

The mechanism of this catharsis is implicit in the action of the storms. The thorough-going disorder of the opening storm gradually yields a ghostly paradigm (to use Yeats's phrase) as the succeeding storms clarify it. A storm is an illusion caused by loosed spirits; it involves the noises, "blowing," and "beating" of a storm; it has a dichotomous effect, depending on the psyche of the characters (who look "up" or "down," seeing, most drastically, either divinities or devils); and it causes similarly dichotomous reactions to the thought of a "higher realm": either an attack of conscience or an expression of loss and longing, as in the ship's crew's panicky prayers (51) and Gonzalo's "the wills above be done but I would fain die a dry death" (1.1.67). The banquet and harpy scene is the most obvious example. The thunder and lightning explic-itly mark the scene as a storm caused by spirits. At the sight of the banquet Alonso invokes heavenly angels (3.3.20), and Sebastian proclaims belief in an opposite divinity, one of fire, the phoenix (20). The deft enactment of the harpy by Ariel causes the conscience-stricken distraction of the king and his "longing" to join his lost, presumably drowned, son.

As Gonzalo, Antonio, Trinculo and Caliban project their illusions under the influence of stormy spirits, so Prospero's spirits in the second half of the play also enact his fancies, as he says. His inner turmoil can be inferred from the performances of his spirits and the cor-responding "natural spirits" of the paired scenes. Again the structural parallels will clarify both the place of spirits and the relationship of Prospero to them.

The parallels between the three performances in the second half of the play are empha-sized by their identical structures. Besides an appropriate prologue, each includes a pair of illusions, now actual performances, with a central metaphorical storm between them and a two-part response—an examination of conscience and a speech of longing and loss. In each case the tempest is suggested by a disorder placed between the two parts of the performance and centrally located in the scene, as I've described above: the beating of Trinculo (line 76 of 152) between the mimicked voice and mimicked song; the thunder and lightning as the ban-quet is whisked away (stage direction after line 52 of 109) before Ariel appears as a harpy; and the "strange, hollow and confused noise" as the dancing nymphs and reapers vanish at Prospero's disquiet (stage directions after line 138 of 266) and the hunt ensues. Each play-within-the-play elicits an examination of conscience—Trinculo's and Stephano's fearful excla-mations (3.2.128–30), Alonso's trespass speech and Prospero's "the rarer action"—and a charged expression of loss—Caliban's dream speech (the loss of imaginary riches), Alonso's trespass speech (the loss of his son and self) and Prospero's renunciation speech (the loss of his magic). The parallel structures emphasize that each of the three performances causes a pyschic storm and that Prospero is as susceptible as the other characters, though he resolves the disturbance in himself. A more detailed look at the scenes will confirm and extend their similarities.

The drunkenness of Caliban's crew (2.2) is paired with a simple two-part performance by Ariel: a mimicked voice and a mimicked song (3.2). We expect from the paradigm some tempestuousness, and here it is the "beating," an attribute of the storm that is mental for Miranda and Prospero (1.1.176–77 and 4.1.164) but fittingly physical in the case of Stephano and Trinculo. The physical spirits of alcohol consumed by Caliban in the central, repeated gesture of 2.2 (86 & 94 of 187) have their effect of mistaken identities dramatized and their corresponding physical effect in the central beating of Trinculo (3.2.76 of 152). The second part of Ariel's performance, the song, is described by Trinculo as "the tune of our catch, played by the "picture of Nobody" (3.2.126), (i.e., it is another mimicry and, like Gonzalo's Golden

Age, is produced by another "nothing"). Stephano and Trinculo have brief attacks of conscience. "O, forgive me my sins!" Trinculo exclaims, and Stephano prays, "Mercy on us!" (128–30). Caliban has the requisite elevated imagining. He generalizes the tune to other noises and sweet airs on the island and makes what is usually judged his most poetic speech, ending:

> ... in dreaming,
> The clouds methought would open and show riches
> Ready to drop upon me, that, when I waked,
> I cried to dream again [3.2.140–43].

The riches Caliban dreams ready to drop on him recall the crown Antonio sees descending on Sebastian and, further, the cloud Trinculo imagined as "a foul bombard" ready to "shed its [celestial] liquor," that is, its spirits of alcohol, whose place has been supplemented in this scene by the mimicry of Ariel. The image of rich clouds and fleeting dreams anticipates Prospero's revels speech and, with the structural parallels, suggest that Prospero's magic is analogous to Caliban's dreams.

Similarly act three, scene three, has a two-part performance divided by a central storm, as mentioned above. The illusory banquet elaborates Gonzalo's earlier description of the Golden Age, the central vision of the paired scene, in which

> nature should bring forth,
> Of its own kind, all foison, all abundance,
> To feed my innocent people [2.1.163–65 of 327].

The banquet vanishing in thunder and lightning makes clear that—as Gonzalo said of his description of the Golden Age—such fantasies are "nothing." It is also a fitting first performance for Prospero to stage, since it subjects the King's party to exactly the deprivation he suffered. Following the central storm, Ariel as a harpy gives the second part of the performance, his accusatory speech, after which Alonso exclaims,

> the thunder,
> The deep and dreadful organ pipe, pronounced
> The name of Prosper; it did bass my trespass.
> Therefore my son i' th' ooze is bedded; and
> I'll seek him deeper than e'er plummet sounded
> And with him there lie mudded [3.3.97–102].

Alonso projects both his guilt and his grief; in his own person he has both the attack of conscience and the expression of loss that were divided among Caliban's crew.

Prospero's Major Speeches

In act four and part of act five exactly the same pattern as in the last two scenes of act three will be repeated. A prologue, a two-part performance (of masque and hunt) with a central "storm" between and a concluding two-part response—an examination of conscience ("the rarer action") and a speech of loss (the renunciation speech). There are two variations to be noted. The prologue to the masque includes not only a review of the lovers' courtship (predictable because the paired scene is of their meeting) but a brief declaration by Prospero of his love for Ariel, suggesting that the masque will also bear on the magician's love for his books and his spirits. Secondly, the metaphorical storm dividing the two performances in act four includes the speeches by Prospero—the revels speech and the nature/nurture speech—expressing his troubled relationships with spirits and with Caliban. These speeches finally reveal Prospero's fallible humanity, his illusory divinities and devil comparable to those of the other characters.

That Prospero's disquiet is a storm is confirmed, again, by the stage directions centrally located in the act and by Prospero's self-described "beating mind" (163) and "vexed" (158) feelings, adjectives associated with the storm. He is stirred both by the thought of Caliban's conspiracy and by reflection on the masque, by the devilish and the (falsely) divine. Remembering Caliban's plot, Prospero suffers, in Ferdinand's words, "some passion that works him strongly" (143–44), and Miranda adds that she has never seen her father so angry. It is not so much the plot as his own forgetfulness, his "transport" by the show, that angers Prospero. Yet he immediately forgets about Caliban again, becoming disturbed by Ferdinand's emotion. Projecting his own engagement with spirits, Prospero takes Ferdinand's dismay as regret that the masque is over. "You do look, my son," Prospero says,

> in a moved sort,
> As if you were dismayed. Be cheerful, sir.
> Our revels now are ended. These our actors,
> As I foretold you, were all spirits, and
> Are melted into air... [4.1.146–50].

Prospero intends a consolatory distinction here between illusion and reality but becomes caught up himself, eradicating the distinction he intended to maintain:

> These our actors,
> As I foretold you, were all spirits, and
> Are melted into air, into thin air;
> And, like the baseless fabric of this vision,
> The cloud-capped towers, the gorgeous palaces,
> The solemn temples, the great globe itself,
> Yea, all which it inherit, shall dissolve,
> And, like this insubstantial pageant faded,
> Leave not a rack behind [4.1.147–56].

In this one brilliant sentence that we too read as both the real world and the world of cloudy nothings, Prospero confuses reality and unreality, the globe and the Globe. Life seems to him at that moment nothing more than an evanescent fancy. Prospero is "transported and rapt" in the metaphysical tempest that has once before cost him his kingdom, as in a comic key it threatens to do now. It is, as the hermetic tradition calls it, his "hodos chameliontis," the path of the chameleon, in which everything slips and slides and shifts and merges, in which all is flux, dissolving into nothing. The momentary madness of Prospero is also confirmed by the imagery of the speech. His metaphor of the world as clouds and of clear sky as nothingness denies the whole force and cumulative imagery of the play. A cloudless sky, clear weather, is symbolic of a "clear life" (3.3.82), free of the storms of guilt, illusion and uncontrolled passions. Prospero's persistence in equating clouds and reality indicates his own continued susceptibility to spirits. The fact that the speech is so admired—it has been called "the Beatific vision of the greatest of all dramatic poets," for example—is itself confirmation of Shakespeare's success in presenting the attraction of a world of spirits. But the revels speech is an expression of the very danger Prospero has been laboring to overcome through the whole play: a metaphysical nihilism. The speech is comparable to the climactic speeches of the great tragic heroes, to the tempest in Lear's mind that would "strike flat the thick rotundity of the world," to Macbeth's vision of life as meaningless, signifying nothing. Even more devastatingly, Prospero's inner storm annihilates all existence.

The implication of Prospero's slide into confusion is that the spirits were the world to him. His love of them lost Prospero the world he is now laboring to regain. Thus his abrupt lecture to Ferdinand and Miranda on chastity is not unmotivated. It comes after a moment of weakness toward Ariel. "Do you love me, Master?" Ariel asks. "Dearly," Prospero replies (4.1.48–49); and, recalling what the love of spirits cost him, Prospero immediately lectures the lovers on the fire in the blood (51). Here as elsewhere we can see one aspect of what Ariel means to Prospero—a beloved. And as spirits provided a comfort against death for the other characters, Ariel and the other spirits provide Prospero with an illusory power over death, as I will show in examining his renunciation speech. Even at the opening of the play the spirits mean so much to him that Prospero can speak in the present tense of "volumes that I prize above my dukedom" (1.2.167–68). Apparently we can take him at his word when he tells Miranda he has done "nothing but in care of thee" (1.2.16); it is not primarily the desire for his dukedom that motivates him but his concern for Miranda. For her sake he will leave Ariel behind and embrace the world. Something of the loss he suffers can be inferred from the drowning analogies I have already mentioned. The drowning of the book that has given Prospero power over the spirits is linked with the imagined drowning of Ferdinand that prompts Alonso to talk of suicide; and Stephano's drowned bottle is an "infinite loss" (4.1.210). Even the tonalities of these losses—mistaken grief and comic exaggeration—seem to inhere in the parallel loss of Prospero's magic, his loss of Ariel, as nuances in the tone of the renunciation speech.

Furthermore, Prospero's own identity is as precarious as his grasp of the world. After dismissing the whole globe as no more than fleeting clouds, Prospero extends the idea of a basic insubstantiality to human identity as well: "We are such stuff as dreams are made on" (4.1.156–57). We easily grant his inclusive pronoun because we have seen all the characters transformed by spirits of one kind or another. Not only the spirit-actors make dreams on them, but the spirits of alcohol, the "nimble spirits" of ambition, the thunderous spirits of guilty consciences and the seeming spirits of the opposite sex—each has caused a change of identity. But to think of Prospero as detached and omniscient here, as articulating some lovely truth about the human condition, is impossible given the dramatic situation and Prospero's own explicit self-description: "I am vexed" (58); he must walk to still his "beating mind" (63). In the midst of this tempest he is transformed from the careful father and adept magus who, only minutes before, seemed so admirable. Now Miranda and Ferdinand hardly know him. The other losses Prospero has suffered—of social identity, of his identity as friend, as brother, as subject—are addressed as he recovers them in act five; but clearly he is even here speaking out of his own experience of spirits in saying that our identities are as shadows, mutable as dreams.

It is also worth noting that, gorgeous as it is, and as delightfully expressive of the union of heaven and earth in Juno and Ceres, the masque itself, like all the illusions of the play, is pointedly disordered. The exclusion of Venus and her son, elaborating Prospero's previous warning to Ferdinand, is an overcompensation for the fiery passion—both lust and anger are figured as fire—of the opening tempest in which Ariel, embodying his master's fancy, appeared as fire. The wished-for year without a winter is another obvious truncation of reality. Most significantly, the masque will appear even more blatantly artificial and irrelevant in retrospect, when Alonso confers his blessing on the couple by taking their hands. Thus the consummate performance of the play, while heightening the enchantment of illusion, also insists on the disorder and unreality of art.

The thought of Caliban continues the storm in Prospero. He describes Caliban as "a born devil on whose nature Nurture can never stick" (4.1.188–89). This judgment is contradicted at the end of the play. When Prospero is himself (i.e., the Duke of Milan), Caliban recognizes "how fine" his "master" is, and not merely because of the change of clothes (5.1.262). Caliban also sees himself clearly—"a thrice-triple ass … to take this drunkard for a god"— and intends to "be wise" and "seek for grace" (295–97). Caliban's conversion is further confirmed by his final willing service (5.1.295), in obvious contrast to his earlier rebelliousness. By every measure of the play Caliban is capable of nurture. By insisting that Caliban is uneducable, Prospero is reacting to his own failure, evaded by imagining Caliban to be a "born devil."

What accounts for Prospero's anger? Caliban is heir to all the impulses of the flesh, of course, and his instinct to procreate has expressed itself toward Miranda. But Caliban also bears Prospero's projected fear of old age, that human reality on which nurture can truly never stick, and by extension of all the ravages of time. "As with age his body uglier grows, So his mind cankers" (4.1.188–89). Prospero punishes Caliban and the crew with his own fearful fancies: "Grind their joints With dry convulsions, shorten up their sinews With aged cramps," (4.1.258–59) acting out the threats of the paired scene: "I'll rack thee with old cramps" (1.2.369). It is this symbol of aging, this embodiment of wasting time (in both senses of the phrase) that Prospero attacks with his spirit-hounds.

The hunt is his catharsis. Between acts four and five he is transformed from detached manipulator, above the action, suppressing his emotions, to engaged and enraged pursuer, from director to actor. According to Andrew Gurr, this act break is unique in Shakespeare in that the same characters leave and re-enter.[6] Clearly, such a decisive break is not warranted by the plot action. It is however warranted by the psychological change in Prospero, a change that is confirmed not only by the difference in him when he re-enters but also by the corresponding change in Ariel, who is uncharacteristically sympathetic toward the sufferings of the King's party. It is not, as some critics have said, that Prospero is guided to some more human feeling by the example of Ariel; it is rather that Ariel had witnessed the humanity— the outraged mortality—of Prospero during the hunt. This spectacle, in which Prospero and Ariel are more than anywhere else in the play equals and equally active, provides the first instance of his master's humanity and fellowship, provides a new script for Ariel. And he may also be brought to a new awareness of himself precisely as not human by Prospero's mirroring of Ariel's earlier mischief. Prospero, on the other hand, has finally become an actor, a word that holds in perfect suspension the simultaneous doubleness of art and nature that could serve as the epitome of the whole play.

Purged of his fear of old age by participation in the hunt, Prospero becomes accepting of it. After Gonzalo, another earthy character like Caliban, is released from the charm, Prospero will say, "Let me embrace thine age" (5.1.121). Even more expansively, he will embrace the "body" of the king (111). As the symbol in Prospero's mind of the body in time, of the inevitability of death, Caliban is a "thing of darkness" (275), a phrase that resonates with the play's complex associations not only of "the dead of darkness" (1.2.130) but also of sleep and dreams and midnight elves, suggesting that the "devil" Prospero sees is simply one more hellish illusion. In fact, in acknowledging Caliban as his own, Prospero may be accepting responsibility for the thing of darkness as his own failed creation. At any rate, the acceptance of Caliban is a necessary accompaniment of Prospero's renunciation of magic, his immersion in emotion and action and his acceptance of his own inevitable death.

While the psychological change in Prospero is accurately signaled by the act break, the structural parallels with the earlier performances are preserved by the re-entry of the same characters, for Prospero will now react to the two-part performance he has just staged and acted in as have Caliban's crew and Alonso earlier, by examining his conscience and by suffering a profound loss. In taking the side of his reason against his fury he successfully harmonizes a disordered conscience; in renouncing his magic, he willingly suffers what is to him a profound loss, the loss of the world of spirits, epitomized in Ariel.

The opening of act five (5.1.1–57) resolves the relationship with Ariel and with spirits generally that was first introduced in the paired scene of act one (1.2.187–304). Both scenes contain three broadly similar elements—Ariel reports the effect of a charm on the King's party; he requests his liberty when Prospero asks for the time; and Prospero discourses about magic. As a consequence of the hunt though, the tone of the scenes is markedly different. Instead of the gleefulness of his earlier account of his shipboard mischief Ariel now expresses sympathy for the sorrowing company. In place of the rage Prospero expressed when Ariel earlier requested his freedom, there is simple confirmation, with no sign of the emotion elsewhere attendant on the loss. And whatever the tone of the renunciation speech it has none of the accusatory anger Prospero directed toward Ariel when reminding him about Sycorax. The cathartic hunt has made Prospero almost genial.

The renunciation speech is his consummate bit of verbal legerdemain. The sticking point of the speech is Prospero's statement that "graves at my command have waked their sleepers, oped, and let 'em forth By my so potent art" (5.1.48–50). Prospero's claim speaks to the Renaissance belief in the possibility of such occult powers. But in the renunciation speech he is clearly "boasting off" his illusory life as he did his daughter earlier. It is a last self-indulgence, a theatrical display with the magus's usual panoply. He inscribes a magic circle and invokes the spirits, invokes them in their most folkloric and in their most sublime guises, in their most earthy and most celestial forms, as elves and as "heavenly music," an "air" as rarified as the music of the spheres (5.1.52 & 58). Prospero here recalls with gusto the whole spectrum of his illusions and rejects them with determination, just as he had earlier taken the part of his reason against his fury "though strook to th' quick" then too (5.1.25).

Prospero's characterization of the elves in his invocation suggests both the nature of his magic and his momentary self-indulgence. They include spirits of night and the moon, reinforcing, as does the paraphrase of Medea's speech from Ovid, the similarity between Prospero's magic and Sycorax's. In their "natural state" elves are innocuous earth and water spirits, such as Ariel will revert to when he is out of harness, of a size to ride a bat's back. They are "demi-puppets" (5.1.36) unless worked by the magus into full-sized puppets, as in the "living drollery" of the banquet (3.3.21). "Weak masters" (5.1.41), however, they are not. Prospero has lost everything because of his susceptibility to them, and his momentary loss of control in the revels speech indicates that the spirits are still capable of "moving" him, of transporting him.

His present nonchalance about the potency of spirits is a kind of dizzy self-congratulation at his imminent success. "Weak masters" is the first of the increasingly grandiose statements in the speech until Prospero finally claims power over death.

The main thrust of the speech is that he has caused storms. After the invocation of the elves, he details his magic:

> I have bedimmed
> The noontide sun, called forth the mutinous winds,
> And 'twixt the green sea and the azured vault
> Set roaring war; to the dread rattling thunder
> Have I given fire and rifted Jove's stout oak
> With his own bolt; the strong-based promontory
> Have I made shake and by the spurs plucked up
> the pine and cedar [5.1.41–48].

This is only to present in overheated rhetoric the central illusion of the play (which was probably written expressly for performance at the Blackfriars, where the noontime sun would indeed be dimmed), and to present it in exactly the metaphors of conspiracy, war and fire that the harmony of the subsequent spell is meant to assuage. In his summarizing phrase, after he has taken pause, Prospero calls his power "rough magic" (50), recalling the storm with considerably less vanity. As he had before equated clouds with reality in the revels speech, so Prospero does now; here however he is not confused but is glorying in the illusions he has created. Having no stage audience to whom any distinction must be made, Prospero speaks from inside the illusion of magical omnipotence.

As he did in the earlier performances, Prospero is enacting his present fancies in the renunciation speech. In his soliloquy "thought is free," (as it was earlier, more comically, for Stephano, 3.2.123), and the artist who has created the masque and the banquet shows no more concern for literal truth now. In the moment of success he speaks metaphorically and without hesitation claims that are literally untrue but perfectly expressive of his feeling of success, of having come back to life. And here he is—to be strictly and rigorously factual about it—lying and malignant, as he accused Ariel of being (1.2.257), false in his claims and, in the most common Renaissance meaning of "malignant," a rebel against the natural order of things. Because of the doubt in the Renaissance mind as to the extent of the magus's powers, the renunciation speech is similar to the "statue" by "Julio Romano" in *The Winter's Tale*—a marvel given credibility because of its extra-theatrical currency—and the play's spectrum of artifice easily shades into outright deception. Like Ariel and like Antonio Prospero, too, is a "deceiver," now of the theater audience as he was earlier of his stage audiences. In his soliloquy he gives his last and most convincing performance: that of the omnipotent magus. His next presentation will be of himself as "sometime Milan" (5.1.86), the first of the visions of reality (to use another of Yeats's phrases) ending the play.

Visions of Reality

All storms are quieted and illusions cleared in the spell-stopped tableau.

> A solemn air, and the best comforter
> To an unsettled fancy... [5.1.58–9].

The "solemn air," just referred to as "heavenly music" (52), is a rendering of the music of the spheres. "Air," earlier said of Ariel as both element and song, has now become (comforting) ethereal music. The spirits are metamorphosed from their various illusory manifestations into the high reality of Ptolemaic harmony. The "heavenly music" and "solemn air" bring the influence of the auspicious star, the immutable and translunar, to the tempestuous and sublunar within the characters, stilling finally the storms of the play.

Having rejected the spirits, Prospero must now people his interior life with flesh and blood. While the king's company are cured of their fancies and restored to their senses, Prospero accomplishes the correspondence of above and below within himself as well. In renouncing magic Prospero has rejected the "false celestial," figured, for example, in the goddesses of the masque. He has now to find an earthly divinity to replace it; like Ferdinand he has to fall in love, so to speak, with the human and the mundane, a caritas to parallel Ferdinand's eros. He finds the epitome of heaven and earth in "Holy Gonzalo" (5.1.62), the man of "charity" (1.2.162) who has from the opening tempest been associated with earth and who like Miranda has been most notable for his compassion.

Upon seeing Gonzalo Prospero cries "fellowly drops" (5.1.64), releasing his long-confined emotions. Here his woodenness ends, for like Ferdinand and Caliban Prospero is also a "logman" (3.1.67). He describes his brother's usurpation: "he was The ivy which had hid my princely trunk And sucked the verdure out on't" (1.2.85–87). Caliban appropriately wants to "knock a nail into his [Prospero's] head" (3.2.61). Prospero has been no more than fantasies and wood, a "living drollery" (3.3.21) in his own person as well as in the "demi-puppets" (5.1.36) he has directed. But with the fulfillment of his labor, Prospero is able to "discase" himself and as a "living prince" embrace the king (5.1.85 and 108).

Prospero's woodenness further suggests a similarity with Ariel's confinement in a pine tree. As Miranda imagines her own compassion even in logs, which, burning, will weep for Ferdinand, Prospero threatens to peg Ariel in "the knotty entrails" of an oak (1.2.295). (The comic version of this anthropomorphism of wood is in the scene with Mistress Line.) The 12 years of Ariel's confinement matches the length of Prospero's confinement on the island with only his daughter, Caliban and deceptive spirits that hate him "rootedly" (3.2.95). Something of Prospero's unexplained pain and rage can be imagined by this tint in his portrait that suggests comparison with the howling of the imprisoned Ariel.

After his apostrophe to Gonzalo Prospero accomplishes his last interior alignment of above with below in taking the part of his "nobler reason" (5.1.26) against his fury, as he explained earlier to Ariel, by forgiving Alonso, Sebastian, and his "flesh and blood" (74), his brother. Prospero thus harmonizes the microcosm of himself with the Ptolemaic macrocosm; his stellar reason stills his sublunar and tempestuous passions.

When the spell clears, Prospero expresses his newly attained harmony in his actions toward the characters of the King's party, repeating the steps of his inner ordering in a different sequence since public priorities take precedence now over private feeling. He first embraces the king, righting in typically Shakespearean fashion order and degree. (The implicit act of forgiveness goes graciously unmentioned.) He next embraces Gonzalo and finally, after revealing his knowledge of their plot to Antonio and Sebastian, forgives his brother. Having attuned himself to the cosmic order and embraced the representatives of the world—having, that is to say, attained the Nuptials of the hermetic tradition—Prospero is now himself again. The recovery of his identity is at the exact center of act five: "I am Prospero" (159 of 319).

There immediately follows the "vision" of Ferdinand and Miranda playing chess, the public enactment of the marriage agreement central in the play. In place of the illusions midpoint in each of the three preceding scenes, Prospero now presents a reality so wonderful as to seem a vision. It is the issue of Prospero's labor, and it has been earned as well by Alonso, who has expressed a willingness to sacrifice himself that the two children might live (5.1.149–52), thus attaining the self-sacrificial love that has marked the lovers and, by inference, Prospero's self-sacrifice for his daughter. The discovery of the pair is not only positioned but also structured as a kind of sketched variation on the previous performances. There is a prologue, a two-part performance with a storm reference between, and a two-part reaction—celestial imagining and guilty conscience. But in this instance the art is dissolved, almost invisible, befitting the play's re-entry into reality. Prospero prefaces the discovery (165–171), Ferdinand and Miranda are disclosed wrangling for the world (reconciling the themes of courtship and conspiracy), the storm is alluded to ("the seas threaten" but "are merciful" [178]) and the second part of the "performance" follows, the young couple viewing the "audience," which has now become the show: "O brave new world" (5.1.183). Alonso expresses both the mistaken divinity reaction ("Is she the goddess…? [187]) and the guilty conscience we have come to expect: "I Must ask my child forgiveness" (197–8). Alonso is corrected in the first mistake by Ferdinand and immediately halted from his guilt by Prospero: "There, sir, stop. Let us not burden our remembrances" (198). Reality and calm prevail.

Of all the lovely intricacies of *The Tempest* none is lovelier than the play's delicate treatment of the human body, of the "rising senses" (5.1.66), as the storms of illusion clear. Though through act four there is more than a little focus on the excrementitious and on the pain and deformity of aging, there is a corresponding affection in the last act for the small manifestations of life, reminiscent in its intimacy, if not in its tone, of the focus on Cordelia's breath at the end of *King Lear*. Most commentators for example have noted the way the "beating" of the storm is modulated through the play, occurring as both a physical and mental rhythm. The varying "beatings" of Trinculo and of the storm in Prospero's and Miranda's minds are the most obvious instances. But the range of the rhythm, whether spoken or enacted, is much wider. Its fullest orchestration is in the stage action of the opening storm, and its diminuendo is in the references to the beating of the pulse in the last act. Free of physical limitations, free in the insouciant unreality of spirit time, Ariel can say he will return "Or ere your pulse twice beat" (103). By contrast a few lines later the king, assuring himself of the reality of Prospero, says, "Thy pulse Beats as of flesh and blood; and since I saw thee, Th' affliction of my mind amends" (113–15).

Through the same kinds of subtle associational shifts that give the whole play its metamorphic shimmer, Alonso's reference to the blood beating at the pulse resolves not only the beating of the storm but the imagery of fire as well. Initially fire symbolizes anger. The first conversation between Ariel and Prospero reveals that the opening tempest is a fiery expression of Prospero's fury, causing the fever and infection of madness. Ariel manifested himself on shipboard exclusively as fire, and Miranda confirms the fire in her description of the storm. In a minor key, Caliban is sometimes tormented by spirits as firebrands (2.2.6) and reciprocally wishes the "red plague" (1.2.364) on Prospero, recalling the fiery infection of the tempest. Act four associates fire with lust, most famously in Prospero's warning to Ferdinand against "th' fire i' th' blood" (4.1.53). This association is extended in "Mars's hot minion," (98), which also begins to intertwine conspiracy and courtship, and in "dusky Dis" (89), suggesting both "dark" and "sooty"; suggesting, that is, how lust smoke-blackened the abductor of Persephone. (As part of the masque these images are of course Prospero's and comment however elliptically on the "thing of darkness," Caliban, who makes the fire and has tried to rape Miranda.) Even as the masque is being performed, Caliban's crew is also enacting in their usual slapstick mode and at a metaphoric remove a violent reaction to love. "Red-hot with drinking," as Ariel reports,

> "they smote the air
> For breathing in their faces; beat the ground
> For kissing of their feet" [171–73].

All these images—"red-hot," "red plaque," "fever of the mad"—are variants of the fire in the blood, both fury and lust. The conflation of the two is succinctly presented in the moment discussed above when Stephano says to Caliban: "Give me thy hand, I do begin to have bloody thoughts" (220–21). This marriage in blood, recalling the parallel moment in the other conspiracy plot, is the final outcome of the fiery tempests and feverish infections of spirits. In Alonso's recognition of the beating pulse of flesh and blood, the psychic storms of anger and of lust—the excesses of conspiracy and courtship—are both calmed to the rhythm of the one reality the play insists on, the felt pulse of quotidian human life.

Furthermore the sense of sight, which has been so much abused by spirits, is now once again trustworthy; as the charm dissolves, the "eyes do offices of truth" (5.1.156). The sight of Prospero cures Alonso's affliction. In a variation of Miranda's wonder at the "goodly creatures" she sees, even Trinculo has his eyes opened: "If these be true spies which I wear in my head, here's a goodly sight" (260). The old strains persist of course in Trinculo's use of the word "spies," suggesting militancy and conspiracy. But in this as in so much else the play discriminates differences of degree as much as of kind and modulates into reality, asking us to find in the unemphasized activities of "day by day" (163) the same impulses previously dramatized on a grander scale in the play. Prospero's inner life, most significantly, will no longer be projected in fantasies enacted by spirit-actors; instead he will tell the story of his life (305 and 313) in his own person and that alone will "Take the ear strangely" (314). In a simple face-to-face narrative are resolved all the angst and effort, all the turbulence of noise and emotion, that have been enacted by the spirits in the play. In the theater of day by day, of eros and caritas, the "fringed curtains" of the "eye advance" (1.2.409). In love Ferdinand and Miranda "chang'd eyes" (1.2.442); in charity Prospero's eyes, "e'en sociable to the show" of Gonzalo's, weep "fellowly drops" (5.1.63–64). The human spirit enacts its subtle dramas in the theater of the eyes.

The final appearance of the boat's crew and Caliban's crew function as codas, restating at their simplest the binding and loosing of spirits: in sleep and in drunkenness. Indeed, the comic coda sums up the effects of spirits not merely loosed but riotous. Seeing Caliban and the others reeling and covered with pond scum, Alonso asks, "Where should they Find this grand liquor that hath gilded 'em?" (5.1.279–80). The King's pun on "gilded," referring to both their flushed drunkenness and the "gilt" coating Trinculo had called "horse-piss" (4.1.199), deftly expresses the falsely golden condition—inner and outer—induced by spirits of all kinds, not only the spirits of "grand liquor." And the efficacy of spirits against death is also comically deflated in Trinculo's, "I have been in such a pickle since I saw you last that, I fear me, will never out of my bones. I shall not fear flyblowing." (282–284). Trinculo's image of flyblowing recalls Ferdinand's contrasting use of the image in his pivotal speech of willing self-sacrifice (3.1.63). Trinculo's joke puts in comic perspective all the illusory attempts to avoid death rather than accept its reality. Gilded and pickled, the three clownish conspirators are the final physical demonstration of transport by spirits.

Acceptance of death and freedom from spirits are exactly the points of the last lines of Prospero's last two speeches in the play proper. Having forgiven his "flesh and blood," embraced Gonzalo's "age" and the king's "body," having acknowledged the "thing of darkness" as his own, and facing the "loss" of his daughter, Prospero can credibly say, "Every third thought shall be my grave" (5.1.312). Finally, with the simple and poignant gesture that ends the play proper, Prospero turns from Ariel—"Fare thou well"—to the King's company—"Please you, draw near" (319).

The paradigmatic presence of spirits that I have tried to trace through the main parts of the play seems to me the essential analogy ordering and proportioning the many other analogies so often intuited by critics, especially analogies between Prospero and the other characters. Identical in their subjection to spirits, it is no surprise that the characters resemble one another in their actions, Prospero above all. He is like Alonso in having usurped another's (i.e., Caliban's) kingdom. He has waked an evil nature in Antonio, as we see Antonio doing in turn to Sebastian. He weeps as Miranda does, finally having the "virtue of compassion" (1.2.27) touched in him. He "moves wood," as do Ferdinand and Caliban. He has his own visions of a devil and of divinities, as others do. And so on, it seems, inexhaustibly. And each analogous detail carries its own shading of emphasis and irony. For example, the courtships are reflected and refracted through parodies, inversions and other variants: the love of Caliban for Stephano and of Stephano and Trinculo for the bottle; the love of Alonso for his son; the largely ineffectual love (i.e., charity) of Gonzalo toward Prospero; the lurking sexuality of Antonio's and Sebastian's plot. These are in turn augmented or qualified by the merely verbal references to still other marriages and couplings—the marriage of Claribel and the abduction of Persephone; the unrealized parodic coupling of Stephano and Miranda, the allusions to Aeneas and Dido, and so on. Through verbal echoes, parallel incidents, analogies at one or two removes, all of these "loves" are more or less brought to bear on Prospero's love for Ariel and his competing courtship of his "dear lady," his fortune—as contrast, as similarity, as contextual coloring. Or consider the analogy with Caliban alluded to above. Prospero, who loves his books above his dukedom and is transported and rapt (from the same root as "rapid") in secret studies, can be said to have "kissed the book," to have been drunk on his spirits as Caliban is reeling drunk on the spirits of the bottle; in his aptly-designated "revels" speech we witness Prospero's intellectual inebriation. Such analogies are endless, dizzying. The fullness, depth, proportioning and detail of Prospero's portrait depends finally on our perception of the entire drama. In the human universe of the play, a commonplace of the Ptolemaic tradition is beautifully realized: the macrocosm and microcosm are joined in Prospero.

It is often commented that Shakespeare uncharacteristically adhered to the classical unities in writing *The Tempest*. More to the point is the fact that the stage time of the play coincides with the real time of the audience. Prospero's afternoon on the island parallels the audience's afternoon in the theater. We have been transported and rapt, possessed by spirits, just as the characters of the play have been. Like them we have been variously engulfed in a storm, drunk with delight, transported with admiration (or woodenly laboring to understand) but in any case subject to an illusion. And when Prospero asks to be released from our spell, it is as a beloved Ariel that he does so. The whole play thus becomes the last of a series of increasingly sophisticated illusions, a series of tempests that now extends to *The Tempest*. In freeing Prospero with the help of our good hands, we are like him foreswearing the isolate illusions of art to return to the peace of the present, to the communal lives we live in charity and mutual forgiveness.

Appendix:
Narrative Analyses

It is universally agreed that Shakespeare's plays are designed in two movements, a rising and a falling action. The turn from one to the other is usually located in the approximate middle, coinciding with or in proximity to a point of "climax" or "crisis." This generalization is subtly varied from one critic to another as they focus on different aspects of the narrative, and consequently provides no precise indication of either the midpoint or the turn. To give some idea of the differing approaches, I will look briefly at the analyses of Gustave Freytag, A. C. Bradley, Emrys Jones, Bernard Beckerman and Richard Moulton.

The "triangle" of Gustave Freytag originated this approach and still approximates the general consensus. It is worth reproducing here as a point of departure.

climax

rising action   falling action

exposition   catastrophe

The diagram is based on the opposing forces of the conflict. The 'triangle' describes the 'rising' and 'falling' movements: the hero's world-affecting action and the world's hero-affecting action in return. The hero's exertion of force in the first movement, "the play," calls forth a "counter-play," the response of the world to the hero. The turn is the climax. A. C. Bradley varies this. He uses the word 'crisis' rather than 'climax' to designate the turning point and defines it as the point at which the protagonist attains his greatest triumph. This is very close to Freytag, except that the hero's continuing exertion of force may be self-destructive instead of triumphal. Consequently, Bradley isolates different turning points than Freytag in some cases. Though they agree that the nomination of Coriolanus to a consulship and the assassination of Caesar are the turning points in their respective dramas, they disagree about the turn in *Macbeth*. Freytag sees the banquet scene as the climax; Bradley chooses the coronation as the crisis. Similarly, Bradley designates the wedding ceremony in *Romeo and Juliet* as the turning point (since the subsequent killing of Tybalt is part of Romeo's decline) whereas Freytag designates the consummation of the marriage.

Emrys Jones bases his analysis of two-part structure not so much on the opposing forces of the conflict as on narrative continuity, most clearly indicated by the interval in performance. He is not interested in the climax or crisis but in the full resolution of the first part of the action. Naturally he finds different dividing points than Freytag and Bradley. It is not the

221

assassination of Caesar or even the funeral speeches that mark for Jones the point at which the first part of *Julius Caesar* ends. It is rather the meeting of the three principals that rounds out the "Rome" action; the scene of Brutus and Cassius in camp begins the second part of the play, which takes place in Sardinia. The second part of *Macbeth* begins for Jones not immediately after the coronation or the banquet but at the re-appearance of the witches in 4.1. (He ignores the Hecate scene as an "excrescence."). The second part of *Coriolanus* begins with the conversation between a Roman spy and a Volsce in 4.3, which signals, for Jones, the beginning of Coriolanus's change in allegiance.

Bernard Beckerman attempts to consider structure as dependent on both narrative continuity and conflicting forces. He distinguishes a "narrative line" ("what happens") and a "dramatic line" ("what the characters undergo"). (These terms coincide with what Una Ellis-Fermor has called the "outer plot" and the "inner plot," but she does not pursue the distinction though entire plays, as Beckerman does.) The narrative progresses linearly to the end, whereas "the dramatic line extends to heights of passion at the center of the play." At the dramatic center Beckerman finds a central plateau rather than a single scene of climax or crisis. In *Coriolanus*, for example, the scene in which Coriolanus is named to a consulship is not the turning point because it is less emotionally intense than the dispute with the Tribunes immediately after. But that dispute is "blunted" because two scenes later the same stage action occurs—a dispute with the Tribunes. Though Coriolanus is banished in the latter scene, neither scene functions effectively as a decisive climax for Beckerman. There is then no single point of demarcation between the two parts of the play but rather a "plateau."

Richard Moulton uses spatial terms in his commentary, but figuratively, since his analyses are based on the same idea of conflicting forces used by Freytag and Bradley. In spite of his terminology, that is, Moulton also sees the action as a temporal unfolding, not as a spatial pattern. In *Macbeth*, however, unlike Freytag and Bradley, Moulton finds the scene of Banquo's murder to be the climax, "the keystone of the arch." It is the point at which Macbeth's successes are at their apex since the murder of Banquo goes off as planned. But Macbeth's downfall is implicit in the same scene because Fleance escapes. In *Julius Caesar* Moulton finds the turning point in the entrance of Antony's servant to the conspirators immediately after the assassination.

Each of these analyses makes its own contribution to our understanding of the narrative shape of individual Shakespeare plays, but none addresses the unvarying thematic structure of paired, reflecting scenes underlying the narrative.

Chapter Notes

Preface

1. Tillyard, *Shakespeare's History Plays*, 218; Melchiori, *Arden Merry Wives*, 32; Bradley, *Shakespearean Tragedy*, 260.

Chapter 1

1. See the Appendix for samples of narrative analysis.

2. Emrys Jones (*Scenic Design*, 82, 81) places the end of the first part of *Troilus and Cressida*, for example, after the eighth of 23 scenes and that of *Coriolanus* after the 18th of 29 scenes.

3. Douglas, *Thinking in Circles*, analyzes chiastic structures from different literatures. For a sampling of the extensive work on chiasmus, particularly in ancient literatures, see Welch, *Chiasmus Bibliography*.

4. For instances of Shakespeare's rhetorical chiasmus, see William L. Davis, "Structural Secrets." And see below.

5. Garber, *Shakespeare After All*, 179.

6. Emrys Jones, *Scenic Design*, 24–25.

7. Rose, *Shakespearean Design*, 36–38.

8. The distinction between a linear narrative structure and a chiastic thematic structure in the plays has an interesting parallel in the sonnets, as analyzed by Helen Vendler (*The Art of Shakespeare's Sonnets*, 29, 30): Shakespeare's "second preferred figure, chiasmus, contends in the sonnets against the natural formulation of a sentence (linear, temporal, ongoing).... It is always worth noting ... whether a Shakespearean statement is being made 'linearly,' in a first-order experiential and 'spontaneous' way, or whether it is being made chiastically, in a second order analytical way. These represent very different stances within the speaker."

9. The *Riverside* divides the Folio scene in three; James Hirsch (*The Structure*, 187–88) further divides it into five scenes.

10. The Hallett's (*Analyzing*, 1–10) express in the subtitle of their book—"Scene Versus Sequence"—the either/or approach that has hampered the analysis of Shakespeare's compositional practice. Rather than incorporating Mark Rose's findings (*Shakespearean Design*) on the spatial thematic structure of most scenes, the Hallett's insist on temporal narrative actions as the sole basis of Shakespeare's dramaturgical composition.

11. Burke, *Kenneth Burke*, 202.

12. The distinction between narrative and theme in *Macbeth* and other tragedies, roughly between the storyline and the protagonist's psychological change, is widely recognized. See the Appendix.

13. Fergusson, *The Idea of a Theater*, 17.

14. *Ibid.*

15. Hallett, *Analyzing*, 6–7.

16. Iacoboni, *Mirroring People*, 15.

17. *Ibid.*, 11–12.

18. Beckerman, *Shakespeare at the Globe*, 40, 237, 62.

19. *Ibid.*, 42.

20. It alters one's sense of Shakespeare to know that, of the mature plays, all but four late works (*Macbeth, Cymbeline, Coriolanus* and *Antony and Cleopatra*) are constructed of 9, 15, 17, 19 or 23 scenes. See below, "Scene Division."

Chapter 3

1. Bevington, *New Cambridge Antony and Cleopatra*, 82.

2. Greg, *Shakespeare First Folio*, 142.

3. *Ibid.*, 143.

4. Warren, *Oxford Classics Cymbeline*, 91.

5. Nosworthy, *Arden Cymbeline*, 7.

6. Bevington, *Arden Troilus and Cressida*, 373, LN on scene 5.8.

7. Evans, *Riverside Shakespeare*, 1140.

8. Wells and Taylor, *Textual Companion*, 290.

9. Gibbons, *Arden Romeo and Juliet*, 123, 127.

10. *Ibid.*, 55.

11. *Ibid.*, 41.

12. Levin, "Form and Formality," 281.

13. My reference text is the *Oxford World's Classics* edition, Roger Warren and Stanley Wells, eds. (New York: Oxford University Press, 1994). Other editions referred to are the *Signet* edition, Herschel Baker, ed. (New York: Penguin, 1998); the *Riverside*, G. Blakemore Evans et al., eds. 2nd ed. (Boston: Houghton Mifflin, 1997); and the *Arden*, J.M. Lothian and T.W. Craik, eds. (London: Methuen, 1975).

14. Turner, "The Text of Twelfth Night," 128.

15. Evans, *Riverside Twelfth Night*, 440.

16. Baker, *Signet Twelfth Night*, 105.
17. Warren, *Oxford Twelfth Night*, 52.
18. Evans, *Shakespeare's Comedies*, 133, quoted in *Arden Twelfth Night*, lxxii.
19. Warren, *Oxford Twelfth Night*, 52–53.
20. *Ibid.*, 182.
21. Lothian, *Arden Twelfth Night*, 107, 271–72.

Chapter 4

1. Stanley Wells, "Shakespeare Without Sources," 58–74. Wells also notes the other similarities included in this paragraph, excepting the fact that the plays are all in nine scenes. Wells is among a numbers of editors and critics who disagree with the traditional division of *A Midsummer Night's Dream*. (See Wells and Taylor, *Textual Companion*, 280.) An argument for the traditional division is implicit in my analysis of the play.
2. I have found only one other instance of scenes cross-related in this way—in *King John*, where it seems to structurally signify the fulfillment of actions no longer desired.

Chapter 5

1. Rose, *Shakespearean Design*, 142–43. Rose has tied this symmetry to the central emphasis of most scenes in the play. See the outline later in the essay.
2. Stirling, *Unity in Shakespearian Tragedy*, 34–35.
3. Ure, *Arden Richard II*, "Introduction," *passim*. All citations are from this edition. The reader might also want to compare Ure's division of the play into four "phases" (p. lxii) with the symmetrical outline provided in this essay.
4. Modern texts of *Richard II* are based on the First Quarto, published in 1597, and add the abdication scene from the Folio, which also supplies, with one exception, the act-scene divisions; Capell introduced the necessary, universally accepted break at 5.4.
5. Altick, "Symphonic Imagery"; Spurgeon, *Shakespeare's Imagery*, 233–35.

Chapter 6

1. Granville-Barker, *Prefaces to Shakespeare*, 366.
2. Citations are from the *Arden Merchant of Venice*.
3. Caroline Spurgeon tallies seven food images in the play (*Shakespeare's Imagery*, Appendix, Chart VII). Her analysis considers only the figurative uses of food, of course, but without the larger context of literal references the figurative tally can be seriously misleading.

Chapter 7

1. Rose, *Shakespearean Design*, 152.
2. Humphreys, *Oxford Classics Julius Caesar*, 67. All quotes are form this edition.
3. Daniell, *Arden Julius Caesar*, 75.
4. Underlying the division of scenes into four balanced and four unbalanced pairs is the number symbolism that Thomas McAlindon has traced in the language, staging and symbolism of the play. ("The Numbering of Men," 373–93, esp. 374–75, 378, 384.) In the Pytha-

gorean-Platonic system, McAlindon reminds us, number provides an "immutable, though hidden, cosmic design," and in that system four is "the constitutive number.... The world was held to be a spatio-temporal cosmos of quadripartite design, four being the number of the elements, the humors, the seasons, the ages of man and the cardinal points of the compass. Four was thus the number of opposites reconciled and of natural unity; in ethical terms it signified amity." And, the central point, "the key number in the play is four." Once pointed out, the number four in *Julius Caesar* is as evident as the number three in *Macbeth*: four main characters in Caesar, Cassius, Brutus and Antony who are "broadly identifiable with the four humoral types"; the two balanced marriages; the four Plebeians at the funeral orations (not observed in modern productions); the stage images of various of four "friends" in stable or unstable concord, as Brutus, Cassius, Messala and Titinius around the candle-lit table; the group of four ending the play in a tableaux of reconciliation: Octavius, Antony, Lucilius and Messala; the repeated references to "quartering," and the uses of "forth." McAlindon further demonstrates a second symbolic number in the play used "less insistently": eight, signifying "justice, regeneration and new beginnings." This includes the number of conspirators and the person of Octavius, whose very name functions in the symbolic design. The division of the scenes into four balanced and four unbalanced pairs accords with this number symbolism. Four, the symbol of friendship, and eight, the symbol of new beginnings, structure at every level the cosmos of *Julius Caesar*.
5. Girard, *A Theatre of Envy*, 194.
6. Knight (*The Imperial Theme*) has exhaustively detailed the instances of love in the play, but he makes few critical distinctions among them.
7. Humphreys, *Oxford Classics Julius Caesar*, 17.
8. Thomas North's *Plutarch's Lives of the Noble Grecians and Romanes* (1579), reprinted in *Arden Julius Caesar*, 334. All references to Plutarch are to this edition.
9. Kaula, "'Let Us Be Sacrificers,'" 197–214;
10. Rose, "Conjuring Caesar," 256–69.
11. Bloom, *The Invention of the Human*, 110.
12. Girard, *A Theatre of Envy*, 223, 205.
13. *Ibid.*, 200.
14. Daniell, *Arden Julius Caesar*, 91.
15. Proser, *The Heroic Image*, quoted in Humphreys, 229 n19.
16. Kahn, "A Voluntary Wound," 176.
17. Daniell, *Arden Julius Caesar*, 360–61.
18. Knight, *The Imperial Theme*, 94.
19. Daniell, *Arden Julius Caesar*, 236 n.
20. *Ibid.*, 224; Humphreys, 152.
21. Humphreys, 153.
22. Daniell, *Arden Julius Caesar*, 226.
23. *Ibid.*, 236 n.
24. Humphreys, 161.
25. Evans, *Riverside Shakespeare*, 1164.
26. Simmons (*Shakespeare's Pagan World*, 93) comments perceptively on Caesar's so-called hubris in this scene. "One can regret that for so many critics the irony of Caesar's blindness parodies rather than heightens a tragic effect. Rather than being merely the final justification for the murder, the metaphor of the northern

star has its place both poetically and politically as the one relieving image in the midst of a chaotic state without a fixed point for guidance." Caesar dies, Simmons goes on, "magnificently defending himself from ever being guilty of Brutus's one reason for murdering him: he cannot change."

27. Traversi, *Shakespeare: The Roman Plays*, 46.

28. Daniell, *Arden Julius Caesar*, 36.

29. *Ibid.*, 324.

30. McCallum, *Shakespeare's Roman Plays*, 219.

31. Liebler, "'Bleeding Piece of Earth,'" 175–196, esp. 183.

Chapter 8

1. Honigmann, *Arden King John*, is the staunchest supporter of the opposing view, that Shakespeare's play is earlier than *TR*, as is, among others, L. A. Beaurline (*New Cambridge King John*).

2. Braunmuller, *Oxford World's Classics King John*, 5. All references are to this text.

3. Honigmann, *Arden King John*, lix.

4. Braunmuller, *Oxford King John*, 1.

5. Tillyard, *Shakespeare's History Plays*, 218, 232, 215.

6. See, for example, Barbara Hodgdon in "Fashioning Obedience" (22–43), who finds only a "semblance" of closure. Sigurd Burckhardt in his seminal essay "*King John*: The Ordering of the Present Time" (*Shakespearean Meanings*) concludes that "even bardolaters have little good to say about the last two acts of *King John*. And I strongly suspect that Shakespeare himself knew that he was not bringing the thing off—not because he was bored with a theatrical chore and wanted to finish it quickly and anyhow, but because he saw no way to put Humpty Dumpty together again" (134)—where "Humpty Dumpty" is any traditional order that does not stand up to Shakespeare's "incorruptible and rich sense of reality" (141). Curren-Aquino ("*King John*: A Modern Perspective") finds the ending to be embodied in the Bastard, who remains, as he has been throughout the play, she posits, "liminal."

7. Bullough, *Narrative and Dramatic Sources*, Vol. IV, 4.

8. Honigmann, *Arden King John*, lx.

9. Bonjour, "The Road to Swinstead Abbey," 253–74.

10. Braunmuller, *Oxford King John*, 76, 78.

11. Beaurline (*New Cambridge King John*) retitles the play *The Tragedy of King John* by analogy with *Richard II* and *Richard III*, which were titled tragedies in their quarto versions only to become, like *KJ*, histories in the Folio.

12. Holinshed may hint at the illegitimacy of John's rule: "Now that king John was thus occupied in recovering his brothers treasure, and traveling with his subjects to reduce them to his obedience, queene Elianor his mother, by the helpe of Hubert archbishop of Canturburie and other of the noblemen and barons of the land, travelled as diligentlie to procure the English people to receive their oth of allegiance to be true to king John" (iii.157/1/11). Shakespeare is obviously much more emphatic.

13. Arthur is called Richard's "posterity" and "his offspring" in 2.1.6 and 2.1.13. "Genealogical confusion" is Braunmuller's phrase in his notes to these lines; the Folger edition's note warns that the words "confusingly suggest a father-son relationship."

14. This reading of the Bastard, of course, departs radically from most recent political analyses of the play, which often romanticize him as the "national conscience" and hero of the play. Though the Bastard comes to appreciate the social order as a Ptolemaic necessity (5.7.78–80), his spiritual confusion is as glaring as his ignorance of the final peace with Louis: at the death of John the Bastard says, "I do but stay behind To do the office for thee of revenge, And then my soul shall wait on thee to heaven" (5.7.70–73). Given the play's emphatic moral distinction between vengeance and forgiveness, the Bastard's destination would not likely be a Christian heaven. His thirst for vengeance, by the way, is Shakespeare's inversion of the character in *TR*, who advises the dying king to "forgive the world and all your earthly foes" (1072), while it is Henry who wants revenge for his father's death at the hands of the monks (1139–42).

15. Curren-Aquino, *Folger King John*, 237.

16. Vaughan, "Between Tetralogies," 418–19.

17. *Ibid.*, 419.

18. Honigmann, *Arden King John*, lxv.

19. I follow Bullough's scene divisions.

20. For a more detailed analysis of the possible interpolation see Braunmuller, *Oxford King John*, 37.

21. While the central narrative incidents of the first two scene pairs are also reflective, they are less obviously so because their import is metaphorical, deriving from the body imagery suffusing the play and especially the identification of the king's body with the body of the kingdom. In the pairing of the first and last scenes the Bastard's initial personal integrity at the cost of lands is extended to the integrity of the "body" of England; in the pairing of the second and penultimate scenes John's invaded lands become his invaded body. See below.

22. Shakespeare is usually considered to have mitigated but not fundamentally contested the anti-Catholic view of *TR*. There are, however, critics who find *KJ* to be pro-Catholic, though on different evidence than I advance, including especially Roy Battenhouse ("Religion in *King John*," 140–149) who emphasizes a salvific providence operating in John's fever and the final storms.

23. Braunmuller, *Oxford King John*, 9.

24. Tillyard, *Shakespeare's History Plays*, 218.

25. This is the Folio reading of the second phrase; Braunmuller prefers Pope's emendation: "*broad-eyed watchful day.*"

26. Honigmann, *Arden King John*, lxviii, and note on 5.1.28–29.

27. Braunmuller, *Oxford King John*, in note to 5.1.29.

28. Larry Champion says that his "last moments evince from John not a hint of remorse or spiritual sensitivity" ("The 'Un-end' of *King John*," 177). While John is much more blatantly conscience-stricken in *TR*, he is no less tormented in Shakespeare's more elliptical (and resonant) rendering. In his penultimate speech John declares the poison to be a fiend from hell, tormenting

his "unreprievable, condemned blood" (5.7.48). (R. L. Smallwood in the *Penguin King John* also suggests that these lines raise the question of John's salvation.) Furthermore, John's physical deterioration is clearly a manifestation of his tormenting conscience, for the first symptoms of his disease appear upon learning that Arthur is dead (as the first hint of his unease is expressed in his re-coronation after ordering Arthur's murder).

29. Spurgeon, *Shakespeare's Imagery*, 245–52.

30. Honigmann, *Arden King John*, lxxii.

31. The *Oxford* editors attribute Mistress Overdone's announcement (which duplicates information provided by Pompey in the same scene) to a late revision of the play by Thomas Middleton (Wells, *A Textual Companion*, 468). The chiastic structure of Folio *Measure for Measure*, outlined in an earlier chapter, and the mirroring actions of the second and penultimate scenes convince me of Shakespeare's authorship.

Chapter 9

1. Baker, *Riverside Shakespeare*, 842.

2. Wimsatt, *Samuel Johnson*, 36.

3. Humphreys, *Arden 2 Henry IV*, xxviii.

4. Shaaber, "The Unity of *Henry IV*," 217–227.

5. Hunter, "*Henry IV* and the Elizabethan," 263.

6. Humphries, *Arden edition of Part II*, Appendix VI, 240.

7. Jenkins, *The Structural Problem*, 19.

8. Jowett and Taylor, "The Three Texts," 31–50.

9. Wells and Taylor, *A Textual Companion*, 361.

10. Humphreys, *Arden Part II*, lxxxii.

Chapter 10

1. Wimsatt, *Sam Johnson*, 82.

2. Melchiori, *Arden Merry Wives*, 32. Citations are from this edition.

3. *Ibid.*, 43.

4. See McDonald, *Merry Wives*, xlv–xlvii.

Chapter 11

1. Barton, *Riverside Shakespeare*, 365.

2. Bate, *Shakespeare and Ovid*, 158.

Chapter 12

1. The portrait of Henry as an epic king, traditionally accepted as unqualified, is in more recent criticism usually considered to be almost savagely ironic. See, for example, Goddard, *The Meaning of Shakespeare*, vol. 1, 266; Knapp, *Shakespeare's Tribe*, 124; and Greenblatt, *Shakespearean Negotiations*, 56–75.

2. Shakespeare's ambivalence is argued in Barber and Wheeler, *The Whole Journey*, 198–236; his subversive ambiguity by Rabkin in "Rabbits, Ducks," 279–96.

3. Kernan, "The Henriad," 272.

4. Baker, *Riverside Shakespeare*, 976.

5. All editors accept the division of the play into 23 scenes. The *Oxford* edition, however, ends 3.2 with the cleared stage at the Boy's exit and extends 3.3 through Henry's Harfleur speech, declining to add a stage direction for the soldiers' exit before Henry's entrance. Though these changes are certainly defensible in terms of the immediate stage action, the altered 3.3 destroys Shakespeare's careful reflection of Fluellen's actions with Henry's in the paired 4.3 as well as the implicit comparison of Henry's Harfleur speech with the "fair show" of the French in the paired scene, 4.2. Again, we see scene divisions thematically rather than narratively determined.

6. Goddard, *The Meaning of Shakespeare*, 254.

7. *Ibid.*, 247.

Chapter 13

1. Kermode, *Riverside Shakespeare*, 1135–36.

2. Jenkins, *Arden*, 128; Hibbard, *Oxford*, 58; and Beckerman, *Shakespeare at the Globe 1599–1609*, 40–42.

3. Except for Quarto-only lines, my reference text is the *Oxford World Classics* edition of *Hamlet*, edited by G. R. Hibbard (Oxford, 1987), which is based on the Folio. To locate Quarto-only lines within entire scenes, I find it more convenient to use a conflated text, the *Arden Shakespeare Hamlet*, ed. Harold Jenkins.

4. *Shakespeare First Folio*, 333.

5. *Prefaces to Shakespeare*, 57.

6. The morality of revenge in *Hamlet* has been much debated. The thematic structure suggests that almost the entire play turns a subtle dramatic irony against Hamlet, which he escapes only when he returns in the last act free of the "memory and purpose" imposed upon him by the father-figures in the central flanking scenes: the imperative to revenge. Claudius's keystone prayer for pardon is realized in the mutual forgiveness of Hamlet and Laertes.

7. Granville-Barker (*Prefaces*, 39–46) discusses the time-structure in detail. See also Hibbard, *Oxford*, 35–7.

8. Particularly in Ophelia's description of him as "loosed out of hell To speak of horrors" (2.1.84–5), but see too Stanley Cavell's sense of a more pervasive haunting of the play by the young Hamlet (*Disowning Knowledge*, 188).

9. Hamlet's biography in Act Five has been commented on by Barbara Everett (*Young Hamlet*, 1–24) and William Kerrigan (*Hamlet's Perfection*, 127).

10. Jenkins, *Arden*, 524–25.

11. This pair of scenes contrasting Rosencrantz's obliviousness and Hamlet's consciousness demonstrates how helpful an awareness of the structure can be to the reading of even apparently small details. Rosencrantz the sponge bears most directly on the relative weights of the two meanings of "conscience" in the paired scene (3.1.84)—its Elizabethan and modern meaning of a sense of right and wrong and the additional Elizabethan meaning, "consciousness." The paired sponge image requires that we weigh the latter more heavily. It is consciousness more than conscience that makes Hamlet, in his estimation, a coward. This then answers the objection that Harold Jenkins brings to the famous opening lines:

To be, or not to be—that is the question:

Whether 'tis nobler in the mind to suffer
The slings and arrows of outrageous fortune,
Or to take arms against a sea of troubles,
And by opposing end them? To die, to sleep—
No more [57–62].

Jenkins comments on the first five lines: "The alternatives put by 'the question,' then, are now restated [in lines 58–61] in metaphorical and amplified form. The difficulty arises because the alternatives do not appear at first to correspond: a choice of 'to suffer' or 'to take arms' does not seem to be the equivalent of 'to be or not to be.' Both are modes of being" (484). This usurps the character's meaning with an insistence on logic. The alternatives for Hamlet are "*in the mind* to suffer" (emphasis added) or "to take arms." These are not for Hamlet both modes of being. To take arms, to act, is not to be. Hamlet exists in his mind, in thought, in consciousness. To act is to be effectively asleep, to lose consciousness. And the very respite from suffering consciousness, sleep, itself threatens an hallucinatory consciousness, a form of madness, i.e., dreams, bad dreams. Death threatens some similar form of torment—not hell necessarily, as some critics think, but any torment of some new and more painful consciousness.

Interpreting action as entailing unconsciousness also explains the phrase in line 61, "by opposing end them" which Jenkins takes to mean "not by overcoming them but (paradoxically) by being overcome by them." This is strained. The phrase reiterates the unconsciousness of action: merely by acting against opposing troubles we lose consciousness of them, as occurs most obviously in the murder of Polonius, a mindless act, done in ignorance of the victim behind the arras. Action is unconsciousness. So "to be or not to be, to suffer in the mind or to lose consciousness in action; not to be, to die, to sleep—no more." Consciousness returns in the form of dreams, whose ills might be worse than those we are already conscious of—ills which are catalogued, and in the very cataloging exquisitely painful: the poetry is the suffering, the consciousness that makes a coward of Hamlet.

12. For an analysis emphasizing the balanced construction and central focus of most of the scenes in the play, see Rose, *Shakespearean Design*, 95–125.

13. It is not strictly accurate to say "through"; Ophelia does not appear in 2.2. It is more accurate to say that the section is bounded by the Hamlet-Ophelia incidents in 2.1 and 3.1. Note the similar pattern in 4.5 "through" 4.7: the two Laertes-Claudius episodes mark the beginning and end of a three-part section with the brief scene of Horatio reading Hamlet's letter in between. This is a common organizational pattern in Shakespeare, the "scene tercets" I have already discussed. The subjects of the three scenes "rhyme" ABA.

14. Among them Emrys Jones, Harley Granville-Barker and the *Arden* editors. Francis Fergusson separates the first and last two "ritualistic" scenes.

15. Mimesis is one of the most strenuously debated topics in Hamlet, and I enter such treacherous waters here merely to reiterate the obvious: structure and character are inextricable. The structural importance of dumb shows is matched by their importance to the character of Hamlet, particularly in marking crucial mo-

ments of his transformation. Notice, for example, that Hamlet's appearance in Ophelia's closet initiates the central movement of the play; the structure, that is, suggests that those critics who take the dumb show as Hamlet's "arrangement," the staging of a scene for Ophelia, rather than as a moment of true anguish, lack a sense of the changes that Hamlet undergoes, reading the achieved poise of "Hamlet the Dane" in Act Five back into the "roleless" and consequently desperate actor in Ophelia's closet. ("Arrangement" is Robert Weismann's word ["Mimesis in Hamlet" in *Shakespeare and the Question of Theory*, eds., Patricia Parker and Geoffrey Hartman, p. 285]. Harold Bloom expresses the same "arrangement" view in *Hamlet: Poem Unlimited*, p. 37–8. Harold Jenkins finds the problem of Hamlet's state of mind while in Ophelia's closet "insoluble" [461].)

16. *Arden Hamlet*, p. 294.

17. That the murder of Polonius is merely a stage play for Hamlet is further suggested by the resemblance to the mummer's play, the killing of the calf. See Todd A. Borlik, "'The Chameleon's Dish,'" 12.

18. Jenkins makes this point of Ophelia's echoing the Ghost (*Arden Hamlet*, 537).

19. Fergusson, *The Idea of a Theatre*, 126–27.

20. The phrase is Stanley Cavell's (*Disowning Knowledge*, 82), reporting on the frequent disparagement of Shakespeare's plots.

21. Jones, *Shakespeare at Work*, 67.

Chapter 14

1. Jones, *Shakespeare at Work*, 62.

2. There is some editorial disagreement as to the number of scenes in *Troilus and Cressida*. In Act Five the battle sequence creates the usual problems of scene designation. The *Arden* (Third Series, David Bevington, ed.) and *Oxford* editions, scrupulously observing each cleared stage, mark 11 scenes; the *Riverside*, adhering to the traditional demarcations, marks 10 scenes. I propose that the traditional designations be retained except for the break at 5.6, which should be ignored. The scene that results from combining the traditional 5.5 and 5.6 has a clear diptych structure. The death of Patroclus occupies the first half of the scene, and the consequent searches by Achilles, "Crying on Hector," and Ajax, "Roaring for Troilus," occupy the second half. The farcical, almost slapstick quality of the immediate action is heightened by the reentry of Ajax and then of Diomedes only seven lines after each of their previous exits, creating a series of entrances, exits and interrupted fighting that rivals the Keystone Kops. Furthermore, the new scene focuses in its dialogue and frenzied action on the same characters as dominate the paired scene: Hector and Troilus. In this way (5.5–5.6) pairs neatly (and ironically) with 2.2, in which Troilus and Hector are the main debaters on the question of returning Helen. (Note that the predominant characters need not physically appear in the scene. Achilles and Hector never appear in 1.3, but they are clearly the generative characters, the one of the debate on dissension in the Greek camp, the other of the challenge.)

The only other disputed scene designations, first introduced in the *Oxford* edition, create two extra scenes in Act Four. Unlike the simple logic of the *Oxford*'s scene designations in Act Five, the breaks in Act Four require some larger editorial tinkering with the text. *Oxford* divides 4.2 at line 76 as a consequence of accepting the Folio SD *Enter Pandarus and Cressida*. This necessitates the previous exit of Pandarus at l. 59, not in either Q or F, and leaves a cleared stage before the entrance of Cressida and Pandarus. Maintaining the traditional view, the *Arden* chooses to change the Folio SD to *Enter Cressida* because otherwise Pandarus, being offstage when the information was disclosed, would not know that Cressida is to be exchanged for Antenor. I would add that other awkward moments are created by the *Oxford* change, particularly in the opening lines of Cressida's conversation with Pandarus, which is much more fluid if Cressida is entering to Pandarus to ask who has just visited. The *Oxford* creates the second extra scene by having Ajax and Hector fight offstage and adding an *exeunt* at 4.5.117 for Agamemnon and the others to rush off to join them, leaving the stage empty. Among the justifications for this change, Taylor advances the difficulty for an audience of focusing on both the Folio's staged battle preparations and the simultaneous dialogue, a description of Troilus by Ulysses. But the play repeatedly stages two events at the same time or one event mediated by one or two choral spectators, as the seduction of Cressida is viewed by Troilus and Ulysses and also by Thersites. The forced linking of Troilus and the staged fight, the overlap of love and war yet again, is surely intended. To sacrifice this linkage to preserve the Folio direction at 159.1, *Enter Agamemnon and the rest*, seems disproportionate when it makes eminent stage sense to merely have, as the *Arden* edition for example does, Agamemnon and the rest *come forward*. As Bevington says, the *Oxford* changes are "highly problematic" (419), and the traditional scene designations in Act Four make more sense in both these instances.

3. This pair of scenes is structurally emphatic in another way that deserves mention. In 1.2 Pandarus extols the virtues of Troilus to Cressida and, in soliloquy, she admits her love. But the scene proceeds by focusing on Hector. He is all the talk. He is the subject of gossip, the standard for Pandarus's praise of Troilus and the most striking warrior in the procession. This intertwining of love and war is ironically paired with the contrasting ten-line scene in which there is not even an allusion to the love story and in which Hector's death is tersely eulogized in two lines by Hector's kinsman, Ajax. The deflation of both love and war could not be more emphatic than in the contrast between the hopeful anticipations of the earlier scene and the vacuity of the later. The lack of a formally structured ending, remarked by Everett in my opening quote, is thus not only anticlimactic in itself but has a precise structural expressiveness.

4. John Jones (p. 61) disputes the *Arden*'s gloss of "arms" as "weapons" and correctly points to instances of another meaning, especially in Nestor's "I would my arms could match thee in contention As they contend with thee in courtesy." Clearly the whole play is like Nestor's welcome of Hector in maintaining the two meanings of arms: for battle and for "embracement."

5. *Arden Troilus and Cressida* (Third Series), 56.

6. By moving—as I think Shakespeare did in the Folio source—the rejection of Pandarus from the end of the play to the end of this scene, the playwright strengthened the staging of this implied, over-subtle defense of Cressida, ironic though it is that Pandarus should be her spokesman still.

7. The quarto gives the line to Troilus and the Folio to Aeneas. Spoken by the emotional Troilus, it would anticipate his speech on the devastating effect of Hector's death on Troy. As the last food image in the play proper, the line would fittingly comment on the end of the love story and would also recall the play's first elaborate food imagery, of Cressida as bread. In its dramatic irony when spoken by Aeneas, who thinks the field is still the Trojans', the line has more edge and heft, commenting on the fates of both warriors and lovers. Though I find the Folio superior, for purposes of my argument it hardly matters which version is final, since the ironic reading encompasses the sentimental.

8. Jones, *Shakespeare at Work*, 70.

Chapter 16

1. A. C. Bradley, *Shakespearean Tragedy*, 183, 184.

2. John Jones, *Shakespeare at Work*, 268.

3. Though the text has the bed curtains drawn by Othello only after the murder, at 5.2.103.

4. Honigmann (*Arden Shakespeare Othello*, my reference text) mentions the domesticity of the meals. For mention of food imagery in character analysis, see, for example, Heilman, *Magic in the Web*, 100; and Adelman, "Iago's Alter Ego," 125–44. For an overview of the investigations of food in Shakespeare's work, see Goldstein, "Shakespeare and Food" 153–74.

5. Emrys Jones, *Scenic Design*, 70, and Bradley, *Shakespearean Tragedy*, 196. The question of intervals has been much debated in connection with the double time scheme in the play. See especially Emrys Jones and Honigmann for a full discussion. I would only point out that the intervals I have indicated are verified not only by the time scheme and the structural markers but also by the intrinsic action of the play traced in this essay.

6. The clown episodes function as more than structural markers, of course. See, for example, Ross, "'Dull Clown,'" 107–128.

7. Not every commentator would agree with this apparently straight-forward summary of narrative events. Based on Iago's shouted obscenities to Brabantio, for instance, Cavell (*Disowning Knowledge*, 131) thinks that the consummation of the marriage occurs during the first scene. Astute as his remarks are, they seem to me contradicted by the action and imagery of the first two Acts. Nor is the obvious contrast between Acts Two and Four always considered, particularly in discussions that generalize from Othello's handkerchief story in Act Four to its initial significance for him. See below.

8. See, for instance, the biting wit of the "carnivores"—particularly Benedick and Beatrice—and the mild amiability of the "plant people"—Dogberry and Verges (i.e., verjuice, the juice of unripe fruit)—in *Much Ado About Nothing*. On meat-eating specifically, see Borlik, "'The Chameleon's Dish.'"

9. Heilman (*Magic*, 142–43) provides a fine-grained analysis of Othello's moral lapse in cashiering Cassio.

10. Janet Adelman ("Iago's Alter Ego," 132) suggestively examines Iago's feeding imagery from a Kleinian perspective, concluding, more sweepingly than I do, that in Iago's view of the body anything "interior [is] a mass of undifferentiated and contaminated matter."

11. Heilman (*Magic*, 142) makes the point: what Othello "lacks ... is the assurance of giving."

12. The handkerchief, of course, becomes a fetish, as it is most commonly referred to, only after Othello's "marriage" to Iago. As a pledge of love see, for example, Boose, "Othello's Handkerchief." Peter Rudnytsky contends that the handkerchief is a floating signifier in "The Purloined Handkerchief." For an association with the Catholic cult of martyrs, see Richard Wilson, "Dyed in Mummy." Harry Berger, Jr. ("Impertinent Trifling: Desdemona's Handkerchief." *SQ* 47, 235–50) finds Desdemona, in her "practical unconsciousness," to be complicitous in the loss of the handkerchief.

13. In a note to 3.3.438 Honigmann (*Arden Othello*) attributes to L. J. Ross in *Studies in the Renaissance* 7, 1960, 225–40.

14. Cavell, *Disowning*, 135.

15. Adelman, "Iago's Alter Ego," 138.

16. Harry Berger, Jr. ("Impertinent Trifling") thinks Desdemona is merely "puzzled" by Othello's tale of magic in the web, but her reaction, though laconic, is certainly much more deeply felt.

17. After Desdemona's response the Folio has a question mark, indicating either exclamation or interrogation. I change the punctuation only to make my reading more explicit. See Hongimann's note, which suggests this reading as a possibility. Berger examines this dialogue using the Quarto reading, "How, sweet Othello?" and concludes that the line is Desdemona's attempt, via its superfluous interrogatory, to show Lodovico that she is a battered wife, though she has not yet been struck.

18. In the event, of course, he decides not to shed her blood, preferring to "revirginate" her as unblemished alabaster or a whole entire chrysolite. See Adelman, "Iago's Alter Ego," 137–38.

Chapter 17

1. The other early text, the 1619 Quarto, is not relevant to my argument.

2. Wells and Taylor, *A Textual Companion*, 510.

3. *The Riverside Shakespeare* (1344) puts the numbers at 288 and 133, respectively.

4. Taylor, *Division*, 429.

5. Thomas, "Shakespeare's Supposed Revision," 506–511.

6. Foakes, *Arden King Lear*, 129.

7. Knowles, "Merging the Kingdoms," 268.

8. Wells and Taylor, *Oxford Complete Works*; Halio, *The Tragedy of King Lear*, Cambridge edition.

9. My reference text for the Folio version is the *Oxford* edition, *The Tragedy of King Lear*, which, unlike most editions, retains the Folio scene designations throughout.

10. See Emrys Jones, *Scenic Design*, 185.

11. The *Oxford* retains the Quarto's "dearer" without comment. The comparative seems subtly wrong to me since Edmond is now effectively fatherless. I have followed the Folio.

12. That Edmond and Lear are exact opposites has been noted by many critics and expressed in many different ways. Stanley Cavell (*Disowning Knowledge*, 68) discusses the split between "inner and outer worlds" as providing Edmond with a "capacity for action" which Lear abdicates. Cavell's view is itself a variation on what has traditionally been expressed as the contrast between power and love. See, for example, Granville-Barker (*Prefaces to Shakespeare*, 318).

13. Cavell (*Disowning Knowledge*, 50) adds to this conventional reading the similar sense of shame in both Lear and Gloucester.

14. Foakes (*Arden Lear*) in his note to 3.2.68, quoting the Cambridge edition (J. Dover Wilson, ed., Cambridge: Cambridge University Press, 1960).

15. Many critics have pointed out the parallel. See, for example, Foakes, *Arden Lear*, 63–4.

16. See, for example, Foakes (*Arden Lear*, 130–31, 132) and Granville-Barker (*Prefaces*, 273–74 n.).

17. John Jones (*Shakespeare at Work*, 209) uses the phrase in an extended consideration of the shortcomings of the scene.

18. Urkowitz, *Shakespeare's Revision*, 54.

19. Warren, *Division*, 59–73.

20. Taylor, "The War in *King Lear*," 27–34.

21. Taylor, *Division*, 30.

22. Knowles ("Merging") thinks that the cuts to Q were made simply to shorten the play and sees the deletion of references to the French invasion as the necessary but not directly intended consequence of larger cuts, therefore as having no significance and as possibly not by Shakespeare at all. Furthermore, in Knowles's estimation, there is no difference in the presentation of the war anyway, for we can still find evidence of a French invasion in the Folio. His premise about shortening the play, as I hope is clear by now, is wrong; and his dismissal of any difference between Q and F in regard to a French invasion, though he points to some real deficiencies in Warren's argument, is overstated. Whether or not we can find evidence for a French invasion is not the point. Rather it is how forcefully and explicitly that invasion is signaled. Certainly the Folio mutes the fact.

23. Warren (in *Division*, "The Folio Omission," 45–57) and John Jones (*Shakespeare at Work*, 220–25), among others, have argued in defense of the deletion of the mock trial.

24. Whether in the standard conflations, Knowles's version ("Revision Awry," 32–46) or Foakes's version in the *Arden* edition.

Chapter 18

1. Wells, *Shakespeare Reshaped 1606–1623*.

2. Muir (*Arden Macbeth*, xxxiii) concedes that the writer of the Hecate passages was "not without poetic talent"; Brooke (*Oxford Classics Macbeth*, 57) says, "Act 3, Scene 5 is strikingly well written; there is no good cause to question its right to be there"; Nosworthy

("The Hecate Scenes," 138–39) thinks the scenes may be Shakespeare's.

3. Paul (*The Torture of the Mind*, 83) comments extensively on the witches' "triplicity," "closely woven into the play." For at least one other instance in which Shakespeare uses number symbolism, see Thomas McAlindon ("The Numbering") on the numbers four and eight in *Julius Caesar*.

4. Muir, *Arden Macbeth*, 174.

5. Paul (*The Torture of the Mind*, 41–57) details the verbal chiasmi as well as the chiastic positioning of the murders in the play. Paul's many perceptive observations, both verbal and structural, remain imprecise, however, because he divides the play into only 22 rather than 27 scenes. As in so many other instances, mistaken structural punctuation obscures the clarity of the action.

6. Muir, *Arden Macbeth*, lxiv.

7. Stirling, *Unity in Shakespearian Tragedy*, 141.

8. Brooke notes, "it is ambiguous whether fate defies Macbeth or supports him" [70–71]; but Muir reads this as defiance of fate.

Chapter 19

1. Kermode, *Riverside Shakespeare*, 1391.

2. Granville-Barker, *Prefaces to Shakespeare*, 370.

3. Ibid., 371.

4. Bradley, *Shakespearean Tragedy*, 260.

5. Rose, *Shakespearean Design*, 167; Bradley, *Shakespearean Tragedy*, 53; Mark Van Doren's opinion is noted in the Cambridge edition of *Antony and Cleopatra*, 31. Emrys Jones (*Scenic Form*, 229–30) agrees with Rose.

6. Neil, *Oxford World Classics Antony and Cleopatra*, 266.

7. Berek, "Doing and Undoing," 303.

Chapter 20

1. My reference text is the *New Cambridge Coriolanus*, Lee Bliss, ed.

2. Van Dyke, "Making a Scene," 135.

3. Adelman, "'Anger's My Meat,'" 134.

4. Ibid., 134.

5. Cavell, *Disowning Knowledge*, 155. My reading of *Coriolanus* shades in and out of Cavell's interpretation so often that I feel a comment is in order attempting to make the contours more explicit. While I agree with Cavell that the play suggests the idea of Christian sacrifice, I find the dynamic of sacrificial action to be stated in the play and intelligible on its own terms, without the necessity of invoking scriptural parallels. That is to say, a reader does not need Cavell's exquisite intuition to confirm most of Cavell's conclusions. Secondly, I find *Coriolanus* more changed in the last scene than Cavell does. As defeat has made Aufidius a man of "craft" and as impotence has schooled the Tribunes and Volumnia in the art of acting, so too Coriolanus, after his defeat by his mother, becomes something of the actor Volumnia recommended before his banishment. Coriolanus, I would say, changes from the unvarying character Cavell describes: "Coriolanus cannot imagine, or cannot accept, that there is a way to partake of one another, incorporate

one another, that is necessary to the formation rather than the extinction of a community.... The play *Coriolanus* asks us to imagine ... a beneficial, mutual consumption" (167). That beneficial consumption is articulated by the Plebeian in Act Two (quoted later in my essay) and understood, if imperfectly, by Coriolanus in the last scene. Thirdly, Cavell sees no difference in the psychic economies of Coriolanus and Volumnia in managing their anger. Obviously, I find a significant difference, fundamental to the structure and meaning of the play. In spite of these divergences of interpretation, I remain indebted to Cavell's work in a way that mere citation does not convey.

6. Adelman, "Anger," 131.

7. Cavell, *Disowning Knowledge*, 155 .

8. Van Dyke, "Making a Scene," 140.

9. Burke, "*Coriolanus*—and the Delights," 197.

10. Adelman, *Suffocating Mothers*, 149.

11. Detienne, *The Cuisine of Sacrifice*, 13.

Chapter 21

1. Evans, *Riverside Shakespeare Cymbeline*. Quotations from plays other than *Cymbeline* are from this edition.

2. Nosworthy, ed., *Arden Cymbeline*, xlix. All *Cymbeline* quotes are from this text.

3. Adelman, *Suffocating Mothers*, 200.

4. I follow the Folio scene divisions with one exception—a break at 2.4.152 creating a separate scene for Posthumus' soliloquy on women.

Chapter 22

1. Pafford (*Arden Winter's Tale*, liv–lv) discusses the common critical perception that there are two parts to the play; Pafford, however, thinks it "better" to distinguish three parts: at the Sicilian court, in Bohemia and again at the Sicilian court. Even critics who distinguish two parts may disagree as to the exact point of demarcation. Pafford says it is usually taken to be the end of 3.2, though he notes that Granville-Barker divided the play after 3.3. Mark Rose (*Shakespearean Design*, 170) thinks the play a "great diptych" but calls the Chorus of 4.1 its "centerpiece." Hallett Smith (*Riverside Shakespeare*, 1612–13) divides the play, as I do, in the middle of 3.3.

2. My reference text is the *Oxford World's Classics The Winter's Tale*, ed. Stephen Orgel.

3. In the etymological root of "a lady's 'verily' 's As potent as a lord's" (1.2.49–50).

4. Orgel (*Oxford Classics Winter's Tale*, 22) collapses all the "nothings" of the play together, finding that "Leontes' nothing is embodied in Perdita, loss personified, but she too is like Polixenes' cipher, 'standing in rich place,' through whom her Bohemian stepfather, 'a most homely shepherd ... from very nothing, and beyond the imagination of his neighbors, is grown to an unspeakable estate'" (4.2.37–40). Orgel concludes that "such reconfigurations ... reveal how controlled the play's terms are by Leontes' mind." But this is true only of the diseased male minds in the play, as even Orgel's examples show. Perdita is named by Antigonus after an

obviously false dream; Polixenes compares himself to a cipher out of an Archidamus-like shame at his comparative poverty; it is the materialistic Polixenes who describes the shepherd as coming from "very nothing." As the most telling example of a "nothing" divergent from Leontes', consider Cleomenes' report of the effect of the sacrifice and the oracle: "I was nothing" (3.1.11). Only after losing his son and wife and doing penance for 16 years can Leontes' mind begin to grasp the profound humility of this nothing.

5. In most cases the "acts" are easily determined by entrances and exits. In the court scene, however, characters remain on stage and move in and out of one another's hearing. So Leontes' first outburst of jealousy is not heard by Polixenes and Hermione; Leontes' expression alone seems to engage the concern of wife and friend. Similarly, Camillo seems to be on stage (there is no direction in the Folio) for the whole scene and to come forward after Leontes sends Mamillius to play. These movements about the stage, emphasizing that the public nature of court life is itself like being on stage, are equivalent to entrances and exits. In the country scene there is some uncertainty in one of the "act designations." The dance of the 12 satyrs, which is almost a free-standing interlude, could be either the end of the Autolycus act (# 2), a comment on the preceding entertainment (though Autolycus has exited), or the beginning of the Polixenes "act" (# 3). The sequence of the three performances in the pastoral celebration—the dance of Perdita and Florizel, the song (and "real" stage enactment by the Clown, Mopsa and Dorcas) of "Two Maids Wooing a Man," and the satyrs dance—suggests a descent into decadence, of artsy bestiality, equally suited to Autolycus and to Polixenes.

6. Pafford (*Arden Winter's Tale*, lxxx) considers that Autolycus "serves as a faint rhythmic parallel to the evil in Leontes" and in a note to this comment explains that "Leontes, centered on himself, acts from irresponsibility to life, and so does Autolycus."

7. Howard Felperin ("'Tongue-tied, our Queen?'" 9) exaggerates the usual attitude and says, of finding "sexual innuendo" in Hermione's speeches, "I am almost ashamed to confess it." Frank Kermode (*Shakespeare's Language*, 275–76) finds Hermione's speech to be poetically too hot, "the figuration as rough as the versification," the tone "hectic." Hermione's passionate presence disquiets critics because, if there is a possible appearance of impropriety in Hermione's behavior, then Leontes' jealousy is, in Orgel's words, "reasonable, an honourable mistake" and the husband's subsequent losses excessive. But, however reasonable, Leontes' jealousy is not, even at the appearance of impropriety, an honorable mistake; Paulina's admonition to Leontes for a just apprehension of the statue is even more aptly true of apprehending Hermione's entertainment: "It is required You do awake your faith" (5.3.94–95).

8. For an extended discussion of grace in the play, see Traversi's *Shakespeare: The Last Phase*.

Chapter 23

1. Citations are to the *Riverside Shakespeare*.

2. Not all critics agree that in the Epilogue the au-

dience is Prospero to Prospero's Ariel. Frank Kermode (*Arden Tempest*), simply compares the Epilogue to the conventional speech of an actor leaving his role: "the magician-without-magic has reference to the actor-without-part." It is true that in certain respects Prospero's magic is like a role, requiring its book and its costume, for example. But in a more important sense the comparison does not hold. Unlike the actor leaving his part, Prospero pointedly retains his recovered identity. Though this is unexpected in terms of the convention, it is perfectly in keeping for a character who has labored so long and hard to recover who he is. While the convention certainly hovers in the background and exerts its own pressure, any sharp cleavage of actor from role, of reality from fantasy, would destroy the precision of the poetry, which I address below.

Harry Berger, Jr. ("Miraculous Harp," 278–82) is similarly impressionistic. He argues that in the Epilogue Prospero "places himself in the same relation to the audience as previously Ariel, the Italians, and also Caliban, had stood to him." But surely this is too indiscriminate. The loss of Prospero's "charms" and his diminished strength are meant to recall Ariel only; such changes have no relevance to Caliban or the Italians. Furthermore, Berger misreads even the allusion to Ariel, taking it to mean that Prospero is "asking to vanish into thin air, or into a cowslip's bell, or wherever he may be far from humanity." On the contrary, Prospero's whole labor in the play is to restore himself to society, and he here states explicitly his desire to return "to Naples." It is not a similarity of character the analogy works to define in this respect but the appropriate environment of each: as elemental nature is to Ariel, society—humans' nature—is to Prospero.

How then does the Epilogue work? As yet another series of suggested metamorphoses. The first ten lines are clearly meant to establish our relationship to Prospero as analogous to his relationship with Ariel. His vanished charms, his diminished strength, his susceptibility to our spell—he is Ariel to our Prospero. The next lines too—Gentle breath of yours my sails Must fill"—continue the same analogy. Though in isolation they could plausibly suggest, as Kermode thinks, that we are Ariel providing "auspicious gales" for the trip to Italy, in context the lines insist on Prospero's comparative diminishment, again like the released Ariel. After all the stormy "blows" of the play, our gentle breath fills a toy-like, fantasy sail. In his "project" too, Prospero is like Ariel, wanting only to please. And to the extent that Prospero is Ariel in the first dozen lines of the Epilogue, we are Prospero the magus with all his powers intact.

At the same time, of course, Prospero, in wanting to please, is courting us in his own person, not as Ariel. His phrase is resonant with all of the play's courtships, so that the Epilogue has a curious intimacy here, reestablishing a relationship with the audience as equals. Like him we then abruptly lose spirits and art—the illusory power over death—and confront the end:

> Now I want
> Spirits t' enforce, art to enchant,
> And my ending is despair....

The final couplet, requesting an almost reciprocal pardon, does not presuppose the Epilogue's earlier relationship of magus and spirit, but, again, one of simple equality: "As you from crimes would pardoned be, Let your indulgence set me free." Momentarily, fleetingly, as our applauding hands free not the actor from his role but the character from his isolation, we enter Prospero's world and he enters ours.

3. Quoted Kott, *Shakespeare Our Contemporary*, 187.
4. Quoted in Mebane's *Renaissance Magic*, 46.
5. See Brown's fascinating study, *Hermes the Thief*.
6. Gurr, "*The Tempest*'s Tempest," 91–102.

Bibliography

Adelman, Janet. "'Anger's My Meat': Feeding, Dependency, and Aggression in *Coriolanus*." In Schwartz and Kahn, eds., *Representing Shakespeare*, 128–49.

———. "Iago's Alter Ego: Race as Projection in *Othello*," *Shakespeare Quarterly* 48, no. 2 (1997): 125–44.

———. *Suffocating Mothers: Fantasies of Maternal Origin in Shakespeare's Plays, Hamlet to The Tempest*. London: Routledge, 1991.

Altick, Richard. "Symphonic Imagery in *Richard II*." *PMLA* LXII (1947), reprinted in C.L. Barber and Richard Wheeler, *The Whole Journey: Shakespeare's Powers of Development*. Berkeley: University of California Press, 1986.

Bate, Jonathan. *Shakespeare and Ovid*. Oxford: Clarendon Press, 1993.

Battenhouse, Roy. "Religion in *King John*: Shakespeare's View." *Connotations* 1 (1991): 140–149.

Beckerman, Bernard. *Shakespeare at the Globe 1599–1609*. London: Collier-MacMillan, 1962.

Berger, Henry, Jr. "Impertinent Trifling: Desdemona's Handkerchief." *Shakespeare Quarterly* 47: 235–50.

———. "Miraculous Harp: A Reading of Shakespeare's Tempest." *Shakespeare Studies* 5 (1968): 253–83.

Berek, Peter. "Doing and Undoing: The Value of Action in *Antony and Cleopatra*." *Shakespeare Quarterly* 32, no. 3 (1981).

Bloom, Harold. *Hamlet: Poem Unlimited*. New York: Riverhead Books, 2003.

———. *Shakespeare: The Invention of the Human*. New York: Riverhead Books, 1998.

Bonjour, Adrien. "The Road to Swinstead Abbey: A Study of the Sense and Structure of *King John*." *ELH* 18 (1951): 253–74.

Boose, Lynda. "Othello's Handkerchief: 'The recognizance and pledge of love.'" *English Literary Renaissance* 5 (1975): 360–74.

Borlik, Todd A. "'The Chameleon's Dish': Shakespeare and the Omnivore's Dilemma." *Early English Studies* 2 (2009): 1–24.

Bradley, A. C. *Shakespearean Tragedy*. London: Macmillan, 1937.

Brown, Norman O. *Hermes the Thief: The Evolution of a Myth*. New York: Random House, 1969.

Bullough, Geoffrey. *Narrative and Dramatic Sources of Shakespeare*. Vol. 4. London: Routledge and Kegan Paul. New York: Columbia University Press, 1957–75.

Burckhardt, Sigurd. *Shakespearean Meanings*. Princeton: Princeton University Press, 1968.

Burke, Kenneth. "*Coriolanus*—and the Delights of Faction," *Hudson Review* 19 (1966): 185–202.

———. *Kenneth Burke on Shakespeare*. Ed. Scott L. Newstok. West Lafayette, IN: Parlor Press, 2007.

Cavell, Stanley. *Disowning Knowledge in Six Plays of Shakespeare*. Cambridge: Cambridge University Press, 1987.

Champion, Larry. "The 'Un-end' of *King John*." In *King John: A New Perspective*. Newark: University of Delaware Press, 1989.

Curren-Aquino, Deborah T. "*King John*: A Modern Perspective." In the New Folger Library Shakespeare *King John*, eds. Barbara Mowat and Paul Werstine. New York: Washington Square Press, 2000, 237–272.

Davis, William L. "Structural Secrets: Shakespeare's Complex Chiasmus." *Style* (Fall 2005).

Detienne, Marcel, and Jean-Pierre Vernant. *The Cuisine of Sacrifice Among the Greeks*. Trans. Paula Wissig. Chicago: University of Chicago Press, 1989.

Douglas, Mary. *Thinking in Circles: An Essay on Ring Composition*. New Haven: Yale University Press, 2007.

Ellis-Fermor, Una. "The Nature of Plot in Drama." In Kernan, ed., *Modern Shakespearean Criticism*, 77–92.

Everett, Barbara. *Young Hamlet: Essays on Shakespeare's Tragedies*. Oxford: Clarendon Press, 1989.

Felperin, Howard. "'Tongue-tied, our Queen?': The Deconstruction of Presence in *The Winter's Tale*." In Parker and Hartman, eds., *Shakespeare and the Question*, 3–18.

Fergusson, Francis. *The Idea of a Theatre: The Art of Drama in Changing Perspective*. Garden City, NY: Doubleday Anchor Books, 1949.

_____, ed. *Aristotle's Poetics*. Trans. S. H. Butcher. New York: Hill and Wang, 1961.

Freytag, Gustave. *Technique of the Drama*. Trans. Elias McEwan. Chicago: Griggs & Co., 1895.

Garber, Marjorie. *Shakespeare After All*. New York: Random House, Anchor Books, 2004.

Girard, Rene. *A Theatre of Envy: William Shakespeare*. Oxford: Oxford Unversity Press, 1991.

Goddard, Harold C. *The Meaning of Shakespeare*, 2 vols. Chicago: University of Chicago Press, 1951.

Goldstein, David B. "Shakespeare and Food: A Review Essay," *Literature Compass* 6, no. 1 (2006): 153–74.

Granville-Barker, Harley. *Prefaces to Shakespeare*, 2 vols. Princeton: Princeton University Press, 1947.

Greenblatt, Stephen. *Shakespearean Negotiations*. Berkeley: University of California Press, 1988.

Greg, W. W. *The Shakespeare First Folio*. Oxford: Oxford University Press, 1955.

Gurr, Andrew. "*The Tempest*'s Tempest at Blackfriars." *Shakespeare Quarterly* 41 (1988): 91–102.

Hallett, Charles A. "Scene Versus Sequence: Distinguishing Action from Narrative in Shakespeare's Multipartite Scenes." *Shakespeare Quarterly* 46 (1995): 183–95.

_____, and Elaine S. Hallett. *Analyzing Shakespeare's Action: Scene versus Sequence*. Cambridge: Cambridge University Press, 1991.

Hassel, R. Chris. *Faith and Folly in Shakespeare's Romantic Comedies*. Athens: University of Georgia Press, 1980.

Heilman, Robert B. *Magic in the Web*. Lexington: University of Kentucky Press, 1956.

Hirsh, James E. *The Structure of Shakespearean Scenes*. New Haven: Yale University Press, 1981.

Hodgdon, Barbara. *The End Crowns All: Closure and Contradiction in Shakespeare's History Plays*. Princeton: Princeton University Press, 1991.

Hunter, G. K. "*Henry IV* and the Elizabethan Two-Part Play." *Review of English Studies* V (1954): 263–75.

Hunter, R.G. *Shakespeare and the Comedy of Forgiveness*. New York: Columbia University Press, 1965.

Iacoboni, Marco. *Mirroring People*. New York: Farrar, Straus and Giroux, 2008.

Jenkins, Harold. *The Structural Problem in Shakespeare's "Henry the Fourth."* 1956.

Jones, Emrys. *Scenic Design in Shakespeare*. Oxford: Oxford University Press, 1971.

Jones, John. *Shakespeare at Work*. Oxford: Oxford University Press, 1995.

Jowett, John, and Gary Taylor. "The Three Texts of *2 Henry IV*." *Studies in Bibliography* 40 (1987): 31–50.

Kahn, Coppelia, *Roman Shakespeare: Warriors, Wounds and Women*. London: Routledge, 1997.

Kaula, David. "'Let Us Be Sacrificers': Religious Motifs in *Julius Caesar*." *Shakespeare Studies* XIV (1981): 197–214.

Kermode, Frank. *Shakespeare's Language*. New York: Farrar, Straus and Giroux, 2000.

Kernan, Alvin B. "The Henriad: Shakespeare's Major History Plays." In Kernan, ed., *Modern Shakespearean Criticism*, 245–75.

_____, ed. *Modern Shakespearean Criticism: Essays on Style, Dramaturgy and the Major Plays*. New York: Harcourt Brace Jovanovich, 1970.

Kerrigan, William. *Hamlet's Perfection*. Baltimore: Johns Hopkins University Press, 1994.

Knapp, Jeffrey. *Shakespeare's Tribe: Church, Nation and Theater in Renaissance England*. Chicago: University of Chicago Press, 2002.

Knight, G. Wilson. *The Imperial Theme*. Oxford: Oxford University Press, 1931.

Knowles, Richard. "Merging the Kingdoms: *King Lear*." *The Shakespearean International Yearbook* 1 (1999): 266–286.

_____. "Revision Awry in Folio *Lear* 3.1." *Shakespeare Quarterly* 46 (1995): 32–46.

Kott, Jan. *Shakespeare Our Contemporary*. New York: Doubleday, 1964.

Levin, Harry. "Form and Formality in 'Romeo and Juliet,'" *SQ* XI (1960). In Kernan, ed., *Modern Shakespearean Criticism*, 279–90.

Liebler, Naomi Conn. "'Thou Bleeding Piece of Earth': The Ritual Ground of *Julius Caesar*." *Shakespeare Studies* XIV (1981): 175–196.

McAlindon, Thomas. "The Numbering of Men and Days: Symbolic Design in *The Tragedy of Julius Caesar*." *Studies in Philology* 81 (1984): 373–93.

McCallum, Thomas. *Shakespeare's Roman Plays and Their Background*. New York: Russell and Russell, 1910.

Mebane, John. *Renaissance Magic and the Return of the Golden Age*. Lincoln: University of Nebraska Press, 1989.

Moulton, Richard. *Shakespeare as a Dramatic Artist*. Oxford: Clarendon Press, 1888.

Nosworthy, J. M. "The Hecate Scenes." *RES* XXIV (1948): 138–39.

Parker, Patricia, and Geoffrey Hartman, eds. *Shakespeare and the Question of Theory*. New York: Methuen, 1985.

Paul, Anthony. *The Torture of the Mind: Macbeth, Tragedy and Chiasmus*. Amsterdam: Thesis Publishers, 1992.

Rabkin, Norman. "Rabbits, Ducks and *Henry V*." *Shakespeare Quarterly* 28 (1977): 279–96.

Rose, Mark. "Conjuring Caesar: Ceremony, History, and Authority in 1599." In *True Rites and Maimed Rites: Ritual and Anti-Ritual in Shakespeare and His Age*, eds. Linda Woodbridge and Edward Berry. Urbana: University of Illinois Press, 1992, 256–69.

_____. *Shakespearean Design*. Cambridge: Harvard University Press (Belknap Press), 1972.

Ross, Lawrence J. "Shakespeare's 'Dull Clown' and

Symbolic Music." *Shakespeare Quarterly* 17 (1966): 107–128.

Rudnytsky, Peter. "The Purloined Handkerchief in Othello." *Psychoanalytic Study of Literature* (1985): 169–90.

Schwartz, Murray, and Coppelia Kahn, eds. *Representing Shakespeare: New Psychoanalytic Essays.* Baltimore: Johns Hopkins University Press, 1980.

Shaaber, M. A. "The Unity of *Henry IV.*" Washington, D. C.: *John Quincy Adams Memorial Studies* (1948): 217–227. Reprinted in *Henry IV*, Part I. Ed. James Sanderson. New York: W. W. Norton, 1969.

Shakespeare, William. *The Arden Shakespeare Cymbeline.* Ed. J. M. Nosworthy. London: Routledge, 1955.

_____. *The Arden Shakespeare The First Part of King Henry IV.* Ed. A. R. Humphreys. London: Metheun, 1960.

_____. *The Arden Shakespeare Hamlet.* Ed. Harold Jenkins. London: Thomas Nelson, 1982.

_____. *The Arden Shakespeare Henry V.* Ed. T. W. Craik. London: Thomas Nelson, 1995.

_____. *The Arden Shakespeare King John.* Ed. E. A. J. Honigmann. London: Metheun, 1951.

_____. *The Arden Shakespeare King Lear.* Ed. R. A. Foakes. London: Thomas Nelson, 1997.

_____. *The Arden Shakespeare Julius Caesar.* Ed. David Daniell. London: Thomas Nelson, 1998.

_____. *The Arden Shakespeare Macbeth.* Ed. Kenneth Muir. London: Metheun, 1951.

_____. *The Arden Shakespeare Measure for Measure.* Ed. J. W. Lever. London: Methuen, 1965.

_____. *The Arden Shakespeare The Merchant of Venice.* Ed. John Russell Brown. London: Methuen, 1955.

_____. *The Arden Shakespeare The Merry Wives of Windsor.* Ed. Giorgio Melchiori. London: Thomas Nelson, 2000.

_____. *The Arden Shakespeare Much Ado About Nothing.* Ed. A. R. Humphreys. London: Thomas Nelson, 1981.

_____. *The Arden Shakespeare Othello.* Ed. E. A. J. Honigmann. London: Thomas Nelson, 1999.

_____. *The Arden Shakespeare The Second Part of King Henry IV.* Ed. A. R. Humphreys. London: Metheun, 1966.

_____. *The Arden Shakespeare Richard II.* Ed. Peter Ure. London: Metheun, 1956.

_____. *The Arden Shakespeare Romeo and Juliet.* Ed. Brian Gibbons. London: Metheun, 1980.

_____. *The Arden Shakespeare The Tempest.* Ed. Frank Kermode. London: Thomas Nelson, 1997.

_____. *The Arden Shakespeare Troilus and Cressida* (Third Series). Ed. David Bevington. London: Thomas Nelson, 1998.

_____. *The Arden Shakespeare Twelfth Night.* Eds. J.M. Lothian and T.W. Craik. London: Metheun, 1975.

_____. *The Arden Shakespeare The Winter's Tale.* Ed. J. H. P. Pafford. London: Routledge, 1963.

_____. *The Merry Wives of Windsor.* Ed. Russ McDonald. New York: Penguin, 2002.

_____. *The New Cambridge Antony and Cleopatra.* Ed. David Bevington. Cambridge: Cambridge University Press, 2005.

_____. *The New Cambridge Coriolanus.* Ed. Lee Bliss. Cambridge: Cambridge University Press, 2000.

_____. *The New Cambridge King John.* Ed. L. A. Beaurline. Cambridge: Cambridge University Press, 1990.

_____. *The New Cambridge King Lear.* Ed. Jay Halio. Cambridge: Cambridge University Press, 1992.

_____. *The New Folger Library Shakespeare King John.* Eds. Barbara Mowat and Paul Werstine. New York: Washington Square Press, 2000.

_____. *Oxford World Classics Antony and Cleopatra.* Ed. Michael Neil. Oxford: Oxford University Press, 1994.

_____. *Oxford World's Classics Cymbeline.* Ed. Roger Warren. London: Clarendon Press, 1998.

_____. *Oxford World's Classics Hamlet.* Ed. G. R. Hibbard. Oxford: Oxford University Press, 1987.

_____. *Oxford World's Classics Julius Caesar.* Ed. Arthur Humphreys. Oxford: Oxford University Press, 1984.

_____. *Oxford World's Classics King John.* Ed. A. R. Braunmuller. London: Clarendon Press, 1994.

_____. *Oxford World's Classics Macbeth.* Ed. Nicholas Brooke. London: Clarendon Press, 2008.

_____. *Oxford World's Classics Twelfth Night.* Eds. Roger Warren and Stanley Wells. New York: Oxford University Press, 1994.

_____. *Oxford World's Classics The Winter's Tale.* Ed. Stephen Orgel. Oxford: Oxford University Press, 1996.

_____. *The Pelican Shakespeare Romeo and Juliet.* Ed. Peter Holland. New York: Penguin, 2000.

_____. *The Penguin King John.* Ed. R. L. Smallwood. New York: Random House, 1974.

_____. *The Riverside Shakespeare*, 2nd ed. Ed. G. Blakemore Evans et al. Boston: Houghton Mifflin, 1997.

_____. *Twelfth Night.* Ed. Herschel Baker. New York: Penguin Signet, 1998.

_____. *William Shakespeare: The Complete Works.* Eds. Stanley Wells and Gary Taylor. Oxford: Clarendon Press, 1986.

Simmons, J. L. *Shakespeare's Pagan World: The Roman Tragedies.* Charlottesville: University of Virginia Press, 1973.

Spurgeon, Caroline. *Shakespeare's Imagery.* Cambridge: Cambridge University Press, 1935.

Stirling, Brents. *Unity in Shakespearian Tragedy: The Interplay of Theme and Character.* New York: Columbia University Press, 1956.

Thomas, Sidney. "Shakespeare's Supposed Revision of *King Lear.*" *Shakespeare Quarterly* 35 (1984): 506–511.

Tillyard, E. M. W. *Shakespeare's History Plays.* London: Chatto and Windus, 1959 (1944).

Traversi, Derek. *Shakespeare: The Last Phase.* New York: Harcourt Brace, 1953.

_____. *Shakespeare: The Roman Plays.* Stanford: Stanford University Press, 1963.

Taylor, Gary. "The War in *King Lear*," *Shakespeare Survey XXXIII* (1980): 27–34.

Turner, R. K. "The Text of Twelfth Night." *Shakespeare Quarterly* 26 (1975): 128–38.

Urkowitz, Stephen. *Shakespeare's Revision of "King Lear."* Princeton: Princeton University Press, 1980.

Van Dyke, Joyce. "Making a Scene: Language and Gesture in *Coriolanus.*" *Shakespeare Survey* 30 (1977): 135–146.

Vaughan, Virginia. "Between Tetralogies: *King John* as Transition." *Shakespeare Quarterly* 35 (1984): 407–420.

Vendler, Helen. *The Art of Shakespeare's Sonnets.*

Cambridge: Harvard University Press (Belknap Press), 1997.

Weismann, Robert. "Mimesis in *Hamlet.*" In Parker and Hartman, eds., *Shakespeare and the Question*, 275–91.

Welch, John W., and Daniel McKinlay, eds. *Chiasmus Bibliography.* Provo, UT: Research Press, 1999.

Wells, Stanley. "Shakespeare Without Sources." In *Shakespearian Comedy: Stratford-Upon-Avon Studies 14*, gen. eds. Malcolm Bradbury and David Palmer. London: Edward Arnold Publishers, 1972, 58–74.

_____, and Gary Taylor. *William Shakespeare: A Textual Companion.* New York and London: W. W. Norton, 1987.

_____, _____, and John Jowett. *Shakespeare Reshaped 1606–1623.* Oxford: Clarendon Press, 1993.

Wilson, Richard. "Dyed in Mummy: Othello and the Mulberries." *Performances of the Sacred in Late Medieval and Early Modern England* (2005): 135–53.

Wimsatt, W. K., Jr., ed. *Samuel Johnson on Shakespeare.* New York: Hill and Wang, 1960.

Index